ALLIANCE AGAINST HITLER

Duke Historical Publications

Moscow, May 1935. Left to right: Molotov, Potemkin, Stalin, Laval.

ALLIANCE AGAINST HITLER

The Origins of the Franco-Soviet Pact

WILLIAM EVANS SCOTT

DUKE UNIVERSITY PRESS

Durham, N. C. 1962

Printed in the United States of America
by the Seeman Printery, Inc., Durham, N. C.

To my Mother and Father

PREFACE

The Franco-Soviet Pact of Mutual Assistance, signed in Paris on May second, 1935, was in the center of the origins of the Second World War. Adolf Hitler was the brutal captain of that war and within a year of his accession to power Paris and Moscow began to talk alliance. Nothing but dread of his unbounded ambitions could have brought together the Soviet Union and the Third Republic.

The student of continuity will immediately hearken back to the "old" Franco-Russian alliance, itself partly created by fear of Germany. The fall of Bismarck in 1890 and the lapsing of his "ReInsurance Treaty" with Russia made the Tsar and his advisers receptive to French advances. A year later, the renewal of the Triple Alliance and reports of British adherence to it destroyed the last Russian inhibitions. In Paris there was no hesitation. Russia was the only power strong enough to enable France to stand against Germany and to return to her traditional duel with England. The Franco-Russian Entente of 1891 and the Military Convention of 1892 forged a powerful and controversial alliance.

The Franco-Soviet Pact is one of the few examples of Soviet alliances with western nations. In the interwar period Russia joined hands with only two great powers: Germany from 1922 to 1933, France from 1933 to 1939, Germany again in August 1939. Many scholars have helped to acquaint us with the Rapallo mystique and the Nazi-Soviet Pact. No study has yet appeared of the French collaboration with the Kremlin.

The Quai d'Orsay must have been astounded at the flexibility of Soviet policy. In the first two years of the rapprochement, Moscow's response was slow and grudging. When Hitler came to power and the Russians suddenly realized that he meant what he had said in *Mein Kampf,* they moved rapidly and forcefully. All the violent denunciations of French capitalism and imperialism were heard no longer; they had served their purpose for a decade, they might serve again, but now they were dismissed. Russia was threatened by Hitler; Russia turned to France—it was as simple as that.

Yet for France it could not be as simple as that, because Stalin was the effective head of the Communist International. The interaction between domestic politics and foreign policy is one of the richest aspects of this inquiry. The outset found the French Communists sunk in futility, a factor of utmost significance in easing the acceptance of the pact. The misery produced by the depression and the need for left-wing unity against semifascist movements revived the fortunes of the Communists. They exploited the opportunity with skill and vigor and became the driving force behind the Popular Front. Ironically, the evidence of this resurgence did not appear until the pact had been signed.

Here, too, there was historical continuity. The Franco-Russian alliance of 1892 was not the exclusive creation of "cabinet diplomacy"— there were currents beyond the control of the diplomats. It was buttressed, almost bought and rebought, by staggering French investments in Russian securities. It, too, was troubled by an ideological conflict, between Tsarist orthodoxy and autocracy and the anticlerical, bourgeois, democratic Third Republic.

Public diplomacy and the Marxist dialectic of history are supposed to eliminate the accidental influence of individuals, of diplomats and ministers in this case. This study confirms just the opposite tendency. In Moscow, there was very little room for independence, yet Maxim Litvinov knew how to find it. Stalin certainly approved every important move, but he did not have much experience in foreign policy and he was preoccupied with the vast problems of the Five Year Plans. There were powerful critics of Litvinov on the Politburo but they guessed wrong—on Germany—whereas Litvinov quickly sensed the true nature of Hitler's threat. Stalin apparently allowed him some freedom of initiative so long as he was successful. Maxim Litvinov seems to have increased significantly the pace of Franco-Soviet rapprochement.

On the French side individual preferences had much to do with the timing and the form of negotiations. M. Joseph Paul-Boncour took the decision to open the alliance talks on his own, consulting only the Secretary-General of the Quai d'Orsay, M. Alexis Saint-Léger Léger. The latter appears in the role where he learned so much of men's hopes and follies. The diplomacy of Alexis Léger was as subtle as the poetry of Saint-John Perse, but less effective. Léger approved the alliance with Russia, but he wished to enclose it with several strings which France might tighten or loosen as she wished.

The most vigorous champion of the pact was Édouard Herriot, an amiable, solid professor turned politician and, like Paul-Boncour, a man of "good will." Leader of the largest party, the Radical-Socialists, Herriot occupied the key position in French politics from 1932 to 1936. He was obsessed by the prospect of German vengeance and by the weakness of France. The combination of his strategic position and his full commitment to the necessity of the Russian alliance form a striking reminder of the power of contingency in history.

Paul-Boncour and Herriot were men of the Left; paradoxically the Right was more important to the conclusion of the Franco-Soviet Pact. M. Pierre-Étienne Flandin was Premier at the time of signature. He was overshadowed on the conservative side of the stage by MM. Louis Barthou and Pierre Laval, neither men of good will. Minister and Premier in the days of the first Franco-Russian alliance, Barthou set to work to build another ring around Germany. Nor was it merely aged reflect, for he was one of the few European statesmen who had read

Mein Kampf. Another was Maxim Litvinov, and the two hit it off well. Cynical and fearless, Barthou regained the diplomatic initiative for France and managed Russia's entry into the League of Nations. He could not have stopped the depression or solved the bitter Left-Right rivalry in France; he did not know how. But he thought he knew how to stop Hitler and he was not afraid to try.

No such attraction adheres to Pierre Laval, but he draws our interest with his skill. Here is a chance to look at his technique before he decided to serve his country at the side of the devil. The opportunism, the desire for an understanding with Germany are already prominent, but in a much different context. Laval suspected the Franco-Soviet Pact, for its provocation of Hitler and for its aid to communism in France. When he replaced Barthou, he displayed a remarkably fine touch in the art of spinning out the negotiations. But Hitler jarred the sleepers awake by his proclamation of German rearmament; and before they relaxed, Laval had been forced to sign the Franco-Soviet Pact.

France and Russia had no monopoly on controversial figures; Mussolini, Marshal Pilsudski, Colonel Beck, and Edward Beneš moved in and around the negotiations. Sir John Simon hardly moved at all, but this too played its part. Laval's favorite scheme was an entente with Italy. Mussolini needed French friendship, and the twin French approaches, to Russia and to Italy, ran on parallel roads to success. Poland is doomed to be affected by all that affects Russia. For two years the Franco-Soviet talks were complemented by a Polish-Soviet rapprochement; then the Poles took the bait of a truce with Hitler. The French sharply resented that move and the Poles felt that the Russians were taking their place. One of the revelations of this study is the disintegration of the Franco-Polish alliance. On the other hand, the Czechs so far approved the motives of the French that they too made an alliance with Russia. Dr. Edward Beneš here took the first step on a road which proved to have many turns.

Throughout the entire Franco-Soviet rapprochement runs the thread of misunderstanding between Paris and London. Sir John Simon should not be singled out; given no effective lead by Ramsay MacDonald or Stanley Baldwin, he wavered between the French and German positions. The French turn to Russia had a deeper cause, but no stranger to it was frustration at the vacillation of the British cabinet.

This book originated in a suggestion of Hajo Holborn, Sterling Professor of History at Yale University; his criticism and encouragement have been essential to its conclusion. I am deeply grateful for his example of scholarship and judgment, which turned me to the study of history. Arnold Wolfers, Director of the Washington Center for Foreign Policy Research of The Johns Hopkins University, taught me the fascination and complexity of international relations and encouraged this study in many kind ways. I should like to record my debt to the late Professor Cecil Driver for his provocative introduction to French politics. Professor Luther Allen, of the University of Massachusetts, has given very generously of his knowledge of the Radical-Socialist, Socialist, and Communist parties in France. The publication of this book has been greatly aided by the wise counsel of Professor John Alden, of Duke University, and by the unfailing interest and support of Professor William B. Hamilton, Chairman of the Committee on the Duke Historical Publications, and by a generous grant from the Duke University Council on Research and the encouragement of its chairman, Professor John Tate Lanning. I should like to express my appreciation to Dr. G. Bernard Noble and Dr. E. Taylor Parks, of the Historical Division of the Department of State, for their assistance and permission to use the records of the Department. I am grateful to Mr. Ashbel G. Brice, Editor and Director of the Duke University Press, and to Mr. John C. Menapace and Mr. William G. Owens, for advice and assistance. Finally, I could scarcely have written this book without the criticism and aid of my wife, Marian.

WILLIAM EVANS SCOTT

CONTENTS

PRINCIPAL ABBREVIATIONS

British Blue Book,
   Cmd. 5143

Great Britain, Foreign Office, Miscellaneous No. 3 (1936), Correspondence showing the course of certain Diplomatic Discussions directed towards securing an European Settlement June 1934 to March 1936, Cmd. 5143.

B.F.P.

Documents on British Foreign Policy, 1919-1939, Second Series, 9 volumes to date (London, 1946 *et seq.*)

D.I.A.

Documents on International Affairs, annual volumes (London).

F.R.U.S.

Foreign Relations of the United States, Diplomatic Papers, annual volumes (Washington, D. C.)

G.F.P.

Documents on German Foreign Policy, 1918-1945, Series C, 3 volumes to date (Washington and London, 1957 *et seq.*)

J.O., Chambre, *Débats*

Journal Officiel, Chambre des Députés, *Débats Parlementaires* (Paris).

J.O., Sénat, *Débats*

Journal Officiel, Sénat, *Débats Parlementaires* (Paris).

L.N.T.S.

League of Nations. *Treaty Series.* (Geneva.)

Rapport Torrès

Journal Officiel, Chambre, *Documents Parlementaires*, 1935, Session Extraordinaire, Annexe No. 5792, 10 Decembre 1935, pp. 161-169, Rapport fait, au nom de la Commission des Affaires Étrangères chargée d'examiner le projet de loi portant approbation des Traité et Protocole signés le 2 Mai 1935 entre la France et l'Union des Républiques Soviétistes [*sic*] Socialistes, par M. Henry Torrès, Député.

"Revue de la presse," *J.D.*

"Revue de la presse," in *Journal des Débats* (Paris, daily newspaper).

S.I.A.

Survey of International Affairs, annual volumes (London).

Pour la France et la Russie, être
unies c'est être fortes; se trouver
séparées, c'est se trouver en danger.
En vérité, il y a là comme un im-
pératif catégorique de la géographie,
de l'expérience et du bon sens.

CHARLES DE GAULLE, 1944

One

THE END OF INDIFFERENCE

In a speech of 26 June 1930, Joseph Stalin, dictator of Russia, called France "the most aggressive and militarist country of all aggressive and militarist countries of the world."[1] A few months later an outcry against Soviet "dumping" gave the French government the occasion to flaunt an equally low opinion of Stalin's regime. Premier André Tardieu announced, on October third, decrees restricting a long list of Soviet imports. The Russians retaliated by decree, and a small-scale tariff war was on.[2] The ill-will which had marked the contacts between France and Soviet Russia since 1917 seemed as virulent as ever. Instead, the new year saw the inauguration of a rapprochement.

Both countries stood to profit from a return to normal trade and the establishment of friendly diplomatic relations. The Russians were dependent on foreign aid for their great program of industrialization. Reporting to the Sixth Congress of Soviets in Moscow, 7 March, V. M. Molotov emphasized the need for close economic relations with the capitalist world in order to fulfil the Five Year Plan. He struck out at the anti-Soviet character of French policy, but he was careful to leave the door open. If the French have had a change of heart, he said, "we are ready to continue our efforts to strengthen our relations."[3] The Soviet Foreign Minister, Maxim Litvinov, echoed this friendly tune. He insisted that, despite the contradictions between communism and capitalism, there was "ample scope" for "economic agreements and dealings between capitalist countries and the Soviet Union, mutually advantageous for all parties concerned."[4] Trade with France

[1] Quoted in Jane Degras, ed., *Soviet Documents on Foreign Policy, 1917-1941*, II (London, 1952), 444-445.

[2] The French and Russian decrees, the latter dated 20 October, were reprinted in *L'Europe Nouvelle* (Paris, weekly), XIV (27 June 1931), 899.

[3] Degras, *Soviet Documents on Foreign Policy, 1917-1941*, II, 478.

[4] Speech at Geneva, 18 May 1931, to the Commission of Enquiry on European Union, *League of Nations Publications*, VII, Political (Geneva, 1931), No. 7, p. 34.

was small, but its favorable balance yielded some of that vital stuff, foreign exchange.[5]

Military weakness was another factor that pointed in the direction of rapprochement with France. Reorganization and expansion of Russian armed forces was barely under way. Internal resistance to collectivization had flared up violently in 1930, and it increased the Kremlin's fear of international tension. The recent installation of Maxim Litvinov as Commissar for Foreign Affairs had introduced a certain change of atmosphere.[6] In E. H. Carr's apt phrase, "Under Litvinov, Soviet diplomacy acquired . . . a new freedom of manoeuvre."[7] "Manoeuvre" is the word, not "policy," for there is no doubt that it was Stalin who made or approved the significant decisions of foreign policy. Yet the Soviet system has room for the influence of personal inclinations, and Litvinov, from his strategic position, could exert such an influence. His contemporaries and students of his policy have discerned differences of preference between him and his predecessor, G. V. Chicherin, who had been attracted to seeking Russia's destiny in Asia. In the West, Litvinov looked less to Germany, whereas Chicherin had clung tightly to the Rapallo policy.

So many reasons impelled the Russians to end the feuding that the question of whether it was they or the French who made the first advance is only a technicality. The decisive initiative had to come from France. What was it, then, that made the French receptive to Russian advances in 1931, whereas previously they had brushed them aside with contempt or indifference?

[5] A. Barmine, a member of the Soviet Commercial Delegation in Paris, 1929-1931, *One Who Survived* (New York, 1945), chap. XXIV.

[6] Consult Raoul Girardet, "Litvinov et ses énigmes," in J.-B. Duroselle, *Les Relations Germano-Soviétiques, 1933-1939* (Paris, 1954), pp. 103-135; Henry L. Roberts, "Maxim Litvinov," Gordon Craig and Felix Gilbert, eds., *The Diplomats, 1919-1939* (Princeton, 1953), pp. 344-377; Louis Fischer, *Men and Politics* (New York, 1941), pp. 127-130; Arthur Upham Pope, *Maxim Litvinov* (New York, 1943); Herbert von Dirksen, *Moscow, Tokyo, London* (London, 1951), pp. 90 ff. M. Litvinov, *Notes for a Journal*, Introduction by E. H. Carr (London, 1955), is apparently a fake; it contains gross errors of chronology, and other signs of spurious manufacture. See Rudolf Schlesinger, "Litvinov's Ghost," *Soviet Studies* (Oxford, quarterly), VII, 373-383, and B. D. Wolfe, "The Case of the Litvinov Diary," in *Encounter* (London, monthly), VI (Jan. 1956), 39-47. The treatment of Franco-Soviet relations in the "Journal" does not seem to me to be genuine.

[7] E. H. Carr, *German-Soviet Relations between the Two World Wars, 1919-1939*, (Baltimore, 1951), p. 98. See *Documents on British Foreign Policy, 1919-1939*, Second Series, VII (London, 1958), 143-146, 213 ff. (hereinafter cited as *B.F.P.*). Litvinov became Commissar for Foreign Affairs 22 July 1930; he had been acting head of the Commissariat since 1928.

From a purely financial standpoint, the losses France incurred by the restrictive decrees could have been endured indefinitely because trade with Russia was small.[8] The decrees, however, had utterly failed to accomplish their chief aim—to make the terms of trade profitable to France.

Over three-quarters of French exports to the U.S.S.R. consisted of finished and manufactured goods, such as machinery, automobiles, and metallic and chemical products. They could be purchased in other countries with relative ease, and many Soviet orders placed in France were canceled and transferred. On the other hand, a large part of French purchases from Russia were raw materials, difficult to cancel because Russia was a major source of supply. By far the most important was oil and its derivatives, purchased by the French merchant marine and navy as well as by commercial firms. France profited from Russian competition against Anglo-Dutch and American oil companies. Russian flax and hemp often found their way to textile mills in Alsace, and other industries counted on Soviet timber, manganese ore, anthracite coal, and furs.[9]

The French decrees of 3 October 1930 primarily restricted imports of Soviet agricultural products destined for consumers' use. These, however, formed only a small part (10-15 per cent) of French imports from Russia. Of the significant imports, only flax and timber were banned. Oil, metallic ores, and furs were discreetly not mentioned. This meant that, at best, French purchases from Russia would only be cut in half. In the early months of 1931 provisional figures demonstrated the failure: imports from Russia were reduced only 40 per cent whereas exports to Russia were off 70 per cent from 1930. The balance of trade was more unfavorable to France than in the previous year.[10] The policy of restriction-with-loopholes, which banned the dumping of wheat but

[8] From 1930 to 1932 French exports to Russia never reached 1 per cent of total French exports, and imports from Russia were never above 1.8 per cent of total French imports. League of Nations, *International Trade Statistics, 1931 and 1932* (Geneva, 1933), p. 120.

[9] *L'Europe Nouvelle*, 27 June 1931, p. 899; H. Slovès, *La France et l'Union Soviétique* (Paris, 1935), pp. 299-301; A. Baykov, *Soviet Foreign Trade* (Princeton, 1946), pp. 65-66; Charles Baron, *Au Pays de l'Or Noir* (Paris, 1934). Oil, flax and hemp, timber, mineral ores, and furs formed at least 70 per cent of total French imports from the U.S.S.R.; oil contributed half of that figure.

[10] *L'Europe Nouvelle*, 4 July 1931, p. 922; *Le Temps* (Paris, daily), 14 Aug. 1931.

smiled at the dumping of oil, merely exaggerated the disequi-
librium in Franco-Soviet trade.

While they systematically shut out the French, the Russians
placed more orders in Germany and Italy. Under terms of the
"Piatakov Accord," 14 April 1931, Soviet negotiators agreed to purchases of 300,000,000 marks from German firms; they would be
financed by credits guaranteed by the German state. This additional business gave Germany such a pre-eminent role in the Russian market that her share of Russia's total imports rose to 37 per
cent in 1931.[11] Trade with Italy had been petty, but a commercial
accord signed in Rome 28 April 1931 provided for Soviet purchases
in Italy up to 350 million lire on state-guaranteed credits. The
agreement revealed that Russian orders would be placed for ships,
airplanes, automobiles, electrical and chemical equipment, all of
which the Soviets had been buying in France.[12] With this boost,
Italy exported to Russia twice as much as did France in 1931 and
six times as much in 1932. In an era of world depression such
commercial agreements were highly prized. They complemented
Russia's diplomatic co-operation with Germany and Italy, a pattern
that had been particularly evident in 1930.

The Soviet agreements with Germany and Italy and the failure
of the tariff war led to a re-evaluation of the French policy. Commercial and industrial groups trading with the Soviet Union protested to the Minister of Commerce, M. Louis Rollin, and to the
Premier, M. Pierre Laval. Early in 1931 the "groupe parlementaire
franco-russe," which had been disbanded in 1927, was re-formed to
work for a rapprochement. Its president and secretary, MM.
Anatole de Monzie and Gaston Bergéry, urged their views on M.
Laval in April, and M. de Monzie twice exhorted the Chamber of
Deputies not to renounce Russian trade in an hour of economic
depression.[13] M. Julien Durand, chairman of the Chamber's Com-

[11] Germany thus became Russia's foremost supplier; in 1930, she had supplied
24 per cent of Russia's total imports, the United States being first with 25 per cent.
Russian business was very important in many German heavy industries hard hit by
the depression. Consult W. Höffding, "German Trade with the Soviet Union,"
Slavonic and East European Review (London, quarterly), XIV, 473-494; *Osteuropa*
(Berlin, monthly), VI, 481 and 539-541; Dirksen, *Moscow, Tokyo, London*, pp.
99-107; Degras, *Soviet Documents on Foreign Policy*, II, 490-492.

[12] Degras, *Soviet Documents on Foreign Policy*, II, 495-497.

[13] Speeches of Bergéry and de Monzie in *Journal Officiel*, Chambre des Députés,
Débats Parlementaires (hereinafter cited as *J.O.*, Chambre, *Débats*), 17 Nov. 1931,
pp. 3896-3898 and 26 Nov., pp. 4092-4094. For de Monzie's earlier speech,
see *ibid.*, 25 March 1931, pp. 2182-2186. See also *B.F.P.*, VII, 245. Bergéry was a

merce Committee, complained that the only result of the restrictive decrees was that other countries had more Russian trade. "We are absent, but replaced. Is this the best way to defend our interests?"[14] The failure of the decrees was conceded by the Minister of Commerce in this debate, 21 February; later the same admission was made on the floor of the Senate by M. Aristide Briand, the Foreign Minister, and by two prominent Senators, MM. Joseph Caillaux and Henry Bérenger.[15]

On previous occasions when rapprochement had been proposed—1924 and 1926—there had been little incentive for France. Lenin's death had released the full force of factional rivalries; reconstruction of the economy had hardly begun. Skepticism greeted the announcement of the Five Year Plan in 1928, and there was severe criticism of Soviet ruthlessness in suppressing opposition to the collectivization of agriculture. A familiar feature in the French press were articles predicting the imminent collapse of the Bolshevik regime. By 1931 the French image of Soviet Russia had begun to change. Hostility remained, but in place of dire predictions there was a tendency towards matter-of-fact observations.[16] Stalin had stabilized the régime by his iron dictatorship. Disaster had come to many peasants, but Russia somehow kept moving. Most French observers now admitted that the Five Year Plan was speeding industrialization and thus providing the basis of military might. Interest in the slowly growing power of the Russian state began to revive.

To this curiosity about better relations with Russia was allied a more powerful force: fear of Germany. The evacuation of the Rhineland by French troops on 30 June 1930 had not been received as a great boon by the German people. They regarded it as

---

left-wing Radical-Socialist, de Monzie a well-known independent Socialist, who had visited Russia in 1923. He published *Petit Manuel de la Russie Nouvelle* (Paris, 1931), a survey of Soviet developments and a plea for rapprochement.

[14] *J.O.*, Chambre, *Débats*, 21 Feb. 1931, p. 1015. M. Durand was a Radical-Socialist.

[15] Speech by M. Rollin, Minister of Commerce, *ibid.*, pp. 1022-1023; speeches by MM. Bérenger, Briand, and Caillaux, *J.O.*, Sénat, *Débats*, 28 March 1931, pp. 682, 690, and 29 March 1931, pp. 752-753. Both Bérenger and Caillaux, the former Premier, attacked Soviet dumping but admitted that the decrees were a mistake.

[16] For example, in addition to the speeches of MM. Durand, Bérenger, and Caillaux, cited above, see article by Senator Édouard Néron, of the Senate's Customs Commission, in *Revue Politique et Parlementaire* (Paris, monthly), 10 April 1931, CXLVII, 5-17; "Vers un Accord Commercial avec l'U.R.S.S.," *L'Europe Nouvelle*, 4 July 1931, pp. 922-923.

long overdue, and they annoyed the French by transferring their agitation to other issues, noisily demanding the end of reparations and revision of their eastern frontiers. But it was the general election of 14 September 1930 that was the shocker. Profiting from the spread of unemployment, Hitler's National Socialists rose from rowdy impotence to poll over six million votes. Vaulting from 12 to 107 seats, they became the second largest party in the Reichstag.[17] Many Frenchmen judged the vote as highly provocative, as an ominous response to evacuation of the Rhineland.

Unfortunately, there was not enough time for these bad impressions to fade out. Instead, they formed the background of a surprise announcement on 21 March 1931 that the German and Austrian governments had just approved a Protocol outlining the framework of a Customs Union.[18] The two Foreign Ministers, Dr. Curtius and Dr. Schober, described it as a purely economic device, a step towards the economic basis of European federation. A generally sympathetic response from Anglo-American opinion was tempered by disapproval of the secrecy involved.

In France there was a remarkably sharp reaction against the project itself. It was assumed to be merely a veil for the coming *Anschluss* of Austria to Germany. Almost all of the Paris newspapers indignantly declared that the vital interests of France were threatened.[19] The official response was unusually blunt: the Protocol would alienate Austria's independence and thus was a violation of Austrian treaty pledges.[20] At the Foreign Ministry Aristide

[17] The Nazi popular vote was 6,379,692, as against 810,127 in 1928. The Communists also profited from depression and unrest, rising from 54 to 77 seats, 3,264,793 to 4,590,160. All the parties in between the two extremes, save the Catholic Center party, suffered heavy losses.

[18] Royal Institute of International Affairs, *Documents on International Affairs, 1931*, edited by John W. Wheeler-Bennett (London, 1932) (hereinafter cited as *D.I.A.*), pp. 3-6; Julius Curtius, *Sechs Jahre Minister der Deutschen Republik* (Heidelberg, 1948), pp. 118-120, 188-197, and *Bemühung um Oesterreich: Das Scheitern des Zollunionplans von 1931* (Heidelberg, 1947).

[19] "Revue de la presse" in *Le Temps*, and *Journal des Débats* for several days following 21 March; Royal Institute of International Affairs, *Survey of International Affairs, 1931* edited by Arnold J. Toynbee (London, 1932) (hereinafter cited as *S.I.A.*), pp. 303-304; W. d'Ormesson, *France* (London, 1939), pp. 83-85. D'Ormesson, former diplomat and advocate of Franco-German reconciliation, felt that the project had a "disastrous effect" upon French public opinion.

[20] French Note to London, 23 March 1931, *B.F.P.*, II, 7-10; even diplomatic phraseology does not conceal the severity of Briand's criticism. The Austrian pledges not to alienate their independence were contained in the Peace Treaty of Saint-Germain, 1919, and the 1922 Protocol governing a League of Nations loan to Austria.

Briand was furious, for not only his work but his pride was involved. Only a few days earlier he had told the Chamber that his policy had scotched the danger of an *Anschluss*. The old man struck back forcefully in the Senate, 28 March.

> I repeat to you, in this affair the position of France is unequivocal: what has been done has been done contrary to treaties and conventions. We shall do everything possible to oppose the realization of this enterprise.[21]

The intensity of the French annoyance was indicated by the fact that the President of the Republic, normally restricted to ceremonial sentiments, was given a serious line to speak. M. Gaston Doumergue denounced the proposed Customs Union as a threat to the peace. A precedent in Germany's own history left no illusions about the significance of the event, namely, the role of the *Zollverein* in preparing the unification of Prussia.[22]

M. Doumergue's term of office was just running out and the election of a new President of the Republic provided another straw in the wind. Briand had been the front runner, but, in addition to other objections, a feeling of doubt about his whole foreign policy now arose. Would not his election amount to an endorsement of weakness? In the secrecy of the vote at Versailles, 13 May 1931, the National Assembly gave the great tribune only 401 votes to 442 for the colorless President of the Senate, M. Paul Doumer.[23] Briand immediately withdrew and drove back to Paris in silence past the thousands waiting to cheer his victory. His resignation was refused by M. Laval, and a week later he had the satisfaction of forcing the Germans to refer the Customs Union Project to the Permanent Court of International Justice. But despite this recovery, his prestige was shaken and he never quite overcame the disappointment.[24]

[21] *J.O.*, Sénat, *Débats*, 28 March 1931, p. 693. For Briand's earlier speech, *J.O.*, Chambre, *Débats*, 3 March 1931, pp. 1525-1526.

[22] Speech at Nice, 9 April, *Le Temps*, 10 April 1931.

[23] Briand lost by about the same margin as Clemenceau in 1920, ironic vengeance for Briand's part in that event. Both losses were examples of the tradition against electing strong personalities as President. However, many observers felt that the collapse of Briand's German policy was the most important factor in his defeat. F. Goguel, *La Politique des Partis sous la Troisième République* (Paris, 1946), I, 338-339; d'Ormesson, *France*, p. 85; Walter Edge, *A Jerseyman's Journal* (Princeton, 1948), pp. 182, 188-195; Georges Suarez, *Briand*, VI, *L'Artisan de la paix, 1923-1932* (Paris, 1952), pp. 361-370.

[24] The double shock of March and May 1931 told heavily on Briand's health; he was forced to take a long rest in August and September.

Heretofore Briand had shown no interest in the Soviet Union. So long as he had faith in Locarno, there was no sense in haunting Germany with the specter of a new Franco-Russian alignment. Now, however, a new situation confronted him. His friend and protégé at the Quai d'Orsay, M. Alexis Léger, has stated that Briand took the Nazi election victory and the Austro-German Customs Union project as clear warning signals. "He had too much clairvoyance ever to let pass the precise moment when conciliation should give way to the exercise of authority." He had in mind "the most concerted diplomatic campaign to assemble all active forces of international authority against the rebirth of German imperialism."[25]

Certainly there is no denying Briand's bitterness at the turn of his fortunes. One night in July he poured out his feeling to the United States Ambassador, Mr. Walter Edge. "For six years he had worked day and night on reconciliation with Germany and... Germany had repaid his efforts by the attempted customs union with Austria which was a mortal blow to his whole policy and furthermore had discredited him with the Chamber and wiped out overnight his political capital in the country."[26] It is very likely that Briand accepted the negotiations with Russia because he had lost faith in his German policy.

There was thus a juncture in time between the failure of the tariff war with the Soviet Union and apprehension of Germany. In the decade just past, France had been indifferent to the value of co-operation with the Soviet Union. This indifference had been a function of French military superiority over Germany, a Germany disarmed and occupied. Now the *poilus* stood no more at Mainz and Trier, and the Germans were talking boldly. As superiority receded, so did indifference.

ii

It was at this moment that the French government decided to terminate the tariff war with Russia. The decision quickly led to developments on the political plane. Exploratory talks began in March or early in April 1931. By the first of May the two

[25] Alexis Léger, *Briand* (Aurora, New York, 1943), pp. 15-16. M. Léger was Briand's *chef de cabinet* as well as Political Director of the Foreign Ministry.

[26] Edge, *A Jerseyman's Journal*, p. 194. Consult also M. A. Hamilton, *Arthur Henderson* (London, 1938), pp. 356-358, and *B.F.P.*, II, 17-18.

governments had agreed to hold negotiations for a provisional commercial agreement and a non-aggression pact.[27] It was decided to announce cancellation of the restrictive decrees of October 1930 after two or three sessions of the commercial negotiations.

The responsibility for the original proposals is still somewhat obscure, but the question is academic. Periodic Soviet offers of commercial accords and non-aggression pacts were standard practice in these years and the real change was the French willingness to listen. Apparently the French suggested the trade talks, and the Soviets countered with the proposal that a non-aggression treaty be discussed at the same time.[28]

During the month of May the Russians' debut on the Commission of Enquiry on European Union, meeting at Geneva, was put to good use. The fact that Maxim Litvinov did not give effective support to the Austro-German Customs Union was appreciated by M. Briand. The two Foreign Ministers discussed Franco-Russian relations at a private meeting 21 May.[29]

On 4 June 1931 Moscow's commercial delegation, headed by M. Dvolaisky, Deputy Commissar for Foreign Trade, arrived in Paris; the next day they began negotiations with officials from the ministries of Commerce, Agriculture, and Foreign Affairs.[30] These talks were announced to the press, but no publicity was given to the fact that conversations on a non-aggression pact were started by M. Philippe Berthelot, Secretary-General of the Quai d'Orsay and the Soviet Ambassador, M. Valerian Dovgalevsky. The trade negotiations did not attract much attention and there were only a few rumors about the non-aggression talks. Paris was absorbed by the swift drama of financial crisis in Austria and Germany and

[27] Soviet Note of 1 May 1931, given as background information to M. Herriot by the Soviet Ambassador, 8 June 1932, a few days after Herriot became Premier. Édouard Herriot, *Jadis* (Paris, 1948, 1952), II, 312-313. See also semi-official French communiqué quoted in *Le Temps*, 27 Aug. 1931; Soviet Tass Agency communiqué, *ibid.*, 29 Aug. 1931.

[28] In addition to the sources cited directly above, consult the interview with M. Louis Rollin, Minister of Commerce, *Le Temps*, 14 Aug. 1931; résumé of negotiations by *Pravda* (Moscow, daily), 30 Nov. 1932, quoted in *Bulletin périodique de la presse russe* (Paris, analysis of the Russian press by the French Foreign Ministry issued irregularly, roughly every two weeks), No. 224.

[29] Articles from Geneva by Gabriel Péri, *L'Humanité*, 21 May 1931 *et seq.*; article by O. Rosenfeld, *Le Populaire*, 6 June 1931; editorial in *Journal des Débats*, 25 Aug. 1931.

[30] Semi-official communiqués quoted in *Journal des Débats*, 6 June 1931, and *Le Temps*, 7 June 1931; see also *L'Europe Nouvelle*, 27 June 1931, p. 899.

by President Hoover's proposal of a moratorium and the fight over its application.

According to their prior understanding, after a few sessions the French and Russian governments announced on 15 July the abrogation of the restrictive decrees of October 1930. [31] The experts then began to search for an arrangement to expand trade between the two countries. The French offered lower customs duties on Soviet goods in return for a large increase in Soviet orders. The Russians countered with the request that the French government facilitate Soviet orders by arranging state-guaranteed credits as did Germany and Italy. [32] Hit by the decline of world markets, a delegation of French industrialists called on the Minister of Commerce early in September to urge the promotion of exports to Russia. The powerful manufacturers' association, La Confédération Générale de la Production Française, suggested an ingenious scheme amounting to indirect credits. [33]

All talk of credits, of course, quickly ran into the debt question, the enormous debts once owed to French investors by the Tsarist government and repudiated by the Soviets in 1918. The French government probably did not seriously consider granting credits, but had it been tempted, the indignation aroused would have given it pause. Upon hearing the rumors of credits, the conservative press launched the familiar cry of treason to the creditors of Tsarist Russia. Indeed, the critics displayed much suspicion of an increase of trade with Soviet Russia on any basis. It would aid the industrialization of a potential competitor and open the door to communist infiltration in French territories. [34] This outcry revealed a dichotomy in the opinion of many French conserva-

[31] *Journal Officiel*, Lois et Décrets, July 1931, p. 7672; *Izvestya*, 16 July 1931, quoted in *Bulletin de la presse russe*, No. 211, and in *Le Temps*, 18 July 1931.

[32] Interview with M. Rollin, Minister of Commerce, *Le Temps*, 14 Aug. 1931; editorial on the negotiations, *ibid.*, 15 Aug.; speech by M. Rollin, *J.O.*, Chambre, *Débats*, 24 Nov. 1931, pp. 4031-4033; *L'Europe Nouvelle*, 4 July 1931, p. 923, and 25 July 1931, pp. 1006-1007.

[33] Communiqué from the Ministry of Commerce, *Le Temps*, 4 Sept. 1931. The group included representatives of railway and electrical equipment and automobile manufacturers, of the Comité des Forges, and other mining and metallurgical firms. Consult the article by R. Millienne, *Le Temps, Économique*, 13 Oct. 1931; *Journal des Débats*, 17 Oct. and 3 Dec. 1931; and *B.F.P.*, VII, 245.

[34] R. Millienne in *Le Temps, Économique*, 13 Oct. 1931; Pierre Gaxotte in *Je Suis Partout*, 12 Sept. 1931; Pierre Bernus in *Journal des Débats*, 17 and 31 Oct. 1931; M. Émile Buré in *L'Ordre*, quoted in "Revue de la presse," *J.D.*, 20 Nov. 1931; M. Louis Marin in *La Nation*, quoted *ibid.*, 12 Sept. 1931; M. Fréderic Eccard, "Dumping et Crise Financière des Soviets," in *Revue des Deux Mondes* (Paris, biweekly), 1 Nov. 1931, pp. 43-65.

tives. They were willing to do away with the restrictive decrees, but, when it came to taking measures for the expansion of Franco-Soviet commerce, the old antagonism returned.

The industrialists, who simply wanted Russian orders for their factories, could not push their credit projects without government aid. However, the government refused to help. The Minister of Commerce twice issued statements that state-guaranteed credits could not be considered until the debt question had been solved.[35] In Moscow there was not the slightest disposition to break the jam by beginning payments on the prewar debts.

These conflicts could not be resolved, and the commercial negotiations were adjourned sometime in the fall of 1931. The sole result was the abrogation of the restrictive decrees. Franco-Soviet trade remained at the very low level it had reached early in the year.[36]

Paris apparently had dismissed the rumors of political talks as too incongruous to be taken seriously. Great was the surprise when the Paris edition of the *New York Herald Tribune* reported on 19 August 1931 that France and the Soviet Union had "concluded" a non-aggression pact.[37] Unable to deny the existence of negotiations, the Quai d'Orsay fell back on the "premature" formula; nothing definite could be expected for several months. In any case, conclusion of the pact would depend upon the success of similar Soviet negotiations with Poland and Romania.[38]

The Quai d'Orsay's explanations, although somewhat embarrassed, were correct. The pact had not been concluded but a draft had been worked out. M. Berthelot and Ambassador Dovgalevsky had initialed a draft of a Franco-Soviet non-aggression pact on or a few days before 13 August.[39] M. Flandin, Min-

[35] Semi-official communiqué in *Le Temps*, 1 Oct. 1931; statement by M. Rollin, *J.O.*, Chambre, *Débats*, 24 Nov. 1931, p. 4032.

French Imports from Russia	French Exports to Russia
1930 886 million francs	170 million francs
1931 496 million francs	59 million francs

League of Nations, *International Trade Statistics, 1931 and 1932*, p. 120.

[37] Quoted in *Journal des Débats*, 20 Aug. 1931; several other Paris papers reprinted the disclosure.

[38] Semi-official notes from the Quai d'Orsay, printed in *Journal des Débats*, 21 Aug., and in *Le Temps*, 27 Aug. 1931. "Bulletin du Jour," *ibid.*, 28 Aug. 1931.

[39] M. Litvinov told the British Chargé d'Affaires in Moscow, Mr. Strang, 13 August, that a "Franco-Soviet pact of non-aggression has been initialled." He said that the French government wished to keep the fact secret. *B.F.P.*, VII, 218. Asked later for information on the negotiations, an official of the French Ministry of Foreign Affairs stated that "the treaty was initialled by M. Berthelot and the Soviet

ister of Finance, told an American diplomat on 19 August that "the fact was that the text of a pact of non-aggression had been worked out in principle between them without committing either government but that no formal action had been taken on this text which presumably will be discussed by the Council of Ministers at its meeting tomorrow."[40] In view of this statement and the criticism aroused by the press reports, it is almost certain that the situation was reviewed by the cabinet. Significantly, it did not repudiate the negotiations.

Apart from Briand, it was a conservative constellation that assumed the responsibility. The Premier, M. Pierre Laval, had started his career on the Left but had made the classical political journey to the Right.[41] His cabinet numbered several notables of the Center and Right, such as MM. André Tardieu, André Maginot, Paul Reynaud, and Pierre-Étienne Flandin.[42] The fact is often forgotten that the first step towards Franco-Soviet rapprochement was taken by a conservative cabinet.

The news of political conversations with Soviet Russia was received with reserve and hostility by most of the French press. Several center and right-wing newspapers denounced the very idea of negotiating with the Soviets. Such action could only lend prestige to the Soviet regime, which was working through its foreign agents to undermine French institutions at home and in the colonies.[43] These were the same quarters who were loudest in decrying the dangers of German nationalism; yet they expressed no interest in securing Russian support or even in breaking Germany's link with Russia. The menace of Rapallo was indeed

---

Ambassador, M. Dovgalevsky last August." Dispatch of 22 Dec. 1931, from the United States Ambassador in Paris, Mr. Edge, 751.6111/11. Archives of the Department of State, Washington, D. C.

[40] M. Flandin to Mr. Theodore Marriner, United States Chargé d'Affaires in Paris. Dispatch of 19 Aug. 1931, 751.6111/3. Archives of the Department of State, Washington, D. C.

[41] See chap. ii, pp. 22-24, for a portrait of Laval.

[42] See chap. iii, pp. 36-43, for Tardieu's later attempt to stall the rapprochement.

[43] During the period when the pact was frequently in the news, 20 Aug.–10 Sept. 1931, such views were expressed in the following journals: on the extreme Right, *L'Action Française, L'Ami du Peuple, Je Suis Partout;* on the Right and Center, *L'Echo de Paris, Le Journal des Débats, L'Ordre, Le Figaro.* At Clermont-Ferrand, a Regional Congress of the *Fédération Républicaine,* the largest party of the Right, passed a resolution asking the government to suspend negotiations until the Soviets stopped subversive activities in France and the colonies. Quoted in *Journal des Débats,* 24 Aug. 1931. Parliament being adjourned, there was no reaction in the Chamber or Senate.

invoked by almost all the writers, but it was used to demonstrate the complete unreliability of the Soviets. M. Pierre Bernus, who wrote a daily column on politics and foreign policy for the *Journal des Débats,* asserted: "A Franco-Soviet pact would merely consolidate the German-Bolshevik alliance; the two partners would then be able to accomplish their designs more easily because France's freedom of action would be restricted."[44] On the Left there was no such condemnation; however, save for the Communists, there was no enthusiasm. Both the Socialists and the Radical-Socialists took a cautious approach to the prospect of co-operation with Soviet Russia.[45]

iii

Critics and supporters of the new tack were agreed on one point: no pact with the Soviet Union should be made at the expense of French allies in Eastern Europe. So said the "Bulletin du Jour" of *Le Temps,* the lead editorial column which was often inspired by the Quai d'Orsay. "It is quite clear that such a pact of non-aggression can only be concluded . . . within the framework of the obligations which link France to Poland and Romania."[46] French negotiators made it a condition that they would not sign the pact until Russian non-aggression pacts with Poland and Romania had been negotiated.[47]

On 28 August the Polish Foreign Minister, M. Auguste Zaleski, stopped in Paris on his way to Geneva. After conferences at the Quai d'Orsay, he stated that his country fully approved the French action and had similar goals.[48] There had been some desultory Polish-Russian discussion about a non-aggression pact, and on 23

[44] *Journal des Débats,* 25 Aug. 1931.

[45] *Le Populaire,* the official Socialist party daily, merely reprinted the original disclosure and the semi-official communiqués. Much resentment had been created among the Radical-Socialists when the Communists refused any co-operation with the other left-wing parties in the 1928 elections. See the bitter complaints of M. Édouard Herriot in a letter to the widow of the late Soviet Ambassador to Paris, in Lubov Krassin, *Krassin* (London, 1929), pp. 274-275. *L'Ère Nouvelle,* a paper often used as a spokesman for Herriot's views, and *L'Oeuvre,* the largest Radical paper, were noncommittal about the pact.

[46] "Bulletin du Jour," *Le Temps,* 28 Aug. 1931.

[47] Verbal report on the non-aggression pact to the Chamber of Deputies, made by M. Henry Torrès, *J.O.,* Chambre, *Débats,* 16 May 1933, p. 2383; Jules Laroche, *La Pologne de Pilsudski, Souvenirs d'une ambassade, 1926-1935* (Paris, 1953), pp. 104-106. Note, however, reports of Soviet denials that such a condition existed; *B.F.P.,* VII, 217, 219-220.

[48] Quoted in "Bulletin du Jour," *Le Temps,* 30 Aug. 1931.

August 1931 M. Patek, the Polish Ambassador in Moscow, proposed that formal negotiations should begin.[49] After some haggling over which draft to use, the negotiations eventually got under way in December.

Poland, in her precarious position, often had to turn from one former master to another. The recent surge of German nationalism made it desirable to lessen the tension in the east. Endless disputes with Berlin over Danzig, the Corridor, and Upper Silesia were bad enough. To these had been added Germany's refusal to ratify a commercial treaty signed in March 1930 and the ominous Nazi election victory. In May 1931 the new German pocket battleship, the *Deutschland,* was sent down the ways at Kiel, to the tune of much talk about re-establishing German hegemony on the Baltic.[50]

The moves towards Russia, for both France and Poland, were measures of deviation from their own alliance. This is a point not generally realized. The Polish rapprochement with Russia had its origins not in French influence, as it appeared, but independently and at a time when relations were deteriorating.[51]

For Poland, rapprochement with Russia could not go very far. For France the limits were much more flexible. No firm answer had ever been given to the question: "Is Poland a satisfactory substitute for Tsarist Russia?" There were groups in the army and foreign office who had never fully approved of the Franco-Polish military alliance of 1921.[52] The Left disliked the authoritarian Pilsudski régime; some friends of Poland on the Right had doubts about her economic viability. It was true that the rapprochements

[49] Statement of M. Patek, quoted in *Journal des Débats,* 28 Aug. 1931; report from the Warsaw correspondent, *Le Temps,* 26 Aug. 1931; semi-official communiqué from the Quai d'Orsay, *ibid.,* 27 Aug. 1931; B.F.P., VII, 219-220.

[50] Consult S.I.A., 1932, pp. 311-394.

[51] The decline of Franco-Polish relations can be studied in the perceptive, documented memoirs of the French Ambassador in Warsaw from 1926 to 1935, M. Jules Laroche, *La Pologne de Pilsudski;* for the later period see especially pp. 101 ff. Consult also Colonel Joseph Beck, *Dernier Rapport: Politique polonaise, 1926-1939* (Neuchâtel, 1951). Although fragmentary, these memoirs reveal many causes of the Franco-Polish misunderstanding.

[52] For different reasons General Weygand and M. Aristide Briand were skeptical of the value of the alliance. Laval's uncomplimentary references to Poland during his visit to Washington are noteworthy: "M. Laval repeated to the Secretary of State [Stimson] the admission that he had made to him in July, that the Polish Corridor was a monstrosity. . . ." Dispatch of 26 Oct. 1931 from the British Ambassador in Washington, B.F.P., II, 307. Consult also *Foreign Relations of the United States, Diplomatic Papers, 1931* (Washington, 1946), I, 549. (Hereinafter cited as F.R.U.S.)

with Russia would strengthen Poland by helping to liberate her from fear of Russia. Even this friendly approach, however, betrayed skepticism about Poland's power.

The reports of Russian negotiations with Poland and France aroused a strong reaction abroad only in Berlin, but the attitude of Italy was also significant. The reaction of Rome was favorable; at last France was following the "realistic" Italian lead. Throughout 1931 Foreign Minister Grandi repeatedly defended Italy's growing trade with Russia; he told a diplomat that "the world must trade with Russia and [he] would like to see France and Germany together make an effort to open up the country."[53] The French rapprochement with the Soviet Union thus did not create a source of friction with her Latin neighbor.

The Franco-Soviet talks had been received fairly calmly in Berlin, but when reports of a Polish-Soviet non-aggression pact followed, there was an outcry. The Russians were accused of "treason to Rapallo"; if the negotiations were successful, Poland would be reinforced in her fight against German revisionism. The German Ambassador in Moscow, Herbert von Dirksen, was called home to report, and the repercussions moved M. Litvinov to stop in Berlin on his way to Geneva in order to offer "assurances."[54]

The Paris press was shocked that the Germans found intolerable a non-aggression pledge between Poland and Russia. An editorial in the "Bulletin du Jour" of *Le Temps* concluded that France could not ignore the disturbing implications of Berlin's reaction. To be sure, one should be cautious about the value of promises by Communist Russia, but they might help to consolidate the balance of power in Eastern Europe. "One might say that a Franco-Russian non-aggression treaty would constitute something of a political counterweight to the German-Russian treaties of Rapallo and Berlin."[55] It had been many years since a rebuke to Germany had been written in Franco-Russian terms.

After the flurry of news at the end of August, the negotiations

[53] Conversation with the United States Under-Secretary of State, Mr. Castle, during Grandi's visit to Washington, 16 Nov. 1931, *F.R.U.S., 1931*, II, 647. For similar statements by Grandi to Secretary Stimson, see *ibid., 1931*, I, 541, 559; also *B.F.P.*, II, 189.

[54] Dirksen, *Moscow, Tokyo, London*, pp. 115-116; extracts from the German press and a statement made by Litvinov in Berlin, 29 Aug., quoted in *Le Temps*, 23-30 Aug. 1931. See the discussion of German-Soviet relations in chap. ii, pp. 27-29, below.

[55] *Le Temps*, 28 Aug. 1931.

for a Franco-Soviet non-aggression pact were temporarily recessed. Certain obstacles had to be removed before any further progress could be made. France would not give a pledge of non-aggression and neutrality to Russia without identical Russian assurances to Poland and Romania. French diplomacy would now have to wait on activity in Moscow, Warsaw, and Bucharest. Thus, in September 1931, the curious phenomenon of a Franco-Soviet rapprochement disappeared from the diplomatic stage almost as suddenly as it had been introduced. There was no telling how far the French would carry their new policy; but they were willing to talk, and that marked the end of indifference.

Two

THE DILEMMA OF GERMANY

One is tempted to say that French relations with Russia were the inverse of those existing between France and Germany. On the Russian side, too, a powerful influence can be attributed to German policy. We have seen how the Nazi election victory and the Austro-German Customs Union Project created a mood of anxiety in Paris at the time when a decision had to be made about Franco-Soviet relations. Let us now return to this question, because the dilemma of what to do about Germany was suddenly modified in the summer of 1931.

The whole tragic complex of distrust and fear between the two countries had started flooding back in September 1930. Indeed, had events proceeded normally, nobody would have dared make the suggestion of inviting German ministers to Paris. Yet they were invited and Brüning even heard the leaders of the French cabinet propose a comprehensive settlement in the privacy of the Quai d'Orsay, 18-19 July. What had changed the situation was the drastic working of the world economic depression.

Financial and economic conditions in Central Europe had been rapidly disintegrating in recent months; and the most serious danger signal was the failure of the Credit-Anstalt bank in Vienna on 11 May. Although this crisis was met by loans from the Bank of England and the Bank of International Settlements, it was only patched up and it had serious consequences for Germany's financial structure. At the beginning of June the Reichsbank began to suffer heavy losses of gold and foreign exchange, mostly withdrawn from abroad, and the failures of several large business concerns became known. Unemployment figures and relief lines swelled by tens of thousands every week. The German government added to the already severe measures of deflation by "economy decrees" of 4 June, but, as Chancellor Brüning told British leaders two days later, "it was very difficult for him to keep control in Germany if he could not hold out any hope. The people were in despair, and the growing power of the Nazis and Communists was a menace."[1]

The desperate circumstances seemed to justify German pleas for help. Some financial aid from abroad might be needed, but, above all, suspension of reparation payments was deemed indispensable to a return of confidence. To the latter, the French would never have agreed, but they were not asked. President Hoover took them by surprise with his dramatic proposal of 20 June 1931 for a year's moratorium "of all payments on intergovernmental debts, reparations and relief debts, both principal and interest. . . ."[2] Most of the world breathed a sign of relief, but in Paris the brusque announcement was acutely resented and decried as an Anglo-American trick. The ensuing negotiations to hammer out a satisfactory formula for French acceptance of the moratorium dragged on until 6 July and undercut the optimism originally produced. Disheartening losses of foreign exchange were again felt in Berlin. On 13 July the Darmstädter and National Bank, one of the largest in Germany, failed to open for business. The panic and runs on other banks forced the government to declare a temporary banking "holiday" and to institute strict control of foreign exchange transactions. It was clear that there would be swift repercussions in Central Europe and in the two centers from which so many loans had been made to Germany, London and New York. No one denied the common peril and plans were hurriedly made. American and British statesmen and financiers converged on Paris, an international conference was summoned for London, and the German Chancellor and Foreign Minister were officially invited to come to Paris for preliminary talks.

Thus, paradoxically, less than four months after the jolting effect of the Austro-German Customs Union Project, the French and German governments were engaged in direct negotiations on the highest level. The immediate problem was a financial one, but it was an open secret that the French would insist that political agreements provide the basis, or the price, for economic and financial accommodations. What was at stake, once again, was the eternal problem of a Franco-German settlement.

[1] Meeting of Chancellor Brüning and Foreign Minister Curtius with British ministers at Chequers, England, 7 June 1931, *B.F.P.*, II, 75. The Nazis had achieved their first control of a Provincial Diet in the Oldenburg elections of 18 May 1931.

[2] Text of the Hoover proposal, *F.R.U.S.*, *1931*, I, 33-34. The spreading of the crisis from one country to another is brilliantly evoked in Arnold Toynbee's section, "Annus Terribilis, 1931," in *S.I.A.*, *1931*.

The French were confronted with a peculiar dilemma. Their suspicion of German intentions was higher than at any time since Locarno. Yet there were several powerful inducements not to rebuff the unexpected occasion. The first was the familiar argument that the collapse of the German economy would produce social upheavals from which only Communism or extreme nationalism could draw profit. Secondly, the evacuation of the Rhineland made it prudent to secure a solid understanding before the Germans took advantage of the absence of foreign troops to begin serious rearmament. Most tempting of all was an advantage of the moment. In 1924-1925, the years of the Dawes Plan and of Locarno, France's severe financial crisis had made it difficult for her to resist American and British plans on the German problem. Now France might be able to impose her own solution, for she still held a good financial position while the United States and Great Britain were staggering.[3] Owing to her relative immunity from the depression, French diplomacy was in the best position to hold out the carrot since 1919.

It was a thesis held in some French circles that, given the withdrawal of America and Britain's refusal fully to commit herself on the Continent, eventually France must reach a "direct" settlement with Germany. Such a settlement would be a two-party affair, in contrast to Locarno, where the basic treaty wove a complicated network among France, Germany, and Belgium and the two guarantors, Britain and Italy. A direct negotiation might offer the opportunity to drive a better bargain. At any rate, it would be more helpful in soothing the rivalry between the two countries than anything achieved by Anglo-American mediation. It was claimed, and with some justification, that whereas the French had made the greater sacrifices in Locarno, the Germans had given the credit to the British. The Hoover moratorium had given a powerful impetus to this belief, for it was taken as a perfect example of the dangers inherent in Anglo-American initiatives on the German problem.[4]

[3] On 1 August the Bank of France gave the Bank of England a gold credit of £25,000,000 (equaled by the Federal Reserve Bank of New York). Commenting on the crisis, Philippe Berthelot, Secretary-General of the Quai d'Orsay, wrote a friend 18 Aug. 1931, "Jamais nous n'avons eu une situation plus forte." Quoted in August Bréal, *Philippe Berthelot* (Paris, 1937), p. 223.

[4] Even Briand, who fully appreciated the necessity for co-operation with England and the United States, told U.S. Ambassador Edge that "he interpreted President Hoover's gesture as another effort of the British and Americans to buy off and

The necessity of a direct settlement with Germany was a thesis that was correctly attributed to Laval. With him, in contrast to others, it was not merely an anti-British reflex, but the product of a sincere desire for an understanding with Germany.[5] If Briand had been in command, his disillusionment might well have led him to let the Germans squirm. But Briand was in physical eclipse in July, and the German crisis thus became Laval's responsibility.

Pierre Laval tried three times to reach an accord with Germany—1931, 1934-1935, and 1940-1944. It is useless, however, to write the history of 1931 in terms of 1940. With France still master of the Continent the situation was completely different, and, in this period, there is no evidence of the attitudes or methods that tainted Laval's later career. If there is nothing to indict, neither is there any reason to attribute lofty aspirations. Laval's motives were simple and practical, the product of his background and ambition.

Laval is an interesting example of a type of political leader new to the traditional European state-system, a man quite truly of the people, from a peasant heritage in Auvergne, to whom abstractions such as "national prestige" and "vital interests" meant much less than considerations of material prosperity and political appeasement.[6] Starting in Paris as a poor Socialist lawyer, elected to the Chamber in 1914 and only thereby given immunity from arrest as a dangerous defeatist, daring enough to speak for a "white peace" in 1917, Laval carved an early career so radical as to be

appease the Reich.... Germany would be able to say that France was forced by the United States and Great Britain to make this sacrifice." *A Jerseyman's Journal*, pp. 194-195.

[5] As Ambassador Edge saw him that summer, "M. Laval believed ... that European peace hinged on cordial relations between France and Germany; and that France and Germany could work out their differences only if the British would refrain from interfering in European affairs in execution of their traditional balance of power policy." *Ibid.*, p. 207. At the Pétain trial, speaking of 1931, Laval said: "J'avais toujours préconisé, comme Briand, de rechercher une réconciliation, une entente, un rapprochement où, en tous cas, un état de bon voisinage avec les Allemands...." République Française, Haute Cour de Justice, *Procès du Maréchal Pétain* (Paris, 1945), p. 196. (Hereinafter cited as *Procès Pétain*.)

[6] Details on Laval's life may be found in Alfred Mallet, *Pierre Laval* (2 vols.; Paris, 1955); David Thomson, *Two Frenchmen: Pierre Laval and Charles de Gaulle* (London, 1951); Henry Torrès, *Pierre Laval* (New York, 1941); Pierre Tissier, *I Worked with Laval* (London, 1942). Consult also Laval's testimony in the Pétain trial and his own trial, *Procès Pétain*, pp. 183-222 and *Le Procès Laval* (Paris, 1946); his apologia, written in prison, *Laval Parle ... Notes et Mémoires* (Paris, 1948); Alexander Werth, *Which Way France?* (London, 1937), chap. vi; M. and Mme René de Chambrun, *La Vie de la France sous l'Occupation, 1940-1944* (Paris, 1957), 3 vols.

notorious. But, while his closest associates went on to become Communists in the split of the Socialist party in 1920, Laval walked out of the party in the other direction. Co-operating with the Radical-Socialists, he backed Caillaux and Briand and gained high posts in three Briand cabinets, 1925-1926. A year later he became an independent senator and by 1930 he was conservative enough to join Tardieu's second cabinet. Despite his evolution to the Right, he remained mayor of the Parisian working-class suburb of Aubervilliers and kept up his personal contacts on the Left.

Nothing in Laval's past created for him the obstacles to reconciliation with Germany which tortured the "traditionalists."[7] He had been a part of the prewar Socialism which so bitterly assailed the army; he carried no memories of facing the enemy's troops; he had no commitment to the Versailles Treaty; indeed, he had voted against it. On the other hand there was much that disposed him to be sympathetic to the policy of reconciliation. He had lived in the lower class milieu of those who had suffered most from the war and were now profoundly pacifist; and he had been apprentice to two men whose names were synonomous with Franco-German friendship—Caillaux, Briand. He was very ambitious and well aware that Locarno and its promise of peace had once given Briand immense popularity.

Finally, Laval bore the stamp of his provincial peasant background and was not too well acquainted with the complexities of international life. He was convinced that formulas which were successful in business and domestic politics were equally applicable to foreign affairs.[8] Was it not a hard-headed policy, this attempt to liquidate a terrible rivalry on which France could no longer squander her limited resources of men and matériel? Laval often made the claim that he looked at the map of Europe from the common sense point of view and that the map taught that France would always be the neighbor of Germany.[9] It was not surprising, then, that the sudden opportunity to reopen the negotiation attracted Pierre Laval. According to M. François-Poncet, then a

[7] Writing of Laval's return in 1934, Flandin made the following remarkable comment: "M. Laval succède à M. Barthou. Il n'appartient pas à la même génération, et n'en a pas hérité la tradition d'un inévitable antagonisme entre la France et l'Allemagne. Il rêve de réconcilier le peuple français et le peuple allemand." *Politique Française, 1919-1940* (Paris, 1947), p. 104.

[8] Torrès reports some interesting comments in this vein made by Laval in 1931-1932. *Pierre Laval*, p. 186.

[9] Werth, *Which Way France?*, pp. 99-100; *Le Procès Laval*, p. 57.

member of the cabinet, Laval was saying that this crisis would make Germany realize at last that she had more to gain by conciliation than by intransigence.[10]

The idea of a direct Franco-German understanding was not openly advertised, but the clear diplomatic clue was M. Laval's successful insistence that private Franco-German talks take place in Paris before the other powers joined the consultation. British displeasure was shown by Prime Minister MacDonald's blunt questioning of the German ministers: "Did it suit them that these conversations should be continued between the two parties [France and Germany] without our intervention or would they prefer that we should intervene? He would remind them that His Majesty's Government were interested politically and it would not do for a settlement to be reached and that His Majesty's Government should be faced with a *fait accompli*."[11] MacDonald's jealousy was simply ignored by Laval. Franco-German talks on 18-19 July preceded the informal six-power talks in Paris; they were continued as the ministers journeyed together to the London Conference and they were renewed in September when Laval and Briand paid an official visit to Berlin.

The French plan was to offer financial aid, in the form of a ten-year loan, in return for Germany's acceptance of "political conditions." These conditions amounted to a moratorium on German revisionism. The most important conditions were tacit renunciation of the Austro-German Customs Union, a guarantee that the loan would not be used to further commercial relations which France considered unwise, a pledge not to insist upon equality of armaments, and the "freezing" of German frontiers.[12] Not all of

---

[10] A. François-Poncet, *De Versailles à Potsdam* (Paris, 1948), p. 178. Laval's open-minded attitude towards Germany was shown by his remarks to Secretary Stimson 24 July 1931: "The underlying problem which would solve everything else was the question of the Polish corridor. If that could only be solved France would have no other real trouble with Germany." *F.R.U.S., 1931,* I, 549.

[11] Conversation among MM. MacDonald, Henderson, Brüning, and Curtius, during visit to Berlin, 28 July, *B.F.P.,* II, 233-237; Curtius, *Sechs Jahre Minister der Deutschen Republik,* p. 222.

[12] Details can be pieced together from the following sources: *B.F.P.,* II, 190-221, 233-245, 254-257, 285-292; *F.R.U.S., 1931,* I, 266, 286-297, 549, and II, 647; *Laval Parle,* p. 89; François-Poncet, *Souvenirs d'une ambassade à Berlin* (Paris, 1946), pp. 22-23, *De Versailles à Potsdam,* pp. 179-180; Flandin, *Politique Française 1919-1940,* pp. 39-40, and testimony in *Le Procès Flandin* (Paris, 1947), pp. 50-51; R. Coulondre, *De Staline à Hitler* (Paris, 1950), p. 194; d'Ormesson, *France,* pp. 85-88; P. Schmidt, *Statist auf Diplomatischer Bühne, 1923-1945* (Bonn, 1949), pp. 219-220; Curtius, *Sechs Jahre Minister der Deutschen Republik,* pp. 219-220.

these had the same value and perhaps the French would have sacrificed all others for a German promise not to rearm.[13] Apparently, the French also proposed, in great secrecy, that a pact of non-aggression and mutual consultation be concluded between the two countries.[14]

The result is well known. Chancellor Brüning hesitated, then rejected the French proposals. Apparently he felt that the French conditions were too severe, that the pressure of resurgent nationalism in Germany was too strong to enable him to accept.

What effect did this dramatic episode have upon French policy towards the Soviet Union? One should not expect to find any decisive influence, for the Franco-German conversations of 1931 were not themselves decisive. They did not yield an accord; on the other hand, they were not broken off and they achieved a momentary *détente*. It is nonetheless possible to detect certain influences and to clarify certain tendencies of the French attitude towards the Russian problem.

One of the French objectives was to cut the Russo-German bonds. Discussing the question of Laval's aims, the British Ambassador in Paris referred to "his desire to turn Germany from Russia, which has, I understand, already met with some response in Berlin."[15] The demand for "assurances" about Germany's commercial policies was specifically directed against her heavy trade with Russia. In June M. Laval had already mentioned in connection with the Hoover moratorium that Germany should not be allowed to use the money she might save for: "1) armaments; 2) competition amounting to dumping; and 3) exploitation of the countries to the east."[16] On 16 July M. Flandin, Minister of Finance, set forth as a requirement of his loan project, "precluding . . . special commercial credits such as those recently made by Germany to Russia

[13] Chancellor Brüning told Sir W. Layton, 22 Aug. 1931, that "he had since received from a very high French source information that if he would undertake not to raise the question of the disparity between French and German armaments no other political condition of any kind would be raised by the French." *B.F.P.*, II, 255.

[14] The authority is M. François-Poncet, then a member of the cabinet and appointed Ambassador to Germany in September, *De Versailles à Potsdam*, p. 179. "Laval et Briand proposent, alors, à Brüning de conclure avec la France un pacte de non-agression et de consultation mutuelle, par lequel les deux pays s'engageraient à se concerter dans toutes les circonstances qui pourraient affecter leurs bonnes relations ou troubler la paix de l'Europe."

[15] Dispatch from Lord Tyrrell, 21 Oct. 1931, *B.F.P.*, II, 301.

[16] Dispatch from the U.S. Ambassador in France, Mr. Edge, 24 June 1931, *F.R.U.S., 1931*, I, 57-58.

and Turkey, which the French financial authorities considered bad policy. . . ."[17]

Any direct Franco-German understanding would be anti-Russian in its impact. At the very least, it would mean the diplomatic isolation of the Soviet Union; she would have lost her only friend among the European great powers. This, of course, was precisely why Moscow was touchy about the mere announcement of Franco-German talks. There is no evidence that the French fancied the accord with Germany as an instrument for *active* use against the Soviet Union.[18] However, they did plan to pull Germany away from Russia. Paris may have thought of this condition as a test of Germany's good faith, a necessary prelude to the reconciliation. If that hope should not materialize, the negative goal of weakening Germany by loosening her bond with the Russians at least would be achieved.

It is a puzzling, delicate task to evaluate Franco-German relations during the interwar years. Perhaps it was already too late for reconciliation. One can be unduly fascinated by a meeting which might have prevented the accession of Adolf Hitler. Yet the talks were not fruitless. They improved the atmosphere between the two countries and created a real measure of confidence between Laval and Brüning. M. André François-Poncet, who owed his October appointment as Ambassador to Berlin to the hopes aroused, reveals that Brüning's sincerity and good faith in pleading his case evoked "confidence and sympathy" in Paris. "With such a Chancellor of the Reich ... how could one not be tempted to believe that it was worth trying to solve the Franco-German problem?"[19] On the eve of the Laval-Briand voyage to Berlin in September, an editorial in *Le Temps* indicated the cautious measure of value that the cabinet attached to the previous negotiations.

The most reliable result of the conversations which MM. Brüning and Curtius had in Paris was to dispel certain misunderstandings, to

[17] Conversation of Flandin, Henderson, and Stimson, 16 July 1931, *B.F.P.*, II, 202. The American record confirms Flandin's intention "to prevent extension by Germany of credits to foreign countries unless the Committee approves. The French say here they have particularly in mind the credits by Germany given not only to Russia but to Turkey." *F.R.U.S., 1931,* I, 266. The French had in mind the "Piatakov Accord" of 14 April 1931, by which the German government guaranteed credits of 300,000,000 marks for Soviet purchases in Germany. See above, chap. i, p. 6.

[18] See Brüning's comments on the Paris talks, *B.F.P.*, II, 254-255.

[19] *Souvenirs d'une ambassade à Berlin,* pp. 17-18. Note Laval's statements during the London Conference, 20-23 July 1931, *B.F.P.*, II, Appendix One.

destroy certain prejudicies, to convince both sides of the possibility of a confident collaboration within strictly limited areas, finally to establish a direct contact between Paris and Berlin, with the will to use it, in all sincerity, to overcome the difficulties of the hour.[20]

Some progress was also made on the level of economic co-operation and a Franco-German Economic Commission was set up as a result of the Berlin talks. It was hoped that on this terrain, where emotions were less involved and material incentives greater, a basis for political rapprochement might be built up.[21]

Incidentally, it was now impossible for London to block the attempt. Economic and financial conditions in the British Isles had grown steadily worse during the summer, and the fall of the Labour government and formation of an emergency National government, 24 August, did not check the slide. Startling news of an "insubordination" in units of the British Navy at Invergordon, 15 September, was followed on the twenty-first by the announcement that the United Kingdom had been forced to go off the gold standard.[22] These cracks in the two most splendid symbols of Britain's power left her prestige and influence at its lowest level in many decades.

The essay at a direct Franco-German settlement did not have a sharp impact on French policy toward Soviet Russia. However, so long as there remained any serious hopes for an understanding with Germany, French curiosity about Russia would be restrained. Earlier in 1931 there had been no hope; now some cautious optimism returned. The re-establishment of good relations between the French and German governments in the summer and fall of 1931 exerted a definite braking influence on the progress of Franco-Soviet rapprochement.

ii

For Russia, too, relations with France were the opposite face of her ties with Germany. No dramatic consultations took place

[20] "Bulletin du Jour," *Le Temps*, 26 Sept. 1931.

[21] On the French visit to Berlin, see François-Poncet, *Souvenirs d'une ambassade à Berlin*, pp. 23-29; Curtius, *Sechs Jahre Minister der Deutschen Republik*, pp. 225-227; Schmidt, *Statist auf Diplomatische Bühne*, p. 229; B.F.P., II, 271-273; F.R.U.S., 1931, I, 326-327.

[22] During the climax of the run on gold, the French Treasury, on Laval's personal decision, put at British disposal a gold credit equivalent to three billion francs. *Laval Parle*, Appendix No. 2 and p. 26; Mallet, *Pierre Laval*, I, 52-53.

between the partners of Rapallo, but their relationship needs to be recalled in order to show its durability under adverse circumstances.

Solid economic bases for this structure had long been established and, as we have seen, they were reinforced by the "Piatakov" Accord of April 1931. The orders therein given to German firms were very important to the success of the Five Year Plan and, for this reason, there was every incentive not to jeopardize their successful completion. The renewal of the Berlin Treaty of April 1926 came due in 1931 and there is no evidence that the Russians thought of letting it drop. On 24 June a protocol was signed prolonging it and the 1929 Arbitration Treaty until July 1933.[23] An editorial in *Izvestya*, 26 June 1931, spoke with great respect of Germany's population and productive power. "This treaty strengthens the position of the Soviet Union in her struggle for the execution of the Five Year Plan, in her struggle for peace."[24] On the other hand, the Russians were disturbed by Germany's financial crisis and feared the changes that it might produce. They were also aware that within the current political and diplomatic leadership at Berlin—notably Brüning and State Secretary von Bülow—there was personal dislike of co-operation with the Soviets.[25] But no alternatives were as yet available to the Russians. On the commercial level, with Britain and the United States unable—and France unwilling—to grant large guaranteed credits, no one came forward to take Germany's place. In September the Reichsbank granted a further support of the credit conditions for trade with Moscow. At Geneva it was Germany that pushed consideration of the Soviet Pact of Economic Non-Aggression against French opposition, and M. Litvinov continued to vote most frequently with Dr. Curtius and Signor Grandi.

Surveying the state of Russo-German relations at this moment, E. H. Carr notes the absence of the "initial enthusiasm and constant preoccupation" of earlier days, but does not underestimate the ties which remained. "What survived was a marriage of con-

[23] Text of the protocol in *L.N.T.S.*, CLVII, 383. It provided that the treaties could be denounced after 20 June 1933 on a one-year's notice. See also Curtius, *Sechs Jahre Minister der Deutschen Republik*, p. 156, and Dirksen, *Moscow, Tokyo, London*, p. 113.

[24] Quoted in Lionel Kochan, *Russia and the Weimar Republic* (Cambridge, 1954), p. 151; long excerpts from the editorial may be found in *Osteuropa*, VI, 671-672, and *Bulletin de la presse russe*, No. 210.

[25] Dirksen, *Moscow, Tokyo, London*, p. 112.

venience, which was kept up partly out of habit and partly because its advantages to both parties were still just great enough to warrant the effort required to maintain it."[26] It must be remembered that the Franco-Soviet negotiations were not a radical departure from general Soviet policy at this time. They fitted easily into the effort to facilitate the Five Year Plan by improving political and commercial relations with as many countries as possible. If this motive counseled the new, it did not condemn the old. It is thus not surprising that at the same time as she sought rapprochement with France, Soviet Russia maintained the "special" relationship with Germany.

[26] Carr, *German-Soviet Relations between the Two World Wars*, p. 101. Consult Kochan, *Russia and the Weimar Republic*, pp. 150-159.

Three

IN THE DOLDRUMS

The negotiations for a Franco-Soviet Pact of Non-Aggression necessarily went into suspension once a draft of the pact had been initialed in August 1931. The conclusion of the pact now depended on two things: improvement of the general relations existing between France and Russia, and the Soviets' negotiation of non-aggression pacts with France's two eastern allies, Poland and Romania. Surprising progress was made by Moscow in her negotiations. On the other hand, this period witnessed the arrival of a new French cabinet clearly hostile to Soviet Russia and in conflict with her on three major issues of the day. When it was replaced by a more friendly cabinet, the latter was immediately distracted from the rapprochement by new and important negotiations with Germany and England.

Diplomatic activity between Paris and Moscow during the winter of 1931 was of a minor nature.[1] The two governments exchanged military information in connection with the forthcoming Disarmament Conference, an exchange of importance owing to the Soviet refusal to communicate this information to the League of Nations.[2] The French government also tried to aid Russia by requesting the United States to drop its objection to Russian adherence to the 1920 Spitzbergen Treaty. This treaty gave Norway sovereignty over Spitzbergen, Jan Mayen, and Bear islands, strategically placed across the North Cape route to the Russian ports of Murmansk and Archangel. Excluded by the militant anti-Bolshevism of 1920, the Russians had no legal entrance to questions concerning the islands. The French suggestions were turned down

---

[1] Questions asked in Parliament in November failed to smoke out the government's intentions about the pact; Laval and Briand refused to comment. Pertinax caused a minor sensation by printing in *L'Echo de Paris*, 21 Dec. 1931, a "résumé" of the draft Pact; the conservative *Le Figaro*, *Le Journal*, *Le Matin*, and *L'Ordre* joined him in demanding the end of the negotiations.

[2] Announcements by the Senate Commissions on Foreign Affairs and Army and the Soviet Embassy, *Journal des Débats*, 19, 21 Jan. 1931; *Soviet Union Review*, X, 19 (hereinafter cited as *S.U.R.*).

in Washington, but they provide evidence of the Quai d'Orsay's willingness to be helpful to the Russians.[3]

It was in Eastern Europe that the significant activity could be found. The Franco-Soviet Non-Aggression Pact was dependent upon similar Soviet pacts with Poland and Romania, and late in December 1931 the Quai d'Orsay assured a foreign diplomat that this condition still stood. "France would not sign the treaty with the Soviets until the other treaties were absolutely assured."[4] Many observers glanced at the strife-laden Soviet frontier and labeled the French condition "impossible," merely a polite way out for France. Times had changed, however.

The key to the whole affair was Poland, and there the tension with Germany showed no signs of abating. Polish leaders were very jittery about the incessant talk of revision surrounding the Franco-German discussions and the visits to Washington made by M. Laval and Italian Foreign Minister Grandi in October and November 1931. These references created the appearance of a serious lack of sympathy among the western powers for Poland's contest with Germany.[5] More than ever did the Poles want to reduce the danger on their eastern frontier. Marshal Pilsudski, at the year's end, ordered Colonel Beck to pay special attention to improving Poland's relations with Russia by means of a non-aggression pact.[6] In Moscow the new Japanese threat added a sense of urgency to the prevailing strategy of concluding non-aggression treaties with all states on the Soviet frontiers.

The formal Polish-Soviet negotiations began in the middle of December 1931 and ran fairly smoothly. The Poles abandoned their previous requirement that Soviet treaties with the Baltic States and Romania be concluded simultaneously with the Polish treaty, a form which would signify Polish leadership in the region.

[3] *F.R.U.S., 1932*, I, 901-902; *F.R.U.S., The Soviet Union 1933-39*, p. 279.

[4] Dispatch from the U.S. Ambassador in Paris, Mr. Edge, 22 Dec. 1931, 751.6111/11, Archives of the Department of State, Washington, D. C.

[5] Note the unusually strong language used by the Polish Ambassador in Washington on the eve of Laval's arrival. "Marshal Pilsudski instructed the Ambassador to say that . . . [if invasion by German irregular troops should occur,] the whole Polish army would be immediately mobilized and march into Germany to settle the thing once and for all, and they would not be influenced by any action of the League of Nations or anyone else." Conversation with Under-Secretary of State Castle, 22 Oct. 1931, *F.R.U.S., 1931*, I, 600. See also *B.F.P.*, II, 307.

[6] Beck, *Dernier Rapport*, p. 10. Beck was Under-Secretary of State in the Foreign Ministry; Pilsudski had recently informed him that he would become minister when Zaleski retired.

In 1926 this had produced a deadlock, but now, five years later, it was a measure of Polish apprehension about Germany that the Poles did not repeat the insistence. Moscow did agree, however, to begin the negotiations for these treaties immediately.[7] The Russians, incidentally, were under repeated pressure from Berlin to give an assurance that they would not guarantee Poland's western frontiers. This was most unlikely but so insistent were the Germans that Stalin, in an interview with Emil Ludwig, 21 December 1931, made a pointed denial: "We never have been guarantors for Poland and never shall be. . . ."[8]

The Polish-Soviet rapprochement was aided by the opening of Soviet negotiations with Finland, Estonia, Latvia, and Romania early in January 1932, and by the unexpectedly rapid progress at Helsinki which produced the signature of a Soviet-Finnish Pact 21 January.[9] The Romanian-Soviet talks quickly reached an impasse, but the Poles did not want to wait. They decided to go ahead and initial the Polish-Soviet Pact but promised the Romanians to make its signature and ratification dependent upon a successful Romanian settlement.[10] This problem postponed, the Soviet and Polish negotiators put their initials to the non-aggression pact in Moscow, 25 January 1932.

The pact contained the usual engagements of non-aggression, neutrality in case of a third party's attack, non-participation in hostile ententes.[11] There was nothing faintly resembling a guarantee of Poland's western frontiers but, by its very existence, the pact weakened the German position and helped to counteract the atmosphere of a Russo-German conspiracy against Poland. The announcement provoked another outburst in the German press. The Russians again tried to appease by having Litvinov stop over in Berlin on his way to the Disarmament Conference. The Polish

[7] *S.U.R.*, X, 21-22, 27, 56; Litvinov statement 22 Nov. 1931, Degras, *Soviet Documents on Foreign Policy*, II, 517; speech of M. Titulescu, then Romanian Foreign Minister, 23 Nov. 1932, *Le Temps*, 26 Nov. 1932; Beck, *Dernier Rapport*, pp. 10 ff. A Polish-Soviet exchange of military information had been made in Sept. 1931.

[8] Degras, *Soviet Documents on Foreign Policy*, II, 517-518; Dirksen, *Moscow, Tokyo, London*, p. 116.

[9] *S.U.R.*, X, 58; *L'Europe Nouvelle*, 20 Feb. 1932, 252-253; *Osteuropa*, VII, 356; League of Nations, *Treaty Series*, CLVIII, 393 (hereinafter cited as *L.N.T.S.*).

[10] Statement in the semi-official *Gazeta Polska* (Warsaw), quoted in *Le Temps*, 27 Jan. 1932; declaration of Prince Ghika, Romanian Foreign Minister, *Le Temps*, 16 Jan. 1932; Laroche, *La Pologne de Pilsudski*, p. 106; *B.F.P.*, VII, 229-231.

[11] The text may be found in *L.N.T.S.*, CXXXVI, 41, and in *L'Europe Nouvelle*, 19 March 1932, pp. 381-382.

press generally welcomed the announcement and, although profess-
ing skepticism about the value of the Soviet signature, hailed it as
a move that would impose caution upon German revisionists.[12]

Pacts with Latvia and Estonia were almost a foregone conclusion once Finland and Poland had come to terms. On 5
February 1932 a Soviet-Latvian Non-Aggression Pact was signed
in Riga. Soviet-Estonian discussions did not open until the end of
January and moved slowly, but on 4 May the treaty was signed in
Moscow.[13] Lithuania took no part in these events. Owing to bitter quarrels with Poland and Germany, she had only one way to
turn and had already concluded a non-aggression pact with Russia
in 1926 and renewed it in 1931.

As expected, it was the Romanian puzzle which could not be
solved. The Romanian occupation of Bessarabia in 1918 had never
been recognized by the Soviets and had blocked all attempts to
restore diplomatic relations. The non-aggression talks started at
neutral Riga 6 January 1932 and took only ten days to reach a
deadlock over the Bessarabian question. The negotiations were
then suspended, and it was agreed to resume contact either directly
at Geneva or through friendly mediation.[14]

Despite Polish assurances, Romanian officials were greatly disappointed when the Poles initialed their pact with Russia, 25 January. They considered it a deviation from the spirit of the Polish-
Romanian Alliance and feared that it would make the Russians less
likely to make concessions on Bessarabia.[15] In Paris there was
apparently no disposition to criticize Romania for the breakdown
of the negotiations. An editorial in *Le Temps* approved Romania's
desire to make Bessarabia as secure as possible and added that it
was obvious that France and Poland should not sign their pacts
until a Soviet-Romanian Pact was concluded.[16]

[12] See quotations in *Le Temps* and *Journal des Débats*, 27 Jan. 1932; *Osteuropa*,
VII, 362.

[13] For the Latvian and Estonian negotiations and the treaties, consult *The
Bulletin of International News*, VIII, 474 (hereinafter cited as *B.I.N.*); *Osteuropa*,
VII, 358-359, 531; *S.U.R.*, X, 59, 142; *L'Europe Nouvelle*, 19 March 1932, p. 382;
L.N.T.S., CXXXI, 297 and CXLVIII, 113.

[14] Litvinov statement, 25 Jan., quoted in *Le Temps*, 27 Jan. 1932, and in *S.U.R.*,
X, 56; Romanian statement, quoted in *Journal des Débats*, 28 Jan. 1932.

[15] Quotations from the Romanian press in *Le Temps*, 28, 29, 30 January, 9 Feb.
1932.

[16] "Bulletin du Jour," 28 Jan. 1932. The conservative nationalist Paris press,
which had denounced the Franco-Soviet negotiations in 1931, remained consistent
and criticized the Polish-Soviet Pact.

The Romanian exception could hardly diminish the significance of what had been accomplished. The Soviet Union had worked out with Finland, Poland, Latvia, and Estonia political accords which had proved impossible to realize for an entire decade. Part of the tension was appeased which had made the western borders of Russia a breeding ground for conflict. Above all, the harsh relations between Poland and Russia, which had come so close to upsetting the Versailles settlement in 1920, were being softened.

ii

Russia's successful negotiations with most of her western neighbors could well have quickened the tempo of her rapprochement with France. The condition that Paris had imposed was being fulfilled. Instead, progress was held back by the hostile policy of a new French cabinet.

The first days of the new year brought the death of M. André Maginot, Minister of War, and the retirement of Aristide Briand. The cabinet resigned 12 January and, when it reappeared two days later, M. Tardieu took over the War Ministry, M. Laval was Foreign Minister as well as Premier, and M. Briand was absent.[17] It was an open secret that Briand's illness and fatigue had become embarrassing and had reduced him to half-efficiency. But his fall was a shock to his friends and followers, who accused Laval of an inexcusable lack of gratitude toward a man whose protégé he had been. The man whose name was already tightly bound to those of Stresemann and Locarno died on March seventh. He left behind no one who could command the same popular following for the policy of reconciliation with Germany, or, indeed, for any other foreign policy. Pierre Laval stayed only thirty days in the Quai d'Orsay he had so long coveted. He was reversed by the Senate 16 February 1932, and was succeeded as Premier and Foreign Minister by his friend, M. Tardieu.[18]

When André Tardieu formed his third government he was at

[17] Briand's remarkably long tenure at the Quai d'Orsay, 17 April 1925–14 Jan. 1932 (with the exception of four days), is an example of the ministerial continuity that mitigates the instability of governments in the French system. Briand closely approached the record tenure of M. Delcassé, 28 June 1898–6 June 1905.

[18] Laval was defeated on a procedural question, but the real issue was electoral reform. The Tardieu Cabinet was a Center-Right combination with almost the same composition as that of Laval. Flandin, Reynaud, and Piétri were, as before, the leading personalities; Laval moved to the Ministry of Labor.

the height of his political power. With brief interludes, a tandem Tardieu-Laval had governed France since 1929. Son of a distinguished Parisian lawyer, Tardieu began his career as an attaché in the French Embassy at Berlin and served briefly under Delcassé at the Quai d'Orsay. He was Waldeck-Rousseau's trusted secretary during the latter's sway, 1899-1902, the most significant cabinet of the prewar republic. Tardieu then turned to carve out a double career as a journalist and as a Deputy Inspector in the Ministry of the Interior. His incisive columns on diplomacy in *Le Temps* exerted so much influence that they won Prince von Bülow's exasperated compliment: "There are the six Great Powers and then there is M. Tardieu." The ebullient young Frenchman, already flourishing a solid gold cigarette holder, sailed into two more professions. He began to lecture on diplomatic history at the École Libre des Science Politiques and at the École de Guerre and, in his first campaign, May, 1914, he won election as a Deputy to the Chamber of Deputies. He was thirty-six and had written six books.

When war came, Tardieu threw himself into staff assignments under Foch and Joffre, then spent a year in the trenches; he was wounded severely and decorated with the Croix de Guerre. Appointed High Commissioner to the United States in April, 1917, he did a superb job of organizing shipments of supplies and munitions to France. Clemenceau rewarded him with delegation to the Peace Conference; and there he demonstrated toughness and skill in negotiation, forming with his friend and fellow trouble shooter, Colonel House, a very useful channel between Clemenceau and President Wilson. Back in politics, Tardieu's chance came in 1926, when he entered Poincaré's Government of National Union. By the time his chief retired in 1929, Tardieu was acknowledged to be the new leader of the conservatives. In so doing he had fulfilled the brilliant promise always attributed to him, but his tendency to carry a chip on his shoulder brought him into more frequent clashes with the Left than necessary.[19]

M. Tardieu's accession was widely interpreted as a return to a

[19] Consult the sensitive study by Rudolph Binion, *Defeated Leaders: The Political Fate of Caillaux, Jouvenel and Tardieu* (New York, 1960), pp. 197-337; V. Goedorp, *Figures du Temps* (Paris, 1943), pp. 201-317; Paul-Boncour, *Entre Deux Guerres*, (Paris, 1945, 1946), 3 vols., II, 213-219; General E. Réquin, *D'une Guerre à l'Autre* (Paris, 1949), pp. 3-5, 157-166; Maurice Gamelin, *Servir* (Paris, 1946), 3 vols., II, xxviii-xxix; Edge, *A Jerseyman's Journal*, pp. 179-180; General Maxime Weygand, *Mémoires* (Paris, 1957), 3 vols., II. *Mirages et Realité*, pp. 24 ff., 344.

more antagonistic attitude towards Germany. His distaste for Briand's policy and his desire to maintain the Versailles Treaty as fully as possible had never been concealed. Despite his distrust of Germany, Tardieu had shown no interest in returning to the prewar pattern of alliance with Russia against Germany. He viewed Soviet Russia with skepticism and suspicion. While Minister of the Interior in 1929, he had personally directed a vigorous repression of the Communist attempt to "seize the streets" on August first. It had been a Tardieu government that had ordered the anti-Soviet dumping decrees of 3 October 1930. Although he had been a member of the Laval government that approved the Russian negotiations, one has the distinct impression that, if Tardieu had been Premier or Foreign Minister, he would not have accepted the Soviet proposal for a non-aggression pact. He believed that co-operation with a country possessing a revolutionary party in France working for revolution was likely to be self-defeating.

As long as Tardieu ruled, 21 February–3 June 1932, no forward steps were taken in the rapprochement with the Soviet Union. He put the negotiations for the non-aggression pact into "cold storage."[20] He insisted upon fulfilment of the most difficult condition—the Soviet-Romanian pact—and he worked to make fulfilment even more difficult. Marshal Pilsudski recently had warned Bucharest that, when the Baltic pacts were completed, he would go ahead and sign the Polish-Soviet pact, without waiting for Romania. Tardieu interfered, objected to the Polish pressure, and encouraged the Romanian government in its resistance.[21]

The French Premier did have an interview with M. Litvinov in Geneva, 16 March, in which the fate of the non-aggression pact was discussed; it was reported that Tardieu gave him no assurance that it would be concluded.[22] Formulation of foreign policy on all issues was held up by the campaign for the general elections in May. Tardieu was hardly likely to push the Soviet pact at the same time that he led an "anti-Marxist" front.

Just at this moment an accidental event gave Tardieu another excuse for blocking the rapprochement. France was shocked when

[20] Dispatch from the British Chargé d'Affaires in Paris, Mr. Campbell, 27 Sept. 1932, *B.F.P.*, VII, 244, also 246-247; *Le Temps, Journal des Débats*, 18 March 1932.

[21] Laroche, *La Pologne de Pilsudski*, pp. 109-110; Beck, *Dernier Rapport*, Appendix, p. 283; *B.F.P.*, VII, 244-247. Pilsudski resented Tardieu's interference and said that Poland and Romania could arrange their own affairs.

[22] *Journal des Débats, Le Temps*, 18 March 1932; *B.F.P.*, VII, 237.

the President of the Republic, M. Paul Doumer, was assassinated, 6 May 1932, by a Russian emigré named Gorgulov. The Rightist press cried "neo-bolshevism" and claimed to see the sinister hand of the O.G.P.U. Moscow immediately denounced the crime as a White Guard provocation.[23] Gorgulov himself announced that he was president of the "Russian national fascist party."

I love Russia. I love Hitler. I love Mussolini. No longer do I love France, who has become the friend of the Bolsheviks, who have ruined my country. I fired on the President of the Republic because France is turning socialist and in order to compel France to make war on the Bolsheviks.[24]

This open avowal of an anti-Soviet motive undercut the campaign for "reprisals" against the Communists. However, the immediate reaction was violently anti-Russian, Red or White.[25]

A semi-official editorial in *Le Temps,* with which Tardieu had intimate connections, bluntly declared that the event should inspire the most serious reflections about Soviet policy.

At this moment, the policy of the Soviets must be given very special attention. The state of trouble in which one sees the world, the moral disarray which one finds everywhere and which aggravates so danger-ously the situation created by the financial and economic crisis, these are general conditions which the Moscow leaders reach out to exploit to the best interests of universal revolution.... There are certain gov-ernments that imagine they can bring the Soviets into their own design against other powers, without any danger to themselves. Instead, they are in reality serving the Soviet power and contributing to the develop-ment of its influence in the world.[26]

This deep fear of the long-run dangers of co-operation with Soviet Russia was the principal motive of Tardieu's desire to block the non-aggression pact.

Tardieu's personal antipathy was enough to slow down the rapprochement. But it was reinforced when French and Soviet policies clashed on three major issues. The first of these concerned Central and Eastern Europe and was created by the "Tardieu Plan"

[23] *Pravda,* 8, 9, 12 May expressed the fear that Tardieu would use the incident to start an anti-Soviet campaign. *Bulletin de la presse russe,* No. 215.
[24] Statement during first interrogation, *L'Echo de Paris,* 7 May 1932.
[25] M. Albert Lebrun, a timorous conservative, was elected the new President of the Republic. Gorgulov was executed late in the year.
[26] The governments named were Germany, Turkey, Persia; and the United States was clearly implied, in its anti-Japanese policy. "Bulletin du Jour," *Le Temps,* 9 May 1932.

for a Danubian economic entente. Following repeated economic
and financial crises in that area, a French memorandum presented
to the British, German, and Italian governments, 5 March 1932,
proposed that immediate measures of financial relief and economic
reconstruction be taken.[27] Considering a Customs Union too slow,
M. Tardieu suggested preferential tariff agreements between Austria, Czechoslovakia, Hungary, Romania, and Yugoslavia plus financial aid from the four great powers.

The aim of reinforcing French bastions in the East was obvious.
This aid to the status quo—symbolized by the predominance of the
Little Entente, the absence of Bulgaria, and the "aegis of France"
—was poor fare for Germany and Italy. Berlin saw only a move to
prevent the *Anschluss* with Austria, Rome a blow to Mussolini's
ambition to play the leading role in Southeastern Europe. Great
Britain, while approving the goal of relief for Central Europe, was
financially unable to match the French and suspicious of an extension of French continental hegemony. Seeking a polite way out,
the British succeeded in convoking a four-power conference which
met in London 6-10 April 1932. The conference quickly reached a
deadlock, and the French were forced to give up the plan.[28]

In the Tardieu plan there was "no chair" for the Russians,
although their economic interests in the Danubian area were tra-
ditionally strong. The plan was sometimes billed as bolstering the
small Danubian states against bolshevism. This exclusion was
feared and resented in Moscow. The French presentation of the
plan as fitting into the framework of Pan-European progress and
the emphasis on European "economic solidarity" were regarded as
references to common measures against Soviet trade reminiscent
of the "anti-dumping" campaign.[29] In an editorial 4 May *Pravda*
admitted the plan's bias against Germany and Italy, but harped on
its danger to Russia. "The Tardieu plan pursues other designs. It
has the goal of extending the anti-Soviet bloc in Southeastern
Europe."[30] Actually, the Tardieu plan was not an aggressive move

[27] French Aide-Mémoire, 2 March 1932, printed in *Le Temps*, 17 March and
in *L'Europe Nouvelle*, 2 April; consult Flandin, *Politique Française*, pp. 97-99;
S.I.A., 1932, pp. 22-23; also reports in *L'Europe Nouvelle*, 26 March, 9, 16 April
1932.
[28] See, in addition to the sources cited above, the Paris and London press, 5-10
April 1932; *F.R.U.S., 1932*, I, 849 ff.
[29] Quotations from the Russian press in *Osteuropa*, VII, 481-483 and in *Bulletin
de la presse russe*, No. 215.
[30] Quoted in *Bulletin de la presse russe*, No. 215.

against Russia. But it was a demonstration that much of the French desire to keep Russian influence out of Central Europe still existed.

A second and more important source of friction was kindled by antagonistic policies on disarmament. No sooner had the Disarmament Conference opened in Geneva than M. Tardieu unrolled an elaborate project, 5 February 1932. It proposed the internationalization of civil aviation, compulsory arbitration and definition of the aggressor, placing a state's most aggressive weapons at the disposition of the League of Nations, and the creation of an international police force for enforcing League decisions.[31] The latter was the key to the plan, said M. Tardieu; by it the French precedence of security over disarmament would be achieved. As one of those who had fashioned the League in 1919, he argued that the international force would restore to the League its original virility. "As we see it, . . . a fully organized League of Nations is the only power capable of prevention and repression."[32] To the Germans and Italians and, to a lesser extent, to the British and Americans, the French draft appeared another ingenious device to avoid French disarmament. The Germans immediately opposed it with their familiar demand for "equality of rights," the Americans, British, and Italians submitted programs that aimed at immediate substantial reductions of armaments, and the delegates were off on their tedious circuit of plans and resolutions and drafts.

There was nothing new about Franco-Soviet opposition on disarmament, but the Tardieu plan was a nightmare to Moscow. Particularly disturbing was the idea of an international police force under control of the League which would possess, by virtue of Article 11 of the Covenant, a mandate for taking preventive measures in an international crisis involving a non-member of the League. Accordingly, when M. Litvinov rose to speak, he began with an acid criticism of French motives.

What are the guarantees that . . . an international army would not be exploited in the interests of some state which has won for itself a

[31] *Le Temps*, 7 Feb. 1932.

[32] Speech of 8 Feb. 1932, presenting the plan. *Le Temps*, 9 Feb. 1932; *Conference for the Reduction and Limitations of Armaments. Records* (Geneva, 1932), Series A, I, 12. This was made in Tardieu's capacity as Minister of War; although he relinquished the War Ministry after becoming Premier, 20 February, Tardieu continued to handle the disarmament negotiations.

leading position in the international organization through separate alliances, ententes, and agreements?[33]

The Soviet minister declared that Russia wanted total disarmament but would welcome "any proposals tending to reduce armaments." He added significantly that he would support "the equal rights of all participants in the Conference."[34]

The French delegates were not overly concerned about Litvinov's barbs, but they resented his support of the German theses: "equality of rights" and immediate reduction of arms. The Soviet stand was a rather serious matters for France because it added to Italian, British, and American sympathy for the Germans on these matters. The very next day *Le Temps* struck back, declaring that the Soviets' ardent advocacy of disarmament and, indeed, all their foreign policies were only designed to gain time.

They need external peace in order to try to consolidate their power. But their bolshevik passion, their hatred of so-called capitalist civilization, their revolutionary imperialism remain the same as before, and there is a grave danger for all nations that they may be taken in by certain appearances which Moscow tries to create....[35]

Whoever else might be tricked into co-operation, France would not.

Throughout the debates in the spring session of the Disarmament Conference, the Soviet delegates consistently spoke and voted against the proposals and strategy of France. M. Litvinov and his cohorts were almost invariably to be found on the German side, and they frequently supported British, American, and Italian initiatives to which the French were opposed. This was the type of obstruction that raised doubts about the very existence of the Franco-Soviet rapprochement.

The French, incidentally, were irritated by other signs of the survival of Russo-German ties. The tenth anniversary of the Rapallo Treaty, 16 April 1932, was celebrated by a luncheon in Geneva of the Soviet and German Delegations to the Disarmament Conference, and an editorial in *Izvestya* declared that "the relations between the U.S.S.R. and Germany will continue to be strengthened and developed on the basis of the principles of Rapallo."[36] Russo-German trade continued to thrive. German ex-

[33] Speech of 11 Feb. 1932, *ibid.*, Series A, I, 85.
[34] *Ibid.*, A, I, 86.
[35] "Bulletin du Jour," *Le Temps*, 13 Feb. 1932.
[36] 16 April 1932, quoted in *S.U.R.*, X, 102. To be sure, there was ill-will under

ports to Russia, bolstered by supplementary credit arrangements on 22 December 1931 and 15 June 1932, grew to gargantuan proportions. Germany supplied 46 per cent of Russia's imports in the year 1932.[37]

A third source of friction had been formed by Japan's invasion of Manchuria, launched in September 1931. The new expansion was a menace to the Soviet Far Eastern provinces. France, on the other hand, was far away and even her great Asian colony, Indo-China, was distant from Japan. Friendly feelings between the two countries had been created by the alliance of the World War, French backing for the Japanese intervention in Siberia, co-operation at Versailles, and a common stand against disarmament.

For two reasons this source of friction did not become irritating until 1932. The first was that French policy was hardly distinguishable from British and American during the period September–December 1931; all three powers demonstrated caution and forbearance towards Japan. Even more striking was the passivity of Moscow's first reaction. Soviet-Japanese relations had been improving since the settlement of 1925. The Russians gratefully remembered that Japan had remained benevolently neutral throughout the Sino-Russian Manchurian dispute of 1929. In its early stages the main Japanese thrust seemed to be aimed down along the coast into the northeastern provinces of China. Owing to these factors and to military weakness in the Far East, spokesmen in Moscow repeatedly characterized the Soviet reaction as "a policy of strict non-intervention."[38]

The latent antithesis between French and Russian purposes emerged only in the new year of 1932. The occupation of the main line of the Chinese Eastern Railway, and of Tsitsihar and Harbin, the most important cities of north Manchuria, made it obvious that

---

the surface. The Russians resented the German government's failure to ratify the prolongation of the Berlin Treaty, signed in 1931. Brüning was reluctant to agree to the luncheon, according to Dirksen, *Moscow, Tokyo, London*, pp. 76-77; Kochan, *Russia and the Weimar Republic*, pp. 161-162.

[37] Degras, *Soviet Documents on Foreign Policy*, II, 521, 533-534; Höffding, "German Trade with the Soviet Union," *Slavonic and East European Review*, XIV; *Osteuropa*, VII, 610, 627-644; *B.F.P.*, VII, 228-229, 233-234; League of Nations, *International Trade Statistics, 1931 and 1932* (Geneva, 1933), p. 256.

[38] Statement by Karakhan, Vice-Commissar for Foreign Affairs, 29 Oct. 1931, Degras, *Soviet Documents on Foreign Policy*, II, 512. Consult *F.R.U.S., 1931*, III, 67 ff. and *1932*, III, 557; *B.F.P.*, VII, 674 ff.

Japan was determined to push her columns north and west to the borders of Russia. What really alarmed Moscow was the proclamation, 1 March 1932, of the puppet state of Manchukuo. Permanent Japanese control of Manchuria would threaten the security of the Trans-Siberian railway and would be a challenge to Soviet control over Outer Mongolia. Four days later an *Izvestya* editorial bluntly warned that Soviet garrisons in the Far East would be reinforced, owing to "the extraordinarily grave character of the events which are taking place." "The Soviet Union will [not] permit anyone whomsoever to violate the security of Soviet frontiers, to invade Soviet territory or to seize even the tiniest portion of Soviet land."[39] During the spring of 1932 a Russo-Japanese clash seemed a distinct possibility.

Just at this time French policy became pro-Japanese and began to stand out clearly from the new anti-Japanese line of the United States. The permanent officials of the Quai d'Orsay and the French military services were reported to look kindly on the Japanese expansion. The French "nationalist" press was almost unanimously pro-Japanese.[40] Briand had been a major counterweight, trying to block Japanese expansion by means of the League of Nations, but now André Tardieu had taken his place.

France gave no support to Secretary Stimson's "Non-Recognition" Doctrine against Japan as it emerged on three occasions in January and February 1932. Throughout the spring of 1932, a series of editorials in *Le Temps,* which was very close to Tardieu, argued that the Powers should recognize the paramount political interest of Japan in Manchuria as a desirable force. "It is necessary that . . . certain powers—notably the United States—lend themselves to a solution of the Manchurian conflict based on Toyko's views."[41] Indo-China became actively involved in the affair when long-drawn-out negotiations with Japan on her commercial relations with that colony were re-established in March 1932. Agreement was soon reached, and on 13 May in Paris M. Tardieu and Japanese Ambassador Nagaoka signed a Treaty of Commerce with respect to Indo-China. It was judged a clear indication of Tar-

[39] *Izvestya,* 4 March 1932, reprinted in *S.U.R.,* X, 91-93.

[40] *Le Figaro, Le Matin,* and *Le Petit Journal* were particularly strong in their support of Japan. For evidence of this sentiment in the French military and diplomatic services see *F.R.U.S., 1931,* III, 165, 361, 388, and *1932,* IV, 70-71; Gamelin, *Servir,* II, 84-85.

[41] "Bulletin du Jour," *Le Temps,* 23 March 1932. See also editorials of 12, 19, 29 March, 1 May 1932.

dieu's pro-Japanese policy that a solution was found for issues which, for several years, had defied conclusion.[42] Referring to this period, the French Ambassador in Washington later stated: "Japan had definitely and formally offered to make an alliance with France . . . the Manchurian market would be open to France and . . . Japan would do all in its power to throw Oriental business into the hands of France."[43] M. Herriot, who succeeded Tardieu as Premier and Foreign Minister, made roughly the same claim.[44]

Moscow, of course, was well aware of the public side of French pro-Japanese policy. France was given a leading place in the diatribes of the Soviet Press against the "imperialists." The most prominent denunciation was delivered by Karl Radek in an article in *Foreign Affairs,* "War in the Far East: A Soviet View," published in July 1932.

> The attitude of France toward Japan is plain. It is determined by French hostility toward the nationalistic movement in the Orient, a movement which threatens the French position in Indo-China. It is also determined by France's hostility to the Soviet Union. French imperialism would like to see Japan strengthened in the hope that this will lead to a struggle with the Soviet Union.[45]

With France openly pro-Japanese and Great Britain reluctant to antagonize Tokyo, the Soviet Union, possessing no diplomatic relations with China and the United States, found itself in almost complete diplomatic isolation on the Far Eastern crisis.

French foreign policy under André Tardieu thus revealed a pervasive hostility to Russia. M. Tardieu would have insisted on the difficult condition of a prior Soviet-Romanian pact before concluding the Franco-Soviet Non-Aggression Pact. Inasmuch as Romania was reluctant to continue negotiations, this condition might well have amounted to an excellent way for letting the pact die. M. Tardieu, however, was not to make the decision, for he fell from power.

iii

May 1932 was a month of political fatality in Paris and Berlin. On its first day French voters turned thumbs down on Tardieu and

[42] Article by R. Lévy, *L'Europe Nouvelle,* 6 Aug. 1932, p. 961; article by A. Dubosq, *Le Temps,* 16 March 1932; *F.R.U.S., 1932,* IV, 218.

[43] Conversation with Under-Secretary of State Castle, 10 Oct. 1932, *F.R.U.S., 1932,* IV, 295-296.

[44] Conversation with Mr. Norman Davis, in Paris, 28 Nov. 1932, *ibid., 1932,* I, 486.

[45] *Foreign Affairs* (New York, quarterly), X (July 1932), 553.

its last but one became the day of reckoning for Heinrich Brüning. In France, foreign policy did not play a major part in the campaign.[46] The real fighting centered on domestic issues, where Tardieu felt the chill winds of the depression which were at last reaching French shores. The *Cartel des Gauches,* an electoral alliance of left-wing parties, won a distinct victory. Both Socialists and Radical-Socialists gained heavily at the expense of the Communists and the center parties. The Socialists won the highest popular vote for any one party but, thanks to the play of the electoral laws, the Radicals elected the largest group of Deputies.[47]

M. Édouard Herriot, leader of the Radicals, formed the new government, but the Socialists did not join. M. Léon Blum intoned the Socialist formula: "Support but not Participation"—rejecting power in a bourgeois cabinet but remaining free to support it in its "progressive" aspects. A disturbing weakness thus continued to plague the Third Republic: the Socialists and Radicals could win elections together but would not wield power together. When Herriot made up his third cabinet, 4 June 1932, it thus was packed with Radical-Socialists, at their head such stalwarts as Chautemps, Sarraut, and Daladier. Herriot himself took the Foreign Ministry.

Édouard Herriot was one of the most successful academic invaders of French politics, whose rise had inspired Albert Thibaudet's satire, *La République des Professeurs.*[48] Born in 1872, the son of a commandant in the infantry, Herriot was turned from a military career by his intellectual promise. After studies at the famed École Normale Supérieure, as classmate of Charles Péguy and a year behind Léon Blum, he won the high degrees of Agrégé and Doctor of Letters. He started his teaching career in 1895, at

[46] Tardieu denounced the Socialists' fondness of disarmament and they made him the symbol of an "adventurous," intransigent foreign policy. However, the fact that Herriot made much of his patriotism rendered impossible a straight fight between right-wing nationalism and left-wing internationalism. The rapprochement with Russia did not become involved in the campaign.

[47] The Communist party refused to join the *Cartel;* owing to this intransigence, internal weaknesses, and other reasons, the party did very poorly. Popular vote (on the first turn) and seats in the Chamber won by these parties, with 1928 figures in parentheses, were: Communists—756,000 (1,070,000) and 10 (12); Socialists—1,964,000 (1,690,000) and 130 (111); Radical Socialists—1,837,000 (1,650,000) and 160 (125). The *Cartel* won 340 seats against 260 for the Center and Right.

[48] Biographical material on Herriot may be found in his memoirs, *Jadis*; Suarez, *Briand,* VI, 46-50; Paul-Boncour, *Entre Deux Guerres,* II, chaps. iii, iv, v; Francis P. Walters, *A History of the League of Nations* (London, 1952), I, chaps. xxi-xxii; Francis de Tarr, *The French Radical Party, from Herriot to Mendès-France* (London, 1961), chap. iii.

Nantes, then moved to the Lycée Ampère at Lyons, where he had the ironic experience of preparing a future rival in the Radical party, Édouard Daladier. One of the few politicians who kept up the great French tradition of combining politics and scholarship, Herriot published frequent volumes of essays and biography.

Here was another Frenchman whose life had been profoundly shaped by Captain Dreyfus. The Affair smashed the idols of Herriot's conservative, clerical, nationalist background. He became an ardent Dreyfusard, and turned in liberal and anti-clerical directions, but stopped short of the antimilitarism of many who did likewise. Édouard Herriot remained a "patriot"; his Radicalism was in the main stream, a Jacobin Radicalism always sensitive to the appeal *la patrie en danger.*

A member of the Radical-Socialist party from its founding in 1901, the young Herriot plunged into politics in his adopted city of Lyons, became its mayor in 1905, and was still mayor in 1932. He made his appearance on the national scene in 1912, as a Senator, had a portfolio in the second Briand war cabinet 1916-1917, and in 1919 struck out on the high road. Elected a Deputy and then President of the Radical-Socialist party, he became head of the left-wing opposition, the *Cartel des Gauches,* and led it back to power in the general elections of 1924. As Premier and Foreign Minister for nine months, he merely fenced with a growing financial crisis, but his liquidation of the Ruhr occupation and his part in setting up the Dawes Plan won him praise as "the man who made peace with Germany." Herriot's essential moderation was revealed in 1926 when the *Cartel* broke up over the financial crisis; Poincaré came in to save the franc and formed a conservatively oriented government of National Union. Despite the disapproval of Radical "young Turks," Herriot joined the Poincaré government and loyally served in it for two years.

Gourmand, inseparable from his pipes, which were as dear to cartoonists as was his expansive silhouette, Herriot was a happier, less intense person than either Tardieu or Blum. Though he came between the prewar and postwar generations, he partook more of the former with his interest in ideals, traditions, and general issues rather than in details and techniques, in problems inherited from the past rather than the new problems of industrialization, in politics rather than economics. Little of a doctrinaire, he was a republican and a Frenchman above all. A "man of good will," with the virtues and weaknesses that label has come to imply in the ruthless twentieth century.

The arrival of the Left under M. Herriot's benign direction was generally hailed as a change that might improve the chances of Franco-German reconciliation. He sincerely hoped for an understanding, and he was under pressure from the Socialists whose faith was still high in an entente with "German democracy." But there were signs that Herriot's views were changing. He was apprehensive of the resurgence of German nationalism and his pride had been wounded by the recently published Stresemann papers. As he told an American diplomat, "In 1924 he had made peace with Germany and had evacuated the Ruhr, and had made the Agreement of London . . . and now when he read the memoirs of Stresemann, he found that they called him a 'jellyfish.' "[49]

M. Herriot also had a Russian reputation—the man who had recognized the Soviet Union in 1924. His later disillusionment with the ruthless tactics of French Communists against other left-wing parties had cast doubt on his attitude towards Moscow.[50] At any rate, there was literally no time for him to re-examine Franco-Soviet relations. The Herriot government had barely presented itself to Parliament when it was confronted with the German problem—in the form of a Conference on Reparations at Lausanne.

The moment seemed inauspicious, for the small but real Franco-German détente of 1931 had been deflated. President von Hindenburg's brusque New Year's Day claim to "equality of rights" and, a week later, the announcement that Germany could no longer pay any reparations had dissipated trust in Dr. Brüning's government. "The charm was broken," wrote the French Ambassador in Berlin, M. François-Poncet. "The idyll of the gentle, modest, captious Brüning had vanished."[51] Publication of extracts from the Stresemann papers in the French press was undermining belief in German good faith.

With this background it may well be asked why the French leaders had any interest in sitting down with the Germans at Lau-

[49] Conversation with Mr. Norman Davis, Paris, 28 Nov. 1932, *F.R.U.S., 1932,* I, 477. Norman Davis reported on May 22 that Herriot was "deeply under the impression of the *Stresemann letters.*" *Ibid., 1932,* I, 139. Translation of the Stresemann papers began in *L'Illustration* and in *Revue de Paris,* during March 1932.

[50] When asked about the Soviet Pact in a pre-election interview, Herriot replied that he was still studying the whole matter. *Le Temps,* 22 March 1932.

[51] *Souvenirs d'une ambassade à Berlin,* p. 33; B.F.P., III, 67.

sanne. Perhaps the most compelling reason was that they were awakening to the fact that France, in her turn, was being smitten by the world economic depression. In addition to a generally high level of cost of production, the British devaluation in September 1931 made French goods more and more expensive on the world market. Exports now began to decline rapidly, creating a much more unfavorable trade balance than had been expected; unemployment, which hitherto had risen very slowly, jumped up sharply at the turn of the year.[52] By June 1932 it was evident that the new government would be faced with a budgetary deficit of large proportions; Herriot immediately proposed all-round economies and even a 10 per cent cut in military expenditures. The effect on French diplomacy was to create an attitude of caution, to reinforce those who argued against a break with Germany. Another substantial incentive lay in the realm of personalities. It was a new Chancellor with a pro-French reputation who took the train to Lausanne.

Brüning had been waging a courageous but losing fight against a horde of troubles. "When the ghastly summer of 1931 . . . had shaded into autumn, the Brüning Government had become the most unpopular ever known in Germany."[53] Winter was disheartening enough, and with it came the fourth major Emergency Decree with bleak economies and a new depth of unemployment –5,500,000. Feeding on the unrest, the Nazis and the Communists grew ever more aggressive.

The presidential election gave Hitler a great opening; it took Hindenburg and Brüning two campaigns full of corroding bitterness to win the former's re-election, 10 April 1932. Hitler pushed his vote to 13,400,000, more than double the Nazi party total in September 1930. On 24 April the National Socialist surge continued with smashing gains in provincial elections, particularly in the Prussian Diet, where they became the largest party. In lockstep the Nazis had marched with unemployment; now those dread statistics rose to 6,129,000. Brüning had a last chance to recoup by producing a dramatic success in the disarmament negotiations, but

[52] W. Arthur Lewis, *Economic Survey 1919-1939* (London, 1949), pp. 98-100; Martin Wolfe, *The French Franc between the Two Wars, 1919-1939* (New York, 1951), pp. 103-107; League of Nations, *World Economic Survey 1932-1933* (Geneva, 1933), pp. 84-87, 107, 110, 114; Herriot, *Jadis*, II, 288 ff.

[53] John W. Wheeler-Bennett, *Hindenburg: The Wooden Titan* (London, 1936), p. 349.

he returned to Berlin with empty hands.[54] This failure mixed with Hindenburg's resentment at owing his re-election to Brüning and to the Socialists, with his senile suspicion of "agrarian Bolshevism" in Brüning's new program, and with the intrigues of General von Schleicher and those around the President. In this brew Brüning's position decomposed, and on 30 May in a pathetic interview Hindenburg told Brüning to resign.

The world was dumbfounded to learn that the President's choice had fallen upon Franz von Papen, formerly a cavalry officer. He was repudiated by his own party, the Center, and had no qualifications save his friendship with Hindenburg. The real power was the new Minister of Defense, General von Schleicher. He intended to come to grips with the Nazi problem, either by "harnessing" the "better" elements of the party or, if that failed, by attack. Schleicher also nourished the hope that the new Chancellor would be "persona grata" in Paris. Coming from the Catholic Westphalian aristocracy, with important French contacts through marriage ties and industrial holdings in the Saar, Herr von Papen had long advocated better relations with France.[55] Schleicher and other Reichswehr leaders were impatient for a deal with France which would lift some of the restrictions on the German rearmament. Brüning had been rebuffed, but perhaps Papen with his contacts could cajole the French.[56] This western orientation might well mean the end of Rapallo, for Papen was known to one intimate observer of Weimar Germany, Mr. Wheeler-Bennett, as "an ardent exponent of the idea of a Franco-German industrial rapprochement and a military alliance against the Soviet Union."[57]

[54] Brüning, Tardieu, MacDonald, and U.S. Secretary of State Stimson had agreed to meet at Geneva, 29 April. Tardieu fell ill and could not come, the French elections took another week and MacDonald and Stimson could not wait longer. Tardieu has been accused of having a "diplomatic cold" and conniving at Brüning's fall; this charge has not yet been proved. Consult *F.R.U.S., 1932*, I, 108 ff; Wheeler-Bennett, *Hindenburg*, pp. 382-383; François-Poncet, *Souvenirs d'une ambassade á Berlin*, pp. 41 ff; Edge, *Jerseyman's Journal*, pp. 215-216.

[55] The British Ambassador in Berlin reported that von Papen "had constantly boasted of his influence with the D'Ormesson group in France and with certain French industrial leaders in Lorraine and elsewhere." *B.F.P.*, III, 166. The French Ambassador writes of von Papen: "Il se déclare francophile et partisan du rapprochement franco-allemand." François-Poncet, *Souvenirs d'une ambassade á Berlin*, p. 43.

[56] *Ibid.*, pp. 47 ff; Wheeler-Bennett, *Hindenburg*, pp. 385-397; Franz von Papen, *Memoirs* (London, 1952), p. 156; Georges Castellan, *Le Réarmement Clandestin du Reich, 1930-1935* (Paris, 1954), pp. 457-458.

[57] *Hindenburg*, p. 397; Pertinax in *L'Echo de Paris*, 5 June 1932; *Journal des Débats*, 7 June 1932.

The long-term tendencies were against Franco-German friend-ship. The promise of the previous summer had turned brown and died. But Papen and Herriot were new men, and the coinci-dence of their arrival created the psychology of a clean slate.

The Lausanne Conference convened on 16 June on the beau-tiful shores of Lac Léman, amidst great publicity and a crowd of celebrities—Prime Minister MacDonald, Premier Herriot, Chan-cellor von Papen; and in the second line, Sir John Simon, Neville Chamberlain, Baron von Neurath, Georges Bonnet, and Dino Grandi. The conference turned on the British attempt to mediate between Germany's request for the cancellation of reparations and the French resistance. Woven into the dreary rounds of unrealis-tic statistics was an intriguing political strand.

The British government, in the hope of softening the French attitude, had sent up, before Lausanne, a trial balloon—a "political truce" on a multilateral basis.[58] The reception had been tepid, but the project was revived in the middle of the Conference. As a result of this and other initiatives, a series of private discussions between Herr von Papen and M. Herriot took place.

Once alone with Herriot, the German Chancellor suddenly left the polite framework of a multilateral agreement and proposed a comprehensive direct settlement between France and Germany. He had already made an advance at the beginning of the Confer-ence, and, according to Herriot's notes, had alluded to an "accord directed against communism, in fact against Russia" and to general staff contacts.[59] Now Papen offered Herriot a Customs Union and a Consultative Pact in return for cancellation of reparations and recognition of Germany's "equality of rights" in arms.[60]

The sensational part of the German Chancellor's proposal to M. Herriot was a military accord. Apparently, this was not to be a regular alliance but rather an understanding on armaments backed

[58] Sir John Simon described the project as ". . . an agreement between European States to pursue no policy which was calculated to raise controversial political issues. Such an agreement . . . would be a form of assurance which might be valuable in return for an adjustment of the reparation and disarmament positions." *B.F.P.*, III, 153, also 135, 161-162, 172.

[59] Herriot's notes of this introductory meeting, 16 June, may be found in *Jadis*, II, 321-322.

[60] Papen described the Consultative Pact as one which "might provide that no questions interesting Germany (i.e., the Corridor and Upper Silesia) could be broached without prior consultation." Conversation with MacDonald and Herriot, 28 June 1932, *B.F.P.*, III, 279-280. According to Herriot, *Jadis*, II, 339, Papen also said that Germany would not bring up the *Anschluss* without prior consultation.

by organized contacts between the French and German general staffs. This extraordinary overture has been described by the two men in the following terms:

[Papen's memorandum—29 June] We were ready for a customs union with France which would bring both countries great advantages, and in the field of security we could give no greater proof of our sincerity, in my opinion, than that we were thinking of an entente between the French and the German Armies. This entente must have no aggressive tendency at all directed against any one, but would simply make possible an exchange of views and information between the General Staffs, and would bring a feeling of security about the present situation. The prerequisite for such an entente was naturally the restoration of equality which I had repeatedly demanded.[61]

[Herriot's notes—24 June] He offered to aid us in the disarmament affair by establishing a Franco-German accord. He demanded equality of rights, even if it is only a formula on paper; it would permit the conclusion of an accord within the limits admitted by the two General Staffs.

[Herriot's notes—29 June] The Chancellor proposed to me a customs union in exchange for equality of rights and, if not an alliance, at least a military entente between the two General Staffs....[62]

In their talk of 29 June, Herriot claims that Papen again brought the conversation around to Russia. "Cautiously but precisely he spoke to me about the Russian question and proposed an accord to eliminate credits to the Soviet Union."[63]

The audacious opening of the Papen-Herriot talks did not long stand the test. Rumors of a Franco-German "alliance" leaked to the press and, when he returned to Berlin for consultation, Chancellor von Papen was sharply attacked in the nationalist press. He

[61] Papen's memorandum of a conversation with Herriot at Lausanne, 26 June 1932, quoted in *Documents on German Foreign Policy, 1918-1945, Series C, 1933-1937* (London, 1957), 3 vols., I, *January 30-October 14, 1933*, 91, n. 2. (Hereinafter cited as *G.F.P.*) In his memoirs, Papen says that he proposed "something like a combined general staff. I suggested that on a basis of reciprocity, French General Staff officers should be allowed access to all the departments of our General Staff. France would then be informed on all German military matters." *Memoirs*, pp. 175-176.

[62] Herriot, *Jadis*, II, 338, 347. Herriot told MacDonald on 27 June that "Herr von Papen had spoken to him of a military alliance between France and Germany and of continuous contact between the General Staffs." *B.F.P.*, III, 271.

[63] Herriot, *Jadis*, II, 347. Herriot adds that Papen dropped the hint, " 'Il y a des traités.' " This was apparently a suggestion that Germany would not ratify the prolongation of the Berlin Treaty of 1926; the prolongation had been signed in June 1931 but had not been ratified. Foreign Minister von Neurath later denied that Papen's offer had any anti-Russian bias. *G.F.P.*, I, 91, n. 2.

came back to Lausanne in a guarded frame of mind. He required a comprehensive settlement all at once, including the accord on armaments, which was impossible on short notice. On the French side, Premier Herriot apparently was interested in the consultative pact and the customs union but suspicious of the military accord and the hints of anti-Soviet co-operation.[64] There was, of course, an underlying distrust of German motives. When Papen became equivocal, doubts of his sincerity rose quickly among Herriot and his colleagues.

The British threw their whole weight against the project, for they were sharply displeased.[65] Prime Minister MacDonald was shocked, and he protested to Papen in a tone which approached a dressing-down:

> He saw . . . in the Press suggestions of a military alliance. Any such idea would upset everything. . . . He felt himself in a state of bewilderment. . . . Things were going from bad to worse and [he] emphasised the dangers to Germany which failure to reach agreement in Lausanne would have.[66]

The British also pressed Herriot hard not to consider a direct accord, one which would run counter to British interests and might imperil Franco-British friendship.[67] As Herr von Papen recalls it, "Herriot told me that to his regret it would not be possible to continue our negotiations. France could not afford to risk a break with Great Britain."[68] Too much emphasis should not be placed on the British "veto," but it was a significant factor in the French decision to turn aside Papen's advances.

Papen and Herriot thus found it even more discouraging to talk reconciliation than had Laval and Brüning in 1931. Under British prodding, the Lausanne Conference eventually agreed on a formula which set up, as "an end to reparations," a lump-sum payment

[64] Herriot, *Jadis*, II, 338 ff; Papen, *Memoirs*, p. 176; *B.F.P.*, III, 271; *G.F.P.*, I, 91, n. 2; *Le Temps*, "Bulletin du Jour," 28 June 1932.

[65] MacDonald had confirmation of the German proposals from Herriot, 27 June. Papen has complained that his suggestion was "a confidential offer which he [Herriot] should not have passed on to MacDonald." *Memoirs*, p. 183.

[66] Conversation of 27 June 1932, *B.F.P.*, III, 274. Papen's recollection is that MacDonald was "not only surprised but appalled. . . . He informed me tersely that any such Franco-German pact was entirely unacceptable to the British Government. He begged me to abandon the whole idea, giving it as his idea that a close *rapprochement* of this kind between France and Germany would upset the balance of European power." *Memoirs*, p. 177.

[67] Herriot, *Jadis*, II, 345 ff.

[68] Papen, *Memoirs*, p. 181; *G.F.P.*, I, 91, n. 2.

of 3,000,000,000 R.M., to be made by Germany under numerous conditions dependent upon the recovery of her credit. All the political talks, however, did not fall on barren ground. Out of them came a striking improvement in relations between London and Paris, the "Anglo-French Declaration regarding future European Cooperation."

Stung by the Papen-Herriot talks, the British promptly proposed a Consultative Pact among the six Inviting Powers of the Conference—Great Britain, France, Germany, Italy, Japan, and Belgium. When this balloon was shot down by various marksmen, MacDonald and Simon told Herriot that they would be happy to sign a consultative accord with France, and the Premier accepted on the spot. The Anglo-French Declaration, announced in London and Paris, 13 July 1932, merely stated that the two countries would exchange views and information on "any questions . . . similar in origin to that now so happily settled at Lausanne. . . ." They would also work for a disarmament solution "beneficial and equitable for all the Powers concerned."[69] M. Herriot gave his enthusiastic approval but not on account of these platitudes. What sent him back to Paris flushed with optimism was the secret explanation of how the British government would interpret the declaration.

The crucial part of the secret interpretation ran as follows:

> On all points raised by Germany and arising, now and in the future, in connection with the liberation of Germany from her obligations under the Treaty of Versailles, His Majesty's Government would return no definite answer to the German Government until they had first talked the matter over with the French Government. It would be understood that the French Government would act in a similar manner should they be approached by the German Government in such a matter.
>
> It would not be a question of an agreement to agree, or to make joint representations. What we should undertake to do would be, not to reach any conclusions with regard to any such particular question until we had talked it over with the French Government. What I [MacDonald] have in mind is, in fact, a preliminary exchange of views with the French Government, coupled with a general desire to come to an agreement. We should undertake, and we should expect the French Government to do the same, to report any such advances made to us on the part of Germany. The object of this understanding would be to protect both Governments against the dangers of piecemeal ap-

[69] The English text may be found in *D.I.A., 1932*, p. 23, and *B.F.P.*, III, 438. In France it was called "L'Accord de Confiance Franco-Britannique"; text in *Le Temps*, 15 July, and in *L'Europe Nouvelle*, 30 July 1932.

proaches by the German Government, the development of which no Government can, at present, foresee.[70]

Herriot could hardly believe his eyes and, before this gift should vanish, he agreed to adopt the same attitude.

In view of the ripe record of Anglo-French discord on the German question, this was a unique document. It can be read as a confession as well as a proposal. True, it had been provoked by a momentary British fear of French concessions to Germany. But the French had suffered from the British tendency to argue the German case, not once, or twice, but for years. Indeed, much of the history of the twenties could be written around "piece-meal approaches by the German Government" to London.

What had led the British to such a startling reversal? Basically, it was a reflection of their traditional role as the balancer. They were upset by the talk of a direct Franco-German understanding; it sounded too much like a continental alliance. From an outsider's view, the efforts of Papen and Herriot looked like frail bits of good-will in the face of a disheartening problem. But the same sort of exploration had occurred in 1931, and on both occasions British diplomacy showed acute sensitivity.

As usually happened when they were startled, the British chose France. Mr. Ramsay MacDonald freely admitted to Herriot that "in recent years he thought Franco-British relations had considerably deteriorated.... He was still anxious to come to the understanding...."[71] Sir John Simon seemed to go out of his way in assurances: "The French Government now had the British Government's promise about their attitude to Germany. That was a promise and would be kept."[72]

The Anglo-French Declaration did not directly concern Russia, but the Franco-German talks had touched intimately on the question. Although the Soviet government did not know the nature of Papen's confidential proposals at the time, one danger was immediately clear—isolation. For nearly a month European politics at the highest level were played out at Lausanne, without the slightest influence being exerted by Soviet diplomacy. The absence of the U.S.S.R. was somewhat accidental, owing to the fact that

[70] *B.F.P.*, III, 368-369. This interpretation was read by MacDonald to the French, 5 July, and communicated to them in written form, 11 July. Other paragraphs dealt with disarmament and economic and commercial relations.
[71] Conversation of 8 July 1932, *ibid.*, III, 418.
[72] Conversation of 8 July 1932, *ibid.*, III, 419.

the conference dealt with the reparation chapter of the Versailles treaty, but there was a more important point. Moscow had no friend at the conference. Papen's attitude meant that the German link was vulnerable; Anglo-Soviet relations had never been close, and the rapprochement with France was still in its infancy.

The Russians were pained by this diplomatic isolation and were especially fearful of the Franco-German negotiations. Soviet diplomats were gloomily predicting that Papen's appointment meant the end of Rapallo.[73] Several months later Herriot apparently informed the Russians of the anti-Russian character of Papen's proposal. Despite German denials, Maxim Litvinov, the Soviet Foreign Minister, personally confronted the German Foreign Minister, Baron von Neurath, with the accusation. "M. Litvinov . . . said that the uneasiness in Moscow had begun to be felt as early as the summer of last year, in consequence of the statements of the then Chancellor von Papen to M. Herriot regarding a German-French alliance, the purpose of which was to be the attack on communism in Germany and to the East."[74] Litvinov was unimpressed by Neurath's denial and he belabored the German Ambassador in Moscow about Papen's "proposals to Herriot which were at the expense of the Soviet Union."[75]

The Anglo-French Declaration was regarded in Moscow as a slight to Soviet prestige. Germany, Italy, and Belgium were urged by the British to adhere to the Declaration, but the Soviet Union was not invited. On a smaller but closer issue, the Lausanne Convention did not include Russians on a committee created to propose measures for "the financial and economic reconstruction of central and eastern Europe."[76]

[73] Julius Curtius, the former German Foreign Minister, visiting in Russia, noticed the concern displayed at a reception given by Litvinov on the night of Papen's appointment. *Sechs Jahre Minister der Deutschen Republik*, p. 248. Ernst von Weizsäcker, of the German Delegation to the Disarmament Conference, says that his Russian colleague, Boris Stein, told him: " 'Nun ist es mit der deutsch— russischen Freundschaft zu Ende.' " *Erinnerungen* (Munich, 1950), p. 91.

[74] Conversation of 1 March 1933 in Berlin, *G.F.P.*, I, 91; see also 64, 87. Litvinov told the Italian diplomat Baron Aloisi, 23 Feb. 1933: "von Papen voulait conclure à Lausanne un accord avec la France contre la Russie." Conversation at Geneva, 23 Feb. 1933, Baron Pompeo Aloisi, *Journal (25 Juillet 1932–14 Juin 1936)* (Paris, 1957), p. 71.

[75] Dispatch of 11 March 1933, *G.F.P.*, I, 143.

[76] This was not simply the result of duplicating the list of Lausanne Conference members, for some of them were left off the list, whereas other countries, not members, such as Holland and Switzerland, were invited to participate. Lausanne Convention, IV—Resolution Relating to Central and Eastern Europe, *D.I.A., 1932*, p. 20.

On the French side, the negotiations with Germany reflected an interest in reconciliation which, though subdued, continued to exist. The conversations had not been broken off by rudeness or intransigence on either side; they simply had been adjourned. No doors had been shut, and so long as the door to Franco-German friendship remained ajar, just so long would French interest in a rapprochement with Russia remain desultory.

The Anglo-French Declaration, too, was full of potential significance for the French attitude toward Russia. Even without knowledge of the secret interpretation, French public opinion hailed the Anglo-French Declaration as a return to the Entente Cordiale. Herriot and the Quai d'Orsay indulged their hopes that the relations of the victorious allies at last would be placed on a basis of confidence. Such harmony would lend great authority to the French voice on the Continent. For France, in her quest for security, a close understanding with England would be much more attractive than the unsteady prospect of relying on Soviet Russia.

By the time the Lausanne Conference was over, a year had passed since the Franco-Soviet Non-Aggression Pact had been initialed. In the interval no tendency of progress in the rapprochement could be discerned. Some things had gone forward, others backward. Unexpected speed and success had been the hallmark of the Soviet negotiations with Poland and the Baltic States. But the Romanian tangle remained, an "out" for the French should they wish to use it. The Tardieu government had distrusted the rapprochement and had ignored it. Tardieu himself had fallen, but French and Russian policies still clashed on three current questions: aid to Central Europe, disarmament, and the Japanese invasion of Manchuria. Herriot was now back in power and his record encouraged the expectation that he would pursue the negotiations with Russia. Yet Herriot's first moves in foreign policy had been to explore the German road and to come home with British gifts. In short, the Franco-Soviet rapprochement was in the doldrums.

Four

THE FRANCO-SOVIET
NON-AGGRESSION PACT

While the oracles of the Quai d'Orsay contemplated the German problem, they were startled to find that events in Eastern Europe were moving along without them. The awakening came from Warsaw's decision to go ahead with the Polish-Soviet Non-Aggression Pact. The Polish government, like the French, was preoccupied with Germany, but it had no offer of friendship to ponder. The tension along the Polish-German frontiers was becoming more acute every day. At Danzig the situation became really touchy in June because of turbulent Nazi demonstrations and a dispute over the entry of Polish and German destroyers. Herr von Papen's cabinet, with its Junker tone, was regarded in Warsaw as the advent of those elements most hostile to Poland.

The Polish government might have urged further postponement in deference to Romania, but it made no attempt to conceal its impatience with the latter. Pilsudski had agreed to postpone the signature of the Polish-Soviet pact until the Romanians had a second chance. Romania had consented, in return, to use Polish mediation. By this means, indirect negotiations were established between M. Litvinov and M. Titulescu when the Disarmament Conference met again at Geneva in June, but after the session had adjourned, 23 July 1932, the two parties were no closer to settlement than ever before.[1] Warsaw also was uneasy about her Baltic politics. Latvia and Finland ratified their non-aggression pacts with the U.S.S.R., 21 June and 7 July respectively, and early Estonian ratification was certain, once her northern and southern neighbors had acted. Poland's claim to leadership of a Baltic Bloc would be publicly deflated by any further delay on her part.

[1] Account of M. T. Schaetzel, Chief of the Eastern Division, Polish Foreign Ministry, who was the intermediary, Beck, *Dernier Rapport*, Appendix, p. 313; *B.F.P.*, VII, 244-248; Degras, *Soviet Documents on Foreign Policy*, II, 543; *Le Temps*, 2 and 6 July 1932.

The Polish decision certainly was not the result of co-operation with Paris, as it is often interpreted. On the contrary, it was reached in an atmosphere of exasperation. The direct Franco-German conversations at Lausanne, the discussion among the great powers about the future size and arms of the German army, the Anglo-French Declaration—all these stimulated fear that France might concede something of the Polish case.[2] The Poles felt that Paris was losing interest in their problems, that Poland was being left to herself. The move to improve relations with Russia was therefore considered to be risky but necessary. Tension had to be lessened on one frontier, and the Russians were making advances.

This was the background as the Polish minister and Assistant Commissar Krestinski put their signatures to the Polish-Soviet Pact of Non-Aggression, in Moscow, 25 July 1932. The Polish cabinet announced that it would not ratify the pact until conclusion of a Romanian-Soviet treaty and assurances were sent to Bucharest that the alliance between the two countries remained as strong as ever.[3] In Romania the official reaction was polite, but the press was quite free with accusations that Poland was betraying its obligations as an ally and making it doubly difficult for Romania to negotiate with the Soviets.[4]

In Paris the response was cool and treated the Poles' decision as their own doing and not the product of French suggestions. The nationalist papers, hostile to the Franco-Soviet pact, took the same stand on this case, and deplored the Poles' breach of solidarity with Romania.[5] In addition, an important editorial in the semi-

[2] Franco-Polish relations were hurt by recriminations about a loan to Poland which the French government refused to give without parliamentary ratification, and by the sudden Polish decision to terminate the French military mission in Warsaw. See Léon Noël, *L'Aggression contre la Pologne* (Paris, 1946), pp. 120, 123; Laroche, *La Pologne de Pilsudski*, pp. 110-114.

[3] Press interview of Count Szembek, Polish Minister to Romania, *Le Temps,* 30 July 1932; Polish government communiqué of 25 July, *ibid.,* 27 July; *Osteuropa,* VII, 724; *B.F.P.,* VII, 240.

[4] Excerpts from Romanian press in *Le Temps,* 27, 28 July, *Journal des Débats,* 27 July, 8 Aug. 1932. The Romanian paper *Curentul* stated: "Nous comprenons la situation de la Pologne, mais quelque primordiaux que soient les besoins d'un État, il existe des éléments impondérables d'ordre moral qu'exigent qu'on ne pratique pas avec une hâte aussi brutale la désolidarisation et le reniement jugés utiles pour un instant." Quoted in *Le Temps,* 27 July 1932.

[5] M. Buré in *L'Ordre* called it "un pacte inutile et dangéreux," "Revue de la Presse," *J.D.,* 29 July 1932. M. Pierre Bernus in *Journal des Débats,* 27 July, could discern only a victory for Soviet diplomacy in dividing two nations to whom reason clearly dictated a common front against the Soviets.

official "Bulletin du Jour" of *Le Temps* warned Poland that the Quai d'Orsay would not be hurried.

France, as far as she is concerned, has constantly subordinated any pact of non-aggression with the Soviets to the guarantee of the security of Poland and Romania.... It is known that the Franco-Russian pact is still in the state of a project having been the object of preliminary discussions but not yet having been submitted to the scrutiny of the governments and, therefore, in no way binding their responsibility.[6]

Thus, far from being the creature of French designs, the Polish rapprochement with Russia was so independently conducted as to create another source of friction between Paris and Warsaw.

At the moment, French diplomacy showed no inclination to follow the Polish lead. It remained passive, waiting upon fulfilment of the condition of a Romanian-Russian treaty. Even a month later, the acting chief of the Quai d'Orsay stated confidentially that "the French Government had no intention of signing [the Franco-Soviet pact] ... until the Soviet-Romanian Pact had been signed."[7] By the end of September 1932 the mood had changed. Paris became anxious to remove the obstacle and for the first time put pressure on the Romanian government. What had happened in the meantime? Suddenly, once again Franco-German relations had deteriorated. Three months after the hopeful discussion at Lausanne, M. Herriot and his cabinet had become thoroughly alarmed about Germany. It was in this new atmosphere of anxiety that their concern about the rapprochement with Russia again became active.

Having failed to make a deal with the French and faced with predictions of defeat in the approaching general elections, the Papen government decided to open a full-dress campaign for "equality of rights" in armaments. General von Schleicher launched it with a broadcast to the nation, 26 July 1932. In a sarcastic, badgering tone, Schleicher scored the French for their negative attitude and said that, since they would not disarm, Germany must see to her security by the "reorganization" of her armed forces. "I wish ... to leave no doubt that we shall take this course if full security and equality of rights are further withheld from

---

[6] *Le Temps*, 27 July 1932. The Polish press replied to this criticism by saying that if the Soviet signature was worthless, so, too, were the German signatures which the French were always collecting.

[7] Conversation of M. Alexis Léger with the Counsellor of the U. S. Embassy, 27 Aug. 1932, Dispatch of 2 Sept. 1932, 751.6111/15, Archives of the Department of State, Washington, D. C.

us."[8] Chancellor von Papen resurrected the old Imperial cry that Germany must again take "a place in the sun."[9] The formal German demand for equality of rights, presented in August, was accompanied by public commentary from General von Schleicher on four separate occasions. The Reichswehr, he insisted, must have some of the weapons forbidden by the Versailles Treaty, specifically military aircraft, tanks, heavy artillery, and anti-aircraft guns. If they were refused, Germany would leave the Disarmament Conference and "assure its national security by national means...."[10]

These militant words were punctuated by unnerving political events. The forcible ouster of the Social-Democratic administration in Prussia 20 July and the temporary vesting of executive power over Berlin and Brandenburg in the Reichswehr sounded like the prelude to a military dictatorship. The general elections, held on 31 July, again boosted the extremists. The Communists cut deeply into the Socialist vote, and Hitler routed the Nationalists. The Nazis more than doubled their poll in the general elections of September 1930, swirling up to the spectacular total of 13,765,781 votes. Their two hundred and thirty seats made them by far the largest party in the Reichstag.[11] The elections were followed by ten days of political terrorism loosed mainly by the Nazi stormtroopers, proud of their murders at Königsberg and Potempa.

At the end of this tumultuous fortnight came President von Hindenburg's interview with Hitler, 13 August, the climax of efforts to pull him into the government as a minister but not as Chancellor. Hitler rebuffed the offer, but the incident startled the French by the realization that they might some day find themselves negotiating with a National Socialist government. Finally, the traditional nationalists' organization of war veterans, the *Stahlhelm*, held an

[8] *D.I.A.*, *1932*, pp. 184-185. For the background of Schleicher's intervention consult Wilhelm Deist, "Schleicher und die deutsche Abrüstungspolitik im Juni/Juli 1932," *Vierteljahrshefte für Zeitgeschichte*, VII, April 1959, pp. 163-176.

[9] *Journal des Débats*, 29 July 1932; *B.F.P.*, IV, 102.

[10] The quotation is from Schleicher's article of 31 Aug. in the Italian journal, *Il Resto del Carlino*, reprinted in *Le Temps*, 20 Sept. 1932; for his statements to the press during maneuvers in East Prussia and in an article in the review, *Heimatdienst*, 30 Aug., consult *B.I.N.*, IX, 162; *B.F.P.*, IV, 134-135; *Le Temps*, 1 and 8 Sept. 1932.

[11] The Nazi popular vote had been 6,379,692 in 1930, their Reichstag seats 107. The Communist vote rose from 4,590,160 to 5,282,626 and their seats in the Reichstag increased from 77 to 89.

immense rally, about 150,000 strong, in Berlin, 2-4 September.
German military virtues were extolled in numerous speeches, and
the Chancellor himself lent the government's prestige, attending
the opening meeting and the great review at Tempelhof.[12]

The formal German démarche, 29 August 1932, proposed that
France and Germany should engage in confidential discussions
about the immediate application of equality of rights in armaments.
It would have been a difficult negotiation under the best auspices,
as Lausanne had shown; dropped into the current atmosphere of
tension its only effect was to intensify the bad feeling on both
sides. The German note insisted upon full recognition of the principle of equality, but offered to compromise on actual execution.
Germany wished to have "samples" of weapons hitherto forbidden,
particularly tanks and heavy artillery, anti-aircraft guns, and eventually military aircraft, submarines, and heavy cruisers. Reichswehr
service would be cut from 12 to 6 or 4 years and a militia of
30,000–40,000 men conscripted to be trained three months an-
nually. If conversations were not accepted by the French, it was
clearly implied that Germany would not continue to participate
at the Disarmament Conference.[13]

This was precisely the type of "piecemeal approach" envisaged
in the secret interpretation to the Anglo-French Declaration, and
the French were in no mood to throw away British assurances. M.
Herriot virtually fell over himself in his haste to demonstrate
French loyalty. He sent to London the substance of the German
note, and stated categorically that he would enter no such negotiations without British participation or full prior consultation.[14] On
its own merits, too, the German program struck fear in Paris; it
might be couched in terms of "equality of rights" but it amounted
to rearmament. Whatever their doubts about their ability to keep
Germany disarmed forever, the French leaders could not bring
themselves to approve what they feared so much. M. Herriot told
the British that the solution could only be "equality of status in

[12] On 14 August, 25,000–50,000 former soldiers of Rhineland units met at
Pirmasens, near the French border, and General von Clauss reportedly evoked their
mission to make Alsace-Lorraine German once more. For the shrill French press
reaction see "Revue de la presse," *J.D.* and "Revue de la presse," *Le Temps*, 16
Aug. *et seq.*
[13] Text in *D.I.A, 1932,* 185-188; *B.F.P.,* IV, 121-124. Further details supplied
by German officials may be found *ibid.*, IV, p. 104 ff. François-Poncet, *Souvenirs,*
pp. 51-52.
[14] *B.F.P.,* IV, 104-105, 118-119, 124-125.

eventual disarmament"; "there must be no rearmament by Germany."[15]

The French note in reply, 11 September, repeated Herriot's stand, and rejected the invitation to talk alone. France could not give "an isolated answer to so vast a question."[16] The German government thereupon notified the Bureau of the Disarmament Conference that the German delegation would not come to its meeting of 20 September. Simultaneously, orders were issued that the construction of the third 10,000-ton cruiser, which had been postponed by Brüning as a conciliatory gesture, should begin 1 October.

There were observers who perceived in the German ferment some elements of "traditional" nationalism, which they hoped might draw the strength from Hitler's fanatical brand. It might have been the better part of wisdom for the French to make this distinction, but most of them did not. They could see only manifestations of German nationalism. All of them were hostile to France, so what matter the variety?

Beginning with General von Schleicher's broadcast 26 July, French observers detected a new note of defiance, a new cynicism. Their alarmed reactions were voiced repeatedly by M. Herriot, officials of the Ministry for Foreign Affairs, and the press. The acting Secretary-General of the Quai d'Orsay, M. Alexis Léger, said that the French spirit of conciliation had been frozen by "a public pronouncement by General von Schleicher which could only be described as provocative. . . ." Léger resented the constant pressure; "each concession . . . was promptly followed by fresh and yet more extravagant demands."[17]

[15] Part of the French alarm came from the realization of the extent of German clandestine rearmament. It was just at this time, incidentally, that the French army's intelligence service finally accepted the validity of evidence revealing the operations of the secret training stations maintained by the Reichswehr in Russia. Consult Castellan, *Le Réarmement Clandestin du Reich, 1930-1935*, especially pp. 177-195. The training stations in Russia are discussed below, chap. v, pp. 95-97.

[16] *D.I.A., 1932*, pp. 189-194; *Le Temps*, 14 Sept. 1932. When shown a rough draft of the note, 9 Sept., Sir John Simon said that it would be better simply to reject "the discussion *à deux*. More than two countries are affected and the French Government might therefore think it well to suggest that discussions should proceed not only with France but with Britain and Italy as well." *B.F.P.*, IV, 152.

[17] Conversation with the British Chargé d'Affaires, Mr. Campbell, who noted that M. Léger "spoke with unusual gravity and is clearly seriously alarmed." 23 Aug., *B.F.P.*, IV, 101-102, also 112. See *F.R.U.S., 1932*, I, 418-419.

While he was devising his reply to the German note, M. Herriot confided his fears to foreign diplomats.

He was profoundly disappointed that his efforts ... for a better understanding between France and Germany should have borne this bitter fruit, and that Germany should have chosen most inopportune moment and most aggressive manner in which to prosecute her claim to equality of status.[18]

Furthermore, he said that any nation that could on a Sunday produce a demonstration of disciplined men to the extent of 120,000, as the Stahlheim [*sic*] demonstration at Tempelhof, only lacked the arms to make them a menace to Europe.... France at the moment was more disturbed with reference to Germany's activity and state of opinion than for many years and in examining his conscience he thought that these fears were justified.[19]

Herriot frequently ended his interviews with predictions of another arms race, even another war. He also showed apprehension about the Russian manufacture of "forbidden categories of arms" for Germany and about the prospect of "German and Italian aggression possibly supported by Russia."[20] In a major speech at Gramat, Herriot told his audience that he could not get away from an historical memory, Prussia profiting from the restrictions that Napoleon had imposed on her to create a new type of army. "In the same fashion, does not Germany today seek to create a new army, or even a double army, with the design of striking to the heart of the adversary by a decisive blow?"[21]

On the day after the Stahlhelm rally an outspoken lead editorial in *Le Temps* said that the character of the German note was revealed by the atmosphere in which it had been conceived.

This offensive return of the elements responsible for the catastrophe of 1914, this slipping of an entire people into the worst nationalistic passions, these are signs that no one can mistake.[22]

For Pertinax in *L'Echo de Paris*, "this is Germany of the *revanche* which is passing before your eyes."[23] Leading an almost unan-

[18] Conversation with Mr. Campbell, 1 Sept. 1932, B.F.P., IV, 118-119, also 130-131, 166-169, 229-231.

[19] Conversation with American diplomats, 9 Sept. 1932, F.R.U.S., 1932, I, 430. Herriot told the Italian diplomat, Baron Aloisi, in Geneva, 28 Sept., "La difficulté ne réside pas d'après lui [Herriot] dans le principe de l'égalité, mais dans la volonté de l'Allemagne de réarmer et de dominer complètement l'Europe." Aloisi, *Journal*, pp. 10-11.

[20] F.R.U.S., 1932, I, 430, 438.   [21] Le Temps, 26 Sept. 1932.

[22] Le Temps, 5 Sept. 1932, "Bulletin du Jour."

[23] L'Echo de Paris, 4 Sept. 1932.

imous press denunciation of the German note, M. Émile Buré sounded the call, "Back to alliances." The usually moderate *L'Ère Nouvelle,* connected with Herriot, said that the German note amounted to saying, "Whatever you won't give us, we'll take."[24]

This was the frame of mind which prevailed at the time of the French decision to push the non-aggression pact with the Soviet Union. There is no need to pretend an exclusive cause-and-effect relationship. Other factors were involved, but it is not surprising that in the face of stormy words and sudden diplomatic pressure from Germany, closer relations with Russia should have become more attractive. It is also likely that Herriot was thinking specifically about depriving the Germans of Russian supplies in a new armament race or a future war.

The rumblings from across the Rhine might not have sounded so menacing had the French been able to stand arm in arm with the British. Many Frenchmen had hoped that the Anglo-French Declaration heralded a real change. The government of the United Kingdom certainly lived up to its obligations to report to Paris "piecemeal approaches" from Germany. But it had not promised to change British policy itself. The secret interpretation referred to "a general desire to come to an agreement," but it included also the disclaimer: "It would not be a question of an agreement to agree." The Declaration was an agreement to consult, a promise of "a preliminary exchange of views" before taking any action.[25] The German withdrawal from the Disarmament Conference tore the cloak of ambiguity from the Declaration and revealed that "a preliminary exchange of views" meant only that.

The plain fact was that British policy still favored the satisfaction of some important German desires. From the middle of September onwards, British diplomats made almost daily efforts to bring Germany back into the Disarmament Conference. They took, superficially, the form of pressure for a four- or five-power meeting to examine the question. But, since the Germans could never return without some satisfaction of their claims, the British efforts were equivalent to pressure on the French to grant Germany some measure of equality of rights in arms.[26] The French cabinet

[24] M. Émile Buré in *L'Ordre,* quoted in "Revue de la presse," *J.D.,* 8 Sept.; *L'Ère Nouvelle* quoted in "Revue de la presse," *Le Temps* 2 Sept.
[25] *B.F.P.,* III, 368.
[26] Consult *ibid.,* IV, chaps. iii and iv and *F.R.U.S., 1932,* I, 416-528.

was not eager for a complete break-up of the conference, and it probably recognized British services as essential to avoid this end. These considerations, however, did not efface the disillusionment of seeing London once again pleading what was in effect the German case. However sympathetic the British manner of urging their views, the substance of policy remained much the same. The French valued the change in atmosphere achieved by the Declaration, but they were beginning to realize that it was not a new Entente Cordiale.

ii

By the end of September 1932 the French government had discarded its passive attitude towards the rapprochement with Russia. It now began to take steps to hasten the conclusion of the non-aggression pact. The Quai d'Orsay, which had hitherto restrained its influence on the Romanian-Soviet dispute, took up an active role in promoting the renewal of negotiations. In a conversation, 27 September, an official at the Foreign Ministry confirmed the initial success of these efforts and also disclosed an important change in the status of the Franco-Soviet pact.

He added that the text of the Franco-Russian pact of non-aggression had been examined and approved by the French Government and the Soviets, and that the signature would occur either at the same time or immediately following the signature of the Russo-Roumanian Pact.[27]

Diplomatic accords, when strongly backed by the Premier and Foreign Minister, usually were given quick approval by the cabinet. The significance of the cabinet's approval thus lies in its revelation of M. Herriot's decision to push the affair to conclusion.

To bring back Romanian and Russian diplomats to the same table required not only French but Polish mediation. A "rolling" interview was arranged, 14 September, between M. Cadère, Romanian Minister to Poland, and M. Litvinov, as the latter journeyed *"en wagon-lit"* between Bialystok and Warsaw.[28] They decided to

[27] Dispatch from the U.S. Embassy in Paris, 27 Sept. 1932, 751.6111/17, Archives of the Department of State, Washington, D. C.

[28] Resumé by M. Vaida Voivod, Romanian Premier, *Le Temps*, 12 Oct.; Degras, *Soviet Documents on Foreign Policy*, II, 543-546; Beck, *Dernier Rapport*, pp. 11-12, 313; *B.F.P.*, VII, 246.

renew direct negotiations; these talks, again between M. Litvinov and M. Cadère, sent as special envoy, began about 25 September at Geneva. They proceeded favorably, thanks in part to M. Herriot, who was in Geneva for the Disarmament Conference and who exercised influence on both sides in favor of a compromise formula on Bessarabia.[29] Urged on by French and Polish diplomats, the Cadère-Litvinov negotiations had almost succeeded in producing agreement when they were overtaken by the ramifications of a bizarre episode in Romanian politics.

On 28 September Nicholas Titulescu, the leading figure of Romanian diplomacy, resigned dramatically from his post as Ambassador to Great Britain. When M. Titulescu announced that he had been spurred by conviction that the non-aggression pact with Russia was a serious error, there was great excitement in Bucharest; the Geneva negotiations were hurriedly interrupted and M. Litvinov returned to Moscow in a huff.[30] The unorthodox result was the appointment of M. Titulescu as Foreign Minister 10 October, and the resignation of the government he had attacked. With the smiling M. Titulescu making policy, it was obvious that there would be little hope for the negotiations.[31]

The cabinet in Paris was now in a quandary. No one could pretend that Romanian-Soviet compromise was just around the corner. Should France drop her own pact with the U.S.S.R. or go ahead without fulfilment of the Romanian "condition"? For the rest of the month of October there was no clear indication on which side M. Herriot would descend.

While the Premier was pondering this dilemma, the Poles helped him to make up his mind. Dispatches from Warsaw and Bucharest revealed in unmistakable fashion that Pilsudski would wait no longer on the Romanians. The Polish Foreign Office refused a Romanian request that it again lend its services to renew the negotiations.[32] This refusal became public knowledge, 31 October, and provoked much press criticism in Bucharest and Paris.[33]

[29] Report from Geneva in *Le Temps*, 1 Oct. 1932; *B.F.P.*, VII, 246-247.
[30] See 28 Sept. *Le Temps*, and thereafter almost daily dispatches from England until 10 Oct., and from Bucharest throughout Oct. Consult also Henry L. Roberts, *Roumania* (New York, 1951), pp. 173-174; Titulescu's statements to *La République*, quoted in "Revue de la presse," *J.D.*, 14 Oct. 1932.
[31] See the declaration of policy by the new Maniu cabinet, in which Titulescu was Foreign Minister, *Le Temps*, 23 Oct. 1932.
[32] Havas Agency report from Bucharest, *Le Temps*, 1 Nov. 1932.
[33] See dispatches from Bucharest, 1 Nov. 1932 *et seq.*, *Le Temps*. Among the

The jibes directed at Colonel Beck subsided, however, when his appointment as Foreign Minister, 2 November, made it clear that he enjoyed Marshal Pilsudski's full confidence.[34]

At some point after the suspension of the Cadère-Litvinov negotiations, according to Beck's account, Warsaw asked for a clear-cut answer on whether or not Romania seriously intended to conclude the pact with Russia. The Romanian government responded in the negative, adding that it would not stand in the way of the Polish Pact.[35] It was reported by a diplomat in Bucharest that the Polish minister told the Romanian Foreign Ministry: "Poland had done everything in the past to help Romania find a formula which would allow it to sign a pact similar to the Russo-Polish and Russo-French pact, but that as Romania demands special conditions, Poland is now obligated to dissociate itself from further Romanian-Soviet negotiations."[36]

Polish insistence on winding up the whole affair was also urged directly on Paris. An official French parliamentary report revealed that, after Titulescu's maneuver, "Poland insisted to us [France] that we should sign our pact of non-aggression."[37] It is thus clear that in the move to improve relations with Russia, France was not forcing Poland into something that the latter did not desire. In fact, just the opposite; at the end the Poles were forcing the French hand.

Another development which eased the way for the rapprochement at this time was the complete reversal of French policy in the Far Eastern crisis. M. Édouard Herriot, with his devotion to the League of Nations and to the concept of collective security, did not approve of French support for Japan; as he told Mr. Nor-

---

Paris critics were Jacques Bainville in *L'Action Française*, M. Saint Brice in *Le Journal*, *L'Ordre*, *La Journée Industrielle*, quoted in "Revue de la presse," *J.D.*, 3 and 5 Nov. 1932, and Pertinax in *L'Echo de Paris*, 3 Nov.

[34] Beck's later career led to the charge of his being pro-German, and it is thus worth pausing to note that when he first gained public notice the charge was that he was pro-Soviet.

[35] "Cela nous força en fin de compte à poser une question catégorique à Bucarest: 'oui ou non?' " Beck, *Dernier Rapport*, p. 12.

[36] Dispatch from the U.S. Ambassador in Bucharest, Mr. Wilson, 11 Nov. 1932, 761., 7111/32, Archives of the Department of State, Washington, D.C.

[37] Verbal report by M. Henry Torrès, *rapporteur* of a resolution on Franco-Soviet Treaty of Non-Aggression, *J.O.*, Chambre, *Débats*, 16 May 1933, p. 2383. In a speech, 11 Feb. 1936, M. Torrès recalled Poland's "intercession pressante et passionnée auprès de la France pour que celle-ci se hâte de signer avec le gouvernement des Soviets, le pacte de non-agression." *Ibid.*, 11 Feb. 1936, p. 350.

man Davis in May 1932, such sympathies "had never been the desire of the parties of the Left...."[38] In September Herriot assured American diplomats that he would discourage the efforts of French banks to arrange a loan to Japan or Manchukuo; "France, Great Britain and America ought all to discourage any further loans to Japan at the present time."[39] At this same time M. Léger stated that, among the reasons for the change in policy, "France had no desire to bring on difficulties with Russia by any attempts to assume responsibilities in the Manchurian region."[40]

During the autumn months, after Japanese recognition of Manchukuo, 15 September, and publication of the Lytton Report had again inflamed the issue, Paris announced sympathy and support for American declarations of policy, which were anti-Japanese, and for the League's decisions. On 10 October 1932 the French Ambassador to Washington, M. Claudel, stated that France felt that the maintenance of treaties was just as essential in the Japanese case as in the German case. "The French Government ... is willing and intends to follow the lead of this country [the United States] undeviatingly."[41] Support for the Japanese expansion into Manchuria thus disappeared from French policy after Herriot's accession to power. One of the conflicts which had embittered Franco-Soviet relations earlier in the year was eliminated.

iii

After waiting the better part of a month, the French government decided to go ahead without Romania. The Premier chose the 29th Congress of the Radical-Socialist party, at Toulouse 3-6 November 1932, to give the public signal that the Franco-Soviet non-aggression pact would soon be concluded. M. Édouard Herriot reminded his party of the insecure international situation, and it was in a spirit of mending fences that he spoke of two former allies—Italy and Russia.

Some people have spoken about Italy. Nothing could be more distressing than the persistence of a misunderstanding which has put us in opposition to a great people, who entered the war with us and to whom perhaps we have not been morally just....

[38] Conversation at Lyons, 22 May 1932, *F.R.U.S.*, *1932*, I, 138.

[39] 19 Sept. 1932, *ibid.*, *1932*, IV, 265-266, see also pp. 67-68, 71-72, 234.

[40] 8 Sept. 1932, *ibid.*, *1932*, IV, 234.

[41] Conversation with Under Secretary Castle, *ibid.*, *1932*, IV, 295. See also *1932*, IV, 298-299, 318, and Herriot's talk with Davis, 26 Nov., *ibid.*, *1932*, I, 486.

I am now negotiating a pact of non-aggression with the [Russian] government.... We have reached agreement on the essential points and I shall be happy if we are able to pursue, in that direction, a work of peace profitable to all.[42]

Le Temps followed up this announcement with an editorial which spoke warmly of Italy and justified the Russian pact as "a supplementary guarantee of security."[43] It is noteworthy that the pact was presented to the French public in the company of an advance towards Italy.

Meanwhile, the final act in the Russo-Romanian negotiations was being played out—this time via Paris. Poland having refused its services, the French government forwarded to Moscow, 1 November, the conditions on which Romania would resume the parleys. Ten days later the Soviet government replied by simply sending a list of its own conditions and leaving Romania the option of signing a pact so defined any time in the next four months.[44] These moves were merely for the record, and M. Titulescu hurried to present a long defense of Romanian policy before Parliament, 23 November. Basically, his argument was that the pact should be avoided because it would weaken the legal standing of Romania's occupation of Bessarabia. Titulescu conceded, however, that he understood the reasons which were leading France and Poland to arrange treaties with Russia and did not wish to stand in the way of their conclusion.[45]

The stage thus was set to bypass a Romanian-Soviet pact, upon which both the Polish and French treaties originally had been made dependent. Warsaw and Paris pressed on immediately. The President of the Polish Republic ratified the Polish-Soviet Pact of Non-Aggression on 26 November 1932. The next day, this act and the corresponding ratification by the Soviet Central Executive Committee were announced simultaneously in the Polish and Russian capitals. *Izvestya's* comments reflected satisfaction with the fact that relations had been repaired with the strongest state on Russia's western frontiers.[46] The event completed the chain of non-

[42] Speech of 6 Nov. 1932, 7 Nov. *Le Temps.*

[43] "Bulletin du Jour," *ibid.,* 7 Nov. 1932.

[44] Soviet communication to Romania, 9 Nov., Degras, *Soviet Documents on Foreign Policy,* II, 547; speech of M. Titulescu, 23 Nov., *Le Temps,* 25 Nov. 1932; F.R.U.S., 1933, II, 666; B.F.P., VII, 285.

[45] Speech of 23 Nov. 1932, *Le Temps,* 25 Nov.

[46] *Izvestya,* 28 Nov. 1932, quoted in *S.U.R.,* XI, 3, and in *Le Temps,* 30 Nov. 1932.

aggression treaties which now linked Russia with Finland, Estonia, Latvia, Lithuania, and Poland. Despite Romania's absence, it was a heartening development in the politics of Eastern Europe. For the moment, there was stability in a troubled area. The key factor had been the first substantial rapprochement between Poland and Russia since the war of 1920.[47]

On 29 November 1932, with appropriate ceremony at the Quai d'Orsay, Premier Herriot and Ambassador Dovgalevsky signed the Franco-Soviet Treaty of Non-Aggression and the Conciliation Convention. Both texts were published on the following day.[48] Simultaneously, it was announced that French and Russian negotiators had returned to the thorny problems of a commercial treaty.[49]

Only a brief analysis of the pact is profitable, for its importance was primarily symbolic. The two governments promised "not to resort . . . either to war or to any aggression by land, sea or air" against each other. "Should either High Contracting Party be the object of aggression by one or more third Powers, the other High Contracting Party undertakes not to give aid or assistance, either directly or indirectly, to the aggressor or aggressors during the period of the conflict." The Russians hoped that this provision would prevent French support for a Polish attack; the French hoped that it would prevent Russian support of Germany.

The controversial sections of the treaty were the definitions of economic and political non-aggression. Article IV was criticized in Paris because it contained a pledge not to participate in any "international agreement" against the other party's foreign trade. That would forbid France to wage a campaign against Soviet "dumping," such as the Tardieu cabinet had done in 1930. The government replied that the restriction was balanced by the promise not to exclude totally the other country's commerce, a form of pressure easily applied by the Soviets, owing to state monopoly of trade. Friends of anti-Soviet Russian groups in Paris, such as the White Russian military associations and the Georgian émigrés, feared the

---

[47] Note M. Beck's statement in Paris, *Le Temps*, 30 Nov. 1932, and his remarks to the British Minister in Warsaw, *B.F.P.*, VII, 284.

[48] Texts of the Treaty and Convention may be found in *Le Temps*, 1 Dec. 1932, *L'Europe Nouvelle*, 3 Dec., and *L.N.T.S.*, CLVII, 411. See Appendix I.

[49] *Le Temps*, 27, 29 Nov.; *Journal des Débats*, 6 Dec. 1932. French exports to Russia declined from 59 million francs in 1931 to 47 million francs in 1932; imports from Russia rose from 496 million francs in 1931 to 519 million francs in 1932. The disadvantage to France thus increased. League of Nations, *International Trade Statistics, 1931 and 1932*, p. 120.

engagement in Article V, "not to create, protect, equip, subsidise or admit in its territory" hostile military organizations or exile governments. In defense, the Quai d'Orsay claimed that this article provided the means to reduce Communist propaganda in France and her colonies: a pledge not "to promote or encourage agitation, propaganda or attempted intervention designed to prejudice its territorial integrity or to transform by force the political or social regime of all or parts of its territories."[50]

The reception that Parisian journals gave the pact showed no change from the pattern which had been revealed in 1931. The conservative nationalist papers, such as *Le Figaro, Journal des Débats, L'Echo de Paris, Le Journal,* though much alarmed about the resurgence of German nationalism, were still not attracted by a deal with Russia in order to weaken Germany.[51] Pertinax, in *L'Echo de Paris,* complained that at the beginning of the negotiation the French government had two objectives: improvement of the commercial balance and separation of the Red Army from the Reichswehr. "In this double design we have not succeeded to any degree."[52]

Nor had opinion changed on the Left. The Radicals, of course, came forth in praise of their chief, "le bon président Herriot."[53] In *Le Populaire,* however, the Socialist welcome was still tepid. "Even if, practically speaking, it brings nothing new, it has, nonetheless, a moral value."[54] Writing in *L'Humanité,* M. André Ferrat ascribed another palm to Soviet diplomacy, but indignantly denied that the rapprochement could be expected to gag the Communist party. "If it is necessary to change something in our activity we will make it even more ardent against French imperialism."[55] The pact, said

[50] The quotations are from the text in *L.N.T.S.,* CLVII, 411. Article III reserved prior treaty rights and obligations, Article VI was a pledge to use, as an instrument for pacific settlement of disputes, the Conciliation Convention. As stated in Article VII, the treaty was drawn up for an indefinite duration; no denunciation of it could take place until two years had passed.

[51] See articles by M. Pierre Bernus, 28 Nov.–2 Dec. 1932, *Journal des Débats;* extracts from *Le Figaro* and *Le Journal* in "Revue de la presse." The extreme Right *L'Action Française,* of course, disapproved violently.

[52] *L'Echo de Paris,* 30 Nov. 1932. See also his articles of 27 Nov. and 1 Dec.

[53] *L'Oeuvre,* the most important Radical paper, but not controlled by the party, based its approval primarily on the hope of promoting Franco-Soviet trade. 27 Nov. 1932.

[54] O. Rosenfeld, *Le Populaire,* 27 Nov. 1932; here, too, the interest was primarily economic.

[55] Article of M. André Ferrat, *L'Humanité,* 1 Dec. 1932; see also article of M. Gabriel Peri, 27 Nov.

the Communist journal, could not be relied upon, because one of the signatories was French imperialism, "the most aggressive and the most militarist of imperialisms, the gendarme of Europe and the bloody tormentor of sixty million colonial slaves."[56]

It was assumed by many Frenchmen that, because Herriot put through the recognition of the Soviet Union in 1924 and concluded the Franco-Soviet pact in 1932, the two projects must have been conceived in the same spirit. Actually, Herriot's approach had changed by this time. In 1924 he had been influenced by favorable impressions of the Soviet experiment gathered on his tour in 1922, by a romantic comparison of the Russian and French revolutions. Now, after watching the unscrupulous battles waged by the French Communists, he knew that they had no romantic illusions about the Third Republic to which he and his party were devoted. In place of sentiment, calculation appeared. Herriot was moved by the conviction that, in the game of European power politics, France was not strong enough to ignore the advantages of political co-operation with Russia.[57]

The Premier continued to be disturbed by the German challenge. Speaking with Norman Davis three days before he signed the pact, Herriot said that once "he had honestly believed in the possibility of an entente between France and Germany. He no longer had that belief." Davis reported that in the interview "he [Herriot] repeated again and again, 'I am afraid.' It seemed to him that France was walking in the darkness towards a goal which it could not clearly ascertain."[58]

Herriot's decision to improve relations with Russia was taken from the point of view of security: to strengthen France, to weaken Germany. These goals were admitted by Herriot in an essay entitled "France in the World," written just a few weeks after signature of the Franco-Soviet pact.

[Russia] calls up each year 1,200,000 conscripts, of whom 400,000 are for the regular army and 800,000 for the territorial army.... Aviation, more than any other arm, is the object of vigorously pursued

[56] *L'Humanité*, 30 Nov. 1932.

[57] Compare Herriot's account of 1922, *La Russie Nouvelle* (Paris, 1922), which was almost entirely devoted to an analysis of the Communist regime, to his treatment of Russia in *La France dans le Monde* (Paris, 1933). In the latter, Herriot concentrates on Russia's economic and military power.

[58] Conversation of 26 Nov. 1932, *F.R.U.S.*, 1932, I, 476-481; see also Herriot-Davis conversation 28 Nov., pp. 481-486.

studies.... Thus, one can understand why a French minister thought it important to conclude with the Soviet Union a pact of non-aggression similar to that which Poland already had signed.[59]

Herriot claimed that by the Polish and French treaties with Russia, "the liaison between the Red Army and the Reichswehr was broken."[60]

On the Russian side the signature of the pact was announced with "the deepest satisfaction." After fifteen years of enmity and disdain, the Soviets welcomed the coming of friendly relations with France, "one of the strongest powers in Europe." At the same time, the editorial in *Izvestya*, 30 November, was careful to add explicit assurances to German readers:

> Just as the signing by Germany of a similar pact at Locarno did not remove those interests out of which was created the friendly attitude between the German people and the Soviet Union, similarly the policy of rapprochement between the Soviet Union and France should not injure these relations. Our relations with Germany have been and still are directed to the mutual interests of both peoples.[61]

This cautious verdict indicated how pragmatically the Soviet leaders viewed the new relations with France. Litvinov, however, gave an interview to *Le Petit Parisien* in which he hinted that the Soviets might move closer to the French on the old quarrel: security versus disarmament. "We are not indifferent to the idea of security . . . ," said Litvinov. "Given the doubtful success of the Disarmament Conference, it is important that all states make serious efforts to find other methods to maintain peace."[62] For the Soviets to say a good word about security, the French thesis that they had denounced for years, was a hopeful sign.

It would be an exaggeration to speak of a "reaction" to the pact from any of the great powers except Germany. There the news was received with gloom and predictions that it would mean the end of Rapallo. Polish official circles expressed satisfaction with the treaty because it complemented and reinforced their own. In the Little Entente, only Czechoslovakia showed enthusiasm for the new

[59] *La France dans le Monde*, pp. 79-83.
[60] *Ibid.*, pp. 41-42; see also *Le Temps* "Bulletin du Jour," 28 Nov. 1932.
[61] Quoted in *S.U.R.*, XI, 6; also in *Osteuropa*, VIII, 224 and *Bulletin de la presse russe*, No. 224.
[62] Interview with Georges Luciani, Moscow correspondent for *Le Petit Parisien* and *Le Temps,* reprinted in Georges Luciani (Pierre Berland), *Six Ans à Moscou* (Paris, 1937), pp. 332-336.

development; criticism and skepticism were the rule in Bucharest and Belgrade.

The conclusion of the Treaty of Non-Aggression brought to an end the first phase in the Franco-Soviet rapprochement.[63] The length and vicissitudes of the negotiations, alone, bore sufficient testimony to the provisional character of this new association. On the Soviet side, the operation required no special motive. It fitted into the general pattern of improving political relations and increasing trade with as many of the great industrial powers as possible. This was a pattern dictated to Soviet diplomacy since 1928 by the absolute need for peace and foreign aid in order to realize the industrialization of the Five Year Plan. In this particular case, the attempt to increase trade had so far failed, but the pact made it unlikely that France would again take the lead in any movement against Soviet trade, as she had done in 1930. As for the effect on Russia's relations with Germany, even her first steps towards France blurred the symbolic value of the ties begun at Rapallo. But the bond with France was light and completely untested. The Soviet leaders were not disposed to make a choice between the old and the new when there was no necessity to do so.

For France, too, the non-aggression pact did not signify a major change in policy. The negotiation had been accepted with limited aims. Memories of Brest-Litovsk and Soviet repudiation of the prewar debts still rankled. Many Frenchmen who were willing to waive the past were held back by fear that co-operation with Russia might produce a stronger Communist movement in France. A lively interest did exist in one aspect of the rapprochement, but it was a negative aspect—the possibility of breaking the Russo-German link. Even this interest was confined to governmental circles, and was not shared by the traditional nationalists. The new friendship was of secondary importance in the scheme of French diplomacy, but the indifference of the previous decade had disappeared. The slate had been cleared and it would depend upon other circumstances what would be written upon it.

[63] French ratification will be covered in chap. vi below because its form indicated a change in the situation. Although parliamentary approval was not necessary for such a treaty, an official of the Quai d'Orsay stated confidentially that "The French Government will in fact request the approval of the Parliament for these treaties [including the Conciliation Convention]." Dispatch from the U.S. Chargé in France, Mr. Marriner, 5 Dec. 1932, 751.6111/24. Archives of the Department of State, Washington, D.C.

Five

HITLER, THE SPUR TO FRANCO-SOVIET RAPPROCHEMENT

Writing in 1934, Arnold Toynbee labeled the Franco-Soviet Non-Aggression Pact an "epoch-making ... event in the international history of Europe."[1] He hardly would have written these words when the pact was signed in November 1932. What had intervened was the appointment of Adolf Hitler as Chancellor of Germany. It was Nazi foreign policy which insured that the non-aggression pact would be only the beginning and not the end of Franco-Soviet rapprochement.

Ironically, the last act of Hitler's struggle for power had opened with failure. The general election of 6 November 1932 revealed that the Nazi flood at last was receding. Hitler was again offered a place in a coalition cabinet but on no more attractive conditions than in August; tantalized for the second time, he still refused. But the denouement came as a surprise to everyone. Instead of Papen continuing as Chancellor, it was General von Schleicher who turned suddenly against his friend and took over the top position.

Schleicher's accession was blessed by a striking success in foreign policy. On 11 December, after protracted negotiations, the British, French, and Italian governments declared their willingness to grant Germany "equality of rights in a system which would provide security for all nations ...," and Germany agreed to return to the Disarmament Conference.[2] Hitler's break with one of his top lieutenants, the popular Gregor Strasser, over Strasser's wish to join the Schleicher government, a string of Nazi losses in provincial elections, and the party's admission of financial insolvency appeared to confirm the decline of National Socialism.

Schleicher might have hastened to smother the infant Franco-Soviet rapprochement, for he had been associated with the military side of the Rapallo policy. But within a few weeks the only ques-

[1] S.I.A., 1934, p. 381.
[2] Text of the Declaration, D.I.A., 1932, pp. 233-234.

tion was that of his survival. He turned the Junkers frantically against him by land reform schemes, and his crafty plan of "harnessing" the better elements among the Nazis yielded only a handful who were willing to follow Strasser's lead and break with Hitler. And Schleicher no more than Papen could escape from the dread lines of unemployed, whose numbers rose over the six million mark in January 1933.

When it was seen that Schleicher had no magic touch, Hitler's stock revived. Financial aid to the Nazis was renewed by wealthy nationalist and industrial circles. From all angles came helping hands to open the way for Hitler: Papen's resentment of being dumped by Schleicher; business leaders, such as Hugenberg, Schacht, and Thyssen, and military men such as General von Blomberg, who had decided that "the Nazi experiment had to be tried"; and in the President's entourage, co-operation from Oskar von Hindenburg and State Secretary Meissner. On 28 January 1933 President von Hindenburg, by refusing Schleicher full powers to deal with the Reichstag, forced him to resign. To the last minute there were clever maneuvers for position. Hindenburg and his advisers wanted to make sure this would be a "controlled experiment." After all, didn't they have Hitler hemmed in, by Papen as Vice Chancellor and "sound men" as Ministers of Defense, Foreign Affairs, and Economy? True, and there were only three Nazis in the government; but—Hitler was Chancellor. The fateful decision was revealed at noon on 30 January 1933, and that evening an ecstatic torchlight parade of Nazi stormtroopers set the tone for his regime.

The immediate reaction in and out of Germany was simply "Wait and see." But there was no "wait." Within six months the extremist nature of Hitler's aims and methods was demonstrated by what was no less than a National Socialist revolution. A rapid-fire sequence of events: the immediate dissolution of the Reichstag and call for new elections; a high-powered election campaign; intimidation and terror against left-wing and moderate parties and their press; the use of the Reichstag fire as pretext to put aside civil rights—by all these tactics the Nazis revealed a dynamism which overshadowed their competitors.

When the 5 March elections gave the Nazis large gains, though not an absolute majority, Hitler determined to ride the psychological momentum to complete control. He extracted from the Reichstag, 23 March, approval for the Enabling Act, which gave the government almost unlimited power to enact laws without the Reichstag's consent for four years. With his mandate secure, Hitler laid about with a will. The non-Nazi governments of the German states were ousted and replaced by Nazi Reichs-Governors to make doubly sure of Berlin's control. A ruthless *Gleichschaltung* was quickly extended to the trade unions, and to the political parties. Triumphantly surveying the wreckage of his colleagues and enemies, Hitler decreed: "The National Socialist German Workers party constitutes the only political party in Germany."[3]

It was an extraordinarily rapid revolution and its callous use of force, its disregard for the pledged word, its contempt of tradition and convention could not fail to arouse fear abroad. Nor can any summary chronicle reproduce the primitive tone of Nazism. The world was shocked by pictures of political prisoners "exercising" in concentration camps, by bonfires of books in the courtyards of honored universities, and by the persecution of Jews, culminating in a nation-wide boycott of all Jewish enterprises as punishment for foreign criticism.

The first hints of Nazi foreign policy were also alarming. While Hitler's early comments were relatively mild, his lieutenants were aggressive. Goering thundered about the necessity to restore Germany to her place in the air, and Herr Kube, the Nazis' head man in the Prussian Diet, announced: ". . . by order of Herr Hitler I declare that the Prussians are pan-German, . . . and that we shall have attained our goal only when all Germany, including German Austria, is united with the Fatherland in one great State that can thus serve Germany's world mission."[4] Almost every day in February, March, and April brought new incidents. Attacks on foreigners in Germany, provocations such as the S.A.'s occupation of barracks in the demilitarized zone at Kehl, and exuberant pro-Nazi demonstrations in Austria and in German colonies in Denmark and Holland produced by accumulation a state of acute international tension.

German policy at the Disarmament Conference now became pugnacious and intransigent. Although the British Draft Conven-

[3] Law of 14 July 1933, *Dokumente der Deutschen Politik*, I (Berlin, 1937), 63.
[4] Goering's speech at Essen, 11 March 1933, quoted in *B.F.P.*, IV, 520. Kube's speech quoted in Norman H. Baynes, *The Speeches of Adolf Hitler: April 1922-August 1939* (London, 1942), II, 1014-1015.

tion had provided for doubling the size of the German army, making it 200,000 men, Herr Nadolny demanded amendments which completely altered the essence of the Convention. When this behavior brought on a complete deadlock by 8 May, he refused to change his position in any way.

On 11 May 1933 the British War Secretary, Lord Hailsham, told the House of Lords that any unilateral German rearmament "would be a breach of the Treaty of Versailles and would bring into operation the sanctions for which that Treaty provides."[5] Vice Chancellor von Papen shot back that Lord Hailsham's talk of sanctions was "hypocrisy" and extolled the traditional German preference for dying in battle.[6] These shocks, hitting into an atmosphere of nervousness about the nature of this new regime, created rumors of the imminence of war. Mr. J. W. Wheeler-Bennett, who commented on European affairs every fortnight, wrote that "the week which opened on 14th May was one of the most momentous in the post-war history of Europe."[7]

This war-scare, and war-scare it was, was resolved only by Hitler's "peace speech" of 17 May 1933. The German dictator discussed the main issues of the crisis in measured terms and protested his "earnest desire" to avoid another war. "The outbreak of such infinite madness... would necessarily cause the collapse of the present social and political order." Europe would sink into "communistic chaos."[8] Such fair words, and Germany's acceptance of the British Disarmament Convention as a draft for discussion, created an excellent impression and the tension immediately subsided.

In the next two months the Four Power Pact, and a Concordat governing the position of the Catholic church in Germany, symbolized Hitler's acceptance in international society. The former, a "Pact of Entente and Collaboration," was signed by the four leading western powers—Great Britain, France, Italy, and Germany. Originally proposed by Mussolini to improve Italy's position as mediator, the treaty had been reduced to platitudes by French caution; but its token value was considerable. Given up for dead

[5] *House of Lords, Parliamentary Debates, Official Report,* 11 May 1933, vol. 87, col. 898.

[6] Speech of 12 May at Münster, quoted in John W. Wheeler-Bennett, *The Pipe Dream of Peace* (New York, 1935), p. 116; also *D.I.A., 1933,* p. 406.

[7] Wheeler-Bennett, *Pipe Dream of Peace,* p. 117.

[8] Quoted in *D.I.A., 1933,* pp. 196-208, and in Baynes, *The Speeches of Hitler,* II, 1041-1058; German text in *Dokumente der deutschen Politik,* I, 79-91.

during the May crisis, the Four Power Pact, concluded on 7 June 1933, was a measure of British and French willingness to deal with Nazi Germany. Soon after, Papen and Hitler collaborated on a program of concessions and pressure for a quick decision, and they won the Vatican's agreement to the Concordat, 20 July 1933. The crisis provoked by Hitler's accession thus ended peacefully, and Europe settled down to live with the revolutionary newcomer.

ii

"Hitler in power"—this headline had a special meaning for Frenchmen and Russians. No man was less secretive about his plans; he spelled them out for all to read in *Mein Kampf*. "The German people's irreconcilable mortal enemy is and remains France." The fragmentation of Germany and the occupation of the Rhineland are essential to the French "hegemony status in Europe."[9]

I do not believe for a moment that France's intentions with respect to us can ever change; because they have their deepest motive nowhere but in the French nation's sense of self-preservation. Were I a Frenchman myself . . . I could not and would not act otherwise than Clemenceau himself did in the end.[10]

The conflict was above all determined by geography. Because Teuton and Gaul live where they do, the "final, decisive battle" and the "destruction" of France are inevitable.[11]

There was an important qualification here. Hitler did not have in mind the destruction of France as a nation (a fate in store for others), but as a great power. The real issue lay "elsewhere," and the battle with France would be significant only if it provided "the rear cover for an enlargement of our national domain of life in Europe."[12]

Only when this is fully understood in Germany . . . will it be possible to bring to a conclusion our eternal struggle with France, in itself so fruitless; on condition, of course, that Germany really sees in France's destruction a means of subsequently and finally giving our nation a chance to expand elsewhere.[13]

[9] *Mein Kampf* (New York, 1941), pp. 902, 899-900. The book was originally published in Munich in two volumes, 1925 and 1927.
[10] *Ibid.*, p. 978.   [11] *Ibid.*
[12] *Ibid.*, p. 949.   [13] *Ibid.*, pp. 978-979.

France was to be crushed for a purpose—to eliminate forever her pretense to European domination. It is this aspect which holds such great import for our story. Nothing could more precisely fill the qualifications of French "hegemony status" than a Franco-Soviet alliance.

Where is "elsewhere"? *Mein Kampf* gives the directions clearly.

> With this, we National Socialists consciously draw a line through the foreign-policy trend of our pre-War period. We take up at the halting-place of six hundred years ago. We terminate the endless German drive to the south and west of Europe, and direct our gaze towards the lands in the east.[14]

This eastern drive was dictated by Hitler's two fundamental aims: the unification of the German *Volk*, or race, and the acquisition of sufficient territory to serve as *Lebensraum* for their expansion. The largest German colonies were in the east, conveniently strewn like stepping stones down the Danube valley and up along the Baltic coast. As for living space, "if we talk about new soil and territory in Europe today, we can think primarily only of Russia and its vassal border states."[15] What is meant by the latter is unclear, probably the Ukraine and the Baltic states. In any case, the countries that stand between Germany and Russia were simply taken for granted. Emotional intensity was lent to this eastern drive by Hitler's hatred of the Slavs and his fear of bolshevism.

Germany was too weak to strike out alone and Hitler intended to seek alliances with England and Italy. Their great common value was an aversion to French ambitions, while England also nursed a traditional hostility towards Russia. "The alliance [with England and Italy] . . . would give Germany a chance to make quite calmly those preparations which, one way or another, must be undertaken within the bounds of such a coalition for a reckoning with France. . . . Thereby the mortal enemy of our nation, France, is left in isolation."[16]

In February 1933, after his accession to power, Hitler made it plain that his designs remained the same. He told the chief of the

[14] *Ibid.*, pp. 950-951. "Neither western nor eastern orientation . . . but an eastern policy signifying the acquisition of the necessary soil for our German people." Pp. 965-966.

[15] *Ibid.*, pp. 950-951. Hitler's prescription for German policy before 1914 was the same: "If one wanted land and soil in Europe, then by and large this could only have been done at Russia's expense." *Ibid.*, p. 182.

[16] *Ibid.*, pp. 964-965.

German Navy, Admiral Raeder, that "he had no intention of contesting England's claim to a position of naval power corresponding to her world interest. . . . The comparative strength of the *French* and *Russian* navies had to be the first *basic consideration* for the coming construction of the German Navy."[17] To a group of the Reichswehr's top brass, the chancellor said:

> How should political power be used, once it has been won? Not yet possible to say. Perhaps the winning of new export possibilities, perhaps—and, indeed, preferably—conquest of new living space in the east and ruthless Germanization of the latter.[18]

Hitler's arrival thus held an ominous meaning for France and Russia. This new disruptive force, preparing to harness the energies of Germany for its designs, henceforth became the spur of the Franco-Soviet rapprochement.

iii

The most important repercussion of Hitler's policy was the decline of German-Russian collaboration. Before we look at that development, so much an invitation to Franco-Russian collaboration, it is necessary to study Hitler's impact on the *existing* French alliance system. If Poland and the Little Entente now became more effective allies, France might not need to go further with Russia.

At first it looked as if this hope would bear fruit, for on 16 February 1933, the Czech, Romanian, and Yugoslav governments signed the "Permanent Statute of the Little Entente."[19] The statute provided for greater unity among the foreign policies of the three states by means of a Permanent Secretariat at Geneva and more

---

[17] Memorandum written by Admiral Raeder during detention in Moscow in 1945, "The Development of German Naval Policy—1933-1939," *Nazi Conspiracy and Aggression,* 8 volumes with supplements A and B (Washington, 1946-48), VIII, 684. Note also Raeder's testimony, International Military Tribunal, *Trial of the Major War Criminals before the International Military Tribunal, Nuremberg, 1945-46, Proceedings and Documents in Evidence,* 42 volumes (Nuremberg, 1946-1949) (hereinafter cited as I.M.T., *Proceedings*), XIV, 21-22, and the partially contradictory statements in his memoirs, *Mein Leben* (Tubingen, 1956), I, 281-282.

[18] Address of 3 Feb. 1933, to a group of officers, notes by Lt. Gen. Liebmann. Thilo Vogelsang, "Neue Dokumente zur Geschichte der Reichswehr, 1930-1933," *Vierteljahrshefte für Zeitgeschichte,* II, 434-435. In a very interesting letter to Colonel von Reichenau, 4 Dec. 1932, Hitler totally rejected the Rapallo policy of collaboration with Russia and said that his goal remained "a tight alliance" with Italy and England. Thilo Vogelsang, ed., "Hitlers Brief an Reichenau vom 4 Dezember 1932," *ibid,* VII, 1959, 434-435.

[19] *L.N.T.S.,* CXXXIX, 233.

systematic consultation among their statesmen. But paper could not remake geography nor trade routes and traditions.

The three small countries which made up the Little Entente had no common enemy save Austria and Hungary. When the Romanian Foreign Minister asserted that "a single diplomatic front" had been formed, his next words made his claim absurd. The new federation, he said, represented "the superimposition of three points of view": Romania's desire to have a veto against the recognition of Russia, Czechoslovakia's concern over the arrival of Hitler, and Yugoslavia's feud with Italy.[20] Three capitals and three different foes! Later in the year there were a few changes, but most of the contradictions remained. Romania continued to flirt with Mussolini, the stalker of Yugoslavia; and the latter openly sought more trade with Nazi Germany, the new threat to Czechoslovakia. The Permanent Statute increased the stature of the Little Entente only in the League of Nations, and it was not votes at Geneva that the French needed now.

If not the Little Entente, perhaps at least Czechoslovakia and Poland would be welded together by Hitler's menace. The French had bet rather heavily on Prague. A strategic geographical position on Germany's eastern side, internal stability, and a significant concentration of heavy industry made Czechoslovakia a much more valuable ally than Yugoslavia or Romania. For Prague and Warsaw to become friends no more powerful incentives could be asked: Hitler's personal hatred of the Slavs, his program of expansion to the east, and the large German minorities within both states. A solid Czech-Polish front, closely supported by France, would be no mean obstacle.

Unfortunately, the mistrust and bad feelings which had grown up between the two countries since 1919 were only momentarily diminished by the new threat. If the Polish and Czech leaders had recognized the menace to an equally strong degree they might have joined hands. Ironically, they came to the conclusion that the Nazi lightning might not strike them, at least not first.

The Czech hopes derived from the good economic relations which had been worked out with Weimar Germany and the relatively moderate character of the German minority problem up to

[20] Conversation of M. Titulescu with Baron Aloisi, Chief of Cabinet in the Italian Foreign Ministry, in Geneva, 27 Feb. 1933. Aloisi, *Journal*, pp. 75-76. See also *G.F.P.*, I, 67-70 and *B.F.P.*, V, 64.

1933.[21] All this stood in marked contrast to the semi-permanent
state of tension between Germany and Poland. No part of Czechoslovakia had been subjected to the relentless pressure of German
propaganda, so that, as one wag put it, the word "Polish" was automatically associated with "Corridor." What about Hitler's coveting
of Austria? The Czechs were aware of that threat, but the past
distorted their image of the present. Their greatest fear was a
Hapsburg restoration, for independence had been born of the
Hapsburg collapse in 1918. Hitler, at least, was violently anti-
Hapsburg. With tragic oversight, many of the Czechs shared the
feelings of Beneš—if worst came to worst, "he preferred even an
Anschluss to the restoration of the Hapsburgs."[22]

The Czech leaders were reluctant to jeopardize the satisfactory
relations with Germany simply because of Hitler's arrival.[23] So
said their capable and energetic Foreign Minister, Dr. Edward
Beneš, in a speech on 1 March 1933.

> We have not had a single grave conflict with Germany in fourteen
> years, we have no frontier dispute with her and we wish to be on the
> same terms of friendship with the Germany of today as with that of
> Stresemann.[24]

When he had a chance to pour out his troubles privately to Sir
John Simon and MacDonald, Beneš was all anti-Mussolini; "M.
Beneš had no serious fears as regards Germany; there was no issue
between the two countries."[25]

A certain smugness about the troubles of the Poles was revealed
in Beneš' confidences to the British statesmen.

[21] At the Nuremberg trials, Gerhard Köpke, Director of Western Affairs in the
German Foreign Office, stated: "Our economic and political relations with Czechoslovakia were, so long as I was in office [through 1935], very good. We had no
occasion whatsoever to change them, not even the slightest." I.M.T., *Proceedings*,
XVII, 112.

[22] Remark made in 1931 to M. Pierre-Étienne Flandin, French Minister of Finance, *Politique Française*, p. 238. See reports of the same formula in *B.F.P.*, V,
447; Jules Laroche, *Au Quai d'Orsay avec Briand et Poincaré* (Paris, 1957), pp.
185-186; and Elizabeth Wiskemann, *The Rome-Berlin Axis* (London, 1949), pp.
41 and 116.

[23] Castellan, *Le Réarmement Clandestin du Reich, 1930-1935*, pp. 491-492.

[24] Address to the Foreign Affairs Committees of the Czechoslovakian Chamber
and Senate, *D.I.A.*, 1933, pp. 420-421.

[25] Conversation at Geneva, 17 March 1933, *B.F.P.*, V, 63-66. The fact that
these remarks were made the day *before* Mussolini's proposal of the Four Power
Pact makes Beneš' preoccupation with Mussolini rather than Hitler the more remarkable.

He feared an incident between Germany and Poland. He had had a long talk quite recently with M. Beck. He had told him that Czechoslovakia would not make an alliance with Poland against Germany, because he thought it would be very dangerous to give Germany clear cause for fearing encirclement.[26]

One of his worries about Mussolini's desire to crush Yugoslavia was that it would leave Czechoslovakia isolated between Germany and Austria-Hungary. "This would push her [Czechoslovakia] into the arms of Poland, and...he had already declined an alliance with Poland."[27]

Hitler, then, was not enough to push the two countries together. What made it possible was Mussolini's sensational proposal, 18 March, of the Four Power Pact, that dream of collaboration among France, Great Britain, Italy, and Germany. Both Prague and Warsaw were irritated by the idea of a great power Directory and angered by the prominence of "revision" in the pact.[28]

In Poland, Marshal Pilsudski was furious and his instinctive reaction was to band together all those menaced. "He was even prepared to pull down the wall erected between us and Prague, despite his profound distrust of the policy of M. Beneš."[29] Foreign Minister Beck was instructed to make contact with President Masaryk and Beneš, the Czechs responded cordially, and by 24 March it had been arranged that Beck would make a visit to Prague and Paris. Then, suddenly, a few days later, both trips were postponed, and the propitious moment was lost.[30]

For a month the project was still in the air. Beneš roundly condemned the Four Power Pact and spoke warmly of a Czech-Polish accord based "on the principles of a policy of eternal and lasting friendship."[31] In May, however, the drift began. Already Hitler had surprised the Poles by his conciliatory speech of 23 March; now he aroused their hopes for a deal by making unusually sympathetic comments to the Polish ambassador, 2 May 1933. The

[26] 13 March, Geneva, *ibid.*, IV, 521.

[27] 17 March, Geneva, *ibid.*, V, 64.

[28] Mussolini's draft, handed first to the Germans, 14 March, to the French and British 18 March, during the visit to Rome of MacDonald and Simon, may be found in *G.F.P.*, I, 162-163; *B.F.P.*, V, 67-68; and Ministère des Affaires Étrangères, *Pacte d' Entente et de Collaboration, paraphé à Rome le 7 juin* (Paris, 1933), p. 3. Consult also Aloisi, *Journal*, pp. 83 ff.

[29] Beck, *Dernier Rapport*, p. 41.

[30] *Ibid.*, pp. 41-43; Laroche, *La Pologne de Pilsudski*, pp. 122-123; Aloisi, *Journal*, pp. 101, 104; *B.F.P.*, V, 114, and VI, 860.

[31] Speech of 25 April, quoted in *S.I.A., 1935*, I, 287-288.

Four Power Pact was gradually emasculated under French pressure; because of these changes and the desire to please Paris, the Little Entente states reversed directions. A communiqué approving the amended pact was issued, 30 May, and a week later Czechoslovakia received from France formal assurances about the interpretation of the pact.[32] Poland refused to make this or any other compromise, and the semi-official *Gazeta Polska* derisively commented: "It is regrettable that the first serious act of the Little Entente should be a gratuitous diminution of its own importance."[33] After that divergence, consideration of a Polish-Czech rapprochement was adjourned indefinitely. There was no break, but nothing more was heard of Beck's journey to Prague.

M. Beneš later claimed that, during this period, he made several offers of a treaty to Poland.[34] However, it is very likely that this was merely a treaty of friendship. There are no contemporary documents to show that the Czechs offered Poland a clear-cut defensive alliance in 1933. Yet that was the only type of treaty which Pilsudski, with his military orientation, would appreciate. Indeed, considering the dangers to be faced, only an alliance would have had practical value. One has the distinct impression that the Czechs wanted reconciliation with Poland, but not sufficiently to pay a good price.[35] There were some plausible reasons for this attitude, but the fact remains that they did not jump at the rare opportunity.

That said, the greater share of the responsibility for this failure must be attributed to Poland. Pilsudski never renewed his advances after the postponement of Beck's trip to Prague. His resentment of the Czechs' acceptance of the Four Power Pact should not be taken lightly; but this was not the prime reason. The tempting hints from Berlin, revealing the chance of a bargain, killed the Polish interest in a common front with the Czechs. If the Polish leaders were to sup with the devil, they could hardly be impudent.

Some of the motives and chronology of these episodes are still obscure, but the result is not. An auspicious occasion had been

[32] *Pacte d'Entente et de Collaboration*, pp. 19-20 and 23-28.
[33] Quoted in *Le Temps*, 1 June 1933; note other criticisms of the Little Entente in the Polish press quoted in *Le Temps*, 2, 8, and 9 June 1933.
[34] Letter from Beneš to L. B. Namier, 20 April 1944, reprinted in L. B. Namier, *Europe in Decay, 1936-1940* (London, 1950), pp. 281-285; Compton MacKenzie, *Dr. Beneš* (London, 1946), p. 163.
[35] *B.F.P.*, IV, 521 and V, 63-66, 334-336; Laroche, *La Pologne de Pilsudski*, pp. 122, 133, 146; Beck, *Dernier Rapport*, pp. 51-54.

wasted. Even the combination of a Pan-German fanatic and the Four Power Pact had not inspired co-operation between Poland and Czechoslovakia. When Hitler turned to the East, instead of a wall, he found an inviting breach. This concerned not only the two young succession states; it was depressing news in Paris. The French alliance system in Eastern Europe was still an army with two headquarters, an affair of right hand, left hand.

iv

Of all the reactions to Hitler, the most disappointing for Frenchmen was the Polish.[36] Everyone expected the Nazis to fan the most stubborn feud of postwar Europe. Instead, by the time summer had passed, tension had given way to soothing words of good will.

The challenge that Hitler represented was badly distorted in Polish eyes by resentment against France, England, and Italy.[37] Warsaw had been highly annoyed by the Declaration of 11 December 1932, which granted Germany the principle of equality of rights in armament. Then the British Draft Convention, of 16 March 1933, allowed for an increase in the German army to 200,000 men. Two days later, Rome spawned the Four Power Pact, twice abominable to Poland as a Great Power Directory and as an invitation to revision.

Warsaw counted on the French to rebuff the Four Power Pact, but it was soon evident that, after important amendments, the new Premier, M. Daladier, wanted to accept the pact. The Polish press now began sharply to censure the French government's "weakness." Beck's visit to Paris and Prague was postponed and a chance to clear the air was lost. Beck's protests to the French Ambassador, 6 April, show the indignant Polish emotions.

If any state, alone or with others, . . . tries to seize a square meter of our territory, there will be war! They understand that in Berlin and

[36] Consult Henry L. Roberts, "The Diplomacy of Colonel Beck," in Craig and Gilbert, eds., *The Diplomats 1919-1939*, pp. 579-614.

[37] Polish leaders suspected French willingness to bargain with Germany at Poland's expense. In October 1932, Marshal Pilsudski complained bluntly to the new French military attaché, Colonel d'Arbonneau: " 'Oui, oui, gare à nous! La France va nous abandonner, la France va nous trahir! Voilà ce que l'on pense et je devais vous le dire. . . . [France, Hungary, Turkey], trois pays contre lesquels la Pologne ne pourrait faire quoi que ce soit, mais à l'égard de la France il y a un peu de relâchement. . . .   C'est la faute de sa politique et ce qui a été mal fait ne peut se refaire.' " Laroche, *La Pologne de Pilsudski*, pp. 111-113.

they do not question it. I am afraid that they do not really understand it in London and Rome, nor even in Paris. . . . It was foreign intervention which led to the disappearance of the old Poland.[38]

Beck went on to remark on the "prudence" of Hitler's recent declarations on foreign policy, and even hinted that it might be better to reach an understanding with Hitler immediately rather than wait for him to grow strong.[39] For the next two months, as Daladier moved steadily towards conclusion of the Four Power Pact, Polish-French relations deteriorated.

Until recently, it was widely believed that the deterioration was furthered by the French government's rejection of an audacious Polish "offer": a proposal for joint action to suppress the Nazi regime. Pilsudski's offer has been described as everything from deliberate "preventive war" to a proposal "to bring Germany's rearmament before the League as a violation of Article 213 of the Treaty of Versailles."[40] It is said that the approach to Paris was made twice, in the spring and fall of 1933. Yet no Polish or French document purporting to be the whole or part of this proposal ever has been published.[41] The absence of any account of it in the memoirs of the Polish Foreign Minister and Under-Secretary of State, Colonel Beck and Count Jan Szembek, and in those of the French Ambassador in Warsaw, Jules Laroche, has cast serious doubt upon the story.[42] The evidence suggests that the Polish

[38] Laroche, quoting a dispatch of 6 April, *La Pologne de Pilsudski*, pp. 123-124.

[39] Beck was referring to Hitler's address to the Reichstag, 23 March, where he said that Germany was ready "to extend a hand in sincere understanding to every nation that is ready finally to make an end of the tragic past. . . . Even in cases where our mutual relations are encumbered with difficulties, we shall endeavour to arrive at a settlement." Baynes, *The Speeches of Hitler*, II, 1017-1019.

[40] The quotations are from J. W. Wheeler-Bennett, *Munich* (New York, 1948), p. 283, and S. H. Thomson, "Polish Foreign Policy," in Bernadotte E. Schmitt, ed., *Poland* (Berkeley, 1945), p. 399. The credibility of the story rests upon rumors at the time and later affirmations, notably by the prominent Polish diplomat, M. Joseph Lipski. See for example *B.F.P.*, VI, 80-81.

[41] The problem is admirably analyzed by Zygmunt Gasiorowski, "Did Pilsudski Attempt to Initiate a Preventive War in 1933?," *Journal of Modern History*, XXVII (June 1955), 135-151. Gasiorowski concludes that there was no offer to France of a preventive war. An impressive case for the contrary thesis—that Pilsudski did make such an offer to France—has been made by Hans Roos, "Die 'Präventive kriegspläne' Pilsudskis von 1933," *Vierteljahrshefte für Zeitgeschichte*, III (October, 1955), 344-363.

[42] Beck, *Dernier Rapport;* Count Jan Szembek, *Journal 1933-1939* (Paris, 1952); Laroche, *La Pologne de Pilsudski*. Nor is there an account of the offer in the memoirs of the head of the French Army, General Weygand, *Mirages et Réalités*, nor in those of the French Foreign Minister, M. Joseph Paul-Boncour, *Entre Deux Guerres*, II.

government did not make a proposal to the French government for joint preventive action against Hitler in the spring of 1933.[43]

There remains an intriguing question—did Pilsudski at any point make plans for preventive war by Poland alone? He did consider this alternative as well as others, but it never reached the stage of a practical project in his thinking.[44] He himself pointed out to Beck certain weaknesses in the Polish army which would be serious hazards in such an enterprise.[45] The French Ambassador, M. Laroche, who sent out his military attaché to investigate the rumors, came to the conclusion that the Polish army had made no special preparations.[46]

There is, to be sure, no doubt that many German leaders, including Neurath and Hitler, were seriously worried about a Polish attack. They were impressed by the recent Polish use of force in the Westerplatte incident, a quarrel over Danzig harbor rights, 6 March 1933.[47] However, Berlin overestimated indirect information and rumors, while underestimating the calm analyses of the German Minister at Warsaw, Count von Moltke.[48] Naturally apprehensive, Moltke made frequent soundings among the diplomats and military attachés to determine the reliability of the rumors. His conclusion was: "Another probing of the available sources of information showed there are no positive signs of a systematic preparation of a preventive war."[49]

Instead of a Polish attack, Europe was astounded to see a flirta-

[43] In late October 1933, following Hitler's withdrawal from the Disarmament Conference, Pilsudski did send a special request for the French dossier on German rearmament and for information on French policy towards future German rearmament. The French quickly complied with the request and that was the end of the matter. This strictly limited communication may have become the basis for the preventive war rumors. See p. 157, n. 10.

[44] There is no doubt that Pilsudski had the audacity and courage to order the invasion of Germany; see his warning in 1931, p. 31, n. 5.

[45] Beck, *Dernier Rapport*, p. 66.

[46] Laroche, *La Pologne de Pilsudski* pp. 124, 127, citing a dispatch of 8 May 1933.

[47] See *S.I.A.*, *1935*, I, 215-218; Beck, *Dernier Rapport*, pp. 25-27; Laroche, *La Pologne de Pilsudski*, pp. 120-121; G.F.P., I, 111 ff.; François-Poncet, *Souvenirs d'une Ambassade à Berlin*, p. 165.

[48] This subject must be studied on a day-to-day basis in the German documents, G.F.P., I; see also B.F.P., V, 150, 202, and F.R.U.S., *1933*, I, 87.

[49] Report of 25 April 1933, G.F.P., I, 342-343. Moltke reported 23 April: "All the diplomats and Military Attachés that I have sounded out personally or through others have unanimously answered the question [whether Poland was preparing a preventive war] in the negative." *Ibid.*, I, 332.

tion develop as the year matured.[50] On the German side, the policy was entirely that of Hitler. It is amusing to hear the Foreign Minister, Baron von Neurath, pontificate that "an understanding with Poland is neither possible nor desirable," just as Hitler adopted the opposite assumptions.[51] Hitler's motives are still a matter for speculation. The rumors of preventive war worried him, but they stopped after May and do not explain the continuity of his policy. Upon reflection, the maneuver fits into his obsession with concentration in foreign policy: one thing at a time. For the moment top priority went to the consolidation of the Nazi regime and to rearmament—friendly relations with Poland could only facilitate these tasks. An arresting passage in *Mein Kampf* may provide the clue: "If we will not ally ourselves with England, owing to the fact that she stole colonies from us, or with Italy, because she has the South Tyrol, with Poland or Czechoslovakia on general principles, then there remains nobody else in Europe but France."[52] One day in May, when the German Ambassador to Russia, Herbert von Dirksen, was back in Berlin arguing for good relations with Russia, Hitler seemed rather bored. Walking suddenly to the window, he nearly floored Dirksen with the remark—"'If only we could come to an agreement with Poland! But Pilsudski is the only man with whom that would be possible.'"[53]

The Poles were given their first clear-cut indication of Hitler's new policy when he assured the Polish Minister, M. Wysocki, 2 May, that he would respect existing treaties and went out of his way to be sympathetic.

The Chancellor does not share the view which questions Poland's right to exist; on the contrary, he recognizes and understands that right. Poland, for her part, should also endeavour to understand the rights and interests of Germany. If their judgment of each other is marked by a certain moderation, many interests common to both States will become apparent. The Chancellor recently examined statistical tables showing the number of births in Russia. The astonishing fertility of that nation caused him to reflect seriously on the dangers to Europe and, therefore, to Poland which might arise from this fact. The Chancel-

---

[50] Note that as early as 12 April Beck made an overture which Moltke considered "a veiled proposal for direct contact with Germany." *G.F.P.*, I, 306-310.

[51] Neurath's briefing on foreign policy to the German cabinet, 7 April 1933, *G.F.P.*, I, 259.

[52] Hitler, *Mein Kampf*, pp. 925-926. Note Hermann Rauschning's report of Hitler's willingness "to make a treaty with the Poles," Aug. 1932, *The Voice of Destruction* (New York, 1940), p. 28.

[53] Dirksen, *Moscow, Tokyo, London*, p. 121.

lor mentioned this to give me an example of his unprejudiced attitude towards our country.[54]

In his "Peace Speech" of 17 May 1933, Hitler solemnly asserted: "The mentality of the past century which made people believe that they could make Germans out of Poles and Frenchmen is completely foreign to us."[55] After fourteen years of German curses, it is not surprising that the Chancellor's friendly approach and anti-Russian line tempted his listeners in Warsaw.

Danzig was currently the hottest spot, and there Hitler gave orders that Nazi policy should not be provocative. Early in July a Danzig Nazi delegation came to Warsaw to seek a comprehensive settlement, and a compromise on several issues was reached by 5 August.[56] To the retiring Polish Minister, on 13 July, Hitler hinted at profitable commercial relations, and again brought up the menace of Russia.[57] Shortly after these events, at a Polish government conference the question was posed: ". . . if it might not be appropriate to profit from the internal revolution of the Reich to improve our relations with that country . . .?" Pilsudski forthwith ordered Beck to reconnoiter the terrain.[58]

The effects of this decision can be clearly seen in Beck's behavior when the diplomatic conclave at Geneva opened in September. In talks with Baron von Neurath and the Propaganda Minister, Joseph Goebbels, Beck warmly and repeatedly expressed his pleasure at the relaxation of tension, particularly at Danzig. "He was firmly resolved not to let the direct wire to Berlin break off again. With good will one could gradually solve most of the pending questions in a direct way."[59]

This "feeler" executed, there the affair marked time. A major crisis in German policy was brewing as the Disarmament Confer-

[54] Dispatch of M. Wysocki, 2 May 1933, Polish Ministry for Foreign Affairs, *Official Documents concerning Polish-German and Polish-Soviet Relations 1933-1939* (London, n.d.), p. 12 (hereinafter cited as *Polish White Book*). Compare the shorter version by von Neurath, *G.F.P.*, I, 365-367.

[55] Baynes, *The Speeches of Hitler*, II, 1046-1047; for favorable effects of the speech in Warsaw, see *G.F.P.*, I, 470-471.

[56] *S.I.A.*, *1935*, I, 218-222; Beck, *Dernier Rapport*, p. 27; Rauschning, *Voice of Destruction*, pp. 86, 116-118, and *Germany's Revolution of Destruction* (London, 1939), pp. 251-259; *Polish White Book*, p. 16; *G.F.P.*, I, 164, 470, 782, 840.

[57] *Polish White Book*, pp. 15-16; no record in the German files, *G.F.P.*, I, 650. Vice-Chancellor Papen spoke to Mussolini, 20-21 July, of "an accord with Poland at Russia's expense. . . ." Aloisi, *Journal*, p. 140.

[58] Beck, *Dernier Rapport*, pp. 27-28.

[59] Conversations of 25 and 26 Sept. 1933, *G.F.P.*, I, 840, 842.

ence approached a critical test. The Polish leaders were puzzled as to just how much credit should be given to the German Chancellor's profession of good will. But enough had happened to arouse lively curiosity in Warsaw about a deal with Germany. Even to this extent, the Polish reaction was a nasty surprise for Frenchmen. It mingled with Poland's opposition to the Four Power Pact to create what the British Ambassador in Paris called "a further tension of Franco-Polish relations."[60] The depth of the ill-feeling can be judged by Premier Daladier's startling remark to a Czech diplomat that continued Polish obstruction might mean the end of the alliance.[61] This outburst was inspired by a passing fit of anger, but it is certain that the Polish flirtation with Hitler seriously upset French governmental circles. It seemed that those who had been skeptical of the new Poland were right.

The French system of taking Poland, Czechoslovakia, Romania, and Yugoslavia and rolling them all up to make an *alliance à revers* had never been entirely satisfactory. It had been adequate for dealing with a disarmed democratic Germany. Could it handle National Socialist Germany? Six months after the fateful day of 30 January 1933, Poland and Czechoslovakia were as far apart as ever, perhaps further, and Polish leaders were responding eagerly to Hitler's advances. The fragility of Poland and the Little Entente was exposed. As the French desire for a solid alliance in the east grew, thoughts turned inevitably back to the old pattern, to the Russian alliance.

V

Of all the reactions to Hitler, the Russian is the most difficult to trace. Contradictory events follow close on one another and the same Soviet editorial can be quoted as proof of two different policies. These hesitations, which plague the historian, are reflections of the doubts which plagued the Soviet leaders. Stalin and his colleagues in the Kremlin must have reached anxiously for the telegrams from Berlin. For the German Communists, by their bitter fight against the Socialists and the Weimar Republic, had helped to smooth the path of the Nazis.

[60] Conversation 29 May 1933 between Lord Tyrrell and the Secretary-General of the Foreign Ministry, *B.F.P.*, V, 281. The tension is copiously documented in the account of Ambassador Laroche, *La Pologne de Pilsudski*.

[61] Report of the Czech Minister in Paris, M. Osusky, 8 June 1933, Friedrich Berber, ed., *Europäische Politik 1933-38 im Spiegel der Prager Akten* (Essen, 1942), p. 24.

Russia's first reaction to Hitler's appointment as Chancellor was passive, "watchful waiting" as the German Ambassador in Moscow called it.[62] This was true of Comintern policy as well as of Russian foreign policy. In the crucial seven weeks of the Nazi conquest, 1 February–23 March, the German Communist party ordered no uprising, no general strike, and refused to join hands with the Social Democrats in resistance. Indeed, the Nazi surge was interpreted as a useful destruction of their Socialist rivals. On 14 February 1933 *Pravda* declared that "the proletarian revolution is able to liquidate the Fascist dictatorship only over the corpse of Social Democracy." Its fairy-tale response, 7 March, to the Reichstag fire and the Nazi election victory was, "Let reaction rage! . . . The contradictions of Germany's capitalism, internal and external, are sharpening."[63]

Although nervous, Soviet officials at first were inclined to attach some credit to German promises that nothing would be changed in foreign policy.[64] The German Ambassador in Moscow, Herbert von Dirksen, used every possible device to allay Russian suspicion; faithful to the example of Brockdorff-Rantzau, he constantly warned his superiors and tried to talk Hitler into greater appreciation of the Rapallo policy. Hitler himself made a few friendly gestures. He approved a Soviet request for an important credit extension, and in his Reichstag speech of 23 March 1933 he declared: "The elimination of Communism in Germany is a purely domestic German affair. . . . The Government of the Reich are ready to cultivate with the Soviet Union friendly relations profitable to both parties."[65]

But the Nazis' incredibly rapid destruction of their opponents, including the mightiest Communist party in Europe, soon began to

[62] Ambassador von Dirksen's dispatch of 20 Feb. 1933, *G.F.P.*, I, 62-65. This volume is by far the most important source on the decline of Russo-German cooperation. The best study, written before publication of the German documents, is that of Jacques Grunewald, "L'évolution des relations germano-soviétiques de 1933 à 1936," in Duroselle, *Les Relations Germano-Soviétiques de 1933 à 1939*, pp. 7-42.

[63] *Pravda*, 14 Feb., quoted in G. W. Millikan, "The Science of Soviet Politics," *Foreign Affairs*, XXXI (April 1953), 481.

[64] Hitler told Foreign Minister von Neurath that "he would allow no change to take place in the political, economic, and military policy with respect to Soviet Russia." Neurath to Dirksen, 22 Feb. 1933, *G.F.P.*, I, 71-72.

[65] Quoted in Baynes, *The Speeches of Hitler*, II, 1015-1019; see G. Castellan, "Reichswehr et Armée Rouge 1920-1939," in Duroselle, *Les Relations Germano-Soviétiques de 1933 à 1939*, p. 203, n. 8. For the credit extension on large Soviet payments due in March and April, see *G.F.P.*, I, 92, n. 7.

sow the seeds of fear in Moscow. Where would this whirlwind end? The spectacular Reichstag fire was pinned on the Communists. In his campaign speeches Hitler attacked the Marxist menace to Europe with a fervor that suggested a crusade against headquarters as well as against the German branch.[66] Raids on the Soviet commercial representations and on their gas and oil distributing agencies in Germany (DEROP) took place repeatedly during March and April.[67] These raids and those on the Communist party offices frequently involved the mistreatment of Soviet citizens. By the end of March Soviet policy began to turn. It was expressed in two ways: a spasmodic deterioration of relations with Germany and the exploration of other routes to security. Dirksen was warned that the Kremlin was "very uneasy and uncertain" about German policy.[68]

The Soviet press now began to insist on the discrepancy between Hitler's words and Nazi acts, to highlight the blatant anti-Russian passages in *Mein Kampf* and in the books of Alfred Rosenberg, and to ask the German government: "Where is it going?"[69] After a particularly big raid on the Berlin offices of DEROP, 1 April, Moscow retaliated with a sharp note of protest and Litvinov told Dirksen that "these events had caused great agitation. The impression had been created that an organized anti-Soviet campaign was in progress in Germany. Confidence in the statements made by [Hitler, Neurath, and Dirksen] ... concerning the unchanged German policy with respect to the Soviet Union was

[66] Hitler was not the sole problem. The Soviets had not forgiven Papen for his talk of a Franco-German military alliance at Lausanne, and they feared that Hugenberg, as Minister of Economics, would discourage trade with Russia. *G.F.P.*, I, 14-15, 64, 91-92.

[67] DEROP, the Deutsche Vertriebsgesellschaft für russische Ölprodukte A.G., was "an organization for marketing Soviet petroleum products set up as a German corporation with exclusively Soviet capital; it operated some 2,000 filling stations in Germany." *G.F.P.*, I, 241, n. 3.

[68] Dispatch of 20 March, *G.F.P.*, I, 189-190. Litvinov told Dirksen: "While the Soviet Government had sought to prevent a German-French alliance in the past by bringing influence to bear on the German side, it would now endeavour to attain the same objective through closer relations with France." Dispatch of 11 March 1933, *ibid.*, I, 144.

[69] *Izvestya*, 22 March 1933, quoted in *Bulletin de la presse russe*, No. 228. Karl Radek in *Izvestya* quoted the anti-Russian declarations of Hitler and Rosenberg and recalled the harsh provisions of the treaty of Brest-Litovsk. Article by G. Luciani, Moscow correspondent, *Le Temps*, 8 April 1933; Paul Miliukov, *La Politique Extérieure des Soviets* (Paris, 1936), pp. 418-419. For Rosenberg's discussion of foreign policy, *Der Mythus des XX Jahrhunderts* (Munich, 1930), pp. 637-677. More important is *Der Zukunftsweg einer deutschen Aussenpolitik* (Munich, 1927); consult pp. 9-21, 61-98, 142-144.

thereby shaken."[70] Significantly, *Izvestya* aired these charges before the world in a scathing editorial attack.[71] As the German Ambassador in Moscow saw it, the Soviets had abandoned their "waiting attitude . . . and the offensive had commenced. The most favorable psychological moment for a restoration of normal relations had been allowed to pass."[72]

Now came an event seemingly made to order to end the crisis. Following the recommendation of the career diplomats, Hitler ratified the long-delayed Protocol of June 1931, which prolonged the Berlin Treaty of 1926.[73] The ratifications were exchanged in Moscow, 5 May, but on the following day an important editorial in *Izvestya* revealed that the clock would not be turned back all the way. When the Franco-Soviet Non-Aggression Pact had been signed, the Soviet press had been careful to present it as not directed against Germany. Now the shoe was on the other foot: France was assured that the prolongation of the Berlin Treaty was not directed against her. The editorial ended like a perfectly balanced seesaw: "The Berlin accord, in the future, must constitute the basis of our policy in Europe, parallel to the pacts of non-aggression which we have signed with the great powers."[74] Dirksen warned his superiors in Berlin not to hope that the ratification would itself overcome Moscow's "rather deep-seated uncertainty or mistrust of Germany." He reminded them that Germany was in competition for Russian favor. When the Soviets had been isolated, settling quarrels had been fairly easy; now it was "the deliberate policy of the French and Poles, pursued in every possible way, of furthering the cooling off between Germany and Russia."[75]

One reason why the ratification did not clear the air was that Hitler had just revealed his "friendly" Polish policy. The Soviets

[70] Conversation of 4 April, *G.F.P.*, I, 241-242; protest by Ambassador Khinchuk in Berlin, 253.

[71] *Izvestya*, 4 April 1933, quoted in *Le Temps*, 5 April 1933; parts of the editorial were almost verbatim quotations of what Litvinov told Dirksen.

[72] Dirksen, *Moscow, Tokyo, London*, p. 122.

[73] *G.F.P.*, I, 252 ff.; Kordt, *Wahn und Wirklichheit* (Stuttgart, 1948), p. 65; information from Dr. Friedrich Gaus, quoted in Castellan, "Reichswehr et Armée Rouge," in Duroselle, *Les Relations Germano-Sovietiques de 1933 à 1939*, p. 203, n. 8. For the conclusion of the Protocol, 24 June 1931, consult chap. ii, pp. 28-29 above.

[74] *Izvestya*, 6 May 1933, quoted in *Le Temps*, 7 May 1933.

[75] Dispatch of 5 May 1933, *G.F.P.*, I, 385-389. Krestinsky, Soviet Deputy Commissar of Foreign Affairs and "one of the warmest adherents of German-Soviet friendship," told Dirksen that "it would take months yet before the old relations were restored."

could not know about his anti-Russian remarks to the Polish Ambassador, M. Wysocki, but they knew from the public communiqué, 3 May, that he had suggested that Germany and Poland should discuss "their common interests." And they listened to his 17 May speech when he stressed his rejection of the traditional Prussian hostility towards Poland. This was most sensitive territory; a common hostility to Poland had been one of the origins of the Rapallo partnership, as it had been in previous Russo-German ententes. If Hitler intended to revise German policy towards Poland, it suggested a revised policy towards Russia.

The month of May also witnessed a fundamental shift in general Soviet policy, a move against Germany and in favor of France. Ever since 1919 Moscow's propagandists had scored the Versailles peace treaties and championed the cause of revision, Germany's cause. It was thus an unwelcome surprise in Berlin when the foremost Soviet journalist, Karl Radek, announced that Moscow no longer favored revision because it would lead to "a *new world war*."[76]

It was then the turn of a German Minister to drive the wedge deeper. On 16 June Herr Hugenberg, Minister of Economics, Food, and Agriculture, created a scandal at the World Economic Conference in London. In a memorandum on Germany's economic recovery, Hugenberg blandly suggested that Germany be allowed to colonize in Africa and in Russia.

The second step would be to open up to the "nation without space" [*Volk ohne Raum*] areas in which it could provide space for the settlement of its vigorous race and construct great works of peace.... War, revolution, and internal decay made a beginning in Russia and large parts of the east.... This destructive process is in the meantime still going on. It is necessary that it be stopped.[77]

The memorandum was quickly disavowed, as Hugenberg's personal initiative, by the German Foreign Office, but this excuse (though apparently true) was given scant credit abroad. Nor did Hugenberg's resignation, 29 June, caused by other factors, quiet the furor in Moscow and the capitals of the small eastern European states.[78]

[76] Article entitled "Revision of the Versailles Treaty," *Pravda*, 10 May 1933, translated directly for the writer; see *G.F.P.*, I, 419, 449-450, and *B.F.P.*, VII, 551-555, and 557-558. This change and an equally important change in Soviet disarmament policy are treated in detail in chap. vi below, pp. 107-110.

[77] Text as released by the W.T.B., *G.F.P.*, I, 562-567; slightly varying translation in the London *Times*, 17 June 1933.

[78] On Hugenberg's earlier versions of the scheme and on the controversy, see

Whatever the case, the proposal was an uncanny echo of *Mein Kampf*.

On 22 June the Russian Ambassador in Berlin delivered to the German government a sharp protest which charged that the memorandum amounted to "an appeal for war against the USSR."[79] *Pravda* struck out in a tone of exasperation.

The racists may amuse themselves as they please, but we have had enough of these pleasantries. Is it possible that people have forgotten in Germany the result of the first move made against the Soviet Ukraine in 1918, at a moment when our country was less strong than today? . . . Let these gentlemen, who have lost all sense of proportion, bear in mind our force, and let them know that our country will defend itself against those who dream of seizing a part of Soviet territory.[80]

From Ambassador von Dirksen's listening post, Hugenberg's indiscretion "was the last straw for Moscow, and constituted the final inducement, to all those who had hitherto adopted a patient attitude, finally to abandon their pro-German policy. . . ."[81]

Signals of the new directions of Soviet policy now began to appear all over Europe. Litvinov's visit to Paris, Radek's journey around Poland, Soviet invitations to the former French Premier, M. Herriot, and to the French Air Minister, Pierre Cot, and the red-carpet treatment they received on their tours through Russia in August and September—all these revealed the Kremlin's desire to prepare the ground for an alternate alliance. In a major diplomatic maneuver, the Soviet Union concluded Conventions for the Definition of Aggression with Poland, Romania, Czechoslovakia, Yugoslavia, Estonia, Latvia, and Lithuania.[82]

None of these events was as portentous as that which took place in the secret domain of Russo-German military collaboration. Of that extraordinary chapter of history, the best-kept secret was the existence on Russian soil, near Lipetzk, Kazan, and Saratov, of train-

---

G.F.P., I, 293-297, 413-414, and 562 ff.; Anton Ritthaler, "Eine Etappe auf Hitlers Weg zur ungeteilten Macht, Hugenbergs Rücktritt als Reichsminister," in *Vierteljahrshefte für Zeitgeschichte*, VII, 1960, 193-219.

[79] *G.F.P.*, I, 591-592.

[80] *Pravda*, 19 June 1933, quoted in *Journal des Débats*, 20 June 1933.

[81] *Moscow, Tokyo, London*, p. 126. Krestinsky told Dirksen that "during the 12 years that he had been occupied with German-Russian affairs he had never had such a serious and unpleasant question to discuss." G.F.P., I, 581-582; and see also pp. 640-642, 650-651, 695-696; B.F.P., VII, 595-596; and Gustav Hilger and Alfred G. Meyer, *Incompatible Allies* (New York, 1935), p. 257.

[82] The Conventions and the other events mentioned above are covered in chap. vi.

ing stations for aviation, tanks, and gas warfare. There Reichswehr officers conducted tests and gave instruction for both German and Russian personnel. About eighty German officers a year came to Russia over a period of eight or nine years. In later years the training received by these officers and the opportunity to test prototypes were of great value to the Luftwaffe and the Panzer divisions.[83] On the other side, the Red Army had the opportunity to observe and test the newest German designs, and high-ranking Soviet officers, notably Tukachevsky and Yegorov, occasionally attended German staff schools and maneuvers.[84]

These military relations survived the first months of tension created by Hitler's arrival, but they were liquidated in September 1933. Who broke them off is an intriguing problem. The revelations of the recently published German diplomatic documents made it reasonably certain that it was the Russians who took the first step.[85] It was on 27 April 1933 that Ambassador von Dirksen received the first jolt—operations at one of the training stations were to stop. Then, inexplicably, a few days later the Russians reversed their move.[86] All was cordiality during the visit to Russia, May 8-28, of Lt. General von Bockelberg, Chief of the Army Ordnance Office.[87] He was assured that the Red Army "placed the greatest value on close cooperation with the German Army and German technology." However, the General was warned by the Soviet

[83] Consult the valuable article by Hans W. Gatzke, "Russo-German Military Collaboration during the Weimar Republic," *American Historical Review*, LXIII (April 1958), 565-597. General Koestring, German Military Attaché in Moscow, 1931-1932 and 1935-1941, told M. Georges Castellan: "Le développement de notre Luftwaffe, en particulier des Stukas, et de notre arme blindée a été grandement aidé par nos stations en Russie." Castellan, "Reichswehr et Armée Rouge," p. 209.

[84] Marshal Tukachevsky, Deputy Commissar of Defense, headed a Soviet delegation to the German maneuvers in Sept.-Oct. 1932. *Ibid.*, pp. 192-194, and Castellan, *Le Réarmement clandestin du Reich 1930-1935*, pp. 484-486. Erich von Manstein recalls his observation of the Red Army's maneuvers in the Caucasus in autumn 1932, *Aus einem Soldatenleben* (Bonn, 1958), pp. 146-159.

[85] In addition to the evidence in *G.F.P.*, I, 362 ff., the thesis that the Soviets took the initiative is supported by the recollections of Dirksen, *Moscow, Tokyo, London*, p. 123; Hilger and Meyer, *Incompatible Allies*, pp. 256-257. That Hitler ordered the break is asserted by Helm Speidel, who was an aviation staff officer in Berlin and received flight training at the Lipetzk station in Russia, "Reichswehr und Rote Armee," *Vierteljahrshefte für Zeitgeschichte*, I (Jan. 1953), 40-41; and by General Koestring, Castellan, "Reichswehr et Armée Rouge," pp. 206-207.

[86] Dirksen's dispatches of 28 April and 14 May 1933, *G.F.P.*, I, 362-363, 421. The first termination may have applied only to the gas station at Saratov, considerably less important than the tank and air stations at Kazan and Lipetzk.

[87] *Ibid.*, I, 273, n. 5 and 467, n. 12.

Commissar for Defense, Voroshilov, that "the armies were members of their respective states, and *that a close cooperation was only possible if the high policy of the Governments pursued the same goals.*"[88] Bockelberg, who recommended continuation of the training stations as "urgently desirable,"[89] had scarcely returned to Berlin when the blow fell again, this time for good. Some time between 28 May and 3 June 1933, "in a rather sudden and unfriendly manner," the Soviet government gave notice that it wished to terminate the training stations as soon as possible.[90] A few days later the Soviets canceled plans for Soviet officers to attend summer training courses in Germany and in July the Germans canceled their participation in the Russian fall maneuvers.

The termination negotiations were conducted with generosity by the Germans, and in late August and September a series of farewell banquets marked the end of the three training stations. Reichswehr and Red Army officers toasted each other "like good friends who part not of their own free will but under the pressure of adverse events."[91] A Soviet Air Force Commander congratulated the Reichswehr for having "kept and developed after the war its high degree of aeronautical competence in a tactical and technical respect, and [said] that the Red Army had been able to derive great benefit therefrom."[92]

It was the end of an era when a Reichswehr officer made the laconic report, 29 September 1933: "The liquidation of the military stations in Soviet Russia has been completed."[93] True, the growing self-sufficiency of both armies made it likely that their co-operation would decline. Yet the fact remains that it was suddenly and

[88] General Bockelberg's report, 13 June 1933, his italics, *ibid.*, I, 467, n. 12. The same warning was made by Tukachevsky to the German Military Attaché in Moscow, Colonel Hartmann, report of 16 May, *ibid.*, I, 464-467.

[89] "Cooperation with the Red Army and the Soviet armaments industry is, in view of the extent of Russian plans and their demonstrated energy in carrying them out, urgently desirable not only for reasons of defense policy but also for technical reasons with respect to armament." Report of 13 June 1933, *ibid.*, I, 467-568, n. 12.

[90] Dirksen's dispatch, 5 June 1933, *ibid.*, I, 520. Consult also Col. Hartmann's reports of 28 June, 19 and 26 Sept. 1933, pp. 609, 820-824, 856-862; and the conversation of German Chargé d'Affaires, Twardowski, with Marshal Tukachevsky, 1 Nov. 1933, *ibid.*, II, 81-83.

[91] Dirksen, *Moscow, Tokyo, London*, p. 123.

[92] Report by Col. Hartmann, 26 Sept. 1933, *ibid.*, I, 856-862; see also pp. 767-768, 820-824, 875, and II, 81-83, and Speidel's account, "Reichswehr und Rote Armee," *Vierteljahrshefte für Zeitgeschichte*, I (Jan. 1953), 40-43.

[93] *G.F.P.*, I, 875.

swiftly terminated in the year of Hitler's accession to power. With this event one of the cornerstones of Rapallo was destroyed.

Against this tide of antagonism economic factors continued to work profitably for both sides. The volume of trade declined from its high point of 1932, but the German position in Soviet foreign trade was still pre-eminent. Germany again acted as the largest supplier to the Soviet Union, and the punctual Soviet payments on their commercial loans were much appreciated in depression-ridden Germany.[94]

In each country some men maneuvered to prevent a complete break. In Moscow a faction including Krestinsky, Deputy Commissar of Foreign Affairs and former Ambassador to Germany, and apparently Voroshilov and Yenukidse, was alarmed at the growing tension and tried to facilitate a reconciliation.[95] With Dirksen's co-operation it was arranged that Krestinsky should use the opportunity of his annual journey to Bad Kissingen for the cure, to have an interview with Hitler. Hitler gave his reluctant consent but, at the last moment, something happened in Moscow, Krestinsky went home via Vienna instead of Berlin, and the interview never took place.[96]

On the German end, collaboration with Russia was backed by industrialists, diplomats, and soldiers—notably State Secretary von Bülow, Ambassador von Dirksen, and General von Seeckt, the famous retired chief of the Reichswehr. In a pamphlet entitled *Deutschland zwischen West und Ost,* published in February 1933, Seeckt invoked the geographical dilemma of Germany and the terrible precedent of the two-front war in 1914-1918. He drew from them a prophetic exhortation not to pull down the wire to Moscow.

Do we wish to be taken by two enemies once again? ... Or will a Polish fleet on the Baltic Sea threaten and cut off East Prussia? Will

[94] Soviet imports from Germany declined from 327,700,000 rubles in 1932 to 148,100,000 rubles in 1933. Nonetheless, the latter figure represented 42.5 per cent of total Soviet imports. League of Nations, *International Trade Statistics, 1933* (Geneva, 1934), p. 254.

[95] There is no question about Krestinsky; see the following note. For indications of pro-German feelings on the part of Voroshilov, Politburo member as well as Commissar of Defense, and Yenukidse, a close friend and secretary of Stalin's, consult the report of the British Ambassador in Moscow, *B.F.P.,* VII, 717-718; *G.F.P.,* I, 421-422, 875, and Dirksen, *Moscow, Tokyo, London,* pp. 95-96, 126-129.

[96] On Krestinsky's attitude and the proposed interview with Hitler, see *G.F.P.,* I, 388, 418-423, 519-524, 747, 848-851, 884-885, 902-904, and II, 14-19, 21-22, 40, 76-77; Dirksen, *Moscow, Tokyo, London,* pp. 126-129; Hilger and Meyer, *The Incompatible Allies,* pp. 260-261.

Poland advance to the Oder? Such possibilities take on tangible form if we exclude Russia from our calculations. . . .

It is said that Count Schlieffen murmured during his dying hours: Keep the right wing strong! So we call on German policy: Keep the rear covered![97]

Hitler, however, was deaf; he could hear nothing but the call to conquest in the east.

The men of the Rapallo line were feeble in face of the distrust and resentment which scarred German-Russian relations. The prospects for collaboration can be judged by the tone in which they were dismissed by Litvinov and Hitler. The Soviet Foreign Minister told a German diplomat, 14 September, that "he was convinced, and this conviction could be changed only by deeds and no longer by words, not even words in official speeches, that Germany had entered upon an anti-Soviet course."[98] In Berlin at a conference 26 September, State Secretary von Bülow asked the Chancellor to receive Krestinsky in the interests of conciliation. Hitler said he would talk to Krestinsky, but "he did not expect that it would do any good."

The Russian government will never forgive Germany for our having smashed communism in Germany, for the fate of Soviet Russia has been decided by our revolution. The rulers in Moscow know that very well. In the relations with Russia the liabilities have always exceeded the profits.[99]

So much for the decade of Rapallo and the work of Seeckt and Rantzau!

The most familiar feature of the Russian reaction to Hitler was uncertainty. Its effect upon Soviet leaders was partly a function of acute Soviet anxieties in two other spheres. Had the Soviet Union been internally strong and in a strong international position, the risk would have seemed smaller. Just the opposite was the case.

Russia lay at the climax of a great famine, caused by the ramifications of forced collectivization. It had started in 1930, but did

[97] General Hans von Seeckt, *Deutschland zwischen West und Ost* (Hamburg, 1933), pp. 41, 45. Consult Kochan, *Russia and the Weimar Republic*, p. 171. In addition to General von Bockelberg, General Koestring and State Secretary Milch in the Air Ministry supported the Russian orientation. Castellan, "Reichswehr et l'Armée Rouge," p. 207, and *B.F.P.*, V, 393-394.

[98] Litvinov to the German Chargé d'Affaires, von Twardowski, *G.F.P.*, I, 816-818.

[99] *Ibid.*, I, 850-851.

not reach its most acute stage until the winter of 1932-1933. The starvation in some regions—one of them the very Ukraine which Hitler and Rosenberg coveted—was in danger of reaching the proportions of the 1921 famine. The second sore spot was the Far East. The Nazis' victory in Germany coincided with another period of sharp Russo-Japanese tension, stimulated by the Japanese invasion of the province of Jehol, the gateway to Soviet-controlled Outer Mongolia. A measure of the Soviet anxiety was the offer, 2 May 1933, to sell the Russian share of the Chinese Eastern Railway to Manchukuo, the Japanese puppet state. These two perils—famine and the Japanese threat—constantly stimulated Soviet sensitivity to the news from Berlin.

Hitler's accession to power thus created uncertainty about Germany's future policy at a moment when the Russians could not stand uncertainty. The Russians did not make a clean break with Nazi Germany. But they became deeply suspicious of Hitler's intentions and began to ponder a return to the old pattern, to the French alliance.

Six

THE TEMPO QUICKENS

The alarm aroused by Hitler's arrival led the French government to fashion closer relations with Russia and to begin a rapprochement with Italy. But these changes were not the children of aggressive emotions. The French reaction to Hitler was defensive to the core.

For years many sections of French opinion had cried, "Wolf, Wolf!" at every sign of German nationalism. Now, when the worst fears were realized, "opinion here [Paris], outwardly at least, has become extraordinarily calm."[1] The measured French reaction was reflected in the government's policies, in parliamentary debates, and in the unsensational treatment that the Paris press gave to the event. Economic and financial troubles at home, and a related parliamentary crisis which had seen two governments fall in forty days, claimed as much attention and emotion as did Hitler. Many of the commentators made no recommendation of new policies, confining themselves to warning the nation of the grave new peril. The most popular suggestion for a new policy was a negative one: that French diplomacy should make no more concessions to Germany.[2] Not one important voice was raised to suggest military action; Right and Left protested their abhorrence of preventive war.[3]

The serenity of the French reaction was most striking on the Center and Right, hitherto the bailiwick of vigilant nationalism.

[1] Dispatch from Lord Tyrrell, British Ambassador in Paris, 19 May 1933, B.F.P., V, 267-269. He concluded, "France has, in fact, fallen back on a policy of extreme caution...." Consult his other long, sensitive reviews of French opinion, 20 March, IV, 462-466, and 17 May, V, 330-334.

[2] For declarations in this sense, mostly in the conservative press, see extracts from Saint-Brice in Le Journal, C.J. Gignoux in L'Ami du Peuple and L'Ère Nouvelle, quoted in "Revue de la presse," J.D., 1 and 2 Feb. 1933; Jacques Bainville in L'Action Française, 2 Feb. 1933; Journal des Débats, 6 Feb. 1933.

[3] Speech of Léon Blum at Bourges, 26 March, quoted in Le Temps, 28 March 1933; Pierre Gaxotte in Je Suis Partout, 10 March 1933; Georges Mandel, speech of 9 Nov., J.O., Chambre, Débats, 9 Nov. 1933, p. 4041; two notes by the British Military Attaché in Paris, 15 and 16 May 1933, B.F.P., V, 259-261.

Observers noted a feeling of satisfaction, verging on complacency, that Hitler at last had cured the British and Americans of their incorrigible tenderness for the Germans. It was in this vein that M. Pierre-Étienne Flandin reassured the Paris correspondent of the *Manchester Guardian.*

> He has made Germany unpopular in England and in America with his sabre-rattling, his flag-waving, his atrocities and his Jew-baiting. No, honestly, I see nothing to worry about. Hitler's Germany has been a revelation to England; it has not been to us. In many ways, we prefer Hitler to Von Papen or Schleicher.[4]

And that implacable chauvinist, M. Franklin-Bouillon, asserted that "Hitler is our best friend," because he had forced British opinion to recognize "that militarism is a German product, and only a German product, and that the danger of the next war can come from Germany, and from Germany alone."[5]

On the Left, strong moral aversion to Hitler was often negated by anti-militarism and by pacifism.[6] It was an awkward combination that M. Léon Blum offered: "We shall combat Hitler, but we shall see to it that France does not succumb to nationalism."[7] The distinguished Socialist leader rejected any forceful reply to Hitler, even French rearmament, in a speech to the Chamber of Deputies, 6 April 1933—a speech alternately noble and pathetic.

> I beg you, gentlemen, in the name of peace, do not reply to one danger by another danger which multiplies the first. Do not reply to campaigns of nationalist excitation by parallel campaigns, reflecting each other and feeding on each other. At the moment when the worst danger for the peace of Europe is the rearmament of Germany and all the consequences to which it may lead elsewhere, persuade yourselves,

[4] Interview given to Alexander Werth in the last week of March 1933, quoted in *France in Ferment* (London, 1934), pp. 23-24.

[5] Interview with Werth, last week of March 1933, *ibid.*, p. 23. Note the annual report on the foreign affairs budget for 1933; "Félicitons-nous, peut-être, des excès commis par les tenants de la Swastika en ce qu'ils dissipent en effet les nuées internationalistes et forcent les opportunistes les plus invétérés à ouvrir les yeux." Rapport fait au nom de la Commission des Finances chargé d'examiner le projet de loi portant fixation du budget général de l'exercice 1933 (Affaires Étrangères), par M. Adrien Dariac, *J.O.*, Chambre, *Documents*, 1933, session ordinaire, annexe 1535, p. 512.

[6] The Communists denounced Hitler, but declared that they would continue to battle the Socialists and French imperialism, the "accomplices" of Hitler. See *L'Humanité*, 1 and 16 March 1933; speech of the Communist deputy, Gabriel Péri, 6 April, *J.O.*, Chambre, *Débats*, 6 April 1933, p. 1940.

[7] Speech at Bourges, 26 March, quoted in *Le Temps*, 28 March 1933.

I beg of you, that today more than ever before ... the way to salvation is peace, the will to peace.[8]

Such an appeal, from a man whose sympathies for his fellow Jews and Socialists in Germany gave him abundant justification for demanding action against Hitler, is a token of the profound desire for peace in certain sections of French opinion.

A government determined to react vigorously to Hitler's challenge might have tried to stir up public opinion, but not the French cabinet of the day. M. Édouard Daladier, a young Radical-Socialist who became Premier on the day after Hitler was made Chancellor, brought with him a dislike of "strong-arm," "adventurous" policies, and an acute realization of the cost of the last war to France. He was sympathetic to the ideal of an understanding with Germany, and he was not ready to dismiss this sympathy simply because Hitler had come to power.[9] The Foreign Minister, M. Joseph Paul-Boncour, though deeply antagonized by Nazi Germany, was an ardent internationalist and preferred to rely upon the League of Nations. The government's existence depended upon the support in Parliament of the Socialist party, and that party was committed to a conciliatory foreign policy. M. Daladier revealed the reaction of his cabinet in his first broadcast to the nation, 14 March 1933.

Rest assured that we are following the evolution of international politics with the utmost vigilance. France does not know hatred. Nor does she know fear.... I would insult you ... if I did not recognize the grandeur of the moral forces and the power of the material forces which permit France to observe the events of a troubled world with complete assurance.[10]

Such dignified and soothing words, coming from the man who was Minister of War as well as Premier, reinforced the pacific temper of public opinion.

The French reaction was calm, but that is not to say that it was passive. Two lines of policy emerge in French diplomacy in

[8] *J.O.*, Chambre, *Débats*, p. 1937. Consult the editorials by Blum in *Le Populaire*, 10 Feb., 16 March 1933. Blum's attitudes were shared to a large extent by the left wing of the Radical-Socialist party. Other Radical-Socialists followed the lead of M. Herriot, who was very much alarmed by Hitler's arrival.

[9] For a portrait of Daladier see below, pp. 125-127. The Herriot cabinet had fallen on 14 Dec. 1932, owing to Herriot's insistence that France pay the war debt instalment due the United States government. M. Paul-Boncour then formed a cabinet which fell on 28 Jan. 1933, owing to his attempt to balance the budget.

[10] Radio broadcast of 14 March 1933, quoted in *Le Temps*, 15 March.

1933, both with elements of continuity. The most successful approach was to bolster French security by rapprochements with Russia and Italy. For a time, however, this search for new friends did not preclude the cautious exploration of a direct understanding with Germany, an exploration previously tried by Laval and Herriot. The basic French attitude towards Hitler—awareness of danger but unwillingness to destroy it—was ambiguous enough to permit these contradictory policies. The search for protection was the more powerful, but there lingered a natural hope that the showdown might be avoided.

The Franco-Soviet rapprochement stood ready to hand, in contrast to the dusty state of Franco-Italian relations. Started in the spring of 1931, the connection between Paris and Moscow had been gradually widened and then secured by the signature of the Non-Aggression Pact in Paris, 29 November 1932. Only moderately interested so far, French and Russian leaders began to look upon the rapprochement as valuable property after Hitler's accession to power. A series of advances from both sides coming in quick succession injected real vitality into the alignment.

The first signal was the French government's choice of method in ratifying the Non-Aggression Pact. When the pact and Conciliation Convention were signed, it had been reported that, although not legally required, "the French Government will in fact request the approval of Parliament for these treaties."[11] Instead, the government decided on the quicker method of ratification by the President of the Republic. M. Albert Lebrun complied on 11 February, the Praesidium of the Central Executive Committee of the U.S.S.R. ratified three days later, and ratifications were exchanged by Ambassador Dejean and Deputy Commissar Krestinsky in Moscow 15 February 1933.[12] This action did not preclude parliamentary discussion of the pact, but it meant that the government did not intend to let the ratification be retarded. The quick ratification was much appreciated by Moscow. Hinting at nervousness about the Japanese as well as Hitler, *Izvestya* urged France to join in

[11] Statement of a Foreign Office official to the U.S. Chargé d'Affaires, Dispatch of 5 Dec. 1932, 751.6111/24, Archives of the Department of State, Washington, D.C.

[12] *Le Temps*, 17, 18 Feb.; *S.U.R.*, XI-XII, 61. Text of the promulgatory decree and the official text of the pact and Conciliation Convention, printed in *J.O.*, *Lois et Décrets*, 17 Feb. 1933, pp. 1571-1572.

forging "a concrete policy in the face of threats to the peace, whatever their source."[13]

Following the exchange of ratifications, the Foreign Affairs commissions of the French Chamber and Senate began consideration of the Non-Aggression Pact, with a seriousness somewhat ironical as it was already the law of the land. In the Senate the reception was cool,[14] but in the Chamber a mere formality was turned by accident into an act of political pressure. That accident was the election of M. Édouard Herriot as President of the Commission. The former Premier, who had signed the pact in November 1932, announced that he would immediately turn the Commission's attention to Franco-Soviet relations. On 17 March M. Henry Torrès delivered a favorable report on the pact and proposed that a resolution endorsing it be placed on the agenda of the Chamber of Deputies; vigorously urged by M. Herriot, the resolution was approved by the Commission.[15] Given his keen rivalry with Daladier, there was no chance that Herriot could promote his views by direct influence, but this strategic post gave him a powerful sounding board for indirect influence on Parliament and public opinion.

M. Herriot did not confine his persuasive energies to the corridors of the Palais Bourbon; he took his campaign to the press and the lecture hall. What began as perhaps only an attempt to justify "his" pact became a project suffused with urgency after Hitler's arrival. The British Ambassador, Lord Tyrrell, reported on 20 March that the shock "has already turned M. Herriot into an impassioned advocate of a Franco-Soviet alliance."[16] In speeches to the Chamber of Deputies and to meetings of the Radical-Socialist party, and in newspaper articles, Herriot pleaded for a Franco-Soviet entente in the face of a new German menace.[17] A book published in May 1933, *La France dans le Monde,* gave him the opportunity to take his readers on a "tour d'horizon" of French

[13] *Izvestya,* 18 Feb. 1933, quoted in *Bulletin de la presse russe,* No. 227.

[14] The pact was criticized by several senators including MM. Millerand and Barthou. *Le Temps,* 12 March 1933.

[15] *Le Temps,* 17 March 1933.   [16] *B.F.P.,* IV, 465.

[17] See articles in *L'Ère Nouvelle* and *Le Petit Provençal,* quoted in "Revue de la presse," *J.D.,* 10 and 13 Feb. 1933; speeches to the Comité Exécutif of the Radical-Socialist party in Paris, to the party's Federation du Sud-Est, in Marseilles, and to other groups in Lyons and Miribel, reported in *Le Temps,* 2 March, 20 March, 7 April, 15 May, 30 May 1933; speech of 6 April, *J.O.,* Chambre, *Débats,* 6 April 1933, pp. 1946-1947.

interests. He marshaled Russia's enormous manpower, expanding army and air force to justify the Non-Aggression Pact, and claimed that it had broken the liaison between the Reichswehr and Red Army. His conclusions emphasized the value of Russian friendship in view of French weaknesses in manpower and resources.[18] Although it is difficult to measure the success of such efforts to sway opinion, it was propitious that a man of personal integrity and broad appeal should have become an unconditional champion of a Franco-Soviet entente. Herriot was the first politician of stature to carry the issue to the French public.[19]

Meanwhile, the structure of Franco-Soviet relations was improved by the exchange of military attachés. Colonel Mendras and Commandant Simon arrived in Moscow 8 April 1933, and their Soviet counterpart, General Ventzov, reached Paris a month later, filling posts left vacant since the days of Brest-Litovsk. The Commissar of Defense, Klementi Voroshilov, received Colonel Mendras in "very cordial" fashion and told him: " 'We are very happy to have re-established normal relations with you. We expect that we shall live together as good neighbors, later perhaps even as friends.' "[20] M. Paul-Boncour impressed on the Chamber of Deputies that the Soviet Army must not remain unknown to France, and his remarks suggested that French Army leaders had decided to support the rapprochement.[21] The arrival of French officers was a significant step in the re-establishment of French *présence* in Russia. They came just on the eve of the break between the Red Army and the Reichswehr.

At this same time, the retirement of the French Ambassador in Moscow, Count Dejean, opened the way for the appointment of M. Charles Alphand, 14 March 1933. A career diplomat, M. Alphand

[18] *La France dans le Monde*, pp. 41-42, 78-83, and 243. The book was based on lectures that Herriot had given in January and February.

[19] M. Yvon Delbos, a prominent figure in the Radical-Socialist party, published an account of his trip to Russia in Aug.-Sept. 1932, *L'Expérience Rouge* (Paris, 1933). Although critical of Soviet institutions, he concluded that a Franco-Soviet entente was necessary in view of the danger of pan-Germanism. Another Radical-Socialist deputy who made the trip to Russia in 1932 was young Pierre Mendès-France.

[20] Conversation of 22 April 1933, Report of Colonel Mendras, quoted by Castellan, *Le Réarmement Clandestin du Reich, 1930-1935*, p. 490, n. 1. For details on the exchange of military attachés, see *J.O., Lois et Décrets*, 28 March 1933, p. 3124; *Le Temps*, 16 March, 9 April, 11 May 1933.

[21] For M. Paul-Boncour's remarks and those of M. Herriot on the Red Army, see *J.O., Chambre, Débats*, 18 May 1933, pp. 2438, 2433-2434.

could claim to be an "old Russian hand" by virtue of experience in M. Delcassé's office, in handling Russian affairs during the war, and in the Franco-Soviet Debts Conference, 1926-1927. In a temporary role as Herriot's *chef de Cabinet* at the Quai d'Orsay, M. Alphand had helped put the finishing touches on the Non-Aggression Pact.[22] The new ambassador facilitated a more rapid pace in the rapprochement.

As the structure of the rapprochement was made more solid, the two countries drew closer together in their general approaches to European politics. For years they had sharply disagreed on disarmament *vs.* security and revision *vs.* the status quo. There would always remain a basic ideological rift between Soviet Russia and any capitalist country, but the gap was narrowed when the Russians shifted over to the French side on these two conspicuous issues.

The question of disarmament had been embarrassing the French for a decade; it became a nasty daily problem when the World Disarmament Conference opened in Geneva in February 1932. There, as we have seen, Litvinov had ridiculed M. Tardieu's plan for security and had announced that the Soviet Union would support "any proposals tending to reduce armaments."[23] Such talk was a blessing to the German delegation and continued the long-standing Soviet support of the German position on disarmament.

When the diplomats returned to Geneva in the new year, they found another French plan up for discussion, the Paul-Boncour plan, which consisted of measures for security based on an international striking force.[24] The Soviets were expected to oppose and, therefore, Litvinov's abrupt declaration of support for the French plan awakened many a bored delegate. The Soviet Union, said Litvinov, 6 February 1933, still desired disarmament, but had decided to recognize the "enormous importance" of security.

Apparently there is no escape from this problem, if only because it has been raised by a great and powerful State, whose representatives

[22] M. Alphand arrived in Moscow in June; he stated that his mission would be to facilitate "une politique de sympathie et de compréhension réciproque." *Le Temps*, 16 June 1933.

[23] Speech of 11 Feb. 1932, *Conference for the Reduction and Limitation of Armaments. Records*, Series A, I, 86.

[24] The concept of a striking force, composed of élite troops, equipped with the newest weapons and motorized for mobility, was suggested to M. Paul-Boncour by a young commandant, Charles de Gaulle. Paul-Boncour, *Entre Deux Guerres*, II, 228-229.

have declared that until it is solved they cannot undertake any obligations with regard to the reduction of armaments. If, therefore, we want to advance, and not just go round and round, we shall have to consider with all seriousness the French proposals, and make up our minds whether there is any possibility of reaching an international agreement based upon these and other proposals which may be made on security ... proceeding subsequently to disarmament or whether such an agreement will prove impossible.[25]

Moving to the particular, the Soviet Foreign Minister declared that his country would accept the obligations which the French plan allotted to it and to the United States in the "outer ring" of security. Not required to contribute troops to the international striking force, the Soviet Union was to give "full legal significance" to the Kellogg-Briand Pact by refusing to carry on economic and financial relations with an aggressor.

M. Litvinov insisted that the difficulty of knowing exactly when a State was an aggressor made some definite criteria necessary and he offered a draft "Definition of the Aggressor." This definition in its first part set up conventional criteria of judging an aggressor, but added a second section stating that "no considerations whatsoever of a political, strategical or economic nature ... shall be accepted as justification of aggression." Litvinov requested that these proposals be discussed along with the French plan; they were "not meant to compete with or be substituted for the French proposals but are their logical extension."[26]

In the day-to-day tactical battle of the conference, the Soviet shift carried heavy weight. To the French, a helping hand on the disarmament issue, where they were constantly on the defensive, was no small boon; and as they gained, so the Germans lost.[27] M. Paul-Boncour immediately welcomed the "extremely valuable support" given by the Soviet Union to the French plan and announced approval of the Soviet Definition of the Aggressor.[28] The French

[25] League of Nations, *Conference for the Reduction and Limitation of Armaments. Records,* Series B, *Minutes of the General Commission* (hereinafter cited as *Minutes of the General Commission*), 14 Dec. 1932-29 June 1933, II, 234-235.

[26] *Ibid.,* II, 238-239.

[27] Litvinov's declaration of 6 Feb. 1933 is often cited as a reaction against Hitler. Such an interpretation does not seem justified. Considering the travel time by train from Moscow to Geneva and the period necessary to prepare such a major shift in policy, it is almost certain that the decision was made before 30 Jan., the date of Hitler's accession.

[28] Session of 8 Feb. 1933, *Minutes of the General Commission,* II, 261-262. See also Paul-Boncour's speech in the Political Commission, 14 Feb. 1933. League of Nations, *Conference for the Reduction and Limitation of Armaments. Records,* Series

Delegation supported the Soviet draft in the Political Commission and when it came back to the General Commission in revised form they declared "full and unreserved support to the proposals made for defining the aggressor."[29] From the time of Litvinov's speech in February, Franco-Soviet co-operation became a prominent feature of the Disarmament Conference.

The second general issue of European politics on which Soviet policy changed was that of revision *vs.* the status quo. From the time of their signature, Moscow had denounced the Versailles peace treaties as the instruments by which the spoils of imperialist war had been divided. Poland, Czechoslovakia, Romania, Yugoslavia, and France were the bloated beneficiaries. The Soviets had given favors to the losers, particularly Germany and Turkey, and had joined the revisionist bloc at international conferences. Revision had been admirably suited to the Soviet goal of promoting division among the European powers. However, revision had not yet posed much danger; it had been applied to reparations and other non-territorial questions, and it had been applied by negotiation. In 1933, with the arrival of Hitler, the situation took on a different aspect. Now, the term might mean revision by force and revision of frontiers. The Four Power Pact, which inscribed revision on its platform, excluded Russia, and this implied that Germany's "injustices" were to be repaired in the East rather than the West. Revision suddenly assumed the aspects of a nightmare and Moscow began to perceive unsuspected beauties in the status quo, and in its charter, Versailles.

It was left to Karl Radek to perform the dialectical acrobatics of a change in the line, in a series of articles in *Pravda* and *Izvestya*, 10-24 May 1933. The Soviets still disliked the Versailles treaties, said Radek, but they disliked war far more.

The road to revision of the predatory tortuous Versailles peace leads through a *new world war*. All attempts by the interested parties to represent the matter as if it were a question of the peaceful resolution of old treaties cannot deceive anyone in any way.... *The word "re-*

D, 5, *Minutes of the Political Commission, February 27th, 1932–March 10th, 1933* (hereinafter cited as *Minutes of the Political Commission*), p. 8.

[29] Speeches of M. Paul-Boncour and M. René Massigli in the Political Commission, 4 and 10 March 1933, *ibid.*, pp. 32, 51. This Commission sent the Soviet draft for study to the Committee on Security, from which it emerged 24 May, revised as the "Act relating to the Definition of Aggression." See the statements of Paul-Boncour, 24, 29 May, *Minutes of the General Commission*, II, 496, 552-553.

vision" is only another name for a new world war. There is therefore
nothing surprising about the fact that one of the basic demands of the
revisionists is for the right to those armaments forbidden them by the
Versailles Treaty. Discussion of revision is a smoke screen behind which
imperialism is preparing the most cruel war which the human brain
could think up.[30]

The new stand was frequently elaborated by Litvinov and was
elevated to the status of dogma by Stalin in his speech to the 17th
Party Congress.[31]

Paris made much of these two innovations in Soviet policy. The
annual report on the Foreign Affairs budget, drawn up early in
March, greeted with pleasure Litvinov's support of the French
plan.[32] In May, when the Non-Aggression Pact came up for debate
in the Chamber, the Foreign Minister and several other speakers
welcomed Moscow's conversion to the French thesis of security.
M. Herriot and others quoted passages from Radek's denunciation
of revision and advanced it as one of the bases on which closer
relations with Russia could be built.[33]

The Soviet "Definition of the Aggressor" and support for the
status quo were much appreciated in Warsaw and the capitals of
the Little Entente, where revision was a highly sensitive issue.
The basis was laid for a Soviet rapprochement with Romania,
Czechoslovakia, and even Yugoslavia. This in turn facilitated the
Soviet move towards France.

The Chamber of Deputies debate on the Non-Aggression Pact
accidentally coincided with the climax of the "war-scare" created
by Hitler's accession.[34] A full-dress debate took place, 16 and 18
May 1933, on the following resolution submitted by M. Herriot's
Foreign Affairs Commission: "The Chamber of Deputies welcomes
with satisfaction the exchange between the U.S.S.R. and the French

[30] Article entitled "Revision of the Versailles Treaties," *Pravda*, 10 May 1933.

[31] For Stalin's speech of 26 Jan. 1934, see Degras, ed., *Soviet Documents on Foreign Policy, 1917-1941*, III, 65-72.

[32] Rapport fait au nom de la Commision des Finances chargé d'examiner le projet de loi portant fixation du budget general de l'exercice 1933 (Affaires Étrangères), par M. Adrien Dariac, *J.O.*, Chambre, *Documents*, 1933, session ordinaire, annexe 1535, p. 549. See Premier Daladier's approval, *ibid.*, 6 April 1933, pp. 1929-1930.

[33] Speeches of MM. Paul-Boncour, Herriot, Torrès, Baron, and Moutet cited below, n. 36, n. 37, n. 38, and n. 42.

[34] The pact was debated in the Senate but was overshadowed by a bitter fight on the Four Power Pact. Approval was cautious and mixed with heavy criticism. Consult speeches of MM. Bérenger, Eccard, Gautherot, and Paul-Boncour, *J.O.*, Sénat, *Débats*, 4 May 1933, pp. 785-799, 803.

Republic of ratifications of the Franco-Soviet Non-Aggression Pact, which reinforces the organization of peace, to the benefit of all of Europe."[35] Though often so described, the Chamber's approval of the resolution did not confer ratification. For this reason, much criticism was held back, as useless, and the debate is not a true index of the opposition. It is, however, an opportunity to measure support.

Speaking for the Foreign Affairs Commission, M. Henry Torrès argued that the stipulations of the pact would prevent Communist subversion in France and would counter any secret clauses in the German-Soviet treaties. The pact had already brought dividends: Litvinov's support of the French disarmament plan and Radek's denunciation of revision; soon it would become "a positive pact of collaboration and friendship."[36] For optimism, Torrès was out-classed by M. Édouard Herriot. Pressing his case with few quali-fications, the former Premier said that Russia was an essential ele-ment of security against Germany, and he even called for military co-operation:

It suffices to note the length of military service and the number of infantry batallions, of cavalry squadrons, of artillery regiments ... to realize that the Russian Army is a considerable force. . . . Do you really believe that it would be patriotism to shut one's eyes to such important facts?

With the precision to be expected from a former professor of his-tory, Herriot reached back to the sixteenth century for a notorious precedent to prove that reason of state had often dictated an al-liance with an ideological enemy. "Francis I ... judging that it was in the interest of France to unite with Turkey ... carried out his idea without hesitation."[37]

When the Foreign Minister rose to close the debate he justified the exchange of military attachés by reference to the "powerful" Soviet Army, and he praised the pact. "It is made with a great country, which will always be a capital piece on the checkerboard of the world. By this pact, mighty Russia enters the general system of our accords and our ententes."[38] But it was noted that M. Paul-

[35] *J.O.* Chambre, *Débats*, 18 May 1933, p. 2440. The entire debate may be found *ibid.*, 16 May 1933, pp. 2382-2395, and 18 May 1933, pp. 2428-2441.
[36] *Ibid.*, 16 May 1933, p. 2386.
[37] *Ibid.*, 18 May 1933, pp. 2433-2435.
[38] *Ibid.*, pp. 2437-2438.

Boncour did not adopt the uncritical optimism of Herriot nor the latter's implication that an alliance was just around the corner. Observers remembered that M. Paul-Boncour, in praising the rapprochement before the Senate, had spoken of "the limits within which it is convenient to keep it."[39] The restrained tone of the Foreign Minister, the fact that M. Daladier had not himself spoken, and other indications in the debate left the impression that the government intended to move cautiously along the road of rapprochement. The cabinet's attitude had been well defined by an editorial in the semi-official *Le Temps*. The recent improvement of relations with Russia was all to the good, but no more should be expected for the moment. "It would be an error, we believe, to wish to pursue towards the Soviet Union a policy geared to more positive and immediate results."[40]

The vote in favor of the resolution was almost unanimous, 554-1 with 41 abstentions. Even considering the fact that the resolution had no force, the result was surprising. Leaving aside the ten Communists, who not unexpectedly endorsed Soviet policy,[41] three different positions of approval emerged from the debate and from press comments. The Socialist party (S.F.I.O.) approved the pact but did so from a limited point of view and without enthusiasm. They applauded the renunciation of anti-Soviet policies on the part of France and the opportunity to increase trade, but they were not interested in the diplomatic value.[42] As before, a strong note of suspicion could be discerned in the Socialists' attitude towards the rapprochement. They were most angry at the German Communists' continued attacks on the German Social-Democrats and at Stalin's willingness to renew the Berlin Treaty with Hitler while the latter was smashing the German proletariat. The grandson of

[39] *J.O.*, Sénat, *Débats*, 4 May 1933, p. 803. Paul-Boncour and Torrès both hinted that the government had not shared the Foreign Affairs Commission's desire for a formal debate.

[40] "Bulletin du Jour," *Le Temps*, 10 March 1933. See editorials in the same tone by M. Alfred Bayet in *La République*, Daladier's organ, quoted in "Revue de la presse," *J.D.*, 10, 15 March 1933.

[41] The speech of M. Jacques Doriot, second in the Communist hierarchy, 16 May 1933, revealed the embarrassment that the party felt in having to approve the new French foreign policy. "Nous craignons fort que le pacte ne soit qu'un camouflage destiné à masquer la continuation d'une politique agressive à l'égard de l'Union Soviétique." *J.O.*, Chambre, *Débats*, 16 May 1933, pp. 2390-2395; same position in *L'Humanité*, 17 May 1933.

[42] Consult the speeches of MM. Charles Baron, Marius Moutet, and Pierre Renaudel, 16 and 18 May 1933, *J.O.*, Chambre, *Débats*, pp. 2388-2390, 2428-2432, and 2441.

Karl Marx, M. Jean Longuet, a Socialist, shouted at the Communists: "Stalin's government did not move a hand, did not speak a word for its communist brothers tortured and massacred [in Germany.]"[43] Indeed, the debate had to be momentarily suspended because of the exchange of epithets between the Socialist and Communist benches, which prompted a Rightist to gibe: "Go sign a pact of non-aggression yourselves." The Socialists also resented the fact that Stalin was willing to improve relations with the bourgeois French government and the French army but refused to allow his French Communist legions to make peace with the Socialists. It was ironic that in its early and intermediate stages, the rapprochement with Soviet Russia received only lukewarm support from the largest working-class party in France.[44]

A second source of support, equally reserved, came from certain sections of the Center and Right. Seldom articulated, it was demonstrated by a substantial number of votes from these quarters in favor of the resolution. This support seemed to be based on the hope of profitable trade relations with Russia and on the growing need of security against Germany. However, none of the conservatives indicated that they wished to go beyond the level of a non-aggression pact.[45] Only from the Radical-Socialist benches (in reality, from M. Herriot and his faction and not the whole party) did there come a cry for "full speed ahead." There alone was heard the Jacobin argument of subordinating all considerations, ideological and others, to the threatened security of France.[46] These three attitudes did not, of course, account for all the 554 votes in favor of the resolution. What apparently accounted for many others was

[43] *Ibid.*, p. 2392. Note also the bitter exchanges between MM. Thorez and Péri for the Communists and M. Blum, the Socialist chief, in the debate of 6 April 1933; articles by Blum and O. Rosenfeld in *Le Populaire*, 11 May 1933.

[44] The rank and file of the Socialist party, "les militants," were more favorable to Soviet Russia than were the leaders of the party. This discrepancy later exerted an important influence; see chap. ix, p. 191.

[45] See the speech of M. Louis Rollin, Minister of Commerce in the Laval cabinet which had initiated the rapprochement, *J.O.*, Chambre, *Débats*, 18 May 1933, pp. 2440-2441. Among those voting in favor of the resolution were the following prominent figures of the Center and Right: MM. Cathala, Henry-Haye, Piétri, Fabry, Reynaud, Champetier de Ribes, Ybarnégaray, and Rollin.

[46] M. Herriot was supported by M. Yvon Delbos in an article 20 May 1933 in *La Dépêche de Toulouse*, the most influential Radical provincial daily. Placing himself almost entirely on the plane of security, Delbos argued that France could not afford to ignore a country of 160 million people and growing industrial and military power. "Ainsi, nous nous retrouvons en face de la Russie soviétique dans une situation analogue à celle qui nous a rapprochés de la Russie tsariste, tant il est vrai que la géographie et l'histoire commandaient la politique."

a vague feeling of anxiety about Hitler, stimulated by the momentary tension of the war scare.

Opposition to the rapprochement, though restrained, was not silent. M. Louis Marin, the vigorous president of the right-wing Fédération Républicaine, denounced the pact as useless and dangerous, and he was joined in abstention by forty deputies from the Center and the Right, among them such well-known figures as MM. Flandin, Mandel, Vallat, and Scapini. The lone negative ballot came from the former Premier, M. André Tardieu.[47] Some of the opposition which was not expressed in the Chamber found its way into the conservative press.[48]

As noted above, the debate and vote gave little indication of the solid resistance to Franco-Soviet rapprochement which existed in certain French circles. The Chamber's approval was nonetheless an important event. It was the first clear demonstration that a large number of French political leaders recognized the necessity for friendly relations with Russia. Secondly, the vote was assigned more importance abroad than it deserved. It was regarded as a chance to stand for or against the rapprochement with Russia and the result was looked upon as a decisive endorsement.

It is impossible to know whether or not the Soviet leaders shared in the exaggeration of the vote's meaning, but they quickly made the most of a good thing. M. Litvinov sent congratulatory telegrams to M. Paul-Boncour and to M. Herriot, thanking them for their parts in a manifestation which "greatly increases the value of the Franco-Soviet Pact."[49] An editorial in *Izvestya* interpreted the vote as a striking demonstration of French opinion and suggested that the pact be considered as a point of departure rather than an end in itself.[50]

Capped by the Chamber of Deputies debate, the series of events which had taken place since ratification of the Non-Aggression Pact in February were small but significant steps ahead on the route of Franco-Soviet rapprochement. Their importance lay

[47] For the remarks of M. Marin, see *J.O., Chambre, Débats*, pp. 2438-2440.
[48] See the attack in *Le Figaro*, quoted in "Revue de la presse," *J.D.*, 15 May 1933; Francois Coty's paper *L'Ami du Peuple* had several articles against the rapprochement during May and June. Pierre Bernus in *Journal des Débats* 20 May 1933 pointed to the renewal of the Berlin Treaty as proof that the Franco-Soviet Pact was worthless.
[49] *S.U.R.*, XI, 166-167, and *Le Temps*, 22, 24, 25 May 1933.
[50] *Izvestya*, 22 May 1933, quoted in *Bulletin de la presse russe*, No. 229.

as much in the realm of atmosphere as of substance. Coming in quick succession they lent the rapprochement a vitality that it had hitherto lacked.

ii

A new stage was opened when the Soviet Foreign Minister visited Paris, 6-7 July 1933. Maxim Litvinov had just attracted a flurry of headlines by his extracurricular diplomacy at the World Economic Conference in London. For one thing, he and Sir John Simon had worked out an agreement ending the crisis in Anglo-Soviet relations caused by the "Metro-Vickers" trial of British engineers in Moscow. His conversations with Secretary of State Cordell Hull were widely interpreted as smoothing the way for the recognition of the Soviet Union by the United States. Then on 3, 4, and 5 July the Soviet diplomat signed three "Conventions for the Definition of Aggression" with representatives of Persia, Afghanistan, Turkey, Poland, Romania, Yugoslavia, Czechoslovakia, Lithuania, Latvia, and Estonia.[51] The treaties provided that their signatories "recognize" in their mutual relations the definition of aggression used at the Disarmament Conference, of which M. Litvinov himself had been the original author.

By these accords the Soviet Union improved the security of its long frontiers in Europe and the Middle East, and opened the road to the restoration of normal relations with the Little Entente states. Romania and Yugoslavia were the prizes.[52] M. Titulescu's signature indicated that a way had been found around the Bessarabian question, the obstacle which had blocked the Soviet-Romanian Non-Aggression Pact in 1932.[53] In the case of Yugoslavia,

[51] The Convention of 3 July comprised states on the Russian frontiers: Persia, Afghanistan, Turkey, Romania, Poland, Latvia, Estonia, and the U.S.S.R. Lithuania, because of her quarrel with Poland, signed a separate convention with the U.S.S.R., 5 July. The third convention was signed 4 July by the U.S.S.R., Turkey, Czechoslovakia, and Romania; it was left open for other states, and Finland later adhered to it. Texts of the conventions may be found in *D.I.A., 1933*, pp. 230-233; *L'Europe Nouvelle*, XVI, 29 July 1933, 731-732.

[52] The adherence of Czechoslovakia was not surprising, for it had long favored the restoration of diplomatic relations with the U.S.S.R.

[53] The convention made no reference at all to Bessarabia, which could be taken as a tacit Russian recognition of Romanian sovereignty over Bessarabia. The Romanian Under-Secretary of State for Foreign Affairs "expressed the keenest satisfaction . . . at the conclusion of this pact, which, he said, removed from Roumania the constant nightmare of an attack from beyond the Dniester, which had so long oppressed her." Dispatch of Mr. Palairet, Bucharest, 7 July 1933, *B.F.P.*, VII, 590.

the convention was the first diplomatic instrument of importance signed with Soviet Russia and marked the softening of the most deep-seated anti-Soviet feelings of any government in Europe. Capitalizing on fears of the Four Power Pact and the Hugenberg Memorandum, Litvinov fashioned a diplomatic success of the first order.

The conventions gave another impetus to the Polish-Soviet rapprochement, which now reached a remarkable degree of warmth considering the basic antagonisms existing on both sides. In the spring and summer of 1933 an exchange of air missions took place, a Soviet trade delegation came to Warsaw, and the editor of the semi-official Warsaw journal, the *Gazeta Polska,* journeyed to Moscow.[54] Returning the latter's visit, the Polish-born editor of *Izvestya,* Karl Radek, made a trip to Poland in July. Radek stayed for over two weeks, toured the vital areas of the new Poland such as the Corridor, Gdynia, and Danzig, and had important talks with Polish leaders. Then, as Colonel Beck tells it, the Soviet envoy put forward an audacious suggestion: "the concept of a common protection of the Baltic states."[55] The Poles replied evasively, as they were already weighing the prospects of a deal with Germany, but the very suggestion demonstrates the progress of the *détente* between Warsaw and Moscow.

The Soviet advances towards the Little Entente and Poland made an excellent impression in Paris. Indeed, the "Conventions for the Definition of Aggression" won applause from circles noted for their hostility to the Soviet Union.[56] The treaties were widely interpreted as confirmation that Moscow's shift from revision to the status quo was not merely a matter of words but of action.

It was thus with enhanced prestige that M. Litvinov came to Paris, and he was treated appropriately. He was formally received by the Premier, M. Daladier, and had important conversations with M. Paul-Boncour at the Quai d'Orsay. On 7 July he was guest of honor at a banquet attended by M. Paul-Boncour, M. Anatole de Monzie, Minister of National Education and a prominent champion of the rapprochement, and several other cabinet ministers. The Soviet diplomat responded by issuing a broad invitation.

[54] Beck, *Dernier Rapport,* pp. 35-37; *B.F.P.,* VII, 550, 557, 587, 591; *S.U.R.,* XI, 167; *Le Temps,* 24 July 1933; Wheeler-Bennett, *The Pipe Dream of Peace,* pp. 155-157; *Polish White Book,* pp. 175-178.
[55] Beck, *Dernier Rapport,* pp. 36-37.
[56] For favorable comments from critics, see Pertinax in *L'Echo de Paris,* 29 July 1933; René Puaux in *Revue Politique et Parlementaire,* XLI, 10 Aug. 1933, 383; O. Rosenfeld in *Le Populaire,* 4 July 1933.

We are glad to note that the Soviet Union's peaceful policy is meeting with ever greater understanding in France.... Neither politically nor economically do our interests conflict with those of France in any part of the world, and therefore in our view there is no obstacle to further political and economic rapprochement.[57]

Two days later, in a major speech in the Provence, M. Daladier included a cordial reference to better relations with Russia, the Premier's first bow in that direction.[58]

It is likely that Litvinov exploited his warm reception to broach the idea of putting Franco-Soviet relations on a tighter basis. The probability is suggested by the fact that the Soviet Ambassador in Paris shortly made overtures of this nature, proposing "exchanges of information." The Soviet advances were welcomed and some further talks between Soviet Ambassador Dovgalevsky and M. Paul-Boncour did take place in the summer, but the Quai d'Orsay responded cautiously and did not put these exchanges on a formal basis.[59] There is evidence that future accords between the two countries were also canvassed—one idea, which did not materialize, was that France should adhere to the Convention for the Definition of Aggression which included the Little Entente.[60] The conversations of July and August, then, were only exploratory in nature, but they contained the germ of future negotiations.

These political discussions were not to slumber in leisurely diplomatic channels.[61] They were quickly stimulated by the voyages to Russia of two leading Frenchmen—one on a colorful per-

[57] Degras, *Soviet Documents on Foreign Policy*, III, 30-31; *Le Temps*, 9 July 1933. Text of the communiqué on Litvinov-Paul-Boncour talks, *ibid.*, 7 July.
[58] Speech at Apt, near Avignon, *Le Temps*, 10 July 1933.
[59] Consult the official report to the Chamber of Deputies on the Franco-Soviet Pact. *J.O.*, Chambre, *Documents*, 1935, Session Extraordinaire, Annexe No. 5792, 10 Dec. 1935, pp. 161-169, Rapport fait au nom de la Commission des Affaires Étrangères chargé d'examiner le projet de loi portant approbation des Traité et Protocole signés le 2 Mai 1935 entre la France et l'Union des Républiques Soviétistes [*sic*] Socialistes, par M. Henry Torrès, Député (hereinafter cited as *Rapport Torrès*).
[60] *Le Temps*, 23, 24 July 1933; *Journal des Débats*, 23 July 1933; J. W. Wheeler-Bennett in *B.I.N.*, X, 100.
[61] The Ministry of National Education, headed by M. Anatole de Monzie, aided the rapprochement by starting a program of Franco-Russian cultural exchanges. M. Rodrigues, an official of the Ministry, visited Moscow early in August to make the arrangements. See the extracts from *Izvestya*, 8 Aug. 1933, quoted in *Bulletin de la presse russe*, No. 232; Rapport fait au nom de la Commission des Finances chargé d'examiner le projet de lois portant fixation du budget général de l'exercice 1933 (Affaires Étrangères) par M. Adrien Dariac, *J.O.*, Chambre, *Documents*, 1933, session extraordinaire, séance de 19 Dec. 1933, Annexe No. 2725, p. 501.

sonal tour, the other on an official mission. First away was M. Édouard Herriot, who set sail from Marseilles for the "awakening East." Taking along a small political retinue, he stopped briefly in Greece, Turkey, and Bulgaria, and reached Russian shores at Odessa, 26 August. With stages at Kiev, Kharkhov, and Rostov-on-the-Don, he finally arrived in Moscow 1 September, and spent ten days in the Soviet capital he had first seen in 1922.[62]

M. Herriot traveled with no official instructions; indeed Premier Daladier was annoyed by the trip. Herriot thus could claim that he was merely engaged in an unofficial personal survey. But his prestige, the fact that he was met at Odessa and thereafter escorted by the French Ambassador, his interviews with Litvinov and Molotov, the banquets in his honor attended by Red Army notables such as Voroshilov, Tukachevsky, Budenny—all these created a much different impression. The Soviets did everything possible to magnify the event, emphasizing his powerful positions in party and parliament, and playing up his promises to work for the rapprochement in the future.[63] In the course of his travels M. Herriot investigated state and collective farms, heavy industries, the Dnieprostroi dam, a military school, and the Aero-dynamics Institute in Moscow, not to mention social and cultural institutions, but he fell somewhat short of the critical observer. Determined to court the Russians, he declared himself delighted with everything he saw, even to the point of denying the existence of the famine.[64]

After his return to France Herriot praised the rising Russian power in industry and military forces, and urged his countrymen to take advantage of it. "Because the [Russian] people demand to be the friend of France, because I heard there the most kind and

[62] Herriot was accompanied by three Radical-Socialists, Deputies Margaine and Julien and Senator Serlin. He described his trip in *Orient* (Paris, 1934), translated as *Eastward from Paris* (London, 1935). Daily reports may be found in *Le Temps* and *Journal des Débats*, 28 Aug.–12 Sept. 1933; in special articles by Pierre Berland, Moscow correspondent, *Le Temps*, 21 and 24 Sept.; and in *Bulletin de la presse russe*, No. 232, a very detailed account. Geneviève Tabouis, reputed to be Herriot's confidante in the French press, covered part of the trip for *L'Oeuvre*, 17, 18 Sept. 1933; see also her book, *Ils l'ont appelée Cassandre* (New York, 1942), pp. 162-168.
[63] Report of the German Military Attaché in Moscow, 19 Sept., *G.F.P.*, I, 820-821; extracts from editorials in *Izvestya*, 27 Aug. and 2 Sept. and *Pravda* 2 Sept., quoted in *Le Temps*, 28 Aug., 3 Sept. 1933. For Herriot's statements about working for the rapprochement in the future, see those quoted in 4, 6, 8, 9 Sept. *Le Temps*, *Journal des Débats*, 4 Sept. 1933, and *S.U.R.*, XI, 217.
[64] Speech at Lyons, 14 Sept., quoted in *Le Temps*, 15 Sept. 1933.

most friendly words for our country, I ask you: is it not my duty as a Frenchman and a republican to rejoice at these remarks . . . ?"[65] In his reports to government and parliamentary circles, Herriot transmitted proposals made to him by Litvinov, Radek, and President Kalinin. They consisted of general suggestions that the two countries form an alliance.[66]

Herriot's voyage had more impact on his own resolve and on the public than it did on the government's intentions. His chances of persuading public opinion now were enhanced by the ability to point to a personal survey. Most important, this influential politician came home convinced of the rightness of his campaign for alliance with Russia.[67]

Even as Herriot was disembarking, the French Air Minister, a young Radical-Socialist named Pierre Cot, took off from Le Bourget airfield leading an official aviation mission to the Soviet Union. Taking along the newest Gallic aviation heroes, the world's long distance record holders, Codos and Rossi, M. Cot's squadron flew by way of Kiev and Kharkhov, arriving in Moscow 15 September 1933. The trip was billed as a purely "technical mission," but this was a widely disregarded interpretation.[68] As the first visit of a minister of the French government to the Soviet Union, its political significance was undeniable and was increased by the fact that Cot was the head of a military service. Indeed, the Cot mission had been approved by the Foreign Ministry and by the staff of General Weygand at the War Ministry.[69] This was the second hint,

[65] Speech at Le Blanc to the Radical-Socialist Federation of the Department of Indre, quoted in *Le Temps*, 19 Sept. Note his remarks on arrival at Lyons, and at a meeting of the Conseil-Général of the Rhône, quoted in *Le Temps*, 15, 16 Sept. 1933.

[66] Herriot, *Eastward from Paris*, pp. 213, 273, and *Jadis*, II, 437; *B.F.P.*, VI, 753-754; *Rapport Torrès*, p. 163; Pertinax, "France, Russia and the Pact of Mutual Assistance," *Foreign Affairs*, XIII (Jan. 1935), 227.

[67] "It was imperative to smother all mistrust, forget prejudices, and deal with Russia aboveboard and directly. . . . Such was the talk heard from M. Herriot and in his circle." Pertinax, *ibid.*, p. 227; also Tabouis, *Ils l'ont appelée Cassandre*, pp. 167-168.

[68] Consult *Le Temps*, 27 Aug., 13 Sept. 1933; Pierre Cot, *Le Procès de la République* (New York, 1944), I, 64.

[69] In the ratification debate on the pact, M. Cot stated: "Lorsque je me suis rendu en Russie, il y a deux ans, nous avons consulté non seulement le ministère des affaires étrangères, mais le ministère de la guerre. . . . Et le directeur de mon cabinet était en liaison avec un officier du cabinet du général Weygand, qui fut ainsi au courant de tous nos projets et qui n'a pas fait la moindre objection, bien au contraire." *J.O.*, Chambre, *Débats*, 27 Feb. 1936, p. 627.

after the exchange of military attachés, that French military leaders approved of the rapprochement.

The Cot mission, which included General Barès, Inspector General of the French Air Force, as well as top technical experts, spent a week in Russia visiting aeronautical factories, schools, and technical institutes, and observing the maneuvers of aviation units of the Red Army.[70] The Air Minister himself also had conferences with Litvinov and Tukachevsky. Once again, the Russians gave their guest the plush treatment. "The reception of the Minister in Kiev, Kharkov, and Moscow had the character of an international military tribute, new for Russia: tricolor decorations at the airport and at the hotel; guard of honor reviewed by the Minister as they marched by; honorary escort by a Russian fighter wing of the 20th Air Brigade on the flight from Kharkhov to Moscow. . . ."[71] And again, the Soviet press made great play of the visit. *Izvestya* predicted "a more complete and regular exchange of technical experience between Soviet and French aviation circles," a co-operation which could be "extraordinarily useful for both countries."[72]

The results of the Cot mission were twofold. The French aviators and technicians were surprised and impressed by the technical progress of the Soviet aviation industry in some fields and by experiments in parachute troops and dive bombing.[73] As a result, an exchange of air attachés took place and some form of technical collaboration between the two air forces was established early in 1934.[74] This contact was made just after the Germans departed their air training station in Russia at Lipetzk. Only three days after the Russian military leaders drank farewell toasts to the German officers leaving Lipetzk, they lifted their glasses to M. Cot and the officers of the French Air Force.

[70] *Le Temps*, daily reports, 13-25 Sept. 1933 and the article by Pierre Berland, Moscow correspondent, 27 Sept.: Cot, *Le Procès de la République*, I, 64-65 and II, 226-227; Tabouis, *Ils l'ont appellée Cassandre*, pp. 168-171.

[71] Report of the German Military Attaché in Moscow, 19 Sept. 1933, *G.F.P.*, I, 821.

[72] *Izvestya*, 15 Sept. 1933, quoted in *S.U.R.*, XI, 217; see other extracts from the Soviet press in *Le Temps*, 16, 17 Sept. 1933, in *Bulletin de la presse russe*, No. 233.

[73] Cot's declaration to the press, *Le Temps*, 25 Sept. 1933 and *Le Procès de la République*, I, 64-65 and II, 226-227; article by Max Dekeyser, member of Cot's staff, *Le Temps*, 28 Sept. 1933; Castellan, "Reichswehr et l'Armée Rouge" in Duroselle, ed., *Les Relations Germano-Soviétiques, 1933-1939*, p. 205; *B.F.P.*, VII, 615-616.

[74] In addition to the sources cited above, consult the speech of M. Paul-Boncour, *J.O.*, Chambre, *Débats*, 14 Nov. 1933, p. 4104; Herriot, *Jadis*, II, 389.

Like his predecessor, the French Air Minister served as the bearer of political advances from the Russian bear, in this case of a more definite character. M. Cot handed to M. Paul-Boncour a proposal from Litvinov that the two countries should conclude a security pact. What Litvinov had in mind was a tight, "unconditional" alliance by which France and Russia would automatically come to each other's assistance wherever attacked.[75]

The most intriguing aspect of the various Franco-Soviet talks which took place in July, August, and September 1933 is that the initiative came entirely from the Russian side. Through the Soviet Ambassador in Paris, through Herriot and Cot, Litvinov pressed the French for a tight bond, if possible an alliance. Such insistence is tribute to the degree of insecurity that Hitler and the Japanese had created in Moscow.

To these Russian advances, the government of M. Édouard Daladier opposed a friendly but evasive attitude; they were not turned down but neither were they acted upon. Official French policy towards the Soviet Union at this time was limited to the establishment of cordial relations. A lively desire to profit from the opportunity of Russo-German tension was balanced by skepticism about the need for a further treaty.[76] The cautious attitude of the Quai d'Orsay was revealed by the comments of one of its officials on the Herriot and Cot voyages. It was hoped that the two visits would make an impression in Berlin. "Of course, the idea of any such thing as an alliance between France and Russia, similar to that which existed before the war, was entirely premature and out of the question for the moment."[77]

[75] Paul-Boncour, *Entre Deux Guerres*, II, 364; M. Leger to Elizabeth R. Cameron, "Alexis Saint-Léger Léger," Craig and Gilbert, eds., *The Diplomats, 1919-1939*, p. 385; résumés of Franco-Soviet negotiations made by French and British officials in June and July 1934, *B.F.P.*, VI, 753-754, 769, 776, 778, 804.

[76] This combination was expressed in the frequently inspired "Bulletin du Jour," *Le Temps*, 29 Aug. 1933. After listing the changes in Soviet policy, the editorial warned against illusions. The Soviet Union remained a revolutionary power; only its internal difficulties and fear of German and Japanese aggression forced it to search for political support in Europe. "Il serait téméraire de voir, pour l'instant, autre chose dans l'évolution de la politique des Soviets mais cela n'empêche point celle-ci d'offrir un réel intérêt pour l'ensemble de la situation internationale."

[77] Statement of an official of the Russian affairs section in the Quai d'Orsay, Dispatch of the United States Chargé d'Affaires, Mr. Marriner, 19 Sept. 1933, 751.61/140, Archives of the Department of State, Washington, D.C. See the résumé of Franco-Soviet negotiations, *B.F.P.*, VI, 753-754.

iii

Geography as well as skepticism counseled against trying to brace French security by means of Russia alone. Italy was close at hand; it would be wise to disarm her threat and to seek her support. Recent French cabinets had cherished the intention, but nothing had been done. While still Premier, Herriot had addressed a friendly "gesture" towards Rome in his speech at Toulouse, 6 November 1932, even admitting that France had not treated Italy well after the war. The lack of any response from Rome, incidentally, helped to embitter Herriot against Italy and presumably increased his determination to push hard on the Russian affair.[78] When Paul-Boncour took over the Quai d'Orsay, he appointed a special envoy as the new Ambassador to Rome, Senator Henry de Jouvenel. But the first two months of De Jouvenel's mission, January and February 1933, were also unsuccessful, Mussolini eluding all attempts to pin him down.[79] Simultaneously, Hitler's accession to power turned the French motives from interest to desire.

The French leaders were thus in a delicate position when Mussolini sprang his famous brainchild, the Four Power Pact. They could scarcely say "No" when they had just begun to solicit his good will. The Premier, M. Daladier, welcomed the pact as an avenue to explore conciliation with Germany as well as with Italy. M. Paul-Boncour would have none of Germany; he accepted the pact in order to lure Mussolini from the German to the French side.[80] The Four Power Pact was bitterly criticized, but it received powerful support from several dignitaries who were Italophiles: former premiers Pierre Laval and Joseph Caillaux, the President of the Senate Foreign Affairs Commission, Henry Bérenger, and the Minister of National Education, Anatole de Monzie.

When the pact was concluded 7 June 1933, Mussolini publicly thanked the French government for "an example of collaboration

[78] Herriot's Toulouse speech, quoted in *Le Temps,* 7 Nov. 1932; his memoirs, *Jadis,* II, 319 ff.; Aloisi, *Journal,* pp. 20 ff.; *B.F.P.,* IV, 324, and V, 361-362; *F.R.U.S., 1932,* I, 479.

[79] J. Paul-Boncour, *Entre Deux Guerres,* II, 339-340; Aloisi, *Journal,* pp. 46 ff. Consult Binion, *Defeated Leaders: The Political Fate of Caillaux, Jouvenel, and Tardieu,* chap. xv; Hubert Lagardelle, *Mission à Rome. Mussolini* (Paris, 1955), pp. 3-16.

[80] Speech of 6 April 1933, *J.O.,* Chambre, *Débats,* 6 April 1933, p. 1949; Paul-Boncour, *Entre Deux Guerres,* and testimony to the Parliamentary Commission, *Les Événements Survenus en France de 1933 à 1945,* III, 791.

in the European sphere, of which full recognition is due to her. In the better atmosphere created by the Four-Power Pact, it is perfectly possible to achieve prompt liquidation . . . of the particular questions which separate France and Italy."[81] A few days later, Quai d'Orsay officials told the British Ambassador that the cabinet was anxious "to reach a general settlement [with Italy] without delay." They wanted to include an arbitration treaty, an agreement on Tunisia and Libya, and resolution of the Italian-Yugoslavian feud.[82]

M. Paul-Boncour set to work to carry out this intention, and during the summer the Franco-Italian connection began to develop. In September and early October 1933, the French and Italians joined with the British and Americans to construct a common disarmament program. The Quai d'Orsay also revived the naval negotiations which had collapsed in March 1931, and considerable progress was made towards a Franco-Italian agreement to limit naval construction.[83]

Central Europe was the obstacle. It was an open scandal that Rome gave powerful support to separatist elements seeking to sabotage the new Yugoslavia. Justifiably, the Quai d'Orsay wanted Mussolini "to acknowledge that he will collaborate in a policy of stabilization in Central and South-Eastern Europe rather than pursue any disruptive designs based on the break-up of Yugoslavia or other alterations of the *status-quo*."[84] Mussolini's evasion of a specific assurance about Yugoslavia gave rise to uneasiness in Paris. However, Hitler made it easy for the two countries to co-operate by his coveting of Austria.

Both Italy and France desperately needed an independent Austria. If German troops held Vienna and patrolled the Brenner, the French Army would be cut off from Czechoslovakia and Mussolini would be shut out of the Danube valley. Rome had stoutly opposed the Austro-German Customs Union Plan of 1931 and shortly after Hitler's accession Mussolini stated privately that he must

[81] Quoted in *D.I.A., 1933*, pp. 273-274. See also *B.F.P.*, V, 478-479; Lagardelle, *Mission à Rome. Mussolini*, pp. 43-51; Louis Planté, *Un Grand Seigneur de la Politique: Anatole de Monzie* (Paris, 1955), pp. 175-182.

[82] Dispatch from Lord Tyrrell, 12 June 1933, *B.F.P.*, V, 349, also 383.

[83] Paul-Boncour, *Entre Deux Guerres*, II, 351-353; Aloisi, *Journal*, pp. 163, 169-170, 173-174; *B.F.P.*, V, 478-479, 702, and VI, 20.

[84] Statement of M. Léger to Lord Tyrrell, 30 June 1933, *B.F.P.*, V, 383, also 399; note also Aloisi, *Journal*, p. 136. Aloisi's notes contain many references to Italian support of Croatian separatism; see especially pp. 40, 41-42, 48, 60.

now intensify his vigilance. "The Danube Basin is our European hinterland. That is why we seek a firm position there. Without it we shall be forced to play the insignificant role of a peninsula on the periphery of Europe."[85] Hitler admired Mussolini and wanted an alliance with Italy, but he had conveniently decided that the Italian Empire should be in the Mediterranean. Austria was his homeland, the first step in the reunion of all Germans.

Mussolini reacted quickly to the challenge, warning Hitler as early as 14 March that "as far as Anschluss was concerned, it was well known that Italy could never permit this and therefore had to oppose all efforts in this direction."[86] When this advice failed to soften the Nazi pressure on Austria, Mussolini hurriedly threw commercial and diplomatic support behind the sturdy little Austrian Chancellor, Engelbert Dollfuss. Dollfuss came to Rome twice in the spring of 1933, and when he returned for a special visit with Mussolini at Riccione, he received this promise: "If contrary to Mussolini's expectations an invasion from Bavaria were to occur, Italy would react in a military way."[87] The French had misgivings about Mussolini's methods, but they reasoned that the more he involved himself in Austria the more chance that he might find himself in an open feud with Hitler. For these stakes, the French acquiesced in Italian predominance at Vienna.[88]

The emergence of Nazi Germany thus provided the occasion for French reconciliation with Italy even as it stimulated the Franco-Soviet rapprochement. Although they proceeded at different

[85] Conversation with Prince Starhemberg, leader of the Austrian Heimwehr, a nationalist paramilitary association, Ernst Rüdiger Prince von Starhemberg, *Between Hitler and Mussolini* (New York, 1942), pp. 105-106.

[86] Statement of the Italian Ambassador to Baron von Neurath in presenting the original draft of the Four Power Pact, 14 March 1933, *G.F.P.*, I, 162.

[87] Notes of the Riccione talks, 19-20 Aug. 1933, apparently dictated by Dollfuss for the Foreign Office files. Documents from the Austrian archives presented by Paul R. Sweet, in an Appendix to Julius Braunthal, *The Tragedy of Austria* (London, 1948), p. 194; see also pp. 173-174, 197-198. Compare with *Geheimer Briefwechsel Mussolini-Dollfuss* (Wien, 1949), pp. 34-35, 41. Mussolini's determination to resist *Anschluss* is confirmed in *B.F.P.*, V, 408, 512, 534-535, 646-647, 675, and in Aloisi, *Journal*, pp. 104 ff.

[88] On French support of Italian policy in Austria, consult Charles de Chambrun, French Ambassador in Rome from August 1933 to 1936, *Traditions et Souvenirs* (Paris, 1952), pp. 187-192; Paul-Boncour *Entre Deux Guerres*, II, 359-361; Aloisi, *Journal*, pp. 148, 152; *B.F.P.*, V, 566-567. Mussolini boasted to Hubert Lagardelle, French Cultural Attaché in Rome and one of Mussolini's maîtres during his socialist days, of "le soutien total que j'apporte à l'Autriche contre le Reich, et qui peut me conduire, demain, à une intervention directe." Lagardelle, *Mission à Rome. Mussolini*, p. 75.

speeds, these two movements henceforth ran on parallel lines. The combination was very attractive to French public opinion. The Left was appeased in its hatred of Mussolini by the reminder that France was working closely with Soviet Russia. The Right was distracted from its hatred of Stalin when the Foreign Minister could point to his collaboration with Mussolini. Geographically and ideologically, the rapprochements with Italy and Russia provided balance in the new French design.

iv

The flight of Air Minister Pierre Cot to Moscow was proof enough that the Franco-Soviet rapprochement was a force to be reckoned with. Every diplomat knew that the French government would not have lightly approved such a public demonstration. Why, then, was the government reluctant to take further steps?

One reason for their reticence was the momentary calm of the international scene. In the summer of 1933 neither the Premier, nor the Foreign Minister, nor the high officials of the Quai d'Orsay judged that the circumstances warranted a new pact with Russia. The diplomatic position of France had been strengthened by the public evidence of her collaboration with Russia and Italy, while the Four Power Pact kept the door open to negotiations with Germany. The conciliatory policies of the Daladier government had sensibly improved the tone of Franco-British relations and had minimized financial and economic difficulties with the United States.

The second reason for traveling slowly on the Russian road involved the personal attitude of the Premier himself. Édouard Daladier was, after Laval, the second of the new political generation to reach the pinnacle of French politics. After his cabinet fell in October, he retained the influential Ministry of War in the next two cabinets, and was reappointed Premier in February 1934. From 1933 on, Daladier was at the center of French politics and, indeed, was the most representative French leader of the decade of the thirties.[89]

[89] Consult Daladier's testimony at Riom, Feb.-March 1942, reprinted in *Les Grandes Journées du Procès de Riom*, ed. Pierre Mazé and Roger Genebrier (Daladier's lawyers at Riom), Préface de Édouard Daladier (Paris, 1945); articles in *Minerve*, (Paris, weekly), 5 and 12 April 1946; speech of 18 July 1946, *J.O., Débats de l'Assemblée Constituante*, 19 July 1946, pp. 2678-2710; testimony of 21

Born in 1884 in the old Provençal town of Carpentras, near Avignon, the son of a baker, Édouard Daladier was a man of the provinces, and he never fully exchanged his simplicity for the sophistication of Paris. Singled out as a student by his mother, in 1909 he won the distinguished rank of Agrége, in history, and struck out on a teaching career combined with local politics. His war record was superb. In four years of infantry service—some of it in the murderous exchanges at Verdun—Daladier rose from the ranks to first lieutenant and won four citations for bravery.

He turned definitely to politics in 1919, winning election to the Chamber of Deputies from his department, the Vaucluse, at the top of the Radical-Socialist list. In 1924 his former professor and political patron, Édouard Herriot, gave Daladier his first executive experience by appointing him to the cabinet.[90] But the two men broke on political and personal grounds in 1926, Daladier becoming the focus of a "Young Turk" opposition to Herriot's leadership of the Radical-Socialist party. From this point dated a sour rivalry, lovingly known to Parisian journalists as "the war of the two Edwards."[91]

When the Left returned to power in June 1932, Daladier served in the Herriot and Paul-Boncour cabinets and was the logical choice when the latter's ephemeral combination fell apart. His appointment as Premier and Minister of War, 31 January 1933, was greeted by a good press—the product of his war record, his capable, unpretentious work in Parliament, and several attractive paradoxes. A native of the Midi, famed for its eloquence, he spoke plainly and infrequently; a leader of the Radicals' left wing, he was not an extremist; and, by training an intellectual, he did not look nor talk like one. Short, stocky build, a rather sad, frowning face, and a rough voice had suggested the nickname of "Le Taureau du

May 1947 before the Parliamentary Commission, *Les Évènements Survenus en France de 1933 à 1945*, I, 7-82, see also IX, 2887-2891. Portraits of Daladier are in Yvon Lapaquellerie, *Édouard Daladier* (Paris, 1939), Pertinax, *Les Fossoyeurs* (New York, 1943), I, "Gamelin-Daladier-Reynaud," 107-199; Werth, *France in Ferment*, pp. 27-28, 63-64, 120 ff.; Paul-Boncour, *Entre Deux Guerres*, II, 386; Weygand, *Mirages et Réalité*, pp. 393 ff.

[90] Daladier was Minister of Colonies in the 1924 Herriot cabinet and Minister of Public Instruction in the 1926 Herriot cabinet. Herriot took Daladier along on his trip to Russia in 1922.

[91] Daladier opposed Herriot's participation in Poincaré's Government of National Union, 1926-1928. Herriot was President of the Radical-Socialist party from 1921-1925, Daladier from 1927-1930, Herriot from 1931-1934, and Daladier again from 1935-1940.

Vaucluse," but this image of a bull was partly deceptive, for this was not a man of aggressive charges.

The new Premier's approach to foreign policy was flexible, but one trait was clear: his rejection of uncompromising nationalism, his distaste for the old policy of no concessions to Germany and of reliance on the French alliance system. "With all the force of my convictions, I wish to express and I shall translate into all my actions, my considered and unshakable will to spare our country violence and adventures."[92] This position was partly the result of his desire to walk hand in hand with the British. Deeper and more permanent were his hope of avoiding war and his sense of French weakness. He shared with millions of his countrymen a sincere revulsion against the thought of another ordeal such as that of 1914-1918.[93] Day and night in the trenches, he had seen the unparalleled sacrifices which victory had required. He also took a thoroughly realistic view of French inferiority to Germany in population and in industrial capacity. These sentiments did not tempt Daladier into pacifism; he was concerned that France be well prepared should conflict come. Politics is, however, a question of emphasis, and with Daladier the emphasis was placed on preventing the outbreak of a new conflict.

The new Premier was sympathetic to an understanding with Germany and believed that its prospects should be explored even with the Hitler regime. It was the Four Power Pact which first offered an opportunity. M. Daladier saw in it not only a vehicle of rapprochement with Italy but a means of improving the strained atmosphere between France and Germany.[94] The pact was vio-

[92] Speech at Apt, near Avignon, 9 July 1933, quoted in *Le Temps,* 10 July 1933. Note his statements to the British Chargé d'Affaires, 7 Sept. 1933, *B.F.P.,* V, 575.

[93] "Est-il besoin de dire que ce gouvernement formé d'hommes qui, pour la plupart, avaient connu, dans l'infanterie ou dans d'autres armes combattantes, la guerre de 1914 et avaient vu les effroyables pertes que la France avait subies, avait le désir profond d'essayer d'éviter que, de nouveau, reprenne en Europe une course aux armements dont on savait bien qu'elle se terminerait par une nouvelle guerre?" Testimony in 1947 to the Parliamentary Commission, *Les Événements Survenus en France de 1933 à 1945,* I, 10.

[94] Lord Tyrrell told Mr. Norman Davis that Daladier had said that: "if it were not for Herriot's opposition he [Daladier] would be willing to go to Berlin and to Rome to sit down and have a perfectly frank talk with Hitler and Mussolini now with regard to the proposed Four Power Pact and try to reach an agreement on political questions which would facilitate an early agreement on general disarmament." Letter of Norman Davis to Cordell Hull, 13 April 1933, *F.R.U.S., 1933,* I, 495.

lently attacked in France, and the British Ambassador in Paris, Lord Tyrrell, remarked that it would have fallen through, "had it not been for Daladier's personal courage and his desire to prove Germany's good faith."[95] After negotiations with Daladier 8 June, an American diplomat reported that "... following the initialling of the Four Power Pact it is quite obviously Daladier's intention to attempt to reach political agreement with Italy and following that with Germany."[96]

During the summer contacts between a confidential agent of M. Daladier, M. Fernand de Brinon, and a member of Hitler's entourage, Herr Joachim Ribbentrop, brought out the possibility of direct Franco-German conversations.[97] Although Daladier has denied that he had any serious hopes for this project, the talks progressed to the point where, with Daladier's approval, M. de Brinon journeyed twice to Germany and had two interviews with Hitler, 9 and 27 September 1933, and several talks with Ribbentrop and Reichswehr Minister General von Blomberg. Out of these conversations (which were kept secret from the Foreign Minister, M. Paul-Boncour) emerged vague plans for a meeting between Daladier and Hitler and a detailed proposal by General von Blomberg of a direct Franco-German understanding on armaments.[98] M. Da-

[95] Conversation between Lord Tyrrell and U.S. Ambassador Straus, Paris, 15 June 1933, *ibid.*, I, 420.

[96] Dispatch of Mr. Norman Davis, 15 June 1933, *F.R.U.S.*, *1933*, I, 192. For suggestions of this intention, consult Daladier's speech at Apt, *Le Temps*, 10 July 1933; the "Bulletin du Jour" editorials of *Le Temps*, 11 and 15 July 1933.

[97] The journalist Fernand de Brinon advocated Franco-German rapprochement. He had known Briand and Stresemann and had been in Laval's entourage during the voyage to Berlin in September 1931. Consult his book *France-Allemagne, 1918-1934* (Paris, 1934). He dates his meeting with Ribbentrop in 1932; he was invited to Berlin by Ribbentrop shortly afterwards and visits were exchanged frequently after Hitler came to power. De Brinon was named an officer of the Legion d'Honneur while Daladier was Premier, for "services exceptionnels rendus dans les missions à l'étranger." *Le Temps*, 18 Aug. 1933. On 16 March 1933 M. de Brinon told an official of the German Foreign Ministry that Daladier was willing to meet von Neurath or von Papen "for direct and discreet discussions" about disarmament. *G.F.P.*, I, 173.

[98] My interpretation of this obscure episode is based on the following sources: M. de Brinon's own accounts, in his *Memoirs* (Paris, 1949), pp. 27-29, 84-85; at his trial, 4-6 March 1947, *Les Procès de la Collaboration. Fernand de Brinon, Joseph Darnand, Jean Luchaire* (Paris, 1948), pp. 53-55, 78-80, 179, and 200-202; M. Daladier's testimony at the Riom trial, *Les Grands Journées du Procès Riom*, pp. 36-37; Anonymous, *La Verité sur Fernand de Brinon* (Paris, 1947); Ribbentrop's testimony at Nuremberg, I.M.T., *Proceedings ...*, X, 233; *The Ribbentrop Memoirs* (London, 1954), pp. 33-35; Paul-Boncour, *Entre Deux Guerres*, II, 385-387, 389-390, and testimony to the Parliamentary Commission. *Les Événements Survenus en*

ladier, although apparently more interested than he has been willing to admit,[99] did not feel able to take the long odds. While the project hung fire, a crisis in the Disarmament Conference took place and created a new situation.

The hazards of French politics thus brought to power a man who was sensitive to the fatigue of his country and tempted by the hope of reconciliation with Germany. His suspicions held him back, for he was well briefed by French Army Intelligence on the extent of clandestine German rearmament.[100] But his curiosity remained, and the rhetorical question which he asked in a speech at Vichy, 8 October 1933, was most revealing. "Where is the responsible statesman who could commend to his country . . . a policy of isolation, or throw her into a policy of antagonistic alliances, unless forced by necessity to do so?"[101]

M. Daladier's general approach to French foreign policy and his exploration of an understanding with Germany acted as a brake upon the Franco-Soviet rapprochement. His position should not be distorted. There is no doubt that he desired better relations with Russia as one of several means to reinforce French security. The point is that he preferred to keep the rapprochement within certain definite limits, limits that stopped short of an alliance.

France de 1933 à 1945, III, 790; *G.F.P.*, I, 803-805; *B.F.P.*, V, 432-433, 574-577, 580-584, and VI, 54-58.

[99] Note the remarks made by M. Daladier to Mr. Norman Davis, 19 Sept. 1933. *F.R.U.S.*, 1933, I, 223-224.

[100] George Castellan, *Le Réarmement Clandestin du Reich, 1930-1935.*

[101] *Le Temps*, 9 Oct. 1933; also extracts in *D.I.A.*, 1933, p. 402.

Seven

TALK OF AN ALLIANCE

In October 1933 Hitler again applied the spur to the Franco-Soviet rapprochement. The arena was the Disarmament Conference, which the Powers uneasily had adjourned in June and were now trying to revive. After much discussion throughout the month of September, the British, French, Italian, and United States governments reached a broad agreement on the principles of a Disarmament Convention. Its salient features were: that there should be two periods of four years each; that in the first period there should be no German rearmament in the weapons forbidden by the Versailles Treaty; that the armaments of the other powers should remain frozen during the first period and their destruction begin only in the second period.[1]

Despite vigorous German protests, the four powers, the Italians with reluctance, stuck to their agreement. Surprised at this rare show of solidarity, Hitler decided that "we must not run the risk of negotiating at all on a new draft that was, in the last analysis, unacceptable to us. Otherwise we would find that the others might agree on this plan and try to force us to accept it."[2] Lest such a dastardly example of compromise take place, Hitler made his plans and disclosed them to a special meeting of the cabinet at 6 P.M., 13 October 1933.

The Chancellor said that it was "absolutely impossible" to sign a convention which postponed German equality for four years.

It therefore becomes necessary to defeat the draft and thereby torpedo the Disarmament Conference.... We shall therefore have to leave both the Disarmament Conference and the League of Nations, since the condition that we be recognized as a nation with equality of rights is not fulfilled. In this situation our position can be strengthened

[1] For details on the disarmament negotiations of Sept.-Oct. 1933, consult *B.F.P.*, V; *G.F.P.*, I; *F.R.U.S., 1933*, I; Aloisi, *Journal*, pp. 143-154; Wheeler-Bennett, *The Pipe Dream of Peace*, pp. 164-183.

[2] Minute by State-Secretary von Bülow of a conference with Hitler and General von Blomberg, Berlin, 4 Oct. 1933, *G.F.P.*, I, 887.

if, at the same time as we make the announcement of our withdrawal . . .
we dissolve the Reichstag, call for new elections, and ask the German
people to identify themselves through a national plebiscite with the
peace policy of the Reich government. By these measures we will
make it impossible for the world to accuse Germany of an aggressive
policy.[3]

If there were some timid souls worried about sanctions, Hitler gave
the assurance that "it was only a matter of keeping cool. . . ."

The next morning, 14 October, a Saturday, Sir John Simon read
to the Bureau of the Disarmament Conference in Geneva an outline of the new program. Mr. Norman Davis, M. Paul-Boncour,
and the Marquis di Soragna rose to announce that their governments agreed in principle. But no sooner had the front united than
the blow fell.

Barely three hours after the session, a telegram from Baron von
Neurath arrived, containing the message that Germany was "com-
pelled to leave the Disarmament Conference."[4] Simultaneously,
manifestoes in Berlin told the German people that the government
would also withdraw from the League of Nations, dissolve the
Reichstag, and submit its decisions to the verdict of a national
plebiscite. That evening, in a radio address, the Chancellor based
his whole case upon German inequality, playing skilfully on the
theme of Versailles pledges never honored. He offered to continue disarmament negotiations away from Geneva and then made
a dramatic bid to France. He would have the "two peoples once
and for all . . . banish force from their common life." "I speak in the
name of the entire German people," said Hitler, "when I assert that
we are all filled with the sincere wish to root out . . . [this] enmity."[5]
It was an adroit performance, distracting many people from their
impulse "to accuse Germany of an aggressive policy."

Hitler could have committed no act of greater symbolic contrast to the era of Stresemann than to leave Geneva. Germany had
cast off the ties of international co-operation and was on her own.
The news created universal resentment at Geneva, but when it
came to deciding what to do, the cracks of disagreement quickly
reappeared. The desirability of a brief recess for consultation was
all that could be resolved. Thus, on 16 October, after sending a

[3] Minutes of the cabinet meeting, 13 Oct. 1933, *ibid.*, pp. 923-925.
[4] League of Nations, *Records of the Conference for the Reduction and Limitation of Armaments*, Series B, *Minutes of the General Commission*, III, 646.
[5] Baynes, *The Speeches of Hitler*, II, 1098-1099.

reply to Berlin rejecting the German government's reasons for withdrawal, the Bureau of the Disarmament Conference adjourned for a short period.[6]

There was no reason to expect that the delegates would return to their capitals to forge some firm common action. From Rome came discreet silence, and then hints that there were more ways than one to write a convention. Mussolini, though furious, was doing a rapid backtrack, afraid that he would lose all his influence in Berlin by siding too closely with France and England.[7] In London opinions were divided between the advisability of conciliatory or hostile reactions. Sir John Simon did refute the "very absurd suggestion" from Berlin that it was his speech to the Conference which had decided Germany's withdrawal. However, he added that the British government soon would resume discussions with all interested powers, including Germany.[8] Mr. Norman Davis tried to placate the nervous American isolationists; the United States, he said, was in Geneva for disarmament and only disarmament. "We are not ... interested in the political element or any purely European aspect of the picture.... Such unity of purpose as has existed has been entirely on world disarmament matters."[9]

The least of Hitler's worries were refutations and rejections. As he told the cabinet, 17 October, "threatening steps against Germany had neither materialized nor were they to be expected. Already ... the internal conflicts among the leading powers in the Disarmament Conference were evident. Germany could now let events take their course."[10] He had correctly gauged the flabbiness of his opponents, and the lesson was not lost.

M. Joseph Paul-Boncour led his delegation back to Paris already discouraged by the decision to adjourn at Geneva. He received no inspiration from the Premier nor any clear lead from

[6] *Minutes of the General Commission,* III, 645-648; *B.F.P.,* V, 682-691; *F.R.U.S., 1933,* I, 266-278.

[7] Aloisi, *Journal,* pp. 154 ff.; *B.F.P.,* V, 684 ff.; *F.R.U.S., 1933,* I, 269 ff., *G.F.P.,* II, 28 ff.; Lagardelle, *Mission à Rome. Mussolini,* pp. 58-63.

[8] Extracts from Sir John Simon's speech are quoted in *S.I.A., 1933,* pp. 308-309. Consult Wheeler-Bennett, *Pipe Dream of Peace,* pp. 190-191.

[9] Statement issued to the press in Geneva, by Mr. Davis, 16 Oct. 1933, *F.R.U.S., 1933,* I, 277. The statement had been wired to Davis by Secretary of State Hull; it had been approved by President Roosevelt, who was quite anxious to disassociate the United States from the crisis.

[10] *G.F.P.,* II, 12.

public opinion. French opinion was unanimous on the gravity of the German decision, but, with one or two exceptions, there was no desire for a vigorous rebuff to Germany.[11] Furthermore, Right and Left took up contradictory positions. The latter favored continuation of the disarmament negotiations, preferably at the Disarmament Conference, while most conservatives consigned disarmament to "the ash-can of history" and demanded the strengthening of French military forces and existing alliances. There were rumors that General Weygand, head of the French Army, proposed military measures such as the re-occupation of the Rhineland. Such a recommendation is highly doubtful, for Weygand was already profoundly concerned about the Army's short training period and aging weapons, and was unsuccessfully fighting against severe cuts in the Army budget.[12]

M. Paul-Boncour certainly found no iron in his chief. M. Daladier's first thoughts were that "France should remain calm in the face of yesterday's events in Germany."[13] He was resentful of the shock, but reluctant to take any action. Sensitive to the conciliatory trend of British policy and to the calmness of French opinion, unwilling to shut the door on negotiation with Germany, M. Daladier ruled out any retaliation. When Paul-Boncour urged that the Conference move quickly ahead to complete a detailed Disarmament Convention and face Germany with the choice of accepting or rejecting it, Daladier disapproved. "He did not want to break up anything."[14]

Finally, a sharp retort from Paris was precluded by a cabinet crisis. On 20 October, it was already predicted that the government's new budget would never pass the Chamber of Deputies. Two days later there was trouble in the Paris streets as the debate began, and on 24 October 1933 M. Daladier fell because of bitter

[11] An extensive coverage of opinions on the German withdrawal can be found in the "Revue de la presse" in *Le Temps* and "Revue de la presse" in *Journal des Débats*, 16-19 Oct. 1933. Lord Tyrrell's dispatch of 17 Nov. is instructive for the opinion of government circles, *B.F.P.*, VI, 54-58.

[12] Weygand, *Mirages et Réalité*, pp. 382 ff.; *B.F.P.*, V, 734; *F.R.U.S.*, *1933*, I, 279-281; articles by Pertinax in *L'Echo de Paris*, 15, 16 Oct. 1933.

[13] M. Léger, Secretary-General of the Quai d'Orsay, stated to the United States Chargé d'Affaires, 15 Oct., that this was Daladier's reaction. *F.R.U.S.*, *1933*, I, 270. Lord Tyrrell reported the same impression from talks with Léger and Daladier himself, *B.F.P.*, V, 690-692.

[14] Paul-Boncour's testimony to the Parliamentary Investigating Commission, *Les Événements Survenus en France de 1933 à 1945*, III, 790; also his memoirs, *Entre Deux Guerres*, II, 386-387.

opposition to the economies proposed in his budget. Just ten days after the German stroke, France was without a government.

M. Paul-Boncour stayed on at the Quai d'Orsay in the new cabinet formed by Albert Sarraut, a prominent Radical-Socialist.[15] The new Premier was almost entirely preoccupied with the financial and parliamentary crises, and had no time to dabble in diplomacy. Daladier retained the Ministry of War, and with it an influence on foreign policy, but he lost the control which he could exercise as Premier. The Foreign Minister thus found himself with much more freedom of action than he had previously enjoyed.

For Joseph Paul-Boncour Hitler's sudden withdrawal from the Disarmament Conference and the League of Nations was an unmistakable sign of the Nazi Chancellor's aggressive intentions. A few days passed and there vanished the solidarity of France, Italy, England, and the United States on which he had lavished so much planning and so many hours of persuasion. Hitler's defiance showed that this unity was, at worst, an illusion, at best an accidental crystallization. It was in this frame of mind, contemplating the debris of common purposes, that the French Foreign Minister turned sharply in the Russian direction. "The duty was . . . clear: to fortify our alliances and search out new ones."[16]

All his past pointed Paul-Boncour to this decision; indeed as a "fighting socialist" he was old-fashioned in the 1930's. It had been the action, the élan, of socialism which had attracted him in the first place, not the theories of Marx. He entered politics as an independent socialist and became Minister of Labor in 1911, but the anti-militarism of the Socialist Party kept him from joining it until 1916. Paul-Boncour fought bravely in the ordeal of 1914-1918; he rose to the rank of *chef de bataillon* and won the Croix de Guerre. After the war, he became one of the most successful Socialist orators in parliament and was the author of the famous proposed "Law on the Organization of the Nation in time of War." In 1931,

[15] M. Albert Sarraut, a Senator, was a conservative Radical-Socialist who had made a reputation as a colonial administrator in Indo-China and as Minister of Colonies; he had served in the latter post in the Herriot, Paul-Boncour, and Daladier cabinets. His cabinet, which was confirmed by the Chamber 4 Nov. 1933, was a reshuffle of the Daladier cabinet.

[16] *Entre Deux Guerres*, II, 361; the same explanation was given in testimony to the Parliamentary Investigating Commission in 1948. *Les Événements Survenus en France 1933 à 1945*, III, 793. When I interviewed him in Paris, 25 Nov. 1950, M. Paul-Boncour strongly emphasized the role played by the German withdrawal in his decision to open negotiations with the Soviets.

he decided that the rising influence of anti-militarism made it necessary for him to resign from the Socialist party. Although an ardent advocate of collective security and permanent French delegate to the League of Nations, Paul-Boncour had the realism and the respect for force that so many of his fellow internationalists lacked. A short, intense figure, his face still handsome and crowned with flowing white hair, this vibrant little Jacobin reacted sharply to the threat of *la patrie en danger.*

Paul-Boncour did not allow internal troubles to stifle his determination. As a young secretary to Waldeck-Rousseau, he had watched with admiration while the great man and Delcassé silently strengthened the Franco-Russian alliance and pressed the Franco-Italian rapprochement in the midst of the frenetic Dreyfus Affair. Despite the ill-tempered demonstrations in the streets near his office Paul-Boncour silently took the first step of a second Russian adventure.

A week after he returned from Geneva, M. Paul-Boncour called in his two top aides, MM. Léger and Bargeton, to review the unsettled diplomatic situation. "We set ourselves the following question; would it not be possible to form an alliance with Russia?"[17] As a result of their discussion, Paul-Boncour sounded out the Soviet Ambassador in Paris. On 31 October he made his approach directly to the Soviet Foreign Minister, Maxim Litvinov, who stopped for a day in Paris on his way to Washington.

M. Litvinov must have been delighted when his host opened the conversation by asking: "What do you think of an alliance between our two countries?"[18] But this was the easy part. What form and what scope for a Franco-Soviet treaty? In the preliminary discussions, Paul-Boncour and his aides had concluded: ". . . an accord with Russia could only take the form of a mutual assistance pact, analogous to the one which linked us to Poland, and, if possible, co-ordinated and built into it."[19] Therefore he immediately pointed out the desirability of linking the pact in some manner to the existing French alliances in eastern Europe.

M. Paul-Boncour took great pains to convince Litvinov that the scope of any Franco-Soviet entente must be limited to Europe.[20] France would not undertake any obligations in the Far

[17] *Les Événements Survenus en France de 1933 à 1945,* III, 793. M. Bargeton was Director of Political Affairs in the Foreign Ministry.
[18] *Ibid.*   [19] *Entre Deux Guerres,* II, 362.
[20] This account of the Paul-Boncour-Litvinov interview and subsequent negotia-

East. The categorical manner in which this reservation was made stemmed from fear that France would be drawn into the Soviet-Japanese conflict. In the summer and fall of 1933 tension between Moscow and Tokyo was higher than at any time since March 1932. In the same manner, in 1891, Alexander Ribot had begun the negotiations for an alliance with Tsarist Russia by trying to rule out the Far East.[21]

As the last of his conditions, the French Foreign Minister declared that he could not afford to make a mutual assistance pact with the Soviet Union unless the latter joined the League of Nations. This was not a matter of symbolic importance alone. In the event of war with Germany, Soviet membership in the League would provide a legal means for co-ordinating Soviet action with that of Poland, Romania, and through their territory, with Czechoslovakia. The League Covenant provided for co-operation in imposing sanctions against the aggressor. Article 16 stipulated that members of the League of Nations "will take the necessary steps to afford passage through their territory to the forces of any Members of the League which are co-operating to protect the covenants of the League."[22] The savants of the Quai d'Orsay hoped that the nasty problem of allowing Soviet troops to pass through Polish territory might be acceptable to the Poles if placed under the aegis and control of the League.

The most exigent reason for Soviet entry into the League was to prevent any injury to the Locarno Treaty. Under this treaty, France could not resort to war against Germany except in cases foreseen by Article 15, paragraph 7, and Article 16 of the Covenant of

tions is based on the following sources: Paul-Boncour's memoirs and testimony cited directly above; a personal interview with him, 25 Nov. 1950; his parliamentary speeches in *J.O., Sénat, Débats,* 12 March 1936, p. 264 and in *J.O., Assemblée Consultative Provisoire,* 21 Dec. 1944, pp. 583-585; *Rapport Torrès,* p. 163; Litvinov's statements to Ambassador Bullitt, 21 Dec. 1933, *F.R.U.S., The Soviet Union 1933-1939* (Washington, 1952), pp. 53-54, 60-61; statement by Soviet Ambassador Dovgalevsky, quoted in Herriot, *Jadis,* II, 391-392.

[21] Actually, the French could not afford to insist on the restriction and the Entente of 27 Aug. 1891 was world-wide in scope. However, the more important Military Convention of 1892 stipulated military action only against three European powers: Germany, Austria, and Italy.

[22] Article 16 applied to wars begun by Members of the League. Germany, of course, had just given notice of withdrawal from the League, and this withdrawal would become effective after two years. By Article 17 the provisions of Article 16 were applied to non-members of the League who refused to accept the obligations of the Covenant during the war.

the League, and in cases of "legitimate defence." If she violated these obligations, France would forfeit British assistance and might even cause British assistance to Germany. Therefore, a Franco-Soviet treaty providing for mutual assistance against Germany had to place that assistance squarely within the context of the League Covenant.[23]

From the accounts of his host, Maxim Litvinov did not try to conceal his pleasure at the prospect which now opened. However, he resisted the idea of joining the League, which the Soviet Union had derided for fourteen years. He also argued in favor of a purely bilateral alliance, consistent with his recent proposals. Paul-Boncour insisted upon his duty to protect previous French engagements. Without denying the possibility of meeting the French conditions, Litvinov pointed out that such vital decisions must be referred to Moscow; this was done while he continued on to Washington to negotiate for United States recognition of the Soviet Union.

A short while later the Soviet Ambassador in Paris communicated a favorable reply from the Kremlin, an acceptance hardly surprising in view of Litvinov's previous overtures. The Soviet government expressed its readiness to begin negotiations for a mutual assistance pact and for Soviet entry into the League of Nations.[24] The Soviet government, however, demanded that the preliminary negotiations to be kept absolutely secret. M. Paul-Boncour willingly acceded to this demand because of indiscretions suffered during his work on the Four Power Pact. He kept the negotiations to himself and his two assistants originally involved, and he did not report on the situation to the cabinet. Nor did he inform the British government of his move. What he did do was to inform the new Premier, M. Camille Chautemps, and receive permission to go ahead with negotiations.[25] Chautemps had been appointed 27 November 1933, after the fall of the ephemeral Sarraut cabinet; Paul-Boncour almost certainly waited until the cabinet, in which he retained the Foreign Ministry, was approved by

[23] The problem of squaring the Franco-Soviet pact with the Locarno treaties is discussed in detail in chap. ix, pp. 176-179, and in chap. xi, pp. 246-250.

[24] Paul-Boncour's testimony in *Les Événements Survenus en France de 1933 à 1945*, III, 794.

[25] Paul-Boncour, *Entre Deux Guerres*, II, 365-369; Cameron, "Alexis Saint-Léger Léger," in Craig and Gilbert, eds., *The Diplomats*, p. 385.

the Chamber of Deputies, 2 December.[26] The French and Soviet governments, then, began formal negotiations for a mutual assistance pact in Paris early in December 1933.

ii

M. Paul-Boncour would never have adopted such a bold tactic entirely on his own. He enjoyed the support of the permanent staff of the Quai d'Orsay, notably the erudite and critical Secretary-General, M. Alexis Saint-Léger Léger.[27] And he found the General Staff, in his words, "a warm partisan" of the entente.[28]

Such a patronage was quite surprising in view of the conservative, often reactionary, political views of the Army and especially of its head, General Weygand. However, Weygand and his staff were realistic in assessing the basically inferior resources of France, human and industrial. They were nervously looking ahead to the "hollow years" of 1935-1939, when the French Army's annual levy of conscripts would be cut in half owing to the ravages of 1914-1918.[29] Weygand was very skeptical of the attempt to limit German rearmament by negotiation. His Intelligence reports were constantly warning him of the proliferation of clandestine German rearmament. Indeed, since 1932 Intelligence had been convinced of the existence and serious military value of the Reichswehr's training stations in Russia.[30] For these reasons, French military leaders developed in the year 1933 a lively interest in the rapprochement, an interest revealed by the exchange of military attachés and the visit of Air Minister Cot.

Colonel Mendras, the first Military Attaché, could not have picked a better time for his arrival in Moscow, April 1933. A few weeks later the first cracks in the Reichswehr-Red Army collaboration began to appear, and the Soviet military leaders immediately

---

[26] Sarraut was defeated on the budgetary issue which had brought down Daladier a month earlier. The Chautemps cabinet was merely a reshuffle of the previous cabinet, again dominated by the Radical-Socialist party. Daladier retained his post as Minister of War.

[27] Cameron, "Alexis Saint-Léger Léger," pp. 382-387.

[28] *Entre Deux Guerres*, II, 371.

[29] Weygand, *Mirages et Réalité*, pp. 384 ff.; testimony in *Les Événements Survenus en France de 1933 à 1945*, I, 231-250; Report on the state of the French Army submitted by General Weygand to the Minister of War, 10 Feb. 1934, *ibid.*, *Rapport*, I, 92-119.

[30] George Castellan, *Le Réarmement Clandestin du Reich, 1930-1935*, pp. 186-195.

began to sound out their new French friends. At a dinner offered by the French Embassy, 31 July 1933, Defense Commissar Voroshilov told Colonel Mendras that the Red Army wanted to establish an exchange of officers with the French Army. Voroshilov boldly asked the French Ambassador, M. Charles Alphand, "Why not send us technicians who could help us build submarines, torpedo boats, even cruisers? Our Navy needs them badly; we have a long way to go to make it strong again. Your specialists would be well paid and well treated."[31] Vice-Commissar Tukachevsky pressed Colonel Mendras to expedite a contract for French mortars, "insisting on the symbolic significance of an accord renewing the relations between the Russian Army and French industry which had been so close before the war."[32] There followed the warm reception given to the French Air Mission which toured Russia in September. In that same month, the last German officers and technicians departed from the training stations at Lipetzk, Kazan, and Saratov. A bit later, Colonel Mendras reported that he had been given to understand that "economically and militarily" the role of Germany in Russia was there for the taking.[33]

These friendly gestures from the Russian bear were heady reading; to one of the French military planners it looked as if "Russia is throwing herself into our arms." That officer, Colonel Jean de Lattre de Tassigny, a member of General Weygand's personal staff, maintained close relations with the new Soviet Military Attaché, General Ventzov, and did much to push the military rapprochement.[34] Colonel de Lattre had come to the conclusion that Poland and the Little Entente were too weak, that Belgian aid to France was unreliable, and that only Russia could create a second front against Germany.[35] In order to evaluate the Soviet Army, Colonel de Lattre, "on behalf of General Weygand," started nego-

[31] Letter of Colonel Mendras to the French Ministry of War, 1 Aug. 1933, quoted *ibid.*, p. 490.

[32] Letter of Colonel Mendras, 14 Aug. 1933, quoted *ibid.*

[33] Letter of Colonel Mendras, 25 Oct. 1933, cited in Castellan, "Reichswehr et Armée Rouge," in Duroselle, ed., *Les Relations Germano-Soviétiques, de 1933 à 1939*, p. 205.

[34] Colonel de Lattre's remark, in a conversation of July 1933, is quoted by General Loizeau, "Une Mission Militaire en U.R.S.S.," *Revue des Deux Mondes*, 15 Sept. 1955, p. 253. It seems very likely that Colonel de Lattre, who was a man of great energy and enthusiasm, personally took a much more hopeful view of the military value of the rapprochement with Russia than did General Weygand.

[35] Guy Salisbury-Jones, *So Full a Glory* (London, 1954), pp. 50-52; Colonel de Lattre's statement to the British Military Attaché, 10 Nov. 1933, B.F.P., VI, 50.

tiations for a mission to Russia led by M. Raoul Dautry, noted French transportation expert. Dautry recalls that "the government was thinking about negotiating a military accord with Russia and wished to be certain that the Russian military transport system was really effective."[36]

The most accurate evidence of the French High Command's attitude at this time is the remarks of Colonel de Lattre to the British Military Attaché in Paris, 10 November 1933. Broaching the subject for the first time, de Lattre assured Colonel Heywood that the new move would never be permitted to damage French friendship with England. The advantages which France hoped to secure from the rapprochement with Russia were "mainly negative."

Russia, with its present régime, had become a peace-loving nation, and could not go to war, as war meant the downfall of the present régime and the probable establishment of a military dictatorship. On the other hand, a Russia unfriendly to France but friendly to Germany would provide the latter country with a vast reservoir of raw materials and a not inconsiderable industrial potential.[37]

This sort of calculated appraisal of Russia's potential value to Germany was probably the original stimulus to the Army's interest in Russia. The Russian-German friendship was breaking up, and the French High Command was willing to deal with the Russians in order to make sure that they did not turn back to the Germans.

iii

The secrecy with which the new Franco-Soviet negotiations were conducted makes it difficult to evaluate the public reaction. However, the well-publicized trips of Herriot and Cot to Russia had revealed that the rapprochement was rapidly gaining tempo and had set off many rumors of a future Franco-Soviet alliance. For the first time the subject evoked frequent comment in the French press.

In conservative quarters there were no important adherents to the rapprochement. Although most of the Right and Center groups

[36] Testimony of M. Dautry, in *Les Événements Survenus en France de 1933 à 1945*, VII, 1945. The mission was to be one of "information and assistance" for six months; it fell through, according to Dautry, because of the upsetting effects of the French crisis of Feb. 1934.

[37] *B.F.P.*, VI, 50-51.

had accepted the Non-Aggression Pact, they remained hostile to suggestions of closer relations with Russia.[38] As before, their hostility stemmed from resentment of the Soviet repudiation of debts and from fear of Communist infiltration in France and her colonies. Pertinax, writing in *L'Echo de Paris* in December, admitted the new menace, Nazi Germany—but this was no reason for approaching Russia. "At best, an alliance with the Soviets would be essentially ephemeral and risky: at any moment it might be torn up in the interests of the revolution."[39]

On the Left, the sentiments of the Radical-Socialists remained divided. The factions behind Daladier still backed his conciliatory policy towards Germany. On the other hand, the activities of Herriot and Cot promoted support for the rapprochement among their followers in the party. They also led to the conversion of that colorful journalist Mme Geneviève Tabouis. Niece of the famous diplomats, Paul and Jules Cambon, and correspondent for the most important Radical daily, *L'Oeuvre,* Mme Tabouis wrote a widely read column on foreign affairs. She covered the Herriot and Cot visits in Moscow and returned to write a series of columns full of enthusiasm for tight relations with Russia.[40]

As for the Socialists, who had given only qualified approval to the Non-Aggression Pact in May, their reticence increased as the year wore on. Travailed by pacifist currents, the Socialists disliked the way in which the rapprochement was taking on traditional diplomatic forms and beginning to resemble the prewar Franco-Russian alliance, a symbol of militaristic secret diplomacy.[41] The Cot aviation mission was compared to the exchange of visits by the Russian and French navies at Kronstadt and Toulon in 1891

[38] Note the criticism of the Herriot and Cot trips to Russia in *Le Matin,* André Tardieu in *La Liberté,* and in *Gringoire* and *Je Suis Partout,* quoted in "Revue de la presse," *J.D.,* 16, 20, 22, 24 Sept. 1933; in *L'Action Française* 15 Sept. 1933; in editorials and articles by Pierre Bernus in *Journal des Débats,* 1, 15, 23 Sept. 1933; by Pertinax in *L'Echo de Paris,* 16 Sept. 1933. See also the speeches of MM. Louis Marin and Jean Ybarnégaray, quoted in *Le Temps,* 2 Oct. and 8 Dec. 1933.
[39] *L'Echo de Paris,* 29 Dec. 1933.
[40] See particularly Mme Tabouis's article of 17 Sept. 1933 in *L'Oeuvre;* also her memoirs, *Ils l'ont appelée Cassandre,* pp. 167-171. *L'Oeuvre* was not a party organ such as *Le Populaire* for the Socialists, but rather an independent paper expressing the views of the left wing of the Radical-Socialists. It had a wide range of readers outside the party.
[41] See the detailed analysis of the pacifistic and anti-militaristic currents in the Socialist party by John T. Marcus, *French Socialism in the Crisis Years, 1933-1936* (New York, 1958), pp. 97-111.

and 1893.[42] M. Rosenfeld, foreign affairs columnist for the official Socialist paper, *Le Populaire,* wrote of a rumored trip by Paul-Boncour to Moscow: "There we are deep in secret diplomacy, that diplomacy which, *by military alliances and coalitions,* managed so well to prepare the horrible carnage of 1914."[43]

The Socialists' suspicions were provoked incessantly by their miserable relations with the French Communists. Since 1928, when the Comintern had laid down the line of complete intransigence towards all non-Communist parties and organizations, the French Communists had been engaged in a violent running attack on the Socialists. In no way did the Communists turn off the pressure in 1933, even after Hitler's success in pulverizing the similarly divided German working class. Marcel Cachin continued to denounce the Socialist leaders for their "odious" polemics against the Soviet Union. "Socialist comrades, turn your backs on your leaders, whose basic task is to separate you from the Soviet Union by a curtain of lies"[44]

For some time the Socialists had been invulnerable to these attacks. The general elections of May 1932 had confirmed the declining trend of the French Communist party, weakened by a series of defections and mistrust among its leaders. It had won only 10 seats in the Chamber of Deputies and polled less than 800,000 votes, hardly a serious threat to the Socialists' 130 seats and 1,950,000 votes.[45] But the bad times which were now bedeviling the country made the Socialists start to worry about a Communist revival. The alarming growth of unemployment and the recent street riots in Paris gave the Communists a fine lot of discontent to exploit.

[42] Editorial by Léon Blum, *Le Populaire,* 20 Sept. 1933. Marceau Pivert, a leading figure of the left-wing Socialists, wrote after the Herriot and Cot trips that the rapprochement was leading in the direction of war. *Ibid.,* "Tribune," 28 Sept. 1933.

[43] *Le Populaire,* 13 Dec. 1933. M. Oreste Rosenfeld, who wrote a daily column on foreign affairs, was a Russian emigré, formerly a Menshevik, and personally very hostile to the Stalinist régime. His sharp criticisms of Soviet foreign policy were a source of great annoyance to the French Communists; they continually pointed to Rosenfeld as a symbol of the anti-Soviet attitude of the Socialist press.

[44] *L'Humanité,* 3 Nov. 1933. Editorials and cartoons attacking the Socialist party were daily material in *L'Humanité,* and in the *Cahiers du Bolchévisme,* (Paris, biweekly).

[45] The membership of the Communist party apparently had dropped to about 25,000 in 1932. All observers, including the Communists themselves, agree that the period 1928-1932 was the nadir of the party. Consult Goguel, *La Politique des Partis sous la Troisième Republique,* I, 342-344, and II, 231-233; Gerard Walter, *Histoire du Parti Communiste Français* (Paris, 1948), pp. 232-241.

These were the preoccupations which led even a left-wing Socialist like Marceau Pivert to admit openly that "the rapprochement between the U.S.S.R. and our government disturbs us. . . ."[46] M. Léon Blum, head of the party, constantly prodded Moscow—why were the French Communists not allowed to co-operate with French Socialists?

> Will the Soviet government ever realize that for it the real *security* lies not in diplomatic agreements with governments but in the force of labor, in the power of the organizations of the European proletariat, which is to say, in its unity?[47]

The criticism implied a fundamental question of confidence. How was it possible to support rapprochement with Stalin's Russia when the same Stalin ordered his French Communist allies to sabotage the Socialist party?

Many political observers who were not Socialists also kept their eyes on the Communist party. Would the Communists take a conciliatory attitude towards bourgeois parties, such as the Radical-Socialists, who supported the rapprochement? Would they soften their avowed program of undermining the French State?

The answers to both questions were aggressively negative. The French Communists did not drop their contemptuous attacks on the Radical-Socialist party. Even Herriot was blasted by *L'Humanité* for combining "imperialism" with his praise of the Soviet Union.[48] The contrast between this cut and Herriot's warm reception in Moscow was neatly satirized by a cartoon of the times. It featured a French Communist reading *L'Humanité* seated beside a Russian Communist reading *Izvestya*. French Communist: "Ah, there's that infamous Herriot who is plotting an imperialist war against Soviet Russia!" Russian Communist: "But, no, Comrade, that's our dear little father Herriot. Here we call him 'the indefatigable fighter for peace.' "[49]

Communist hostility to the French State did not waver. The party continued to condemn French foreign policy as imperialistic, to oppose military service, and to spread separatist propaganda urging autonomy for Alsace-Lorraine.[50] *L'Humanité* frankly ad-

---

[46] *Le Populaire*, "Tribune," 28 Sept. 1933.
[47] *Ibid.*, 18 Nov. 1933. [48] *L'Humanité*, 2 Dec. 1933.
[49] *Le Populaire*, 31 Aug. 1933.
[50] *L'Humanité*, 29 Aug., 11, 12, 24 Sept., 15 Oct., 29 Nov., 2, 8 Dec. 1933, 18 Jan. 1934; speech by M. Gabriel Péri, *J.O.*, Chambre, *Débats*, 10 Nov. 1933, pp. 4063-4066; *Cahiers du Bolchévisme*, articles by M. Gitton, H. Cartier, M. Marty, A.

mitted the discrepancy. The Soviet Union made those accords necessary to survive in a capitalist world; meanwhile the Communists of each country pursued their task—"to combat their own imperialism."[51]

Some light was thrown upon the discrepancy by the explanations of M. André Ferrat, one of the top French Communists. His article in the party's journal, *Cahiers du Bolchévisme,* entitled "The Peace Policy of the U.S.S.R. and Imperialist France," apparently was a reply to criticism of the rapprochement from Communist militants. Invoking Lenin's well-known exhortation to exploit the tensions between capitalist countries, Ferrat pointed out that, in order "to prevent anti-Soviet coalitions," Moscow must work with first one country, then another. Today, the danger was an anti-Soviet Western coalition including Nazi Germany, a coalition directed by England and foreshadowed in the Four Power Pact. One way of preventing this coalition was a Soviet rapprochement with France, a move which utilized the tension between France and Germany.

What meaning did the exigencies of Soviet foreign policy have for Communist parties? Ferrat chose the example of a non-aggression pact.

In case the capitalist state accepts, the Soviet government signs the pact with it. But we, as the Communist party, we shall never recognize the good faith of the capitalist government which signs the pact. Our attitude appears different from that of the U.S.S.R.—although it is joined to it as the thumb and first finger of the hand—because we do not work on the same level, even though we have the same enemy.

There is no real contradiction, only one of appearance. On the contrary, in reality there is the most intimate and profound community of view and of goal between the proletarian government and the communist parties.[52]

Ferrat ended by saying that there was no more contradiction between Soviet foreign policy and that of Communist parties than between two armies who marched upon a fortress from opposite directions.

It was of course possible that Communist tactics would change as the rapprochement progressed. But the discrepancy between

Ferrat, editorial of 1 Dec. 1933, X, 1031-1041, 1312-1320, 1350-1351, 1405-1415, 1555-1562.

[51] *L'Humanité,* 8 Dec. 1933.

[52] *Cahiers du Bolchévisme,* X (Oct. 1933), 1414.

the friendly approaches of Russia and the intransigence of the French Communist party, controlled from Russia, remained a disquieting feature of the rapprochement for many Frenchmen.

iv

Nothing which happened in November and December 1933 gave M. Paul-Boncour reason to doubt the necessity of his overture to Russia. As the days passed, American, Italian, and British support for the common disarmament program of October entirely vanished. Early in November, Norman Davis sailed for New York, with an air of leaving Europe to her insoluble quarrels. The United States delegates who stayed in Geneva withdrew to the fringes of the negotiations for reviving the Disarmament Conference.[53] The Roosevelt administration faced vast problems at home and was anxious to tackle them unhindered by international obligations. From Washington blew a cool isolationist wind.

Mussolini still nursed a grudge against Hitler, but he was willing to hide it if he could retain his flattering position as arbiter among the four Western powers. Accordingly he worked hard to repair his standing in Berlin by proposing "realistic" concessions of armaments to Germany.[54] The Italians did continue their negotiations with France on other matters, but their retreat from the common front against Germany was so abrupt that it left an uneasy feeling in Paris.

It was the English who canceled the most highly valued support. Sir John Simon had been the spokesman for the late bloc on 14 October and had roundly asserted that his government could not sign a Convention "which would provide for any immediate rearmament."[55] Yet the British cabinet lost no time in "facing facts," German facts. On 24 November the same Sir John Simon told the House of Commons that the choice now lay between regulation or license in armament. The British government would throw its whole weight "on the side of securing regulated as op-

[53] *F.R.U.S., 1933*, I, 299 ff., especially 310-319.

[54] Not to be outdone by Hitler, Mussolini also turned on a hostile propaganda against the League of Nations. The Italians were much impressed by Hitler's massive victory in the plebiscite and elections of 12 November. Aloisi, *Journal*, pp. 161 ff.; *G.F.P.*, II, 181 ff.; *B.F.P.*, VI, 23 ff.

[55] League of Nations, *Conference for the Reduction and Limitation of Armaments. Records*, Series C, Minutes of the Bureau, II, 183.

posed to unregulated armament."[56] To that end, British diplomats revived their pressure on the French to make more concessions to the German demands.[57] By the end of the year, the solidarity of France, England, Italy, and the United States had turned into a bad joke. The disillusionment reinforced M. Paul-Boncour's quiet determination to find some new way of bolstering French security.

The French Foreign Minister continued to direct the Russian negotiations in secret. The cabinet crises, the long lines of unemployed, and the belligerent tone of Rightist agitation had already created a taut, unpleasant atmosphere in Paris. The new Premier, M. Camille Chautemps, managed to maneuver the budget through the Chamber of Deputies 11 December, but was soon faced with a financial scandal. When Paul-Boncour came to report on his talks with the Russians, he found Chautemps badly tangled in domestic disorders and willing to allow him much latitude on foreign policy.[58]

What were the subjects of the Franco-Soviet talks, the records of which Paul-Boncour guarded so carefully in "a locked iron box"? Alexis Léger, Secretary-General of the Foreign Ministry to whom the drafting was intrusted, described the task as removing "the inadmissible conditions" proposed by the Russians. This was Léger's way of referring to their desire for a purely bilateral alliance. Instead, he tried to persuade them to fit the alliance into the scheme of existing French alliances with Poland and the Little Entente. Léger also had to be careful not to create a conflict with the Locarno Rhine pact. To accomplish these ends, the French proposed that the alliance be enshrined in some sort of a regional mutual assistance pact. It was quite a task; the Russians resented the numerous French conditions and, in Léger's graphic image, Ambassador Potemkin "visited the dentist twice every week."[59] However, the negotiations did make headway and, by the end of January 1934, the broad lines of the design had been sketched in.[60]

[56] House of Commons, *Parliamentary Debates*, Vol. 283, 24 Nov. 1933, columns 435-436.

[57] *B.F.P.*, VI, 64 ff.; *F.R.U.S.*, *1933*, I, 308-309.

[58] Testimony to the Parliamentary Investigation, *Les Événements Survenus en France de 1933 à 1945*, III, 794.

[59] Léger's account in Elizabeth Cameron, "Alexis Saint-Léger Léger," in Craig and Gilbert, eds., *The Diplomats 1919-1939*, pp. 385-386; statement by Soviet Ambassador Dovgalevski, Herriot, *Jadis*, II, 391-392; Paul-Boncour, *Entre Deux Guerres*, II, 372-373; *B.F.P.*, VI, 754.

[60] See further pp. 150-152, below.

The Russians accepted the French condition of joining the League of Nations and began to take soundings. No sooner had the first United States Ambassador to Russia, William C. Bullitt, unpacked his bags in Moscow than Litvinov asked him in strict confidence, 21 December, whether the United States "would have any objection" if Russia joined the League.[61]

> He [said] . . . that the French had asked the Soviet government to make a "regional agreement" for defense against attack by Germany. . . . He said that the Soviet Union considered an attack by Japan this spring so probable that it felt it must secure its western frontier in every way. . . . Therefore the Soviet Government, although still wishing to keep its hands free and not to join the League of Nations, felt that it must pay this price if necessary to obtain the agreement from France.

The Soviet Foreign Minister added that "the conversations were merely preliminary"; nothing had been signed. Herriot and the majority of the French government favored it, but "the entire agreement might fall through as Daladier was opposed to it and the British were opposed."[62]

It was Stalin himself who gave the press its first hint. On 25 December, in an interview with *New York Times* correspondent Walter Duranty, he denied that the Soviet attitude towards the League of Nations was inflexible. "Despite the withdrawal of Germany and Japan from the League of Nations—or perhaps for that very reason—the League may act in some degree like a brake, retarding or preventing the outbreak of hostilities. If that were so, if the League were to turn out an obstacle, even a small one, that made war more difficult, . . . then we would not be against the League."[63]

At this point, the political negotiations were stimulated by a breakthrough on the economic front. The moribund trade talks had been revived in July and seriously pushed since late Septem-

[61] President Roosevelt and Litvinov had made a series of agreements, 16 Nov. 1933, providing for the restoration of diplomatic relations. On his return voyage Litvinov further strengthened the Soviet diplomatic position by a stop at Rome, 3-5 Dec. He and Mussolini discussed the new international situation and agreed to prolong the 6 May 1933 Trade Accord for the year 1934. Ratifications of the Italo-Soviet "Pact of Friendship, Non-Aggression and Neutrality," signed on 2 Sept., were exchanged on 15 Dec. 1933.

[62] Dispatch of Ambassador Bullitt, 24 Dec. 1933, *F.R.U.S., The Soviet Union 1933-1939*, pp. 53-54; note also expanded version of 4 Jan. 1934, pp. 60-61.

[63] Quoted in Degras, ed., *Soviet Documents on Foreign Policy*, III, 1933-1941, 45. Molotov and Litvinov included similar allusions to the League in their speeches to the Central Executive Committee, 28 and 29 Dec. 1933, quoted *ibid.*, pp. 48 and 51.

ber. As a result, a provisional Commercial Accord was signed in Paris, 11 January 1934.[64]

The accord, valid only for the year 1934, revealed that the Soviet Union had agreed to make purchases in France of a minimum of 250 million francs, 200 million francs above the average for the past three years. In return, the French pledged to lower tariff rates and increase quotas on a substantial number of Soviet products and granted diplomatic status to the Soviet Commercial Representation in France. Payments for Soviet purchases were guaranteed by a complicated system of revolving credits; the funds would be created by temporarily withholding French payments for imports of Soviet oil. It was noted that the French government did not guarantee the credits as had Germany and Italy.[65]

The tortuous arrangements for credit, the modest dimensions of the accord, and its provisional nature were signs of the obstacles standing in the way of Franco-Soviet trade. Some of these were commercial in essence: French firms could be undersold by German, British, and American firms on much of the industrial equipment sought by the Soviet Union. In the areas where they could compete, French businessmen were hampered by a nasty legacy. No Paris cabinet could grant loans or guarantee credits unless the Soviets would begin repayment of the enormous Russian debts held in France. From all indications, both sides regarded the debt question as insolvable and agreed simply to put it aside. In reality, the significance of the Franco-Soviet Commercial Accord was political.[66] The first advance since the end of the tariff war in 1931, it showed that even in economic relations progress could be made, given enough incentive.

With the coming of the new year, the commissars in Moscow had a chance to publicize the rapprochement in their annual reviews of policy. V. M. Molotov told the Central Executive Com-

[64] Announcements in *Le Temps*, 23 July, 28 Aug., and 22 Sept. 1933; statement by M. Paul-Boncour, *J.O., Chambre, Débats*, 14 Nov. 1933, p. 4104; *B.F.P.*, VII, 607-608, 615-617.

[65] French exports to Russia declined from 59,000,000 francs in 1931 to 48,000,000 francs in 1932 and then to 44,000,000 francs in 1933. League of Nations, *International Trade Statistics, 1933*, p. 120. For details of the accord see *Le Temps*, 12 Jan. 1934; E. Néron, "L'Accord Commercial Franco-Soviétique," *Revue Politique et Parlementaire*, CLIX, (10 April 1934), 22-26.

[66] This was the sense of the remarks made by M. Paul-Boncour and Ambassador Dovgalevsky at the signature, quoted in *Le Temps*, 12 Jan. 1934. The political implications were also stressed in the "Bulletin du Jour" editorial in *Le Temps* and in *Izvestya*, 12 Jan. 1934, quoted in *Bulletin de la presse russe*, No. 236.

mittee, 28 December 1933, that the Soviet government was "convinced that our collaboration with France has entered upon a new stage and has a bright future."[67] He was followed by Litvinov, who praised the "rapid strides" towards a close friendship. "I am confident that this movement will be accelerated as the factors menacing peace continue to accumulate."[68]

The dictator of Russia did not often give a public address, and Joseph Stalin's words were closely attended when he rose to speak on foreign policy to the Seventeenth Congress of the Communist party, 26 January 1934. He singled out co-operation with France and Poland and recognition by the United States as the most striking recent achievements of Soviet policy. With France the previously "undesirable" relations were giving way to those "which cannot be otherwise described than as relations of rapprochement." Stalin added that this did not mean "that the incipient process of rapprochement can be regarded as sufficiently stable and as guaranteeing ultimate success." He spent much more time discussing Germany and implied that the friendly atmosphere between Paris and Moscow owed much to the impact of events in Berlin.

The point is that Germany's policy has changed. The point is that even before the present German politicians came into power, and particularly after they came into power, a fight began in Germany between two political lines: between the old policy, which was reflected in the well-known treaties between the USSR and Germany, and the "new" policy, which, in the main, recalls the policy of the former German Kaiser, who at one time occupied the Ukraine, marched against Leningrad, and converted the Baltic countries into a *place d'armes* for this march; and this "new" policy is obviously gaining the upper hand.[69]

With his habitual caution, Stalin inserted a brief reference that the Soviet Union did not seek a break with Germany and stood ready to improve relations if Hitler showed such an intention.

In Paris, M. Paul-Boncour was given his forum by the Senate, which indulged in a full-scale foreign policy debate on 12, 16, and 18 January 1934. Harried about the failure of the Disarmament Conference, the Foreign Minister called up in his defense the forward movements of French diplomacy. He dwelt with special pride on the collaboration with Italy and Russia, calling the latter "an important, eminent, capital element" of French diplomacy.

[67] Quoted in *S.U.R.*, XII, 9.   [68] Quoted *ibid.*, XII, 62.
[69] Quoted in Degras, *Soviet Documents on Foreign Policy*, III, 1933-1941, 69-71.

Yes, we have practiced, we are now practicing a policy of rapprochement. . . . I know the respectable prejudices, the painful memories which have long led to hesitation before this policy of rapprochement with Russia. Gentlemen, one does not ignore a country of 165 million inhabitants, which lies on the edges of Europe and of Asia.[70]

France, said Paul-Boncour, was pleased to see that her Polish and Little Entente allies were likewise embarking on friendly relations with Moscow. The recent pacts and conventions of non-aggression had created a "system" of security in that area which bore some resemblance to an Eastern Locarno.

Even as the debate was going on, Rightist agitators fought the police in nearby streets each night. They were attacking the government on a lurid financial scandal created by one Serge Alexander Stavisky. Misguidedly trying to minimize the scandal, Premier Chautemps lost control of the Chamber of Deputies and resigned 27 January. M. Édouard Daladier took over as Premier and Foreign Minister, thus ending Paul-Boncour's tenure at the Quai d'Orsay. But the new cabinet was driven out of office, too, this time by bloody riots which gave Paris a glimpse inside the box of civil war. It was two months before serious decisions on foreign affairs could again be made.

Where was the Franco-Soviet rapprochement on the eve of the riots of 6 February 1934? M. Paul-Boncour has asserted that when he left office the negotiations had reached an advanced stage and that "an agreement in principle" already existed between the two governments.[71] In the light of the available evidence, this claim cannot be accepted. What may well have existed was an agreement on the form of the alliance. It sometimes happens that agreement on the basic formulae to be used in a treaty is reached at an early stage, before one or both sides finally have decided to bind themselves. In any case, the negotiations had not reached a decisive stage in January 1934. Several reasons dictate this conclusion. On the Soviet side the break with Germany was not yet complete. Stalin and some of his aides were skeptical about the

[70] *J.O.*, Sénat, *Débats*, 16 Jan. 1934, pp. 39-40; compare with Paul-Boncour's earlier speech, *J.O.*, Chambre, *Débats*, 14 Nov. 1933.

[71] These were the terms that M. Paul-Boncour used in an interview with the writer, in Paris, 25 Nov. 1950. He said that the Franco-Soviet pact was always thought of as Barthou's work, whereas in reality it was his. In *Entre Deux Guerres*, II, 369, he wrote that Barthou found "un projet tout préparé, auquel il n'eut qu'à donner sa marque"; note also his testimony in *Les Événements Survenus en France de 1933 à 1945*, III, 795.

permanence of French intentions. It was in Paris, however, where the obstacles were concentrated.

In order to guard against leaks, Paul-Boncour had reported the negotiations only to the Premier and not to the rest of the cabinet. Thus the government as a whole was not committed. It was probable that when the project was submitted M. Daladier would oppose it, and his parliamentary position was stronger than that of M. Paul-Boncour. This superiority was demonstrated when Daladier became Premier and Foreign Minister after the fall of the Chautemps government.

One may assume that Édouard Daladier took over the Quai d'Orsay because he wanted to pursue his own foreign policy. That policy remained conciliatory to Germany. After the German withdrawal from Geneva in October, Daladier had not considered it advisable to continue the secret conversations with Hitler and General von Blomberg.[72] Instead, he exerted the influence that, as Minister of War, he still possessed, in favor of disarmament negotiations with Germany through the official diplomatic channels. Against the wishes of M. Paul-Boncour, the French cabinet sided with M. Daladier.[73] The French Ambassador in Berlin called on Hitler, 24 November, and listened to proposals for a convention permitting "limited" rearmament, a settlement on the Saar issue, and German non-aggression pacts with all her neighbors. The Chancellor protested his sincere desire to end the bloodshed between France and Germany. Thus began an exchange of notes on the disarmament problem, proposals from Paris, 13 December and 1 January 1934, replies from Berlin on 18 December and 19 January 1934. So long as these discussions were carried on, there lingered some hope of a direct understanding with Germany. M.

[72] However, the contact between Count Fernand de Brinon and Joachim von Ribbentrop was maintained. It is likely that Daladier approved the publication of an interview between Hitler and de Brinon, published in *Le Matin* 22 Nov. 1933. Hitler abounded in friendly sentiments. "Si elle [France] admet de trouver sa securité dans un accord librement discuté, je suis prêt à tout entendre, à tout comprendre, à tout entreprendre." Reprinted in F. Grimm, ed., *Hitler et la France* (Paris, 1938) pp. 92-98, and in *D.I.A., 1933*, pp. 314-316. See above, chap. vi, pp. 128-129, and de Brinon in *France-Allemagne, 1918-1934*, pp. 213-222; in *Mémoires*, pp. 26, 28-29, 84-85; and in *Les Procès de la Collaboration*, pp. 54-55; *The Ribbentrop Memoirs*, pp. 33-37.

[73] Paul-Boncour, *Entre Deux Guerres*, II, 385-387. This decision was also the result of British pressure; the English strongly urged the French to explore Hitler's conciliatory statements.

Daladier was not the man to shut the door gratuitously by "encircling" Germany with a Franco-Soviet Pact.[74]

A second major handicap to the prospects of an alliance was that the idea had not yet been openly presented to French public opinion. Rumors were current, but no clearcut reference to a Franco-Soviet Pact had been made by the Foreign Minister. It was certain that the move would be bitterly resisted by influential conservative groups. For such a controversial project an extended period of public discussion was essential, and its lack indicates that an advanced stage had not been reached.

Some diplomatic fields also needed cultivation. The formal procedures for bringing Russia into the League of Nations had not been invoked. M. Paul-Boncour had not yet taken counsel with the government whose good will was most valuable to France, the British.[75] Nor had he begun consultations with Poland and the Little Entente, who might be associated with France and Russia and, in any case, would be vitally affected.[76] M. Paul-Boncour had taken the big step—to begin talks for a Franco-Soviet Pact—but those talks were still in a preliminary stage when he walked out of the Quai d'Orsay at the end of January 1934.

[74] For further evidence of Daladier's conciliatory attitude towards Germany during this period, see *G.F.P.*, II, 43; *B.F.P.*, VI, 54-57, 197-198, 354-355, 367, 369-371.

[75] Lord Tyrrell, the British Ambassador in Paris, reported on 8 Jan. 1934: "During recent visits to the Ministry for Foreign Affairs I have more than once endeavoured to find out what exactly has been passing between France and the Soviets. On each occasion, I received the impression that the subject was distasteful, from which I inferred that something was in the wind. . . . I hardly expect the French Government to take us into their confidence until the something, whatever it may be, has taken definite shape." *B.F.P.*, VI, p. 263.

[76] It was announced late in Dec. 1933 that M. Paul-Boncour would make official visits to Poland and the Little Entente states; however, these visits were not to take place until two or three months later.

Eight

THE BOLD DIPLOMACY OF LOUIS BARTHOU

When the Chautemps cabinet resigned 27 January 1934, it was the opening of a fortnight that brought France close to civil war. One consequence was the formation of a cabinet with a new, tough attitude towards Germany, one which speeded the Franco-Soviet rapprochement. The crisis also deeply affected the destiny of the French Communist party.

The world economic depression had spared France to the last, allowing her a moment of isolated pride as the United States, Germany, and England suffered. But the ordeal was only delayed, and since the spring of 1932 her economy had been seriously declining. French exports continued their seemingly endless slide downwards, from a monthly average of 2,536,000,000 francs for 1931 to one of 1,539,000,000 francs for 1933. The same pattern of decline was traced by the indices of prices and production; from June 1933 on, the general index of industrial production slipped downwards each month. Throngs of unemployed workers appeared in the industrial towns; their total rose sharply from 226,000 in September 1933 to a new high of 351,000 in February 1934.[1] Reflecting these problems and increasing them was the budgetary deficit, which grew to an estimated 6,000,000,000 francs.

This economic and financial pressure accentuated political rivalries. The Radical-Socialists and the Socialists completely failed to reach agreement on their financial policies, the former deflationary, the latter inflationary. The two leading left-wing parties, who had joined hands to win the general elections of May 1932,

---

[1] The total value of French foreign trade dropped from 6,537,000,000 francs in 1931 to 4,052,000,000 francs in 1933, and the commercial balance continued to be heavily unfavorable. The general index of industrial production (base of 100 in 1928) dropped from 91 in June 1933 to 86 in February 1934 and on down to 82 in June 1934. Tables in Ministère des Finances, Service National des Statistiques, *Mouvement Économique en France de 1929 à 1939* (Paris, 1944), pp. 147, 165, 177, 223.

thus were unable to co-operate in fighting the depression. Conservative groups under Tardieu's direction deliberately used intransigent tactics to accentuate the dilemma.

From the time of Daladier's fall in October 1933, nervousness and tension rose in Paris. The cabinet of M. Albert Sarraut, dominated by the Radical-Socialists, did not survive a full month and then the same faces reappeared in M. Camille Chautemp's cabinet. There were angry demonstrations by groups of taxpayers, civil servants, war veterans, and shopkeepers. The Rightist and semi-Fascist armed leagues came out on the streets again for the first time since 1926. The Rightist press began an aggressive campaign not merely against the cabinet but against the institution of Parliament itself. Not their views but the violence of their tone was new.

Into this turbulence, at the end of December 1933, came news of the last of a series of financial swindles authored by one Serge-Alexander Stavisky. Stavisky died a week later in circumstances that suggested he might have been murdered to prevent his testimony. It turned out that he had conducted his operations with the compliance of a number of government officials and members of Parliament. Public indignation mounted rapidly and was adroitly fanned by Rightist organizations. On 7 January the monarchist *Action Française* began nightly street demonstrations which were joined by other Rightist groups. Ill-served by his strategy of business as usual, Premier Chautemps was viciously attacked in Parliament and resigned, 27 January 1934.

The new. Premier, M. Édouard Daladier, took the courageous step of dismissing M. Jean Chiappe, the dapper, volatile little Corsican Prefect of the Paris police, who was very popular with the Right. And that proved to be the spark. The armed leagues and veterans' organizations called demonstrations for 6 February, and the Rightist press threw a storm of abuse against Daladier. The Communists too now joined the pack.

There was no conspiracy among the Rightist groups to make a coup d'état on the night of 6 February 1934.[2] Some intended to force Daladier's fall and bring in a right-wing government; others

---

[2] The verdict of Max Beloff on the charge of a Rightist conspiracy is "Not proven." "The Sixth of February," in James Joll, ed., *The Decline of the Third Republic* (London, 1959), p. 35. Charles Maurras's hesitancy and ineffectiveness on the night of 6-7 February was revealed by Samuel M. Osgood, *French Royalism under the Third and Fourth Republics* (The Hague, 1960), pp. 118-123.

also hoped to impose an authoritarian reform of the Constitution. Some men were there simply because they resented unemployment and the series of incompetent governments. As Daladier presented his cabinet to the Chamber of Deputies in the Palais Bourbon, demonstrators began to converge on it from all directions. They were led by organizations of war veterans and by the Rightist leagues, notably the *Camelots du Roi* of the *Action Française,* the *Jeunesses Patriotes,* the *Solidarité Française,* and the *Croix de Feu.*

After a scabrous session, Daladier won his majority, but his fate was being decided outside. The fighting was most savage on the Pont de la Concorde, the bridge over the Seine leading to the Palais Bourbon. There the mob surged against barricades, slung grills at the police, and slashed their horses with razor-tipped sticks; the police and mounted guards were barely able to hold the bridge and twice resorted to firing. Soon after midnight the rioters fell back, but seventeen men had been killed, sixteen from the crowds, and hundreds of demonstrators and police had been badly wounded.

Next day Daladier, terribly upset by the fatalities, announced his resignation. The harried President of the Republic, M. Albert Lebrun, successfully appealed to M. Gaston Doumergue, himself a former President. His appointment as Premier, although denounced by the Socialists and Communists, put an end to the danger of anarchy.

M. Doumergue formed a government heavily weighted to the Right, essentially a coalition of conservatives and moderate Radical-Socialists. It was a curious mixture: André Tardieu and Édouard Herriot as Ministers of State without portfolio, symbolizing conservatism and liberalism, Senator Henry ("Papa") Chéron, huge, round, and complacent; the shrewd, ambitious Pierre Laval; and that sharp-tongued old warrior, M. Louis Barthou, at the Quai d'Orsay. Young Adrien Marquet, bursting with vague ideas of neo-socialism, sat beside the revered seventy-eight-year-old hero of Verdun, Marshal Henri-Philippe Pétain.[3] "C'est tout, sauf un gouvernement," quipped Tardieu.[4]

[3] Other prominent figures in the cabinet were MM. Albert Sarraut, François Piétri, Louis Marin, and Pierre-Étienne Flandin. Doumergue, President of the Republic, 1924-1931, took no portfolio; despite his recent shift to conservatism he was acceptable to the Radical-Socialists because he had been a member of the party until he became President. Only seven out of twenty posts in the cabinet went to the Left, six to Radical-Socialists and one to a Neo-Socialist.

[4] Quoted by Herriot, *Jadis,* II, 383.

On the night of 9 February Paris was again troubled by rioting, this time by the Communists, who were trying to redeem themselves for their participation on the sixth. Three days later a twenty-four hour general strike was called to protest against the rise of "Fascism." All across the country Communists and Socialists dropped their rivalry to march in impressive throngs. It was the last notable agitation. On 15 February Doumergue's cabinet won a solid vote of confidence, 402 to 125, from the Chamber of Deputies.[5] The Premier insisted on speedy consideration of the budget and it was voted through on the last day of the month.

The night of 6 February 1934 brought the French nation to its most troubled hours since 1917. The news that a mob was storming Parliament in Paris had an electric effect across Europe, and French prestige was shaken. Order was restored rather quickly, but hatred and violence had been indulged and they were remembered. At the hour of hazard the unity of France was severely strained. "The dust subsided; so did France."[6]

In its early days the Doumergue government was preoccupied with domestic affairs: voting the budget, investigating the Stavisky scandal and the riots, tackling the interminable financial crisis. For the moment foreign affairs were ignored. The negotiations for a Franco-Soviet mutual assistance pact simply lay dormant for two months.[7] During this period, however, three events of high significance for the rapprochement took place: the German-Polish Declaration of Non-Aggression, 26 January 1934, the final break in German-Soviet relations, and the French disarmament note of 17 April 1934. All three events favored the prospects of a Franco-Soviet entente.

The Polish-German rapprochement was only momentarily shaken by the German withdrawal from Geneva in October 1933.[8] The Polish Ambassador asked Hitler, 15 November, "whether he did not see any possibility of compensating the loss of this element

[5] Doumergue's majority was composed of the Right, the Center, 130 Radical-Socialists (out of 160), and a few Neo-Socialists. The vote against the government included 97 Socialists, 10 Communists, and 9 dissident Communists; there were 67 abstentions. Despite Herriot's participation in the government, 26 left-wing Radical-Socialists abstained.

[6] Lord Vansittart, *The Mist Procession* (London, 1958), p. 473.

[7] *F.R.U.S., 1934*, III, 75; Beck, *Dernier Rapport*, Appendix, pp. 281-283; *Rapport Torrès*, p. 163; Herriot, *Jadis*, II, 382 ff.

[8] For the origins and course of the Polish-German rapprochement beginning in May 1933, see chap. v, pp. 85-90 above.

of security, in direct Polish-German relations." Hitler replied with assurances about his intention to live peacefully with Poland, "an outpost [*Vorposten*] against Asia," and he proposed "to exclude the very idea of the possibility of war from Polish-German relations."[9] The German draft of such a declaration was accepted in principle by Warsaw and, after a month's hesitation, the negotiations were rapidly completed in January 1934. Disappointment with French weakness,[10] fear that the French and British would concede re-armament to Germany, underestimation of Hitler's dynamism, and belief in his "Austrian" deviation from Prussian policies—these were the principal motives that led Pilsudski and Beck to exploit what the latter called a "unique opportunity."[11]

The German-Polish Declaration of Non-Aggression, signed in Berlin on 26 January 1934, pledged the two governments "to reach direct understanding on questions of any nature whatsoever concerning their mutual relations." Never again would Poland and Germany "use force" in order to settle their disputes.[12] If Hitler's objective in making this surprising gesture was to sow confusion, he succeeded—for the declaration made nasty reading in Paris and Moscow.[13]

The shock was taken up a bit for the Russians by the state visit

[9] Report by Ambassador Lipski, *Polish White Book*, pp. 16-19; a summary is printed in G.F.P., II, 128-129.

[10] There is no substantial evidence to support the apparent legend that Pilsudski at this time made the French a second offer of preventive war against Germany. What did happen was that late in October 1933 Pilsudski requested the French to send him their latest Intelligence estimates on German rearmament. This information was promptly conveyed to Warsaw by Colonel Koeltz of the Deuxième Bureau, French Army. Comte Jean Szembek, *Journal, 1933-1939*, pp. 1-2; Laroche, *La Pologne de Pilsudski*, pp. 137-138. See chap. v, pp. 86-87 above.

[11] Beck, *Dernier Rapport*, pp. 28-29. In addition to Beck's memoirs, this interpretation of the Polish-German rapprochement is based on: G.F.P., II, 61 ff.; Laroche, *La Pologne de Pilsudski*; B.F.P., VI, 80-81, 128-133, 357-360 and VII, 617, 633, 639-640; Rauschning, *Voice of Destruction*, 109-110, 116-120; Zygmunt J. Gasiorowski, "The German-Polish Non-Aggression Pact of 1934," *Journal of Central European Affairs*, XV (April 1955), 19-29.

[12] "Each of the two Governments declares that the international obligations hitherto undertaken by it towards a third party ... are not affected by this declaration." G.F.P., II, 421-422; also *Polish White Book*, pp. 20-21. The two governments concluded press co-operation and tariff accords, 26 Feb. and 7 March 1934.

[13] Hitler made similar offers to sign non-aggression pacts with Czechoslovakia and Belgium. Success with these approaches would have hurt the French alliance system as much as the German-Polish Declaration did. G.F.P., II, 22-23, 126-128, 147-148, 893-894, 902; B.F.P., VI, 14, 115-116, 713, 771; letter from E. Beneš to L. B. Namier, printed in the latter's *Europe in Decay*, pp. 281-283; Pierre van Zuylen, *Les Mains Libres* (Brussels, 1950), pp. 308-309, 311-312.

of Colonel Beck to Moscow, 13-15 February 1934. Beck claimed that Poland desired to keep a perfect balance between her two great neighbors, and the visit took place in a cordial atmosphere. Nevertheless, the Soviets were deeply suspicious and by summer the friendly Polish-Soviet relations of the past two years had soured.[14] More profound was the Soviet interpretation of German policy. The Polish question was a touchstone of German-Russian relations; time and again their alliances had been based on a common antipathy to Poland. That Hitler should suddenly decide to lay aside a centuries-old tradition was seen as an ominous confirmation of his hostility to Russia.

On the French side the effect produced was exasperation. The Franco-Polish alliance had been under strain recently, but it was hardly expected that the Poles would make a bargain with Nazi Germany. Pilsudski gave his word that only Polish-German relations were affected and that Poland still held in high honor her alliance with France.[15] But the essence of the declaration was symbolic; it had the effect of withdrawing Poland from the anti-German coalition. Officials of the Quai d'Orsay were very critical of the "encouragement it will give to Hitler" and of the fact that the Poles had kept the whole matter secret until the last moment.[16]

The second event which reinforced the trend towards Franco-Soviet rapprochement was the failure of the last attempt to improve German-Russian relations. The new German Ambassador, Rudolf Nadolny, went to Moscow in December 1933 fortified by a deep personal belief in the Rapallo mystique of Russo-German collaboration. At first Nadolny was rebuffed in his efforts to reduce Soviet hostility.[17] Finally, on 28 March 1934, Litvinov made a formal proposal, a move that probably reflected displeasure with the hiatus in Franco-Soviet negotiations.

Litvinov suggested a joint guarantee of "the independence and

[14] Beck, *Dernier Rapport*, pp. 54-57; Laroche, *La Pologne de Pilsudski*, pp. 152 ff.; *Polish White Book*, pp. 175-179; *B.F.P.*, VI, 707-708; *G.F.P.*, II, 525-526.
[15] Laroche, *La Pologne de Pilsudski*, pp. 148-150.
[16] *B.F.P.*, VI, 349. The French Ambassador in Warsaw, M. Laroche, remarkably patient and objective in a difficult situation, was outraged this time. "Rien dans les propos de Beck n'avait donné lieu de penser que nous serions mis en présence du fait accompli sans avoir été avisés, sinon de la teneur même de l'accord, du moins de ses grandes lignes. Et cela au mépris de ses promesses répétées." *La Pologne de Pilsudski*, pp. 147-148. See also Noel, *L'Aggression Allemande contre la Pologne*, pp. 74-76; Herriot, *Jadis*, II, 395; Vansittart, *The Mist Procession*, p. 469.
[17] The Soviet reaction to Hitler is covered in chap. v, pp. 90-99 above.

inviolability" of Estonia, Latvia, and Lithuania.[18] The Russians, very nervous about Nazi propaganda among the German minorities in the Baltic states, had approached Poland with a similar project twice in 1933.[19] Defense Commissar Voroshilov and the Deputy Commissar of Foreign Affairs, Krestinsky, both sympathetic to Germany, in constrast to Litvinov, pressed the proposal. Nadolny reported that Krestinsky even said that it was "a documentation of the will to eliminate the existing distrust and an appeal to the same will in us [Germany], . . . a negative or evasive reply from us [Germans] would make a very bad impression."[20] Nadolny tried hard to win approval, but on 15 April he had to inform Litvinov of Berlin's refusal to discuss the proposal. Litvinov publicized the rejection, emphasizing the fact that the German government had turned down a "concrete" proposal to improve German-Russian relations.[21]

Soon afterwards Nadolny's mission ended in significant fashion. During the discussions with Litvinov he had suggested that it might be wise to supplant the Berlin Treaty with a completely new general treaty, within which a Baltic guarantee might be included. To promote his plan, Nadolny returned to Berlin late in May and tried to convince Hitler that it was not in Germany's interest to alienate Russia. Hitler refused to argue; he simply laid it down that "he did not wish to have anything to do with those people [Russians]."[22] Nadolny was ordered to take no more initiatives in Moscow; instead he resigned. The fact that Nadolny made such strenuous efforts to improve relations and failed so miserably that he felt it necessary to resign must have greatly increased Soviet suspicions of Hitler.

The Franco-Soviet alignment was also hardened by the consequences of the French Disarmament Note of 17 April 1934. That

[18] Litvinov's draft of a Protocol, *G.F.P.*, II, 683-685. The account of this episode is based on: *G.F.P.*, II, 121 ff.; Rudolf Nadolny, *Mein Beitrag* (Wiesbaden, 1955), pp. 142-169; Hilger and Meyer, *The Incompatible Allies*, pp. 262-264.

[19] Beck, *Dernier Rapport*, pp. 35-37; *B.F.P.*, VII, 630 ff.; *G.F.P.*, II, 314, 333-334, and 367-369. Radek told a German journalist in Jan. 1934, "The machinations of the Nazis in the Baltic area fill us with the greatest concern." *Ibid.*, p. 334.

[20] Conversation of 28 March 1934, *ibid.*, p. 686. See the discussion of Krestinsky and Voroshilov, in chap. v, p. 98 above.

[21] Litvinov's reply to Nadolny, 21 April, reprinted in *Pravda*, 27 April 1934; Degras, ed., *Soviet Documents on Foreign Policy*, III, 79-83. Consult also *G.F.P.*, II, 763 ff., and III, 112.

[22] "Sodann hielt er mir einen längeren Vortrag, dessen Quintessenz war, er wolle mit England gehen, aber mit Russland nichts zu tun haben." Nadolny, *Mein Bertrag*, p. 167.

note closed down the negotiations for an arms convention that had been revived six weeks after Hitler had withdrawn from the Disarmament Conference. British and Italian mediation elicited an offer from Hitler: the other powers would retain their existing arms, while Germany would receive recognition of full "equality of rights" but would agree to apply this equality only for "defensive" requirements. Specifically, Germany would have a 300,000 man short-service army and "defensive" weapons such as artillery up to 155 mm., anti-aircraft guns, tanks up to six tons, and fighter planes.[23]

The Doumergue cabinet, absorbed with the repercussions of the Stavisky scandal and the riots, postponed its decision. Just as it began to study the new compromise, the German government published, 29 March 1934, its military budget estimates for the coming year. These revealed an over-all increase of 356,000,000 RM., or one-third, and the tripling of appropriations for the Air Ministry. Simultaneously, the British pressed the French for precise answers to two questions: could the French government accept the new compromise as a basis for negotiation and, if so, "what is the exact nature of the 'guarantees of execution' [of the Arms Convention] which the French Government propose?"[24]

There is much evidence to show that M. Louis Barthou wished to accept in principle the British-sponsored compromise and then to pin down the British on precise guarantees of execution, i.e., security. As Barthou's general attitude was sharply anti-German, it is very likely that he merely wished to be conciliatory in form, counting on the deep Anglo-French differences over security to prevent any final agreement. Whatever Barthou's motives, his preference for a conciliatory response was overruled by the cabinet. Doumergue, Tardieu, and Herriot were the most intransigent and they were so advised by General Weygand, chief of the French Army.[25] As a result, the French reply was a flat negative.

[23] Accounts and documents on the four-power disarmament negotiations, Nov. 1933-April 1934, may be found in *S.I.A., 1935*, I, 2-33; Wheeler-Bennett, *The Pipe Dream of Peace*, pp. 191-223; *D.I.A., 1933*, pp. 324-384; *F.R.U.S., 1933*, I, 322-355, and *1934*, I, 1-63; *B.F.P.*, VI, 3-685; *G.F.P.*, II, 152-748; Aloisi, *Journal*, pp. 163-187.

[24] Letter from Sir John Simon to the French Ambassador in London, 10 April 1934, *B.F.P.*, VI, 617.

[25] Testimony of M. Daladier, M. Albert Lebrun, and M. le Baron de Dordolot, a Belgian Senator, at the parliamentary investigation, *Les Événements Survenus en France de 1933 à 1945*, I, 13-14, IV, 957-958, and III, 830-831; Herriot, *Jadis*, II,

The French government, in a note dated 17 April 1934, declared that the German budget estimates showed determination to rearm in defiance of the negotiations; that revelation dictated the response of France.

Even before seeking to discover whether an agreement can be obtained upon a system of guarantees of execution sufficiently efficacious to permit the signature of a Convention which would legalize a substantial rearmament of Germany, France must place in the forefront of her preoccupations the conditions of her own security.[26]

The Germans denounced the note but in private they were delighted that Paris had courted the responsibility for ending the negotiations. In London and Rome there was dismay and irritation. British opinion came to attach great significance to the 17 April note, seeing it as a typical example of French obstruction.

The French withdrawal from the arms negotiations is a landmark in Franco-German relations. It ended a series of conciliatory approaches by French leaders, in the tradition of the late Aristide Briand. Laval with Brüning, in 1931, Herriot with Papen at Lausanne in 1932, Daladier and Hitler through their agents in 1933, all had explored the prospects of an understanding.[27] Sometimes there had been real hope, sometimes only curiosity and the desire for a talk. The Doumergue cabinet no longer wanted even to talk. Its tough attitude was trenchantly expressed by M. André Tardieu.

M. Tardieu said he had no belief whatever in Germany's good faith. She had not been slow to violate the Young Plan, and was now openly violating the Treaty of Locarno, both of which she had signed of her own free will. At the very moment when His Majesty's Government were making their recent enquiry, Germany had defiantly announced a vast increase in her military budget. This had been the last straw.[28]

With such feelings there was nothing to do but rearm and build a ring around Germany.

395-420; François-Poncet, *Souvenirs d'une Ambassade*, pp. 174-180; Flandin, *Politique Française, 1919-1940*, p. 71; Weygand, *Mirages et Réalité*, pp. 417-421; van Zuylen, *Les Mains Libres*, pp. 299-300; *F.R.U.S., 1934*, I, 51-53; *B.F.P.*, VI, 593-685; Paul Hymans, *Mémoires* (Brussels, 1958), 2 vols., II, 671-679.

[26] *D.I.A., 1933*, p. 382.

[27] At the Riom trial Daladier criticized the 17 April note and said that Hitler's proposal of a 300,000 man German army should have been accepted. "J'aurais signé cet accord de grand coeur...." Testimony of 27 Feb. 1942, in Mazé and Genebrier, eds., *Les Grandes Journées du Procès de Riom*, pp. 36-37.

[28] Conversation between Tardieu and the British Chargé in Paris, Mr. Ronald Campbell, late in April 1934, *B.F.P.*, VI, 677.

The German-Polish Declaration of 26 January 1934, the German rejection of Litvinov's proposal for a joint guarantee of the Baltic states, and the French disarmament note of 17 April 1934, all smoothed the path of rapprochement between France and Russia. When the two countries renewed their negotiations, the situation was as favorable as possible. The Poles had made a deal with Hitler and thus released the French from their moral scruples. France and Russia had given up their separate efforts to conciliate Germany.

ii

The man who took over command of French diplomacy in February 1934 was one of the last active members of the grand generation of the Third Republic. Clemenceau, Delcassé, Poincaré, Jaurès, Briand, Caillaux had been Barthou's friends and enemies. At seventy-two, the new Foreign Minister had behind him seventeen cabinets and forty-five years in Parliament, as a Deputy and later as a Senator.[29]

Born in 1862 in the province of Béarn, of whose historic glories he was always proud, Louis Barthou had a child's vivid impressions of the disaster of 1870 and grew to manhood in the patriotic atmosphere of the *revanche*. After finishing law school, he immediately went into politics and was elected as a conservative to the Chamber in 1889. Rising to prominence very quickly—he and Poincaré were called *les deux gosses*—he became a minister in July 1894, a few months after ratification of the Franco-Russian alliance. He dipped into the literary and cultural life of Paris, and while in politics he gained a succession of cabinet posts, serving notably under Clemenceau and Briand. Then as Premier in 1913 he pushed through the Three Year Military Service Law which helped to save France from sudden defeat a year later. After the death of his only son in the war, he virtually withdrew from politics, but he continued to write and his literary career was crowned by election to the Académie Française in 1918.

[29] Louis Barthou did not publish memoirs, but there are autobiographical fragments in the following of his works: *Lettres à un Jeune Français* (Paris, 1916); *Le Politique* (Collection *Les Caractères de ce Temps*) (Paris, 1923); *Promenades autour de ma vie, Lettres de la Montagne* (Paris, 1933). For portraits consult: Wilhelm Herzog, *Barthou* (Zurich 1938); Caillaux, *Mes Mémoires*, (Paris, 1947) III, 53-57; Weygand, *Mirages et Réalité*, pp. 362-363; Herriot, *Jadis*, II, 382-459.

As *rapporteur* of the Versailles Peace Treaty in the Chamber of Deputies, Louis Barthou composed a lucid analysis; he recommended ratification but criticized the lack of precision in the guarantees of execution.[30] Barthou returned to the cabinet as Minister of War under Briand in 1921, and then moved to the Ministry of Justice in the cabinet of his old friend, Raymond Poincaré. When the fall of the franc brought Poincaré back to power in 1926, Barthou served in the same post until the former's retirement in 1929. From that time on, as an elder statesman in the Senate he had been content to make life miserable for ministers.[31]

Louis Barthou was an exceptionally agile politician—it was no more safe to bring him into the cabinet than to leave him out of it. However, he had never changed two positions: although conservative, he remained a staunch republican and nothing dimmed his vibrant old-fashioned patriotism. He had another mark of the old school—versatility. Patron of music, ardent bibliophile, like Churchill a stylist who gave his subordinates bad marks for sloppy writing, Barthou published a score of books, including biographical studies of Mirabeau, Danton, Baudelaire, and Richard Wagner. Utterly fearless, he indulged a taste for sarcasm and irony, but it was done with a sprightly touch. Spade beard and a pince-nez disclosed his generation, but he had more verve and energy than men half his age.

It is well to linger over Barthou's portrait, because interpretation of his motives must rest upon the character of his career and upon his actions in 1934: other evidence is inadequate. Everything in his background served to heighten his sensitivity to the threat of Germany. In addition, he was one of the few Frenchmen who had read *Mein Kampf*.[32] Throughout his tenure as Foreign Minister, Barthou expressed faith that France could meet the threat. His optimism has been called a bluff, but it is not so surprising. Here was a man who had lived through all the stages of French recovery after 1870 and then through her staggering, noble drive

[30] The report is reprinted in Louis Barthou, *Le Traité de Paix* (Paris, 1919).

[31] Although Barthou had only been Foreign Minister for one brief period, 23 Oct.–13 Nov. 1917, he had served long terms on the Foreign Affairs commissions in the Chamber and Senate, and he had been head of the French delegations to the Genoa and Hague conferences in 1922 and President of the Inter-Allied Reparations Commission from 1922-1926.

[32] Herzog, *Barthou*, pp. 78, 95-98. For a contrary interpretation, that Barthou's long-term goal was "an understanding with Germany," see d'Ormesson, *France*, pp. 119-120.

to victory in 1918. That recovery, which he himself had helped to lead, could be repeated by tenacity and self-confidence.

Louis Barthou's first task at the Quai d'Orsay had been the disarmament talks. The decision to withdraw from them led logically to the conclusion of the 17 April note: "France must place in the forefront of her preoccupations the conditions of her own security."[33] Accordingly, Barthou turned to examine the state of the French alliance system, and he set off on a series of trips to Brussels, Warsaw, Prague, Bucharest, and Belgrade.

For some time Belgium had been turning aside from intimate collaboration with France. The discontent centered on the secret Franco-Belgian Military Convention of 1920. Many Belgian leaders feared that, through its application, they might be drawn into war against Germany without any choice. They sharply disagreed with the French interpretation that the convention gave the French army the right to enter Belgium in a period of diplomatic tension.[34]

Belgian apprehension was increased by the fact that French military men believed and said that Belgium was the best place to stop the right wing of another Schlieffen Plan attack. Instead of waiting for the Germans, the French Army intended to move up and form a defensive line with the Belgian Army in the narrow corridor between Antwerp and the Ardennes.[35] This disposition seemed to be confirmed by the fact that the construction going on for the Maginot Line stopped at Longwy, 180 miles from the Channel, leaving uncovered the entire Franco-Belgian border.

The Belgian government had secured in 1931 a slight attenuation of the Military Convention. They reopened the question in 1933 and, by a démarche of 8 February 1934, they tried to pin down the French to a more restricted interpretation; the French simply avoided making any reply. The Belgians wanted to sub-

---

[33] *D.I.A.*, *1933*, p. 382.

[34] The accord, signed 7 September 1920 and ratified later in the month, was entitled: "Accord Militaire Défensif Franco-Belge, approuvé par les états-majors français et belge pour le cas d'une aggression allemande non-provoquée." Note that the victim of German aggression is not specified; the convention thus could be applied in case of German attacks on Poland or Czechoslovakia. The key clause provided: "Pour répondre à une prise d'armes générale de l'Allemagne, les deux puissances s'engagent à décréter la mobilisation générale de leurs forces." General von Overstraeten, *Albert I—Leopold III: Vingt Ans de Politique Militaire Belge, 1920-1940* (Brussels, n.d.), pp. 36-37.

[35] Marshal Pétain told the Belgian Ambassador in Dec. 1933 that French troops would enter Belgium without invitation if necessary. When Baron de Gaiffier asked, "Même si nous vous combattons?" Pétain replied, "Nous vous combattrons!" *Ibid.*, pp. 99-100; see also Van Zuylen, *Les Mains Libres*, pp. 101-131, 253-254, 276-277.

ordinate the convention to the framework of the Locarno Rhine Pact, to deny its application in disputes involving France's eastern alliances, and to retain discretion over the timing of its application.[36] This dispute was rendered more difficult of solution by the tragic death of King Albert I in a mountain climbing accident, 17 February 1934. A dominating figure, whose irritation with the French had been balanced by his memories of the common wartime ordeal, was succeeded by a young man whose personal inclinations were unknown, Leopold III.

M. Louis Barthou's visit to Brussels, 27 March 1934, and his talks with King Leopold, Count de Brocqueville, the Premier, and Foreign Minister Paul Hymans were cordial in tone, but he could not in one day repair a long slide. Barthou politely evaded their efforts to modify the Military Convention.[37] Indeed, the trend had gone so far that in the judgment of a French staff officer, "the French must not count on immediate intervention on the part of Belgium in case of German attack."[38] In the spring of 1934, Belgium, for France, was a friend but not an ally.

M. Barthou's second voyage took him to the east. His visit to Warsaw and Cracow, 22-25 April 1934, was a lively personal success, as befitted a negotiator of the Franco-Polish alliance. At the banquets and the talks with Marshal Joseph Pilsudski and Colonel Joseph Beck, Barthou's charm and optimism won a generous response. He, in turn, was impressed by the self-confidence of the regime and the virility of Polish national sentiment.

It is clear, however, that Barthou did not secure any changes in Polish policy.[39] He was assured that there was no secret agreement behind the German-Polish Declaration and that Poland remained faithful to its alliance with France. But he was given to understand that the Polish government no longer considered itself a satellite and would pursue a policy dictated solely by its own estimate of its own interests. Beck gave only vague promises to

[36] *Ibid.*, pp. 247-264, 274-285; Hymans, *Mémoires*, II, 602-636, 929-930.

[37] Van Zuylen, pp. 272, 284-285, 299-300; Hymans, *Mémoires*, II, 676-678, 967; Herriot, *Jadis*, II, 400. The Belgians were so dissatisfied that they tried, unsuccessfully, to secure a British guarantee.

[38] Statement by Colonel de Lattre de Tassigny, a member of General Weygand's staff, to the British Military Attaché, Colonel T. G. G. Heywood, 10 Nov. 1933, *B.F.P.*, VI, 50.

[39] For reports on Barthou's visit to Poland, consult: Laroche, *La Pologne de Pilsudski*, pp. 155-163; Beck, *Dernier Rapport,* pp. 57-61; Szembek, *Journal, 1933-1939*, pp. 3-7; Herriot, *Jadis*, II, 422-424; *F.R.U.S.*, 1934, I, 72; *Le Temps*, 23-27 April 1934.

tone down the feuding with Prague and then belied them by his repeated denigrations of the Czechs. With regard to the Franco-Soviet rapprochement, little was said. When Barthou brought up Russian entry into the League of Nations, Pilsudski replied in a very negative tone and questioned the stability of the Soviet regime.

The second leg of the Foreign Minister's journey, to Prague, was an unqualified success. Barthou was warmly received by the President of the Republic, Thomas Masaryk, and the Foreign Minister, Edward Beneš, 26-27 April; the cliché "perfect accord of views" for once was true. Herriot's comment on Barthou's report was that "nothing separates us from this people."[40] Soviet entry into the League of Nations was fully approved by the Czechs. Dr. Beneš recently had been urging his Romanian and Yugoslavian colleagues towards recognition of the Soviet Union, and at Zagreb, 22 January 1934, the Council of the Little Entente had agreed that recognition should take place in the near future.[41]

M. Barthou did not make his trip to Bucharest and Belgrade until June, and it thus did not contribute to the frame of mind in which he revived the Franco-Soviet negotiations. There were, however, elements of weakness in each of these alliances which already had come to his attention. Both countries were subject to strong commercial attraction from Germany, which the French were unable to counter. A German-Yugoslav commercial accord was signed 1 May 1934 and two weeks later Goering came to Belgrade on a well-advertised "good-will" mission. The Romanian Foreign Minister, M. Nicholas Titulescu, was effusively pro-French but many of his opponents and King Carol did not share his inclinations.[42]

Barthou's investigation showed that the French "alliance system" had no unity and was far too weak to stop Hitler. Belgium and Poland no longer wished to be French sentinels standing watch on Germany's borders. Yugoslavia and Romania did not wish to seek a quarrel. Only Czechoslovakia stood ready to follow as far as France might lead.

[40] *Jadis*, II, 424; see also *Le Temps*, 28-30 April 1934; article by Albert Mousset, *L'Europe Nouvelle*, XVII (5 May 1934), 450-451.

[41] Letter from Beneš to Litvinov, 9 June 1934, printed in *D.I.A., 1934*, pp. 402-403.

[42] Barthou's trips to Romania and Yugoslavia are covered below, pp. 174-175. For evidence of his anxiety at this time, March-May 1934, see Herriot, *Jadis*, II, 395, 426.

France could have adopted the alternative of haughty isolation. Louis Barthou had been intimately connected with Poincaré's experiments in that direction. Perhaps as a result of Poincaré's brilliantly executed but sterile occupation of the Ruhr, Barthou realized that France was not strong enough to go it alone. He set out then to find new allies.

iii

M. Louis Barthou took some time to make up his mind to play the Russian card. Indeed, at the time of his appointment he enjoyed an anti-Soviet reputation, based on his truculent attacks at the Genoa Conference and his prosecutions of French Communists as Minister of Justice. He had criticized the Franco-Soviet Pact of Non-Aggression when it came up for discussion in the Senate Foreign Affairs Commission in March 1933.[43] Upon entering the Quai d'Orsay, he even told the Secretary-General, M. Alexis Léger, that he might replace him for being "too soft with the Russians."[44]

The Foreign Minister reported to the cabinet on Franco-Soviet affairs at least four times throughout February, March, and April 1934. He confined himself to vague expressions of approval and to the question of Russia's entry into the League of Nations.[45] Herriot, who had worked so hard to promote the rapprochement, was discouraged by Barthou's reticence. At the cabinet of 10 April 1934, Herriot noted: "The rapprochement with Russia is again put off. The President of the Council [Doumergue] does not seem pressed to see it come about. Barthou, without appearing hostile, looks around for delays or accepts them."[46]

Sometime at the end of April Barthou made up his mind to grasp the Russian alliance. What did he think about the interaction of foreign and domestic politics? He had always been a bitter opponent of the French Communists; did it bother him to

[43] Reports in *Le Temps, Journal des Débats*, 12 March 1933.
[44] Elizabeth Cameron, "Alexis Saint-Léger Léger," in Craig and Gilbert, eds., *The Diplomats*, p. 385. Barthou soon changed his mind about Léger and the two men worked well together. M. Léger later said that Barthou was the only Foreign Minister from 1932 to 1940 who combined "the vision with the will to carry on 'the great rules of French diplomacy.'" *Ibid.*, p. 382.
[45] Herriot, *Jadis*, II, 389, 395, 401, 403, cabinets of 20 Feb., 8 and 29 March, 10 April 1934. On 20 Feb., the cabinet did take the important decision to send a small aviation mission to Russia, but this was only confirmation of an initiative taken by M. Paul-Boncour in Nov. 1933.
[46] *Ibid.*, p. 401.

seek the friendship of their masters? He, like Herriot and Paul-Boncour, seems to have dismissed the danger as small because the French Communist party was so small, a paltry ten out of six hundred in the Chamber of Deputies.[47]

Here, as on other points concerning Barthou's motives, direct evidence is inadequate and the only recourse is to his background, his character, and the implications of his later actions. Barthou did not jump at the Russian alliance; he considered the disadvantages and he juggled the alternatives. True, there may be increased Communist infiltration in France; true, the Russians may offend the Poles and annoy the British—but who is left other than Russia and Italy? And what will the Russians do if we reject their offers? Some risk attends any policy, France cannot simply watch her own decline, and action has its own virtues—that is the way Barthou's motives may be read. "Long ago Republican France had signed a treaty with Tsarist Russia . . . ," he reminded the British. His memories of the contribution of that alliance to the recovery of France must have aided his decision.[48]

The Franco-Soviet negotiations were resumed in Paris late in April 1934; these talks prepared the ground for the meeting of Barthou and Litvinov in Switzerland.[49] Maxim Litvinov's arrival in Geneva, 18 May, ten days before the Disarmament Conference was to open, caused much speculation. His eagerness to confer with Barthou probably betrayed serious anxiety about the delay, which played into the hands of his critics in Moscow.[50] Litvinov went immediately to a long meeting with Barthou, where he proposed three ambitious schemes: security pacts for Eastern Europe, the Mediterranean, and the Pacific. The latter scarcely drew a breath of life, and the "Mediterranean Locarno," although much

[47] Barthou claimed that "he found that the Soviet Government had stopped their political propaganda in France." Conversation with British ministers in London, 9 July 1934, *B.F.P.*, VI, 804. Barthou was a master at deception and it is impossible to know whether he believed this or not; it was certainly incorrect.

[48] Conversations in London, 9-10 July 1934, *ibid.*, pp. 804-806. "The Doumergue Government . . . considered that they must take guarantees of peace where they could find them. . . . A disappointed Russia might go over to Germany."

[49] *J.O.*, Chambre, *Documents Parlementaires*, 1935, Annexe 5792, *Rapport Torrès*, p. 163; Laroche, *La Pologne de Pilsudski*, pp. 164-165; Beck, *Dernier Rapport*, Appendix, pp. 281-282; *B.F.P.*, VI, 753-754, 804-806, and VII, 669, 676, 677.

[50] Barthou's remarks on his talks with Litvinov, quoted in Herriot, *Jadis*, II, 432, and in Beck, *Dernier Rapport*, Appendix, pp. 281-282.

discussed, never reached the stage of a definite proposal.[51] Litvinov's main business was the Eastern Pact, which came to be known as Eastern Locarno.

Eastern Locarno was the result of several twists since the original Soviet offer, in the summer of 1933, of a bilateral alliance. When, in October, M. Paul-Boncour had decided to move, he had insisted that the Franco-Russian Pact must be "co-ordinated" in some way with the existing French alliances, particularly that with Poland. Litvinov had reluctantly accepted the principle of a multilateral pact; having done so, he insisted upon adding the Baltic States and Finland. Somewhere along the line, the French had decided that, at least for the sake of appearances, there must be a place in the scheme for Germany.[52]

Barthou and Litvinov quickly agreed on the concept of a security pact that would include Russia, Germany, Poland, Czechoslovakia, the Baltic States, and possibly also Finland and Romania. This regional pact would be guaranteed by a Franco-Soviet pact. The two foreign ministers then left Geneva, having decided to continue the negotiations during the forthcoming Disarmament Conference.[53]

M. Barthou returned to Paris to make a vigorous defense of his "policy of alliance" before the Chamber of Deputies, 25 May 1934. After paying tribute to the existing alliances, Barthou spoke of Russia and Italy.

I consider ... that the entry of Russia into the League of Nations should be an eminent event for the peace of Europe. . . . I say plainly . . . that the policy of France tends toward a sincere rapprochement with Russia. . . .

It does not seem to me impossible that France and Italy may concur in a cordial, loyal and definitive entente.[54]

The Foreign Minister's bow to Rome reflected his desire to cultivate the split between Hitler and Mussolini. There were currently some sharp differences between Paris and Rome, especially on dis-

[51] The Mediterranean Locarno was to include the Soviet Union, Romania, Bulgaria, Turkey, Greece, Yugoslavia, Italy, France, and perhaps Great Britain.
[52] See chap. vii above, pp. 135-137, and Herriot, *Jadis*, II, 391-392; *B.F.P.*, VI, 753-756, 769-770. 807.
[53] Herriot, *Jadis*, II, 432; Laroche, *La Pologne de Pilsudski*, pp. 164-165; Beck, *Dernier Rapport*, Appendix, pp. 280-283; *F.R.U.S., 1934*, I, 71-72; *B.F.P.*, VI, 703, 707-708, 804; "Bulletin du Jour" in *Le Temps*, 22 and 24 May 1934; articles by Pertinax in *L'Echo de Paris*, 19 and 24 May 1934.
[54] *J.O.*, Chambre, *Débats*, 25 May 1934, pp. 1257-1262.

armament policy, and Barthou did not take kindly to the Italian tactics. Basically, however, he continued Paul-Boncour's policy of simultaneous approaches to Russia and Italy.[55]

When the stricken Disarmament Conference resumed its sessions in Geneva, 29 May 1934, Litvinov immediately proposed that the delegates admit the failure of disarmament and turn to "other guarantees of peace," in a word, security. To that effect he proposed "regional pacts of mutual assistance." If "dissident states" refused to join a pact, "that should by no means prevent the remainder from coming still more closely together to take steps which would strengthen their own security."[56]

The next day, after Sir John Simon had rejected the Soviet proposal and had restated the British preference for an arms convention with Germany, Barthou created a sensation. He delivered an attack on British policies which astonished one delegate by "its irony, its insolence and its passion."[57] He implied that Sir John Simon lacked the courage to stand up to the Germans, and he lampooned the timidity of British views on security.

Having polished off Sir John, Barthou turned to compliment Maxim Litvinov.

M. Litvinov was not a man who tried to please everybody. . . . He was a man who accepted realities. While there were parts of his speech which M. Barthou would find difficult to endorse, he had to recognize that in M. Litvinov's speech also there was one idea which dominated everything and which he [M. Barthou] was ready to believe had inspired his whole speech—the idea of security.[58]

On 1 June the Turkish Foreign Minister, Tewfik Rüstü Bey, who was working closely with Litvinov and Barthou, proposed that the Conference set up a special committee to work out regional security pacts. France, Russia, the Little Entente, and the recently formed Balkan Entente (Yugoslavia, Romania, Greece, and Turkey) announced their support.[59]

[55] "Bulletin du Jour," *Le Temps*, 28 May 1934; Herriot, *Jadis*, II, 401, 437, 439; Aloisi, *Journal*, pp. 191, 196.

[56] League of Nations, *Minutes of the General Commission*, III, 657-661. See the *Izvestya* editorial of 1 June, quoted in S.U.R., XII, 158-159, and the favorable commentary on Litvinov's speech in the "Bulletin du Jour," *Le Temps*, 31 May 1934.

[57] Major-General A. C. Temperley, a British delegate, *The Whispering Gallery of Europe* (London, 1938), p. 265.

[58] Speech of 30 May 1934, *Minutes of the General Commission*, III, 665-670.

[59] The Pact of Balkan Entente was signed at Athens, 9 Feb. 1934; *D.I.A., 1933*, pp. 408-409, and *1934*, pp. 298-304. The Turks were apprehensive about Mus-

The Franco-Soviet campaign for security was much too strong for the British, United States, and Italian delegations, and a deadlock ensued. A compromise was fashioned laboriously in the form of a resolution that contained equally respectful references to disarmament and security.[60] On 8 June the World Disarmament Conference passed the resolution and adjourned three days later, never to meet again.

Barthou and Litvinov continued their own negotiations on the margin of these debates, and they reached a firm agreement on 4 June 1934. Two treaties were necessary, owing to the awkward fact that France was not in Eastern Europe. An Eastern Pact of mutual assistance would be signed by the Soviet Union, Germany, Poland, Czechoslovakia, Lithuania, Latvia, Estonia, and Finland; it was decided not to include Romania.[61] France and the Soviet Union would sign a separate treaty which, in a sense, would guarantee the Eastern Pact. France would give assistance to Russia as if she were a signatory of the Eastern Pact, while Russia would give assistance to France by a guarantee of the 1925 Locarno Treaty. Litvinov also confirmed the willingness of his government to join the League of Nations.[62]

The Geneva agreement was immediately sent to Paris for submission to a meeting of the cabinet, 5 June 1934. The cabinet approved it and gave Barthou authorization to pursue negotiations on this basis.[63] From Herriot's notes, it appears that only Pierre Laval offered vigorous resistance. "Laval declared himself categorically in favor of an accord with Germany and hostile to a rapprochement with Russia, which would bring us the International

solini's imperial ambitions and they also hoped to use the regional pacts as a means of revising the Lausanne Treaty provisions for the Straits.

[60] *Minutes of the General Commission*, III, 682-683.

[61] If Romania were invited, Turkey would insist on joining and the pact would become more unwieldy than it was already. Romania and Turkey were given the nebulous consolation of the Mediterranean Locarno.

[62] Herriot, *Jadis*, II, 432, 437-439; *Rapport Torrès*, pp. 163-164; Laroche, *La Pologne de Pilsudski*, pp. 164-165; Beck, *Dernier Rapport*, Appendix, pp. 280-283; *F.R.U.S.*, 1934, I, 489; B.F.P., VI, 746 ff. and VII, 706-707; G.F.P., II, 880-881, 902-904.

[63] Notes of a cabinet meeting, 5 June 1934, Herriot, *Jadis*, II, 437-438. Herriot had the impression that Barthou remained "very reserved" about the matter. Litvinov made Barthou a strange offer: "Les Russes ont même proposé de prendre un engagement analogue à celui que nous avions avec l'Angleterre avant 1914...." This presumably was a reference to the Anglo-French staff talks and agreements, 1906-1914. See Barthou's remarks in London, 9 July, B.F.P., VI, 806.

and the red flag."[64] In Barthou's absence, M. Doumergue presented the case for approval of the negotiations and thus indicated for the first time his own support.

The cabinet's approval of Eastern Locarno was a very important step. M. Paul-Boncour had kept his negotiations secret from the cabinet, informing only the Premier, M. Chautemps. Now, for the first time, the French government as a whole was committed. They were committed, however, only to Eastern Locarno, the combination of an Eastern Pact and a Franco-Soviet Pact. They had not agreed to go ahead with the latter if the former should fall through.

Eastern Locarno was given a rather unfriendly reception. The British were especially irritated. With Parliament and public opinion divided on the meaning of Hitler, the cabinet clung to the hope that an accommodation with Germany was still possible. Barthou seemed an anomaly, "a man who had acquired the mental rigidity of age without having lost the animal spirits of youth."[65] The rumors of a new Franco-Russian alliance were shocking; they called up memories of the "encirclement" of Germany before 1914. The extent of British annoyance can be seen in Sir John Simon's remarks to Mr. Norman Davis, 1 June 1934. He had just had lunch with Barthou and they had patched up their personal quarrel but that was all; their policies still rankled.

He furthermore said that they [the British] were not disposed to wait indefinitely for France to complete her so-called Eastern Locarno, which was not a matter for the Disarmament Conference to deal with but which was merely an alliance, and he remarked that if France continues along that line England may make a deal with Germany and Belgium unless a real disarmament agreement can be arrived at promptly.[66]

Eventually, M. Barthou was invited to visit London in July, but that did not disguise the fact that Eastern Locarno got off to a very poor start in British eyes.

[64] Herriot, *Jadis*, II, 437. In April, Herriot heard opposition from Adrien Marquet, a Neo-Socialist, and from the conservative leader, Andre Tardieu, who, as Premier in 1932, had tried to stop the rapprochement. *Ibid.*, pp. 403-404.

[65] Arnold Toynbee, *S.I.A., 1934*, p. 387. To Lord Robert Cecil he was "Monsieur Barthou, with his genius for being wrong." *A Great Experiment* (London, 1941), p. 255.

[66] Conversation in Geneva, 1 June 1934, *F.R.U.S., 1934*, I, 94-95. Barthou was unmoved by the British displeasure; see Herriot, *Jadis*, II, 438-439; *B.F.P.*, VI, 764-768; Pertinax, who was close to Barthou, in *L'Echo de Paris*, 2 June 1934; Hymans, *Mémoires*, II, 682, 968-970.

The French Ambassador in Berlin gave a sketch of Eastern Locarno to State Secretary von Bülow, 7 June 1934, and expressed the hope of a favorable reply. There was not the slightest chance that Germany would join Eastern Locarno, but the Wilhelmstrasse adroitly decided that "it would be well if we did not reject the proposal outright, but treated it in a dilatory manner.[67] The German government thus replied that it would study the proposal; meanwhile, the German press raked it over.

Germany's displeasure had been discounted, but French officials were surprised and disturbed when Eastern Locarno received a poor reception in Rome.[68] Despite their own friendly relations with Russia, the Italians did not like the idea of a Franco-Russian alliance. It would reduce Italy's value to France, and it might goad Hitler into more aggressive policies. Mussolini's opposition to Eastern Locarno meant that the Franco-Italian rapprochement was held back.

Another disappointment was the Polish response. Barthou made every effort to flatter Colonel Beck by special treatment, but Beck gave a noncommittal reply and expressed skepticism about the chances of the pact.[69] On the way home he did the Germans a favor by hinting at the Polish refusal to join the pact.[70]

On the credit side, Eastern Locarno received a boost from the Little Entente. On 9 June Czechoslovakia and Romania announced *de jure* recognition of the Soviet Union. The Yugoslavian government did not follow suit,[71] but it favored the policy of regional security pacts. Meeting at Bucharest, 18-20 June 1934, the Little Entente Council issued a declaration of enthusiastic support for "regional conventions of mutual assistance."[72]

[67] Baron von Neurath's instructions, 8 June 1934, *G.F.P.*, II, 885-886. For the presentation of Eastern Locarno by the French Ambassador, 7 June, and by M. Litvinov, who stopped in Berlin, 13 June, see *ibid.*, pp. 880-881 and 902-903.

[68] A dislike of regional security pacts was one of the few subjects on which Mussolini and Hitler agreed when they met at Stra, near Venice, 14-16 June. *F.R.U.S., 1934*, I, 491-492; *B.F.P.*, VI, 762-763; *G.F.P.*, III, 12-13; Aloisi, *Journal*, p. 200.

[69] Laroche, *La Pologne de Pilsudski*, pp. 164-165; Beck, *Dernier Rapport*, p. 73, and Appendix, pp. 280-283; Herriot, *Jadis*, II, 437, 439; *B.F.P.*, VI, 755, 766, 769.

[70] Conversation between Beck and Baron von Neurath, Berlin, 7 June 1934, *G.F.P.*, II, 879-880.

[71] By the year's end Yugoslavia was the only country in Eastern Europe that had not recognized the U.S.S.R. Anti-Soviet sentiment centered in the court; some members of the royal family were related to the Romanov dynasty and King Alexander had spent part of his childhood at the court of Nicholas II.

[72] *D.I.A., 1934*, pp. 365-367. The letters of recognition exchanged between M. Litvinov and Beneš and Litvinov and Titulescu, are printed *ibid.*, pp. 402-404.

The Czechoslovakian government quickly asserted its intention of joining Eastern Locarno. The Foreign Minister, Dr. Édouard Beneš, welcomed the new development, which would "serve as foundation to our future friendly relations with the greatest of the Slav peoples."

> Our international situation cannot be settled as long as Russia, in full possession of all her rights and of all her responsibilities, shall not, fully and normally, come to play her rôle in the politics of the Continent particularly with regard to Central Europe.[73]

From this time on, Beneš became the most articulate European champion of collaboration with Russia.

M. Barthou had an opportunity to promote Eastern Locarno during his journey to Romania and Yugoslavia, 20-26 June 1934. Passing through Vienna he made the significant gesture of a short talk with Engelbert Dollfuss, the embattled anti-Nazi Chancellor of Austria. Barthou assured Dollfuss that France would do everything possible to support Austrian independence.[74]

In Bucharest the French Foreign Minister was received "with all imaginable pomp."[75] Presenting him to the Romanian Parliament, M. Titulescu inserted an impassioned protest against revision; if anyone asked for a square centimeter of Romanian territory, the response would be "No! No! Never!" Barthou took the cue and replied, to thunderous cheers, "Know that if a square centimeter of the soil of your country is touched, France will be at your side...."[76] His visit to Belgrade was "spectacularly staged" and he pledged with solemn eloquence French devotion to the alliance of 1927. In both capitals Barthou received support for the Eastern Pact and for the concept of a Mediterranean Locarno. Barthou learned at first hand, however, something of the opposition in Romania to the pro-French policies of Titulescu and of the German economic penetration into Yugoslavia.[77]

Barthou was reproached for his aggressive tone, but it is likely that he raised his voice to be sure that he was heard. He was

[73] Speech to the Foreign Affairs Commission of the Czech Parliament, 2 July 1934, *D.I.A., 1934*, pp. 380, 382; see also *G.F.P.*, III, 82-83; *B.F.P.*, VI, 782.
[74] *F.R.U.S., 1934*, II, 28; *B.F.P.*, VI, 768-769, 772; *G.F.P.*, II, 85, n. 7.
[75] Report of the German Minister in Bucharest, 27 June 1934, *G.F.P.*, III, 95-96.
[76] *Le Temps*, 23 June; also *D.I.A., 1934*, p. 312.
[77] For accounts of the two visits, consult the reports of German ministers, *G.F.P.*, III, 92-93, 95-96; *Le Temps*, 23-30 June 1934; *D.I.A., 1934*, 374-377; Barthou's statements in London, *B.F.P.*, VI, 806, 809. See also Herriot, *Jadis*, II, 440, and *G.F.P.*, III, 9-10.

serving notice on friends and enemies alike. His militant backing
for Romania and Yugoslavia was a warning that France had vital
interests on the Danube, on the Black Sea, and along the shores of
the Adriatic. Whether they liked him or not, observers in London,
Rome, and Berlin began to listen carefully when the sprightly old
Frenchman spoke. By the end of June 1934, Louis Barthou had
regained the diplomatic initiative for France.

Nine

EASTERN LOCARNO

After a moment of hesitation, the new French Foreign Minister, M. Louis Barthou, had thrown himself into a bold new course. He had made visits to each of the French allies: Belgium, Poland, Czechoslovakia, Romania, and Yugoslavia. He had revived the negotiations with Russia. He had made the acquaintance of Maxim Litvinov and the two had loosed on a skeptical world a grandiose scheme called Eastern Locarno. Now he was off again, on a trip to London to beard his English critics.

The experts at the Quai d'Orsay had worked out a rough draft of Eastern Locarno. On 27 June, in preparation for Barthou's arrival, the French Ambassador in London gave the Foreign Office a memorandum containing the draft. The first part was a "Treaty of Regional Assistance," to be signed by Russia, Germany, Poland, Czechoslovakia, Finland, Estonia, Latvia, and Lithuania. These states would promise to "lend assistance to one another in the case of attack by one contracting State on another."[1] Other articles provided for consultation in case of a threatened attack and for the "complete application" of articles 10 and 16 of the Covenant of the League. The latter was an ingenious attempt to solve the delicate problem of the passage of Russian troops through Polish territory. By placing that passage under the aegis of the League, the Quai d'Orsay hoped to lessen Polish resistance.[2]

---

[1] "Eastern Pact . . . communicated by the French Ambassador June 27, 1934," Great Britain, Cmd. 5143, Miscellaneous No. 3 (1936), *Correspondence showing the course of certain Diplomatic Discussions directed towards securing an European Settlement,* June 1934 to March 1936 (hereinafter cited as British Blue Book, *Cmd. 5143*), pp. 7-8. The French original is in *B.F.P.*, VI, 776-778; see also pp. 785-787, 801-803. This rough draft was also sent to Warsaw.

[2] Article 6 of the Treaty of Regional Assistance stated, "Where one contracting country could benefit from the provisions of Articles 10 and 16 of the Covenant of the League, the other signatories would undertake to secure a complete application of such provisions by the League of Nations." Article 16, paragraph 3 of the Covenant stated that "The Members of the League agree . . . that they will take the necessary steps to afford passage through their territory to the forces of any of the Members of the League which are co-operating to protect the covenants of the League."

The second part of Eastern Locarno was an "Agreement between France and Russia."

(1) As towards France, Russia would accept the obligations arising from the Treaty of Locarno as though the Soviet Union were a signatory of that treaty on the same footing as Great Britain or Italy.

(2) As towards Russia, France would accept the commitments which would arise for her under Part I, paragraphs (1) and (2), of the Regional Treaty if she were a signatory, in cases where it is a question of action in fulfilment of article 16 of the Covenant, or decisive action taken by the Assembly or the Council in fulfilment of paragraph 7 of article 15 of the Covenant.

Finally, there would be a General Act stating that all obligations were in conformity with the Covenant and that the treaties would not go into effect until Russia's entry into the League of Nations.

The French memorandum of 27 June 1934 revealed a number of ambiguities in Eastern Locarno. The Eastern regional treaty was an awkward jumble, "predators and prey huggermugger."[3] Poland and Lithuania had no diplomatic relations, owing to their bitter quarrel over the Polish seizure of Vilna in 1920. Poland and Finland would never accept Soviet assistance; Estonia and Latvia were very much afraid of it. It was hard to conceive of Poland and Czechoslovakia coming to each other's aid. Finally, there was no reason for Hitler to join; on the contrary, the countries involved were all included in his conception of German *Lebensraum*.

If in Barthou's image the Franco-Soviet pact was supposed to "cover" Eastern Locarno, it was a leaky umbrella. France promised to lend assistance only to Russia. Poland and Czechoslovakia were covered by their alliances with France, but Finland and the Baltic States had no such alliances and, therefore, they would receive no aid from France.

With regard to Russia, the French continued to refuse any commitments in the Far East. Their obligation applied only to an attack on Russia by one of the members of the regional treaty, obviously Germany. The definition of Russian assistance to France—as if Russia were a signatory of the Locarno Rhine Pact of 1925—created delicate problems. It was likely that Locarno would be weakened by associating Russia with it. To say nothing of Hitler's reaction, the British and Italians would resent the intrusion of

[3] Vansittart, *The Mist Procession*, p. 491.

Russia as another "guarantor" of Locarno. Such a position would give Russia a decisive voice in Western Europe.

In July M. Louis Barthou crossed the Channel to explain his ambiguous project and to repair the Entente Cordiale, which had been damaged by his own recklessness. Both sides now regretted the bickering at Geneva. Barthou, though unrepentant, had no desire to perpetuate the quarrel.[4] The British recoiled by instinct, as they recoiled from every sharp stand they took until March 1939. They were newly apprehensive of the clandestine rearmament in Germany and the possibilities of a sudden air attack on London. Barthou also profited from the disgusted English reaction to the Nazi "Blood Purge," 30 June 1934. The macabre elimination of the top leadership of the S.A., including its chief, Ernst Röhm, did not shock as much as the erratic murders of old and new opponents: General von Schleicher and his wife shot "while trying to escape"; General von Bredow; Gregor Strasser, who had broken with Hitler in 1932; the aged frustrator of the 1923 Munich Putsch, Gustav von Kahr, found in a swamp; two of Vice-Chancellor von Papen's aides, Edgar Jung and Herbert von Bose; Erich Klausener, a Catholic leader; and many an unsung enemy of the Nazis. News of these barbarous hours fled the frontiers and spread dismay and bewilderment across Europe. M. Barthou might be nasty, but he did not kill people in the afternoon.

The French Foreign Minister arrived in London, 9 July 1934, and spent two days at receptions and talks with members of the British government. At the working sessions with Sir John Simon and Anthony Eden, Barthou put on his most amiable manner and set out to justify Eastern Locarno. He stressed the fact that the Russians had pressed for a direct alliance, even a military alliance; the French had refused it, insisting on a multilateral pact. He himself had done nothing for two months "in order to show the Soviet government that he was not in a great hurry."

Barthou reminded his hosts that they would certainly prefer Eastern Locarno to a Franco-Russian alliance, and he hinted that, if necessary, he would adopt the latter alternative.

[4] M. Alexis Léger, Secretary-General of the Quai d'Orsay, who was committed to collaboration with the British, softened Barthou's tactics. For Léger "no new ally was worth the price of estrangement from Britain. Her position must be reckoned with, her confidence maintained against all odds, even if necessary at the high cost of sacrificing the initiative for France." Cameron, "Alexis Saint-Léger Léger," in Craig and Gilbert, eds., *The Diplomats*, pp. 383, 385.

If the French Government did not succeed in this matter [Eastern Locarno] ... the problem of security would remain open as between Russia and France. The French Cabinet had not yet deliberated on what would happen in those circumstances. But long ago Republican France had signed a treaty with Tsarist Russia, though the two régimes were very different. Geography, however, commanded history, and there had been a Franco-Russian alliance.

Would the France of today also be obliged to ally herself with Soviet Russia, who would abstain from propaganda in her territory? It was possible that, if the Eastern Locarno failed, the dangers of the European situation would oblige France to do so.[5]

Barthou ended by appealing to Simon and Eden to support Eastern Locarno; they need not join the treaty, merely recommend it. "If the United Kingdom Government could help so that Poland and Germany participated in these arrangements, they would be rendering a great service to the cause of peace."

Sir John Simon replied that he could scarcely recommend Eastern Locarno to the Germans; why should they join a treaty that included a Franco-Soviet Pact directed against them? He might feel differently, however, if Germany were inserted into the Franco-Soviet Pact itself. If the French and Russians were each to extend their guarantees to Germany, the pact would then contain "the necessary element of reciprocity."[6] Barthou blinked, but cynically accepted with good grace. He agreed provisionally for the Russians that their guarantee of Locarno would extend to Germany as well as to France. Equally so, "if Germany wanted to participate in the proposed arrangements and asked for a French guarantee against Russia, France would give it."[7] With a flourish, M. Barthou handed Sir John Simon an empty concession.

There was a second British condition, and here assent from Barthou was less readily forthcoming. Simon strongly urged that Eastern Locarno be linked to a new attempt to negotiate an arms convention giving Germany equality of rights. Barthou tried to slip this demand, but eventually he made a partial concession. He

[5] Anglo-French meeting, 9 July 1934, London, *B.F.P.*, VI, 803-806.

[6] "He [Sir John Simon] was gravely concerned at the idea of a Russian guarantee given to one party of the Locarno Treaty and refused to another, because that destroyed the reciprocal principle upon which the treaty was based." *Ibid.*, VI, 807-808.

[7] Second Anglo-French meeting, 9 July 1934, *ibid.*, VI, 812-813. Barthou added that the Russian guarantee of Locarno would not extend to Belgium. "Belgium had nothing to do with this matter; and, moreover, she did not wish to have anything to do with it." *Ibid.*, VI, 815-816.

would not agree to simultaneous negotiations, but "they could say to Germany that by the conclusion of the Eastern Locarno a better situation would arise in which to consider the rearmament of Germany."[8] The British were satisfied with this loose promise for the future.

The modifications agreed upon were drawn up by Sir Robert Vansittart and M. Alexis Léger, two poets who submerged their love of elegant language to the exigencies of a diplomatic formula.

1. In the view of the French Government, Russia ought to be prepared to give to Germany as well as to France the same guarantees against non-provoked aggression as those which she would be bound to give if she were a signatory of the Treaty of Locarno.
2. In regard to the proposed Eastern Pact, France would be prepared to give the same guarantees to both Germany and Russia.
3. The French Government agree with His Majesty's Government in holding that the conclusion of such a pact and Germany's participation in the system of reciprocal guarantees now contemplated would afford the best ground for the resumption of negotiations for the conclusion of a convention such as would provide in the matter of armaments for a reasonable application of the principle of German equality of rights in a régime of security for all nations.[9]

On that basis the British government promised to recommend Eastern Locarno to the German, Polish, and Italian governments.

Sir John Simon immediately revealed the bargain in a debate on foreign policy at the House of Commons, 13 July 1934. The debate was distinguished by speeches from Sir Austen Chamberlain and Winston Churchill hailing Eastern Locarno as a warning to aggressors.[10] Sir John Simon spoke about it in an entirely different tone. After revealing Barthou's willingness to extend French and Russian assistance to Germany, Simon asserted that the pact was now "in the truest and most complete sense reciprocal. . . . The thing is completely mutual in its structure, and the poison of suspicion . . . is completely eradicated, and removed by the fact that it is a genuinely mutual proposal."[11]

British diplomats called immediately on Mussolini, Baron von Neurath, and Colonel Beck, gave them the French Memorandum

[8] *Ibid*, VI, 812.
[9] *Ibid.*, VI, 821-822; compare to the first proposal, p. 815.
[10] House of Commons, *Parliamentary Debates, Official Report*, 292, 13 July 1934, columns 729-736, 739-746. Churchill warned the House that there ought to be "deep anxiety" about German rearmament.
[11] *Ibid.* columns 696-702.

outlining Eastern Locarno and the London modifications, and recommended the project. Neurath was surprised but still hostile; he would study the new proposals, but he thought them "merely phrases."[12] Beck's reaction was skeptical and noncommittal; "he could not accept proposed Pact even in principle until he had completed exhaustive study of all its implications and liabilities."[13]

In contrast, the British reversal was effective on that sensitive actor, Mussolini. On being informed of the modifications, he made some sarcastic remarks about the Baltic states and Czechoslovakia but put the best face on the matter. He agreed on the spot to a statement of approval which Sir John Simon was able to read to the House of Commons the next day.[14] The Italians promptly suggested to the Germans that they should take the modifications at their face value and thus turn the pressure back on the French. Mussolini was not taken in by the French concessions; his reversal was purely tactical.[15] When England shifted back to the French side, it was prudent, almost necessary, for him to follow. Each month he took more steps towards an adventure in Ethiopia, and such things as the Suez Canal and the French and British fleets began to acquire great significance.

The agreement on Eastern Locarno lifted the recent Anglo-French tension. Both sides were pleased with the results, but only one had a right to be. The British were impressed by Barthou's willingness to include Germany in the Franco-Russian Mutual Assistance Pact. How could they fail to realize that Barthou was conceding an invitation that Germany would never accept? If Germany did not join Eastern Locarno, then the revival of the arms negotiations fell to the ground. Barthou would be able to shrug his shoulders and say, "No Eastern Locarno, no arms convention."

[12] Conversation with the British Ambassador in Berlin, 12 July 1934, *G.F.P.*, III, 164-166; *B.F.P.*, VI, 835, 840-842.

[13] Conversation with the British Minister in Warsaw, 12 July 1934, *B.F.P.*, VI, 839-840; see also Laroche, *La Pologne de Pilsudski*, pp. 168-169. Beck said that "he failed to see how Russia could assist France against Germany across Poland's body."

[14] "... Italy regards with sympathy proposals which are made on a basis of absolute reciprocity between all the countries concerned. This is particularly the case when such proposals offer fresh possibilities in field of a limitation or reduction of armaments and as regards implicit recognition of equality of rights." Conversation between the British Ambassador in Rome and Mussolini, 12 July, *B.F.P.*, VI, 837-838.

[15] *G.F.P.*, III, 170-173, 204-206; *F.R.U.S.*, *1934*, I, 497; Aloisi, *Journal*, pp. 203-204.

The decision of the British to recommend Eastern Locarno did restore some of their influence on French policy and they hoped to use it to prevent a Franco-Russian alliance. But that depended on the success of Eastern Locarno, which had no chance of success. It is difficult to resist the conclusion that the British reversal was due to the desultory quality of Sir John Simon's policy. Given no lead by MacDonald and Baldwin, he wavered back and forth between France and Germany. Under the impress of Hitler's repudiation of the Disarmament Conference in October 1933, he had shifted from opposition to acceptance of German rearmament; now, under the impress of Barthou's dynamism, he shifted from opposition to support of Eastern Locarno.

ii

M. Barthou returned to Paris to receive the congratulations of his colleagues in the cabinet. When he spoke of the inclusion of Germany in the Franco-Russian pact, apparently he treated it in a perfunctory manner: "As for Germany, she will be invited."[16] In a speech at Bayonne, 15 July, he served notice that the promise of arms negotiations was dependent upon Germany's good behavior.[17] When the Foreign Minister received the German Ambassador in Paris to describe the London talks, he repeated this distinction.

Simon had then asked him whether France would be prepared to satisfy the German claim for equality of rights. To this he [Barthou] had replied: "No," adding that he could not agree to negotiations on the Eastern Pact being conducted parallel with negotiations for the recognition of equality of rights. France could only go into this question when the security she desired had been attained.[18]

When Ambassador Köster said that in that case he did not understand why the British government had recommended Eastern Locarno to Germany, "Barthou shrugged his shoulders and said that that was a matter for the British. In any case he could congratulate himself over it."

Barthou, in short, did not take the invitation to Germany seriously. He regarded it merely as a good tactical move, to show that France was not encircling Germany, to put Germany in the wrong

[16] Herriot's notes of the cabinet of 11 July 1934, *Jadis*, II, 445-446.
[17] *Le Temps*, 17 July 1934.
[18] Conversation of 20 July 1934, *G.F.P.*, III, 194-199.

by her refusal. This interpretation is strengthened by the fact that he waited six weeks before giving a written text of the Eastern Locarno proposals to the German government! The French memorandum of 27 June, containing an outline of Eastern Locarno, had been sent only to London and Warsaw, not to Berlin. After the London talks, it was the British who sent to Berlin the memorandum and the formula of modification. The French Ambassador confined himself to some general oral remarks; when he was taxed for this lapse, M. François-Poncet gave a specious excuse.[19] Finally on 20 August, after British prodding, M. François-Poncet sent Bülow the French memorandum containing the original draft of Eastern Locarno. Even then the communication was uncomplimentary. The text of the Franco-Russian agreement had not been reworked to include Germany in each of the articles. Instead, there was only a negatively worded addition:

Although the agreement takes the form of a Franco-Russian agreement, there would be nothing against extending to the benefit of Germany, at the request of the German Government and on their assumption of the corresponding obligations, the guarantees herein provided, whether for the benefit of France or of Russia.[20]

The French handling of the invitation to Germany proves that Barthou did not take it seriously and, indeed, may be seen as a studied discourtesy.

Litvinov also treated the inclusion of Germany purely as a tactical maneuver. To diplomats in Moscow he showed disenchantment with the whole project and stressed the determination of France and Russia to go ahead on their own.[21] The Russians never did send a written text to Berlin. The Russian Ambassador informed State Secretary von Bülow, 21 July, that the Soviet government "agreed to the extension of the guarantees in the supplementary agreement [Franco-Russian Pact] to include Germany."[22] That was the extent of Russian discussion of the proposal with the Germans. The German Chargé d'Affaires in Moscow complained

[19] He told State Secretary von Bülow that "the Eastern Pact project had purposely not been completely drawn up because it had been intended to draw up the text jointly with us [the Germans.]" Conversation of 23 July 1934, *G.F.P.*, III, 220-221; see also *B.F.P.*, VI, 872, 888-889, 892-893.

[20] *G.F.P.*, III, 349-351.

[21] *F.R.U.S.*, *1934*, I, 496-497, 502-508; *B.F.P.*, VI, 889, 896, and VII, 717-718; *G.F.P.*, III, 270-271, 279-280, 292-293.

[22] *G.F.P.*, III, 209-210. The Soviet Ambassador made a similar notification to the British Foreign Office, 19 July 1934. *B.F.P.*, VI, 849.

that "as authoritative Soviet quarters maintain the greatest reserve towards this Embassy in the matter of the Eastern Pact, it is not possible for me to supply any authentic opinion as to the Soviet Government's intentions."[23]

On 25 July 1934, Hitler again applied the spur. That was the day his Austrian comrades almost staged the *Anschluss*. In Vienna, a band of Austrian Nazis seized the Chancellery, shot the Chancellor, little Dollfuss, refused to let in a doctor or a priest, and then, while their coup failed, watched him bleed to death. Coming so close on the Blood Purge, the assassination of Dollfuss roused Europe against Nazi Germany as nothing else had done before. Mussolini, who was preparing to receive Dollfuss at Riccione and was already entertaining the Chancellor's wife and children there, was humiliated and furious. Four Italian divisions were moved up to the Austrian frontier near Tarvisio. The Duce proclaimed: "The independence of Austria, for which he [Dollfuss] fell, is a principle which was and shall be defended by Italy with even more fierceness in these exceptionally difficult times.... The civilized world..., by its moral condemnation, has already struck those who were directly or indirectly responsible."[24] The Italian press was let loose, and it indulged in vituperative condemnation of the barbaric treatment of Dollfuss.

The French and British governments immediately reaffirmed their backing of Austrian independence; Sir John Simon chose the House of Commons as the place to voice "our horror at this cowardly outrage."[25] The reaction of the Doumergue cabinet could best be read in a leading article in *Le Temps*, "To Defend the Peace," by far the most resolute editorial since Hitler's accession to power. The Dollfuss assassination, it said, had crystallized tendencies which had been fluid.

[23] Dispatch from Herr von Twardowski, 11 Aug. 1934, *G.F.P.*, III, 311-314.

[24] Telegram from Mussolini to Prince Starhemberg, Austrian Vice-Chancellor, 26 July 1934, *D.I.A.*, *1934*, p. 293. For reports on Mussolini's personal reaction and Italian troop movements, consult: Aloisi, *Journal*, pp. 205-208; *F.R.U.S.*, *1934*, II, 32 ff.; *B.F.P.*, VI, 869 ff.; *G.F.P.*, III, 251 ff.; Lagardelle, *Mission à Rome. Mussolini*, pp. 85-88.

[25] House of Commons, *Parliamentary Debates*, 26 July 1934, cols. 1942-1944. Neville Chamberlain wrote, 28 July 1934: "I had a great admiration, and almost an affection, for [Dollfuss].... That those beasts should have got him at last, and that they should have treated him with such callous brutality, makes me hate Naziism, and all its works, with a greater loathing than ever." Quoted in Keith Feiling, *The Life of Neville Chamberlain* (London, 1946), p. 253.

Since the assassination of Chancellor Dollfuss, a great change has taken place. Almost all of Europe, Italy in the first rank, is drawn up in front of the disturbers.... No longer will anyone think of tolerating that she [Germany] carry across her frontiers, by force or by ruse, an ideology of which the least one can say is that she is today the only country able to live with it.[26]

The editorial went on to urge the speedy conclusion of security pacts. The time for hesitation was past; something must be done.

For Barthou personally, the Dollfuss assassination was confirmation that *Mein Kampf*, which he had read, was to be taken literally. While on vacation in Switzerland in August he asked the journalist Wilhelm Herzog: "How can I be blind ... to the monstrosities which are taking place before our eyes in Germany? The triumph of organized force, the biologically based brutality, the racial delusion, the persecutions of the Jews, the intellectuals, the socialists and democrats...."[27] Barthou insisted that nothing would stop the Nazis but a powerful coalition. The Dollfuss assassination set the lines of Louis Barthou's resolve.

The Blood Purge and the assassination of Chancellor Dollfuss left Germany isolated. But Hitler was not afraid of moral condemnation. He simply drew back and waited; never again until 1940 did he move before the ground was prepared. His luck came back quickly with the death of President von Hindenburg, 2 August 1934. Immediately, the German government passed a decree which added the office of the President to that of the Chancellor. The leaders of the Reichswehr, who had been pleased to see their S. A. rivals destroyed by the Blood Purge, now fulfilled their part of the implicit bargain. Across the land, officers and men of the Reichswehr took a new oath: "I swear by God this holy oath: I will render unconditional obedience to the Fuehrer of the German Reich and People, Adolf Hitler, the Supreme Commander of the Armed Forces...."[28] Barthou's comment was that now "the situation in Germany had grown definitely worse, but ... clearer, the assumption of supreme

[26] "Bulletin du Jour," 1 Aug. 1934. André Tardieu, Minister of State in the Doumergue cabinet, had been a famous editorial writer for *Le Temps* and maintained close relations with the paper.

[27] Quoted by Herzog, *Barthou*, pp. 94-95. "Es gibt keine andere Lösung, scheint mir, als dass alle diejenigen Völker, die aufrichtig den Krieg hassen und ihm vorbeugen wollen, sich vereinen, um dem Chaos, dass uns alle zu verschlingen droht, entgegenzuwirken. Nicht mit billig gewordenen Friedensphrasen und nebulosen Versprechungen; sondern ganz real und konkret mit äusserster Aktivität und Wachsamkeit." Quoted *ibid.*, pp. 93-94.

[28] Quoted by Alan Bullock, *Hitler: A Study in Tyranny* (New York, 1952), p. 282.

power by Hitler making it certain to the world that no one could count on Germany's peaceful intentions or honest purpose."[29]

The German government was determined to reject Eastern Locarno, but the step was deliberately delayed. Finally, it was decided that an answer had to be given before the fall session of the League of Nations.[30] The German note was presented on 10 September to the foreign ministries in London, Paris, Moscow, Rome, and Warsaw. The rejection of the pact was based on an adroit analysis of its ambiguities. It was not practical, the selection of its members was illogical, and the Franco-German-Russian Pact was hypocritical.

> The German Government cannot consider it a practical reality that Germany, one day, should be defended in her own territory by Soviet-Russian troops against an attack from the west or by French troops against an attack from the east.[31]

The connection of Eastern Locarno with a revival of arms negotiations was rejected as worthless, a vague promise for the future. Although the note was not published, its essence was revealed to the press and restated by Baron von Neurath in a speech at Berlin, 19 September.[32]

The three tiny Baltic states which had been invited to join Eastern Locarno became pawns in a struggle between Moscow and Warsaw. Finland, incidentally, never showed any desire to join the pact and was left out of the negotiations.[33] Estonia, Latvia, and Lithuania were interested but fearful of creating any grounds for the entry of Russian troops. Colonel Beck tried to persuade Estonia and Latvia to co-ordinate their policies with Poland, but his efforts were erased by Litvinov. The Estonian Foreign Minister, M. Seljamaa, traveled to Moscow, 29-30 July, and issued a statement that in principle Estonia favored the pact; the Latvian minister in Moscow made an identical statement. On 2 August the Lithuanian Foreign Minister, M. Lozoraitis, came to Moscow and

[29] To the United States Ambassador, Mr. Jesse Straus, 31 Aug. 1934, *F.R.U.S.*, *1934*, I, 572-573.

[30] The Germans and Poles kept each other informed of their intentions. Beck sharply criticized Eastern Locarno to the German minister, 1 Aug.; the Polish minister repeated this criticism to Hitler, 27 Aug., and Beck told Neurath, 6 Sept., that Poland definitely would not accept the pact. "Both he and Marshal Pilsudski were extremely skeptical about the whole Eastern Pact proposal, and he would make no secret of this in Geneva." *G.F.P.*, III, 277-279, 360-361, 385-386.

[31] German Memorandum on Eastern Locarno, *G.F.P.*, III, 396-402.

[32] *D.I.A.*, *1934*, pp. 331-336.

[33] *F.R.U.S.*, *1934*, I, 494, 502, 518; *G.F.P.*, III, 215; *B.F.P.*, VI, 896.

joined Litvinov in a declaration favoring the pact.[34] Lithuania had been expected to side with Russia, but the "defection" of Estonia and Latvia wounded Polish pride.

Despite French prodding,[35] Colonel Beck did not send an official answer on Eastern Locarno until 27 September 1934, after the German rejection and after the entry of the Soviet Union into the League of Nations, about which he made considerable difficulty.[36] The Polish note, which amounted to a rejection, argued that Eastern Locarno would upset Poland's recent efforts to improve her security by direct relations with Germany and Russia. Poland could consider the pact only on the basis of four reservations: no obligations towards Lithuania; serious reluctance to incur any obligations towards Czechoslovakia; the participation of Germany; and finally "an article stipulating the integral maintenance of the Polish-German Accord of 26 January 1934."[37]

The Polish note, however, did not reveal the deepest and most sincere reason—fear of Russia, specifically fear that Poland might have to grant Russian troops the right of passage across Poland.[38] The Poles were convinced that once on Polish soil the Russians would never go home. Count Jan Szembek, who did not share Beck's anti-French bias, protested to Ambassador Laroche: "Can't you see it, a Russo-German war and Russian troops demanding passage through our territory? That's just the way the partition of Poland began!" And on this issue, Laroche admitted that the whole country shared the government's position.[39] (Was it an unreasonable fear, after all?)

Military co-operation was not the only factor; Russia's new policy posed the whole question of Poland's role in Eastern Europe.

[34] Laroche, *La Pologne de Pilsudski*, p. 172; Beck, *Dernier Rapport*, pp. 77-82; *F.R.U.S., 1934*, I, 497-498, 505-508; *B.F.P.*, VI, 849-850, 880 ff., and VII, 720-721, 736-740; *G.F.P.*, III, 215, 266 ff.

[35] The French Ambassador warned Beck as early as 26 June that France would conclude the pact with Russia even if Poland refused to join. Laroche, *La Pologne de Pilsudski*, pp. 167 ff.; *B.F.P.*, VI, 782-784, 799-800, 892-895; Beck, *Dernier Rapport*, pp. 73-75.

[36] Beck took the opportunity to denounce the 1919 Minorities Treaty; see below, p. 199.

[37] Printed in Beck, *Dernier Rapport*, Appendix, pp. 335-338; *G.F.P.*, III, 447-449.

[38] Polish suspicions were increased by an unsuccessful French attempt in June 1934 to revise the Franco-Polish Military Convention. Laroche, *La Pologne de Pilsudski*, pp. 166-167.

[39] Conversation of 16 July 1934, Laroche, *La Pologne de Pilsudski*, p. 170; see also the report of the British Military Attaché in Warsaw, *B.F.P.*, VI, 859-861.

The French Ambassador in Warsaw evoked the anxiety of the Polish leaders.

They fear that the role of Poland will be diminished, her importance lessened in our eyes and in the eyes of Europe. They fear the use which Russia will make of a tight rapprochement with us and, even more, of an alliance.[40]

Fearless, stubborn, and misled by their recent bargain with Hitler, Pilsudski and Beck thought nothing of provoking the ire of Paris and Moscow.

Eastern Locarno embittered Franco-Polish relations. French officials respected the Polish fear of Russian troops, but they were furious at Colonel Beck's refusal to give a quick answer, his ostentatiously friendly relations with the Germans, and his obstruction of Soviet entry into the League of Nations.[41] M. Alexis Léger, who seldom allowed himself to be excited, complained bitterly that Poland was trying to "wreck" Eastern Locarno. "The Poles not only pursued a policy of their own without consultation with their ally [France], but even put spokes in the wheel of the policy of their ally."[42] Barthou returned from managing the Soviet entry into the League of Nations "embittered" at Beck's tactics. He told the French Ambassador to Warsaw: "I will not leave you in that hornets' nest."[43] After the cabinet had discussed Poland one day in September, Herriot ended his notes with the laconic verdict: "For us, she is no longer a friend."[44] It has been said that the Franco-Polish alliance obstructed the Franco-Soviet rapprochement. On the contrary, the moral collapse of the Franco-Polish alliance helped to bring France and Russia together.

[40] Dispatch of 16 July 1934, quoted in Laroche, *La Pologne de Pilsudski*, pp. 170-171. In April Pilsudski ordered a military-political study of the question: "Of the two countries [Russia and Germany] which one is, or will become, the more dangerous to Poland?" The conclusion was that Russia was the more likely to run the risk of war and, therefore, the more dangerous to Poland. J. Szembek, *Journal, 1933-1939*, pp. 2-3, 65-66; Beck, *Dernier Rapport*, pp. 64-66.

[41] Further friction was caused by severe restrictions on French investments and enterprises in Poland and by the Polish-Czech quarrel. The extent of Polish antagonism can be gauged from Colonel Beck's extraordinary revelation about one of Pilsudski's current projects. "Entre autres choses, il organisa à Moszczenica un exercice de cadres dont le thème était les opérations que la Pologne aurait à effectuer si la Tchécoslovaquie se désintégrait ou capitulait devant l'Allemagne." *Dernier Rapport*, pp. 83-84.

[42] Conversation with Sir George Clerk, British Ambassador in Paris, 25 July 1934, *B.F.P.*, VI, 872-873, 876-877; see also pp. 892-895.

[43] Laroche, *La Pologne de Pilsudski*, pp. 179-180.

[44] Notes of the cabinet of 22 Sept. 1934, Herriot, *Jadis*, II, 452.

By the end of September 1934 Eastern Locarno was dead. Only France, Russia, and Czechoslovakia (aside from the badgered Baltic states) wished to play the game. Something different would have to be devised.

iii

No foreign policy in modern times can be divorced from domestic politics, least of all an alliance with Soviet Russia. M. Barthou's design could not succeed if a large part of French public opinion opposed it. In this year of 1934 there were two domestic developments of direct significance: the favorable evolution of conservative opinion to the rapprochement and the birth of a Socialist-Communist united front.

For the first time the rumors of a Franco-Russian alliance were plausible. The ostentatious co-operation of Barthou and Litvinov at Geneva was front-page news and so were the ups and downs of Eastern Locarno and Soviet entry into the League of Nations. Publicity also was attracted by the exchange of visits so dear to the new public diplomacy. A large delegation of French scientists, headed by Professor Jean Perrin, traveled to Russia in May for the "Franco-Soviet Scientific Rapprochement Week." In August a Soviet Air Squadron flew to France to return the flight of M. Pierre Cot to Russia in 1933. The Soviet mission, headed by M. Unschlicht, chief of Soviet civil aviation, and General Khripin, chief of the Air Staff, spent a week touring factories and watching tests and maneuvers.[45]

On the Left, the Radical-Socialist party continued to provide the most numerous champions of the rapprochement. This attitude was in line with its traditional Jacobin reaction to foreign threats. Many members followed the lead of M. Édouard Herriot, President of the party and leader of the six Radicals who sat in the Doumergue cabinet. Herriot remained convinced of the inescapable necessity of the alliance.[46]

I have reflected on this as best I could. Hitler has taken his stand; he is already in full execution of his program and his maneuvers are only feints and lies. It is on the side of Russia that England and France

[45] *Le Temps, L'Echo de Paris,* 8-16 Aug. 1934; *Bulletin de la presse russe,* No. 242.

[46] Herriot had an unusual private source of information, Litvinov himself. He quotes from four letters written to him by Litvinov throughout 1934; note the contrast between those of 4 June and 4 August. *Jadis,* II, 373, 438, 449, 453.

must seek their security and that of the small states of Europe. The map talks; that is sufficient.[47]

Other prominent Radicals, such as Yvon Delbos, Georges Bonnet, and Pierre Cot, spoke up for the rapprochement. At the annual party congress M. Cot, formerly Air Minister, presented the case entirely in terms of power.

The military power of the U.S.S.R. is considerable and is on the rise. Its army, well equipped and well disciplined, is commanded by young, likeable leaders, who are full of drive and intellectual curiosity. Its bombing force is the strongest in Europe. Its industrial potential already is equal to that of Germany, double that of France or of England.[48]

Nonetheless, some opposition was heard from the left wing of the party by the friends of M. Édouard Daladier, Herriot's keen rival.[49] Daladier himself was now very quiet, letting time dull the memory of his role in the February crisis. He never supported Herriot's all-out Russian policy, and thus maintained intact "the war of the two Edwards."

Farther to the left, all things were overshadowed by the dramatic reconciliation of the Socialists and Communists. After the joint manifestation of 12 February 1934, the bitter struggle of the two parties had been revived in all its intensity. With one exception, the Communists maintained their daily campaign of anti-Socialist abuse; the exception was Jacques Doriot, one of the party's most energetic and popular leaders. Doriot's crime was to be right before the party was right. As mayor of the working-class Paris suburb of Saint-Denis, he organized a "Front Commun" in which local Communists and Socialists enthusiastically joined hands against Fascism. Summoned to Moscow in April 1934, along with Maurice Thorez, head of the party, Doriot refused to go. When Thorez returned to Paris, he carried orders to expel Doriot from the party and to put into practice the heretic's very policy![50]

[47] *Ibid.*, p. 411; G.F.P., III, 421.

[48] Speech of 26 Oct. 1934, at Nantes. Quoted in *Société des Nations*, XVI, 568-569. M. Bonnet, several times Finance Minister, visited Russia during July-August 1934. In a series of articles for *Le Petit Parisien*, he praised the rapid progress of the Red Army. Georges Bonnet, *Defense de la Paix, Du Washington au Quai d'Orsay* (Geneva, 1946, 1948), p. 123.

[49] See criticism from M. Jacques Kayser in *La République*, quoted in "Revue de la presse," *J.D.*, 5, 11 June 1934; also the debates of the special Radical-Socialist Congress at Clermont-Ferrand, *Le Temps*, 12-15 May 1934, and Herriot, *Jadis*, II, 426-430.

[50] Franz Borkenau, *European Communism* (London, 1953), pp. 115 ff.; Walter, *Histoire du Parti Communiste Français*, pp. 264-271.

The Communist party promptly proposed to the Socialist party an agreement on common action against Fascism and exploratory talks began early in June.[51] Once their decision was made, the Communists exploited fully "the emotional intensity of the *mystique* of working-class unity and solidarity." M. Léon Blum, the Socialists' chief, was deeply suspicious of the sudden Communist reversal, but he was "swamped by the enthusiasm of the rank and file."[52]

From the national congress of the Communist party, 26 June, Thorez launched an ardent appeal: "At any price, the Communist party wishes unity of action of the masses against the bourgeoisie and fascism."[53] His article in *Cahiers du Bolchévisme*, 1 July 1934, suggested a series of astonishing leaps, starting from co-operation with the Socialists, then with the lower middle classes, and finally even a bow to patriotism.

We have said and we repeat: *We, the Communist party, are ready to renounce criticism of the Socialist party during the common action.* . . . There will not be the slightest attack against the organizations and the leaders of the Socialist party who are faithful to the accord with our party.[54]

Formal negotiations began on 15 July, and the Socialist leaders were surprised and outflanked when the Communists made all the concessions.

On 27 July 1934, delegates from the two parties signed a "Unity of Action Pact" against "fascist organizations."[55] Thus, fourteen years after their split at the Congress of Tours, Socialists and Communists were united again, not in a single party, but in combat. This unity of action, called "Front Unique" or "Front Commun" at

[51] One Socialist proposal was a collector's item of diplomatic history. *Le Populaire* suggested that the Franco-Soviet Non-Aggression Pact of 1932 should be doubled by a "Pacte de Non-Agression Socialo-Communiste." A draft pact was printed, with a preamble and five articles modeled on those of the 1932 pact. *Le Populaire*, 23 June 1934; the idea originated in the Socialist paper *La Bataille* of Lille.

[52] Marcus, *French Socialism in the Crisis Years, 1933-1936*, p. 77. The popular appeal of unity of action was shown when the National Council of the Socialist party authorized the negotiations by a vote of 3,471 to 366.

[53] *Oeuvres de Maurice Thorez* (Paris, 1951), Livre II, Tome 6, p. 186.

[54] *Cahiers du Bolchévisme*, 1 July 1934, XI, 771-780. "Nous voulons empêcher que les employés des grandes villes, que les fonctionnaires, que les classes moyennes—petit boutiquiers, artisans—et que la masse des paysans—travailleurs ne soient gagnés par le fascisme. . . . Puis, afin de combattre la pénétration de l'idéologie chauvine dans les couches de la petite bourgeoisie, nous avons dit ouvertement 'nous aimons notre pays.' "

[55] For the text of the pact see *Le Populaire*, 28 July 1934.

this moment, was destined to grow into the famous "Front Populaire."

What could have been the motives for the sharp twist in Communist policy and for its approval by Stalin? A fascinating enigma
this remains, provoking completely contradictory hypotheses.
Either Stalin was laying the basis for a left-wing revolution in
France; or he intended that unity of action with the Socialists
would lead to co-operation with the Radical-Socialists, then with
the Center and finally with the Right itself. The latter hypothesis
would be the logical complement to the policy of alliance with
France, because the Doumergue-Barthou government was conservative.[56] Both explanations assume that Stalin foresaw the smashing
success of the new tactic. But this assumption is unlikely; no one
else foresaw it and Stalin was well-known for his low opinion of
foreign communists and his ignorance of conditions in Western
Europe. The most plausible hypothesis is that Stalin had no idea
of where the first step would lead, and that he approved it in
pragmatic fashion—try it out and see what happens. In any case,
he had made a decision that caused an upheaval in French politics.

The Unity of Action Pact did not immediately alter the attitudes of the Socialist and Communist parties towards the Franco-
Soviet rapprochement. M. Léon Blum welcomed Soviet entry into
the League of Nations, but he took a sour view of the security
pacts proposed by Litvinov and Barthou. "Europe thus will be
split into antagonistic clans, each desperately arming."[57] Blum in-
dicted the rapprochement in the most damaging terms possible
for a Socialist: Barthou was stamping on it "the character of the
pre-war Franco-Russian alliance."[58] Communist attacks on French
foreign policy retained all their scorn and violence. The party
bitterly opposed the Doumergue government, "this ministry of high
finance and grand larceny," and Communist deputies continued to
vote against the appropriations for French military services.[59]

[56] Franz Borkenau, *European Communism*, pp. 133 ff. makes a provocative
case for this hypothesis. It cannot lightly be dismissed owing to the prevision of
co-operation with the middle classes and of a patriotic attitude in Thorez' article
in *Cahiers du Bolchévisme*. However, as Borkenau admits, given the seething Left-
Right rivalry in France, it was a wildly impractical idea.

[57] Editorial in *Le Populaire*, 10 June 1934.

[58] "Le parti Socialiste . . . reste hostile aux alliances militaires accélérant la course
aux armements." Editorial in *Le Populaire*, 13 July 1934.

[59] Article of Jacques Duclos in *Cahiers du Bolchévisme*, XI, 1118-1119. M.
Sulpice Dewez, a Communist Deputy, told the Chamber that French workers no
longer believed in national defense. "Ils comprendront que leur ennemi est dans

The other side of the fence witnessed a vital shift of conservative opinion. Many men of the Center and Right had accepted the Non-Aggression Pact, but they had been unwilling to go further and had been shocked by the rumors of a Franco-Russian alliance.[60] Now, in the spring and summer of 1934 some prominent conservatives accepted the necessity of an alliance. They were influenced by the fact that the respectable Doumergue government sanctioned the policy and by reports of the Army's approval. They were shaken by the Blood Purge and the assassination of Dollfuss; it was a tough world and tough, unpleasant allies might be needed to stop Hitler.

Such elderly heroes of the Right as Marshal Lyautey, M. Jules Cambon, and apparently also M. Raymond Poincaré, decided that the alliance was worth courting.[61] For M. Jules Cambon, master of the old diplomacy, the situation was nearly the same as it had been before 1914. "Diplomacy is above all a question of geography. There are some eternal laws. If France wishes to grapple with a greater Germany, then the alliance in the east is indispensable."[62]

The trend in the press was started by M. Henri de Kerillis and M. André Géraud (Pertinax) of *L'Echo de Paris*, and by M. René Pinon of the haughty *Revue des Deux Mondes*.[63] The latter previously had looked with disdain upon the rapprochement; now, preoccupied with Hitler's intentions, he welcomed Eastern Locarno.[64]

Every political act consists of choosing between opposing disadvantages, between contrary perils.... For the moment, the Soviet Union brings powerful assistance to the Powers who, in the presence of a

---

leur propre pays. Ils suivront la route tracée par leurs frères de Russie. Ils repousseront l'union sacrée et préféreront l'insurrection à la guerre, ils détruiront votre régime et vous balayeront." *J.O.*, Chambre, *Débats*, 15 June 1934, pp. 1514-1518.

[60] See above, chap. vii, pp. 140-141.

[61] Article by Henri de Kerillis on Marshal Lyautey, *L'Echo de Paris*, 22 Oct. 1934; Poincaré's unpublished obituary article on Barthou, quoted by Jacques Chastenet, *Raymond Poincaré* (Paris, 1948), p. 289.

[62] Quoted by his niece, Mme Geneviève Tabouis, *Ils l'ont appelée Cassandre*, p. 162.

[63] The "Bulletin du Jour" editorials in *Le Temps* are not representative because they were frequently inspired by the Quai d'Orsay. However, M. Wladimir d'Ormesson wrote several articles in *Le Temps* supporting Barthou's Russian policy; see especially that of 9 Sept. 1934.

[64] "Chronique de Quinzaine," *Revue des Deux Mondes*, 1 July 1934, pp. 235-237. "Il y a là, en quelque sorte, une loi de physique politique qui, dès que l'Allemagne s'agite et devient menaçante, porte ses voisins de l'Est et ceux de l'Ouest à s'épauler."

frenzied and fanatical Germany, deem that they cannot take too many precautions. . . .

The Rapallo policy, the most dangerous menace which has weighed on Europe, is broken. Europe is organizing itself as a consequence of the German peril. . . . Even if Soviet, Russia is Russia.[65]

M. Pinon added a warning, perhaps to Barthou: "Do not forget the proverb: he who sups with the devil must bring a long spoon."

The approval of *L'Echo de Paris* was very significant, because it was the "ultra-conservative paper of the Catholic bourgeoisie" and close to the French Army.[66] Its widely read foreign affairs columnist, Pertinax, had derided the alliance as "ephemeral and risky" as late as December 1933; but he changed over in March 1934 and became its strongest advocate in the Paris press. For Pertinax the clinching argument was the need to weaken the Reichswehr. By Franco-Soviet collaboration, "the Russo-German policy of Rapallo is snapped. Russia will not be a reservoir of raw materials at Germany's disposition."[67]

The editor of *L'Echo de Paris*, M. Henri de Kerillis, an aggressive Right-winger, changed his mind after a flight to Russia. In a series of articles written in October 1934, M. de Kerillis described the giant strides of the Red Air Force and stated that it was "capable of playing a decisive role" in a war against Germany.[68] In accepting the Franco-Russian alliance, there must be no nonsense, only "the coldest of realisms." The risks were unpleasant, but they were overridden by the critical factor of French weakness.

France is too weak to stand alone against Germany, whose population is a third more numerous, whose industrial resources are five or six times larger. France knows what isolation cost her in 1870-1871.[69]

If one had second thoughts, said de Kerillis, it was only necessary to imagine the revival of Russo-German friendship.

Not all of the Center and Right rallied to the rapprochement; for example, the traditional conservative daily, *Le Journal des*

[65] *Ibid.,* 1 Oct. 1934, pp. 712-714.

[66] The description is that of Charles Micaud, *The French Right and Nazi Germany* (Durham, N. C., 1943), Bibliography.

[67] *L'Echo de Paris,* 19 June 1934; see also his articles of 19 May, 10, 12 July, and 13 September 1934. Pertinax's first clear plea for the alliance was made in his article of 22 March 1934. One reason for his shift was a request from General Gamelin, Chief of Staff, to explain the rapprochement to the public. Pertinax, *Les Fossoyeurs,* I, 15; see also Paul-Boncour, *Entre Deux Guerres,* II, 371.

[68] Articles of 17, 18 Oct. 1934, *L'Echo de Paris.*

[69] Articles of 21, 22 Oct. 1934, *L'Echo de Paris.*

Débats, continued to reject its necessity.[70] As for the reactionaries, the extreme Right, they maintained their virulent attacks. *L'Action Française, Le Matin, L'Ami du Peuple,* and the weeklies *Gringoire* and *Je Suis Partout,* bitterly denied that any foreign menace was great enough to justify alliance with communist Russia.[71]

The favorable evolution of conservative opinion was partly caused by the fact that the French Army supported the rapprochement. The Army had backed M. Paul-Boncour's decision to open negotiations for an alliance and it supported Barthou's rapid pace.[72] The Army's approval was demonstrated by the presence of Marshal Pétain and General Denain in the Doumergue cabinet; Barthou could not have succeeded if his policy had been rejected by the Marshal, whose prestige was pre-eminent. André Tardieu and Louis Marin, both regarded as spokesmen for the Army, shared in the Cabinet's collective responsibility. Tardieu told Barthou one day: "You will have the military with you in your Russian policy; they are in a hurry to recover the alliance with Moscow...."[73] When the cabinet gave its approval to sending a "small aviation mission" to Russia, 20 February 1934, the Air Minister, General Denain, asserted: "Soviet aviation is first in the world."[74] In August a Soviet Air Mission flew to France to return the visit made by M. Pierre Cot in September 1933. The cabinet was informed of favorable reports on Russian power from the French Military Attaché in Moscow, Colonel Mendras.[75] Paris was impressed too by the Soviet government's decision to raise the size of the Red Army from 562,000 to 942,000 men.

General Gamelin, Chief of Staff and thus second to Weygand, fully approved Barthou's policy towards Russia. He based his opinion on the decisive aid of the Russian army in 1914, the opportunity to confirm the break between Reichswehr and Red Army, and the strategic advantages of a friendly Russia for the defense

[70] Consult frequent articles on the subject by Pierre Bernus, foreign editor, in *Journal des Débats,* especially 14 June, 25 July 1934. M. Bernus was vigilantly anti-German; he, too, desired to prevent a return to Rapallo but not by making an alliance with Russia.

[71] The approach of writers on the extreme Right was almost invariably ideological. They often denied that Soviet Russia could be treated as a state; for them it was only the headquarters of the Comintern.

[72] See chap. vii, pp. 138-140 above.

[73] At the cabinet meeting of 13 March 1934, quoted by Herriot, *Jadis,* II, 397. Tardieu's personal attitude is not clear; see *ibid.,* pp. 403, 437-438 and chap. ii above, pp. 34-43. It is likely that he was sufficiently impressed by the Army's approval to drop his previous opposition to the rapprochement.

[74] Quoted by Herriot, *Jadis,* II, 389.   [75] *Ibid.,* p. 411.

of Syria.[76] General Weygand's attitude was ambiguous: politically very conservative, if not reactionary, co-operation with Soviet Russia was repugnant to him. He accepted the necessity of some contacts but to what extent is not clear. On Barthou's request General Gamelin discussed the matter with Weygand: "I came to an agreement with him [Weygand] on the opinion that Russia 'represented the only great counterweight vis-à-vis Germany.'"[77]

The High Command's support of the Franco-Soviet rapprochement was qualified. The military did not want a Military Convention, which would set up intimate collaboration between the two armies. They feared Communist infiltration among French troops, and they were influenced by purely military considerations. They were skeptical that the Red Army could take the offensive, and, in any case, they did not think that the French Army needed a Russian offensive.

What, then, did the Army leaders hope to gain from the rapprochement? The answers vary, but they all derive from the completely defensive posture of the French Army itself. Its doctrine based on the superiority of the defensive, its manpower reduced by the wartime losses and by the 1928 one-year service law, the French Army was incapable of taking the offensive.[78] Its war plan was to man the Maginot Line and to move up into Belgium, there also to man a defensive position. It was trained to hold and then to wear down the attacking German armies.[79]

In these circumstances there were several services that the Russians could render. The very existence of war between Russia and Germany would suffice to create a second front to which the Reichswehr would have to divert forces. General Loizeau put it

[76] Gamelin, *Servir*, II, 130-133.

[77] *Ibid.*, II, 132. Consult chapter vii above, pp. 138-140; *G.F.P.*, III, 125; Pertinax, *Les Fossoyeurs*, II, 43-44; Weygand's report on the state of the French Army, 10 Feb. 1934, *Les Événements Survenus en France de 1933 à 1945*, Rapport, I, 92-93. The Franco-Soviet rapprochement is not discussed in Weygand's memoirs, *Mirages et Réalité*.

[78] Consult Richard D. Challener, *The French Theory of the Nation in Arms, 1866-1939* (New York, 1955), chaps. iv-vi.

[79] Weygand told the British Military Attaché, 26 April 1934: "4. The war had taught us two very important lessons:—The first was the superiority of the defence over the attack. The second, the value of permanent fortifications.... 5. As France had no intention of attacking Germany, and as her policy was definitely a defensive one, Germany, in order to wage war victoriously against France, would have to acquire a very considerable margin of superiority before she embarked on this venture.... Germany would not be able, with the weapons known to us at present, to overcome France." *B.F.P.*, VI, 684.

in this form: "The command judged that, in the state of her effectives and her armaments, France . . . had need of a powerful ally capable of creating immediately a serious second front against Germany: obviously, in Europe there were only two possible allies, Italy and the Soviet Union."[80]

A second service was to back up the small French allies in Eastern Europe, Poland, and Romania. M. Paul-Boncour, the former Foreign Minister who had begun the negotiations, told a Polish diplomat that the French general staff was trying to arrange it so that Russia would be the principal route and source of munitions for Poland.[81] The third view, which concerned Russia's raw materials and heavy industries, was explained by Colonel de Lattre de Tassigny, a member of Weygand's personal staff. "A Russia unfriendly to France but friendly to Germany would provide the latter country with a vast reservoir of raw materials and a not inconsiderable industrial potential." To prevent this by detaching Russia from Germany was the object of the French advances to Russia.[82]

These considerations help to explain a paradox—why the French Army wanted an alliance but did not want its logical consequence, a military convention. If the completely defensive nature of the French Army is kept in mind, the paradox is resolved. There was no urgent need for a Russian offensive; merely a second front or even the benevolent neutrality of Russia would suffice to hurt Germany by depriving her of Russian resources and by dividing her army. Thus weakened, German divisions would pound in vain at the Maginot Line and the Franco-Belgian trenches.

[80] General Loizeau, deputy Chief of Staff in charge of Intelligence and Operations, "Une Mission Militaire en U.R.S.S.," *Revue des Deux Mondes,* 15 Sept. 1955, pp. 252-253.

[81] "Les nouvelles conceptions de l'état-major français, établies pour tenir compte du système des fortifications et de l'organisation de l'armée de métier, peuvent empêcher l'armée française de coopérer activement avec la Pologne et notamment de prendre l'offensive contre l'Allemagne." Conversation with M. Komarnicki, Polish delegate at the League of Nations, 11 Sept. 1934, at Geneva, quoted in Beck, *Dernier Rapport,* p. 73, n. 1.

[82] Conversation with the British Military Attaché, 10 Nov. 1933, B.F.P., VI, 50-51. M. Alexis Léger said that "It was impossible to exaggerate the importance to France of being able to draw on Russia's vast industrial resources. In aeroplane construction alone, to mention only one instance, the French Government realised that France could not compete unaided with Germany if it ever came to war." Conversation with the British Ambassador, 20 June 1934, *ibid.,* VI, 770; see also G.F.P., III, 420-421; Van Overstraeten, *Albert I-Leopold III, Vingt Ans de Politique Militaire Belge,* p. 157.

iv

Returning from an August vacation in Switzerland, M. Louis Barthou pressed on with his grand design. First he set in motion the cumbersome machinery necessary for the admission of Russia to the League of Nations. He had persuaded Maxim Litvinov that early Russian entry was desirable and Litvinov had secured Stalin's approval to join the League at its fall session.

There was much skepticism in Moscow about joining an international organization dominated by the "imperialists." Litvinov's success in pushing his policy aroused speculation in diplomatic circles. It was linked to the question of his personal inclinations, which were more anti-German than those of some of his colleagues. Did he really have freedom of action? No, that was impossible; he was not a member of the Politburo, and his power depended entirely on Stalin's favor.

Even Stalin's iron-handed government, however, had room for differences of opinion. There is substantial evidence that different opinions on foreign policy existed in the years 1933-1934. Litvinov, keenly anti-Nazi and perhaps influenced by his Jewish sensibilities, wanted to push the rapprochement with France as fast as possible and enter the League in order to facilitate that policy. Krestinsky, his deputy at the Foreign Ministry, Yenukidse, one of Stalin's secretaries, and Voroshilov, the Commissar of Defense, preferred cooperation with Germany. They had tried to prevent the break and they wished to avoid action that would block a return to the Rapallo policy.[83] There is no evidence of Stalin's preferences; we know only that he decided in favor of Litvinov.

It is likely that Stalin approved Litvinov's policies simply because they were turning out well. M. Alexis Léger believed that Litvinov faced serious opposition; "a number of his colleagues disapproved of the whole business and considered that Russia's future lay in an alliance with Germany."[84] Viscount Chilston, the British Ambassador in Moscow, agreed with this hypothesis and his comments are the most plausible description of Litvinov's relationship to Stalin.

[83] Consult pp. 98 and 159 above for evidence on Krestinsky, Yenukidse, and Voroshilov.
[84] Conversation with the British Ambassador, 2 Aug. 1934, *B.F.P.*, VI, 893, also earlier remarks by Léger and Barthou, *Ibid.*, 875-876, 805.

With regard to M. Léger's remark that some of M. Litvinov's colleagues disapproved of the Franco-Soviet Pact and thought Russia's future was in an alliance with Germany, I have reason to believe it is true that at least two of his colleagues, MM. Voroshilov and Yenukidze, do not see eye to eye with him, and would prefer not to be tied up with France; but such is the intense desire for 'security' that up to the present M. Litvinov is allowed by the Politburo to carry out his ideas of a French alliance. At present, and particularly since his success in obtaining American recognition and generally in international politics, a fairly free hand is given by Stalin and Company to M. Litvinov; but I understand that he has to refer all matters of principle and high policy to the Politburo, without whose assent and decision no important step can be taken.[85]

In considering Stalin's choice, it should be kept in mind that Hitler held out no encouragement of a return to Rapallo. To some extent, Stalin's only choice was between France and isolation.

In the early days of August 1934, Litvinov informed the French, British, Italian, Czech, and Turkish governments that the Soviet Union would join the League if invited and if offered a permanent seat on the Council. Acting as sponsors, French, British, and Italian diplomats turned up considerable support, but they also found reluctance in Belgium and Poland, allies of France, and downright opposition in the Netherlands, Portugal, and Switzerland, the latter host to the League.[86] The Poles and the Swiss provided the fireworks. Without any warning, at a debate of the League Assembly, 13 September, Colonel Beck used Russia's entry as the pretext to denounce the 1919 Minorities Treaty.[87]

Russia's admission tested the wits of the Geneva jurists. In the Assembly a unanimous vote was impossible, but an invitation in the form of a private letter signed by over two-thirds of the Assembly members would allow Russia to qualify for admission by a two-thirds vote of the Assembly.[88] Accordingly, an invitation was sent

[85] Dispatch of Viscount Chilston, Moscow, 10 Aug. 1934, *B.F.P.*, VII, 717-718. The German Chargé d'Affaires in Moscow, Twardowski, held similar views, but the Italian Ambassador in Moscow, Attolico, disagreed. He believed that Krestinsky and the military men had "completely written off" the Rapallo policy. *G.F.P.*, III, 150-151, 313.

[86] *B.F.P.*, VI, 893, 896 and VII, 711 ff.

[87] *League of Nations Official Journal*, Special Supplement No. 125, Records of the Fifteenth Ordinary Session of the Assembly, pp. 42-43; also Beck, *Dernier Rapport*, pp. 67-72.

[88] The matter may be studied in F. P. Walters, *A History of the League of Nations*, II, 579-585; *B.F.P.*, VII, 711 ff.; Aloisi, *Journal*, pp. 212 ff.; Herriot, *Jadis*, II, 452-453; *S.I.A.*, *1934*, pp. 354-404; Max Beloff, *The Foreign Policy of Soviet Russia* (New York, 1947-1949), I, 134-137.

to Moscow, 12 September, signed by the delegates of thirty states, notably France, Britain, Italy, Turkey, Poland, and the Little Entente. M. Litvinov replied that the Soviet Union was willing to accept the obligations of the Covenant. The Council of the League then voted unanimously (with three abstentions—Portugal, Argentina, and Panama) to grant Russia a permanent seat on the Council once she had been admitted.

On September seventeenth the fight came out in the open in the Sixth Committee of the Assembly, a committee of the whole. M. Guiseppe Motta eloquently announced the decision of the Swiss Federal Council to vote against Russia's entry, denouncing the Soviet regime's attacks on religion, the family, and private property. "We cannot sacrifice to the principle of universality the idea of a necessary minimum of moral and political conformity between States."[89] The Argentinian and Belgian delegates also spoke against admission, the latter complaining about the large Belgian investments repudiated by the Soviets. M. Louis Barthou rose to the rebuttal. His countrymen, he said, also abhorred communism and they had suffered by far the heaviest financial losses in Russia. But was this the time to dredge up the past when there were immediate dangers to be faced?

> ... I know there are certain risks and certain objections; but in public life, as in private life, it is necessary to weigh the advantages and the drawbacks. We have to take certain risks and to decide in favour of the advantages when they seem to be greater than the drawbacks.[90]

The vote to recommend Russia's admission was 38 in favor, 3 against—Switzerland, Portugal, and the Netherlands, and 7 abstentions—Belgium, Luxembourg, Argentina, Cuba, Peru, Venezuela, and Panama.

When the Assembly proper took up this recommendation on the following day, 18 September 1934, there was only a short debate and the vote was virtually the same, 39 to 3 with 7 abstentions.[91] The President of the Assembly, Swedish Foreign Minister Richard Sandler, then extended a formal welcome to the Soviet delegation and Maxim Litvinov mounted the tribune. He gave a

---

[89] *League of Nations Official Journal*, Special Supplement No. 130, Records of the 15th Ordinary Session of the Assembly, Minutes of the Sixth Committee, pp. 18-20.

[90] *Ibid.*, pp. 21-24.

[91] The Assembly also approved the Council's decision to grant Russia a permanent seat on the Council by 40 to 0, with 10 abstentions.

moderate speech, relating the Soviet desire for admission to the changing international situation. The League had been a brake on "aggressive elements," who had found it necessary to withdraw from Geneva.

The exponents of the idea of war, the open promulgators of the re-fashioning of the map of Europe and Asia by the sword, are not to be intimidated by paper obstacles. Members of the League of Nations know this by experience. We are now confronted with the task of averting war by more effective means.[92]

The U.S.S.R., said Litvinov, would work in the League to prevent war, a language far removed from Chicherin's abuse of the "capitalist conspiracy."

Thus Russia came to Geneva, in the year after Japan and Germany had departed. There was much talk of "universalism," but in reality the cause had been quite specific—the French condition that no alliance was possible until Russia joined the League. The way was now clear for a Franco-Soviet pact of mutual assistance.

M. Barthou now picked up the other strand of the twin alliance policy. Franco-Italian relations had cooled earlier in the year, but the Italian decision to support Eastern Locarno and the assassination of Dollfuss revived the rapprochement. At Geneva, Barthou and Baron Aloisi worked in very friendly fashion on Soviet entry into the League, the Saar plebiscite, and the critical Austrian question.[93] A communiqué issued by Barthou, Aloisi, and Eden, 27 September, reaffirmed "the necessity of maintaining the independence and integrity of Austria in accordance with the Treaties in force."[94] Indeed, conditions were so propitious that Barthou made plans for an official visit to Rome in the first week of November.

Before he could tie the knot, Barthou had to deal with the Italian-Yugoslav feud. It was a touchy affair and in order to handle it more smoothly he invited the King and Queen of Yugoslavia to visit Paris. King Alexander and his ministers had good reason to fear Mussolini's ill-will and ambitions. Recently, their suspicions had been acutely stimulated by the movement of Italian

[92] *League of Nations Official Journal*, Special Supplement No. 125, pp. 66-69. The next day, according to Mme Geneviève Tabouis, Barthou said: "Ma tâche principale est achevée. Le gouvernement de l'U.R.S.S. va maintenant coopérer avec l'Europe." *Vingt Ans de 'Suspense' Diplomatique* (Paris, 1958), p. 201.
[93] Aloisi, *Journal*, 215-224; Lagardelle, *Mission à Rome. Mussolini*, p. 93.
[94] Quoted in *S.I.A., 1934*, p. 485. Notice the reports of the German Ambassador in Rome, Ulrich von Hassell, *G.F.P.*, III, 300 ff.

troops up to the frontier following the assassination of Dollfuss.[95] If Barthou were not careful, the Franco-Italian rapprochement might alienate Yugoslavia. He might have been willing to pay that price, but he hoped to avoid it by acting as mediator. The Yugo-slavian court also was uneasy about Barthou's collaboration with Litvinov. There are indications, however, that King Alexander had come to understand the expediency of the French move towards Russia.[96] M. Louis Barthou thus faced a delicate task, but he had prepared the grounds by his trip to Belgrade and he went off to welcome King Alexander in his customary jaunty spirit.

[95] *G.F.P.*, III, 274; *B.F.P.*, VI, 871 ff. On Mussolini's anti-Yugoslav policies, consult Aloisi, *Journal*, and Nevile Henderson, *Water under the Bridges* (London, 1945), pp. 182-184.

[96] *B.F.P.*, VI, 806.

Ten

THE FABIAN DIPLOMACY OF
PIERRE LAVAL

King Alexander of Yugoslavia arrived in the harbor of Marseilles aboard the cruiser *Dubrovnik*, 9 October 1934. When he landed on the docks of the Vieux Port, M. Louis Barthou and General Georges escorted him to the car in which they led the procession up the ancient avenue of the Canebière. They had gone only a short way when an assassin burst out of the crowd, jumped on the car, and emptied his gun into it. King Alexander died within a few minutes; M. Barthou succumbed an hour later; General Georges was badly wounded but survived.[1]

The assassin, who was beaten to death on the spot, turned out to be a Macedonian, Vlada Georgiyeff Kerin. He and several Croats had come to France, under the supervision of Eugen Kvaternik, a leader of the Croatian terrorist society, the Ustachi. This band of conspirators was headed by the notorious Ante Pavelić; they were working for an independent Croatia and for years they had tried to kill King Alexander, on whose death they expected Yugoslavia to disintegrate. They maintained a terrorist training camp in Hungary, and had some Nazi contacts, but their main subsidies and protection came from Mussolini. The responsibility for ordering the assassination has never been proved, but, in any case, Mussolini bore a heavy indirect responsibility for harboring the Ustachi.[2] The Italian authorities refused to co-operate with the French and Yugoslav investigations; Pavelić and Kvaternik were arrested in

[1] Vladeta Milićević (head of the Yugoslavian investigation), *A King Dies in Marseilles* (Bad Godesberg, 1959); Herzog, *Barthou*, pp. 247-303; Gaetano Salvemini, *Prelude to World War II* (London, 1953), pp. 168-171; Jean Belin, *My Work at the Sûreté* (London, 1950), pp. 155-166; Paul-Boncour, *Entre Deux Guerres*, III, 21-27. Queen Marie was not in Marseilles at the time, having come to France earlier by train.

[2] Baron Aloisi's diary contains much damaging evidence of Mussolini's patronage of Pavelic and the Ustachi. *Journal*, pp. 25 ff., see especially 48-49, 187, 212, 225-228.

Italy but not brought to trial, and permission to question them was refused.

The double assassination was a harsh blow to French prestige. Yugoslavs could hardly forget that, after years of danger in the Balkans, King Alexander had not survived an hour as the official guest of France. At the funeral ceremonies in Belgrade, General Goering successfully conveyed the impression of a strong, friendly Germany sympathetic to the late King's authoritarian regime. The arrival of King Alexander had been filmed and the picture was shown around the world. The poor organization of security and the confusion in the street after the assassination combined to make a bad impression. The French Ambassador in Berlin, M. François-Poncet, thought that the film, which Hitler and his cronies ran over and over again, helped to convince them that France was decadent.[3] Many Frenchmen themselves lost self-confidence. Coming only a few months after the 6 February riots, the double assassination left doubts and troubled minds. "Dejected cabinet, everyone is disconsolate."[4]

There was a state funeral for Barthou in Paris on October thirteenth, and the same route was followed a few days later by the procession mourning his close friend, Raymond Poincaré. Coupled with the recent death of Marshal Lyautey and with those of Foch, Joffre, Clemenceau, and Briand a few years earlier, these losses meant the end of a generation of leadership. New men were converging on the positions of power; and in another month the Premier's chair was available.

For a successor to Barthou, Premier Doumergue hesitated among Tardieu, Laval, and Flandin. André Tardieu ardently desired the Quai d'Orsay; but he and Herriot, as ministers of state, represented the symbolic balance between Right and Left in the cabinet, and Herriot refused to shift over to the Ministry of Interior. Doumergue then decided upon M. Pierre Laval.[5]

The Marseilles tragedy was only the beginning of the cabinet's

[3] "Hitler et les siens avaient une assez haute idée de la France. Ils la croyaient redoutable. L'assassinat d'Alexandre et de Louis Barthou fut un des événements qui contribuèrent à modifier leur opinion et les amenèrent peu à peu à considérer que notre pays serait, éventuellement, un adversaire moins dangereux qu'ils ne l'avaient supposé." *Souvenirs d'une Ambassade à Berlin*, p. 219.

[4] Cabinet meeting of 9 Oct. 1934, 6 P.M. Herriot, *Jadis*, II, 456-457. Herriot's reaction was: "Comme Français, au souvenir de la confiance aveugle que nous témoignaient les Serbes, j'éprouve autant de honte que de douleur." Note Weygand's comments, *Mirages et Realité*, pp. 428-429.

[5] Herriot, *Jadis*, II, 458.

troubles. Vigorous in foreign policy, it failed to solve the basic problems at home. The period of relative calm after the February riots lasted only a few months. The belligerency of the semi-fascist armed leagues and the "unity of action" sworn by their Socialist and Communist opponents showed that there was no chance for a "truce" between Right and Left. An acid dispute between Tardieu and the Radical-Socialists nearly tore the cabinet apart in July.

The economy suffered the same phenomenon of relapse after a brief improvement. Doumergue had received extensive powers to fight the depression by decrees; he pursued a deflationary policy and reduced government expenses by cutting salaries and pensions of civil servants and veterans and by decreasing government services. However, the economies, though enough to be resented, were not enough to prevent a large increase in the budgetary deficit, nor did they stimulate business activity. In July 1934 the value of French exports fell to its lowest point in six years. Industrial production declined steadily, dropping from an index of 86 (100 = 1928) in February 1934 to 79 in November. In contrast, industrial production in Great Britain, the United States, Germany, and Italy was reviving. Unemployment reached a new high of 375,000 in November. Nineteen thirty-four was the year of deepest depression in France.[6]

Doumergue chose this ill-starred moment to introduce constitutional reform. His major proposal was to give the President of the Republic the right to dissolve the Chamber of Deputies after its first year, with the consent of the Senate. The specter of dissolution gave the Left nightmares of an authoritarian regime based on the semi-fascist armed leagues. The Radical-Socialists, though financially conservative, were devoted to republican institutions; their leader, M. Édouard Herriot, warned Doumergue that they would not accept dissolution. The maneuvers for a compromise produced a curious twist. In order to disarm Herriot, Doumergue, in the middle of a cabinet discussion, suddenly offered him a promise to sign a pact with the Russians. This "oblique procedure" was not appreciated by Herriot, and other efforts at conciliation failed.[7]

[6] Tables in Ministère des Finances, *Mouvement économique en France de 1929 à 1939*, pp. 147, 165, 223. Consult Wolfe, *The French Franc between Two Wars*, pp. 105-112; Charles Bettelheim, *Bilan de l'Économie Française, 1919-1946* (Paris, 1947).

[7] Herriot, *Jadis*, II, 473.

Led by Herriot, the Radical ministers submitted their resignation 8 November.

There had been rumors that the Rightist armed leagues would come out on the streets again if anyone dared touch the Doumergue government. But when the time came, M. Doumergue, who was in declining health, simply followed standard procedure and submitted his own resignation. By evening of the very same day, in order not to leave any time for street demonstrations, a new government had been formed by M. Pierre-Étienne Flandin. M. Flandin was a relatively young, able conservative, who had been Minister of Finance in the Laval-Tardieu governments of 1931-1932 and Minister of Public Works under Doumergue. Personally flexible and the leader of a Center party, L'Alliance Démocratique, the new Premier was well suited to end the crisis.[8]

The Flandin cabinet had the same basic structure as Doumergue's, a coalition of conservatives and moderate Radical-Socialists. André Tardieu, furious at the failure, retired to become a powerful but increasingly embittered publicist for constitutional reform. M. Louis Marin, president of the largest Right-wing party, the Fédération Républicain, replaced him as Minister of State in the symbolic balance with M. Édouard Herriot.[9] Marshal Pétain refused his services, but Pierre Laval continued as Foreign Minister. M. Flandin presented his cabinet to the Chamber of Deputies 13 November 1934; his conciliatory declaration of policy, postponing constitutional reform, was greeted with relief and a heavy vote of confidence, 423-118.

M. Pierre Laval already had introduced the atmosphere of conciliation into the Quai d'Orsay. Laval's policy, as we have seen, was an understanding with Germany, a policy learned under Briand in the days of Stresemann, applied in his talks with Brüning, and still applied to Hitler's Germany.[10] In the words of M. Flandin:

[8] Pierre-Étienne Flandin was born in 1889; his father was a lawyer and politician who served as Resident-General in Tunisia, 1918-1921. Flandin studied at the École Libre des Sciences Politiques and the Faculté de Droit, Université de Paris. During the war he became a pilot and served on an inter-allied aviation board; he was one of the French aviation experts at the Paris peace conference. He entered politics in 1914, serving as Deputy from the Yonne from that date.

[9] Flandin offered the Quai d'Orsay to Herriot, but the latter said he did not want it. "Pour l'instant, il me suffirait d'être délégué, le cas échéant, à Genève et de connaître la correspondance diplomatique." Herriot, *Jadis*, II, 479. This privilege gave Herriot a means of watching over the Franco-Soviet negotiations.

[10] See the portrait of Laval and account of his talks with Brüning in 1931, chap. ii above, pp. 22-24, and also the perceptive analysis of Laval by Leopold von Hoesch, who had been German Ambassador in Paris in 1931, *G.F.P.*, III, 491-494.

"M. Laval succeeded M. Barthou. He did not belong to the same generation and had not inherited the tradition of an inevitable antagonism between France and Germany. He dreamed of reconciling the French people and the German people."[11]

There is no evidence that Pierre Laval was willing to jeopardize French security to reach an understanding. He hoped to guide or channel Germany into a settlement by facing her with a strong front which would require great efforts to overcome. Such a front would be based primarily upon England and Italy; if Germany could be induced to co-operate, the result would be a concert of the four great powers of Western Europe. Laval's goal amounted to a restoration of the Four Power Pact, which he had warmly supported in 1933. Neither Laval nor Mussolini, its author, intended to acquiesce in German predominance. Certainly Germany would be treated with respect, would be given prestige and solid advantages, but the Four Power framework was also a means of containing Hitler. Proof of that is the determination of Mussolini, 1933-1935, to resist Hitler's conquest of Austria, and Laval's willingness to line up solidly alongside Italy.

The new French Foreign Minister quickly made known his friendly disposition. Talking to a journalist, he appealed to the map. " 'Look at this. . . . Do you see this big red patch right in the middle of Europe?' he said, pointing to Germany. 'Do you *really* imagine that we can have peace and collective security in Europe so long as we haven't brought *this* into our peace system?' "[12] In his first conversation with the German Ambassador, Roland Köster, he spoke candidly of his goal.

> His [Laval's] attitude to the problem of France-Germany was known to us. He could only assure us that not only had he not changed this attitude but he was more deeply convinced of its rightness than ever before. Misunderstandings must be eliminated.[13]

The Saar, for example, was a source of conflict, but it could be handled if Germany were reasonable.

The plebiscite scheduled for the Saar Territory fifteen years after the entry in force of the Versailles Peace Treaty might easily

[11] Flandin, *Politique Française*, p. 104.

[12] Interview given by Laval to Alexander Werth, Paris correspondent of the *Manchester Guardian, Which Way France?*, pp. 99-100. See also reports in *F.R.U.S.*, 1934, I, 577-578, 585; Pertinax in *L'Echo de Paris*, 3 Dec. 1934; and the perceptive discussion of Laval's policies by Elizabeth Cameron, *Prologue to Appeasement* (Washington, 1942), pp. 85-104.

[13] Conversation of 7 Nov. 1934, *G.F.P.*, III, 587-591; see also pp. 471-472, 545.

have been a venomous episode. Barthou had annoyed the Germans by taking a stiff attitude, speaking of the special responsibilities for keeping order in the Saar which accrued to France as occupant and which she would not evade. Laval eased the tension by telling Ambassador Köster that "in his opinion, the Saar was one hundred per cent German and that he personally desired nothing more sincerely than that this territory should return to Germany.... [He desired] the establishment of sincere, honest and good-neighbourly relations by a rational attitude to the Saar question."[14] Laval's first speech to the Chamber of Deputies, 30 November, was remarkable for its soothing tone. Hitler would be asked to prove his constructive purpose by collaborating in the organization of peace. "I repeat, it is a true invitation which is tendered [to Germany]. Between France and Germany there is no territorial problem."[15]

The League Council took up the problem in December and Laval immediately requested the formation of international contingents to police the plebiscite. "France would willingly agree not to send a contingent, on the understanding, of course, that Germany would send none."[16] The Germans agreed, and the Council arranged an international force composed of British, Italian, Dutch, and Swedish troops. This compromise had been prepared by an earlier one on the economic and financial arrangements for transfer of the Saar. Working under the mediation of Baron Aloisi in Rome, French and German diplomats concluded an accord, 3 December, of which the most important part was the French cession of their rights in the Saar coal mines for 900,000,000 francs.[17]

When the German cabinet met next day, Baron von Neurath praised the achievement. "For the first time we had succeeded in reaching an agreement in direct negotiations with the French." Laval would have been pleased to hear that; he would have blanched to hear Hitler's Machiavellian comment. "The *Führer and Chancellor* termed the conclusion of the agreement a clear success, for which credit must go to Germany's resurgence as a Great Power. The French had definitely missed the opportunity for a preventive war."[18]

[14] *Ibid.*, p. 588.
[15] *J.O.*, Chambre, *Débats*, 30 Nov. 1934, pp. 2834-2835.
[16] Quoted in *S.I.A., 1934*, p. 612.
[17] For evidence of Laval's conciliatory influence on the economic and police negotiations, consult *G.F.P.*, III, 654 ff.; Aloisi, *Journal*, 229-237; *F.R.U.S., 1934*, I, 204.
[18] Minutes of the German cabinet meeting, 4 Dec. 1934, *G.F.P.*, III, 706.

ii

Where was Russia in all this? M. Laval always inserted a paragraph on co-operation with Russia in his speeches, but his terms were merely correct, never enthusiastic. The Franco-Soviet rapprochement had been started by Laval's government in 1931, but it then involved only an increase in trade and a non-aggression pact.[19] Pierre Laval did not wish to continue the rapprochement beyond that point. When the cabinet had authorized Barthou's negotiations with Litvinov, 5 June 1934, Herriot had noted: "Laval declared himself categorically in favor of an accord with Germany and hostile to a rapprochement with Russia, which would bring us the Internationale and the red flag."[20]

Laval was now in charge of the negotiations he had opposed. Barthou had pushed them so far they could hardly be dropped; Herriot would have fought any attempt to do so. Laval could only play for time, and this he did brilliantly. His first move to revive the Eastern Pact.

Eastern Locarno had come to serve merely as a façade in Barthou's policy, a façade to be discarded after Germany and Poland had rejected it. Barthou had given the Russians some sort of assurance that these rejections would not be allowed to block the negotiations. Litvinov told a diplomat in July that "he had received formal promises from the French and Czechoslovak Governments to enter into a pact of mutual assistance even though any or all other governments concerned should reject such a pact."[21] Litvinov apparently exaggerated a bit; it is almost certain that what Barthou gave him was an informal, verbal promise, an assurance that, if Eastern Locarno failed, France and Russia would conclude a separate accord.[22]

Pierre Laval could afford to take lightly Barthou's promise to Litvinov, presumably because it was verbal. In any case, the cabinet had not approved it. All that the cabinet had approved was the Eastern Locarno project in which the Franco-Soviet Pact was tied to a regional Eastern pact. Laval proposed to take Eastern

---

[19] Consult chap. i above.   [20] Herriot, *Jadis*, II, 437.

[21] "The French Ambassador, Alphand, has given me the same information." Dispatch from the United States Ambassador in Moscow, William C. Bullitt, 20 July 1934, *F.R.U.S., 1934*, I, 496-497; see also *G.F.P.*, III, 111-112, 150-151, 292-293, 311-313; *B.F.P.*, VI, 782, 806, 875-877.

[22] This interpretation is based on the sources cited directly above, plus the fact that no written record of Barthou's promise has been revealed.

Locarno seriously. Instead of treating the German and Polish rejections as definitive, Laval made a careful, sympathetic study of their objections and tried to refashion the scheme. On 27 November 1934, the French Foreign Minister sent a very accommodating reply to the Polish note. All the open Polish objections received satisfaction. An annex to the Eastern pact could stipulate that the obligation of mutual assistance did not apply to states that did not have diplomatic relations, such as Poland and Lithuania. Another annex could provide for the Czech case, stating that "the pact would not include any clause on mutual assistance between these two countries." Finally, France would accept the Polish demand for an insertion in the pact that the German-Polish Declaration of 26 January 1934 would be maintained in its entirety.[23]

The French note was so conciliatory that it caused embarrassment in Warsaw. It could scarcely be rejected out of hand, yet nothing would make the Polish government, with its fear of Russia, accept Eastern Locarno. Colonel Beck merely said he would study the French proposals.[24] Beck's noncommittal response held up the negotiations with Germany. Laval still hoped to persuade Beck if he could talk to him privately, and he planned to do so at Geneva. Beck, however, did not come to the December session of the League so the talk had to be put off until January 1935. For this reason the reply to the German note on Eastern Locarno was delayed.[25] It was quite plausible to use a personal approach with Beck, but it should be noted that Laval also gained time.

When Pierre Laval first referred publicly to Eastern Locarno, he spoke almost entirely of its multilateral, collective character.

We have only one attitude: engaged in an act of international collaboration, we do not intend to substitute for it a bilateral accord.... Franco-Soviet solidarity must be exercised openly, to the benefit of all, for the consolidation of the peace in eastern Europe. Germany has been invited and will be invited again, on the same conditions and for the same motive, to participate in this mutual assistance pact where she is assured of obtaining the same guarantees as she will give to the other states.[26]

[23] French note of 27 Nov. 1934, communicated to the German government by the Polish Ambassador in Berlin, *G.F.P.*, III, 715-719; Laroche, *La Pologne de Pilsudski*, p. 186. See chap. viii above, pp. 187-188, for the Polish note of 27 Sept. 1934.
[24] Laroche, *La Pologne de Pilsudski*, p. 186.
[25] *Ibid.*, pp. 187-189; *G.F.P.*, III, 707-709, 715, 752-753.
[26] Speech of 30 Nov., *J.O.*, Chambre, *Débats*, 30 Nov. 1934, p. 2835.

Laval's audience might have been forgiven for being puzzled: what was he talking about, co-operation with Russia or with Germany?

At first, after the assassination of Barthou, the Russians seemed equally ready for a lull in the negotiations. Indeed, their reaction apparently was to take advantage of the loss of French prestige. The United States Chargé d'Affaires in Moscow, Mr. Wiley, reported that Soviet officials showed no regret over the weakening of French prestige. "France, therefore, will hereafter be dependent to a much greater degree upon the support of the Soviet Union."[27] But as time revealed that Laval was only too willing to be left alone, the Soviets became apprehensive.[28]

Maxim Litvinov, who had faced some opposition in getting his French policy accepted, reacted vigorously when he realized that it was in danger. He complained bitterly when he conferred with Laval for the first time, in Geneva 21 November 1934. He demanded "guarantees against a Franco-German accord intervening in the course of the Franco-Soviet negotiations on the eastern pact." To prevent this, he proposed a protocol promising a full exchange of information and forbidding separate negotiations. Laval suggested an exchange of letters instead, but in the end he acceded to Litvinov's pressure.[29]

The two foreign ministers signed the Franco-Soviet Protocol in Geneva on 5 December 1934. This unusual document, which amounted to "a promise not to betray each other,"[30] stated that the two governments would adopt the following attitude during the negotiation of Eastern Locarno:

1. In their relations with the Governments called to participate in the pact, and notably with those who have not yet given it their adherence in principle, neither of the two Governments will engage in negotiations aiming at the conclusion by them of political agreements, bilateral or multilateral, which might compromise the preparation and conclusion of the Regional Pact of the East or of the

[27] Dispatch of 20 Oct. 1934, from Mr. Wiley, Moscow, 860h.001 AL2/102, Archives of the Department of State, Washington, D. C.

[28] Suspicion of Laval was increased by the following incident. M. Léon Archimbaud, reporting to the Chamber on the War Ministry budget, hinted at the existence of a Franco-Soviet military alliance. The Quai d'Orsay issued an official denial and inspired a semi-official denial in *Le Temps*. Their alacrity and effusiveness made it sound as if the alliance were the last thing Laval wanted. Herriot, *Jadis*, II, 489; Archimbaud's speech, *J.O.*, Chambre, *Débats*, 23 Nov. 1934, p. 2572; *G.F.P.*, III, 692-693; "Bulletin du Jour," *Le Temps*, 25 Nov. 1934.

[29] Herriot's notes of cabinet meetings, 24 and 27 Nov. 1934, *Jadis*, II, 488-489.

[30] Dispatch from Geneva, Mr. Mayer, *F.R.U.S.*, *1934*, I, 204.

agreements connected thereto, or which would be contrary to the spirit by which they are inspired.

2. To this end each of the two Governments will be kept informed by the other of any proposition capable of having that effect....[31]

In case the Eastern Locarno negotiations had to be abandoned, the French and Russian governments would "consult with each other as to the new assurances which it would seem opportune to them to give to each other in the same spirit and with a similar objective in view."

It was a measure of the Czechoslovakian government's desire for more security that it quickly adhered to the Franco-Soviet Protocol.[32] Three weeks later the arrival in Moscow of a delegation of Czech journalists, headed by M. Hubert Ripka, a close friend of Dr. Beneš, provided evidence of the rapid progress of Czech-Soviet rapprochement.[33]

The Franco-Soviet Protocol has been described as an obligation to make an alliance if Eastern Locarno collapsed. That it was not, for the pledge on future action was limited to consultation. The Protocol cannot be construed as the decisive step from which there was no turning back. It was certainly not discussed in this fashion by French diplomats; when communicating it to other governments, they treated it as an interim affair, designed to placate Litvinov.[34] In a speech to his fellow Senators, M. Laval read out the Protocol, but he followed it with a peroration on Franco-German reconciliation.

The French Government will never do anything which justifies Germany in thinking that we intend to practice a policy of isolation towards her. The Franco-German rapprochement in an international framework is an effective guarantee of peace. Let Germany be persuaded of this, let her act accordingly and a great step will be taken towards the necessary reconciliation of our two peoples.[35]

[31] Printed in the British Blue Book, *Cmd. 5143*, pp. 14-15; also Degras, ed., *Soviet Documents on Foreign Policy*, III, 96-97; French text in *Le Temps*, 20 Dec. 1934.

[32] Announcement by M. Laval, *J.O.*, Sénat, *Débats*, 18 Dec. 1934, p. 1398; exchange of letters between Litvinov and Beneš, 7 Dec. 1934, Degras, ed., *Soviet Documents on Foreign Policy*, III, 97.

[33] Litvinov's speech to the Czech delegation, *ibid.*, III, 101-102; *Bulletin de la presse russe*, No. 247; Hubert Ripka, *East and West* (London, 1944), pp. 28-29.

[34] Laroche, *La Pologne de Pilsudski*, p. 187; Aloisi, *Journal*, p. 234; *G.F.P.*, III, 727-728.

[35] *J.O.*, Sénat, *Débats*, 18 Dec. 1934, pp. 1397-1398.

A commentary in the semi-official leader of *Le Temps* emphasized that there was nothing more to the Protocol than what appeared there.[36]

Four days after Laval and Litvinov signed their paper, a Franco-Soviet Commercial Protocol was signed in Moscow. Throughout the year there had been negotiations for revision of the provisional Commercial Accord of 11 January 1934, but the result was very thin. The Protocol merely stated that the two governments intended to negotiate a new commercial accord by 1 January 1935; in case this proved impossible, they agreed to prolong the Provisional Accord of 11 January 1934.[37] These stipulations glossed over the failure to find a compromise. The Soviets made an offer to quadruple their purchases in France, but they insisted on their familiar demand for long-term guaranteed credits.[38] It was a political impossibility for the French government to guarantee credits unless the Soviets started repayment of the huge prewar debts owed to French investors. Moscow would never consent to do that, and so the deadlock was insoluble. Negotiations were revived in Paris, 20 December 1934, and when they made no progress, the Provisional Accord was prolonged.

Owing to that accord, trade between the two countries did increase from the previous puny volume. French exports to the Soviet Union rose from 44,000,000 francs in 1933, to 108,000,000 francs in 1934 and then to 176,000,000 francs in 1935; but this figure came to only 1.1 per cent of total French exports. Russian exports to France were more valuable, but they declined slightly in 1934 and again in 1935. France never took over the leading role in Soviet foreign trade. Germany lost that role in 1935, but it was England, not France, that became Russia's foremost trading partner.[39]

French diplomacy returned at this time to a subject obscure to most countries but not to Russia—the barren, half-frozen island of Spitzbergen, high off the north cape of Norway. On 23 November 1934 the French Ambassador in Washington inquired whether the United States had any objection to the adherence of the Soviet Union to the Treaty of Spitzbergen 9 February 1920. The treaty,

[36] "Bulletin du Jour," *Le Temps*, 20 Dec. 1934.
[37] Text of the Protocol in *ibid.*, 21 Dec. 1934; Dégras, ed., *Soviet Documents on Foreign Policy*, III, 99-100.
[38] Report by M. Marchandeau, Minister of Commerce, who went to Moscow to sign the Protocol, Herriot, *Jadis*, II, 492.
[39] Tables in League of Nations, *International Trade Statistics, 1936* (Geneva, 1936), pp. 119, 280.

which provided for Norwegian sovereignty, was open to Russian adherence but the United States government previously had refused to agree; this time it approved. An invitation was sent to Moscow, under French auspices, and on 7 May 1935 the Soviet Union formally adhered to the Spitzbergen Treaty.[40]

iii

When Pierre Laval was Premier in 1931, he had confided to Henry Stimson that he "wanted to make a general settlement with Mussolini" and that they had plans for a meeting.[41] The meeting never took place, but in the following years the Franco-Italian rapprochement was started by Paul-Boncour and pursued by Barthou. Returning to power in October 1934, Laval had a second chance to make the trip to Rome.[42] He was determined to reach an intimate understanding with Mussolini, and he made it the keystone of his foreign policy.

The assassination of King Alexander of Yugoslavia by a Croatian terrorist group harbored in Hungary and Italy could have ruined the rapprochement. Laval prevented this by skilful co-ordination with the Italian delegate on the League Council, Baron Pompeo Aloisi, who was personally inclined to an entente with France. It was arranged that the League's verdict should place the blame on Hungary rather than Italy.[43] This expediency sapped Yugoslavian loyalty to France more than did the assassination of their king, but it pleased Mussolini.

The questions dividing the two countries—especially Yugoslavia, the African colonies, and the naval rivalry—were complex and touchy, but the will to agree prevailed. Benito Mussolini had made a paradoxical decision. He gambled that he could combine his European ambitions with an imperialist adventure in Africa, reasoning presumably that he could return to Europe before Hitler became too strong.[44] His aim was the conquest of Ethiopia and,

[40] *F.R.U.S., The Soviet Union 1933-1939*, pp. 278-280.

[41] Conversation with Mr. Stimson, United States Secretary of State, in London, 24 July 1931, *F.R.U.S.*, 1931, I, 549-550.

[42] See above, chap. vi, pp. 122-125; and chap. ix, pp. 181 and 201-202.

[43] Aloisi, *Journal*, pp. 232-237; Paul-Boncour, *Entre Deux Guerres*, III, 21-27; *S.I.A., 1934*, pp. 537-577.

[44] After the Saar agreements, Mussolini grew nervous about the prospect of a Franco-German understanding. Notice his sharp reproaches to the German Ambassador, 6 Dec. 1934, *G.F.P.*, III, 710-713.

on 5 December 1934, his "peripheral" pressure produced a clash between Italian and Ethiopian forces near the settlement of Wal-Wal in southeastern Ethiopia. French and British benevolence were indispensable to the operation. The French Mediterranean fleet could threaten Italian troop transports, and the French-owned railway from their Somaliland port of Djibouti to the Ethiopian capital, Addis-Ababa, could be used to supply the Ethiopians. On Christmas day, Mussolini told Aloisi: "This affair of Abyssinia will ripen when we have concluded the accord with France." When the negotiations reached a stalemate a few days later, he gave instructions to reach an accord "at any price."[45] In Paris, Laval was equally contemptuous of his experts; overriding the objections of M. Alexis Léger, who almost resigned, he decided on 2 January to go to Rome.[46]

Pierre Laval's "voyage de Rome," 4-8 January 1935, was colorful and successful. He was very proud to be received by the Pope, Pius XI; and once he and Mussolini slipped away from their experts for a secret talk that set everyone guessing. On 7 January Mussolini and Laval signed a series of agreements, known as the Rome Accords. No general alliance was made, nor were there any agreements on the naval rivalry and Yugoslavia; they concentrated on Africa and Austria where compromise was easier. In the African settlement, France ceded to Italy: a large chunk of desert to round off the southeastern corner of Libya, a tiny slice of coastline to be added to Eritrea, and 2,500 shares of stock in the Djibouti to Addis-Ababa railroad. These concessions were relatively small and in return the French received a major Italian concession, renunciation of the extensive Italian rights in Tunisia.[47]

The African settlement was so favorable to France that it was widely assumed that Laval had made Mussolini a secret concession on Ethiopia. Laval, in fact, did make such a concession, but he

[45] Aloisi's notes of 25 and 31 Dec. 1934, *Journal*, pp. 239-241.

[46] Cameron, "Alexis Saint-Léger Léger," in Craig and Gilbert, eds., *The Diplomats*, p. 384; see also Herriot, *Jadis*, II, 492-493; Flandin, *Politique Française*, p. 104.

[47] D. C. Watt has recently revealed the texts of the four secret accords in his valuable article, "The Secret Laval-Mussolini Agreement of 1935 on Ethiopia," *Middle East Journal*, XV, Winter 1961, 69-78. The public accords may be found in *D.I.A., 1935*, I, 19-24. Consult William C. Askew, "Secret Agreement between France and Italy on Ethiopia, January 1935," *Journal of Modern History*, XXV, March 1953, pp. 48-49, and Lagardelle, *Mission à Rome. Mussolini*, pp. 275-287 for important additional documentation.

always insisted that he consented only to economic penetration and not to conquest.

We made an accord—that was the famous secret clause in my dossier, but it was an open secret—by which France renounced all aspects of a sphere of influence in Ethiopia and abandoned to Italy all possible economic advantages. . . . I said to M. Mussolini: "From now on, you have a free hand, but a free hand on the peaceful plane."[48]

The Italians on the other hand claimed that Laval gave Mussolini an unqualified "free hand." It is doubtful that Laval agreed to war in Ethiopia, because he needed Italian military co-operation in Europe. His mistake was to assume that Mussolini would be content with gradual expansion into Ethiopia, as the French had been in Morocco.[49]

The European side of the Rome Accords centered upon Austria. Mussolini and Laval proposed a "Danubian Pact," a pledge of non-interference in domestic politics. The pact would be signed by Austria, Germany, Czechoslovakia, Yugoslavia, Hungary, and Italy, and would be open to the adherence of France, Poland, and Romania. In case Austria's independence should be threatened before conclusion of the pact, the French and Italian governments would consult each other on the appropriate countermeasures. They also made an important pledge concerning German rearmament. "In the event of Germany wishing to free herself unilaterally from the treaty and reserving to herself complete freedom to rearm, the two Governments, animated by the desire to act by common agreement, will consult together on the attitude to be adopted."[50]

[48] Laval's speech, "Comité secret du Jeudi 14 Mars 1940," first printed in *J.O.,* Sénat, *Débats,* 2 Aug. 1948, p. 7. Laval also said that he told Mussolini: "Imitez l'exemple du Maréchal Lyautey." Haute Cour de Justice, *Procès du Maréchal Pétain,* p. 184. See also his testimony at his own trial, *Le Procès Laval,* pp. 46-47, 55-56; his speech, *J.O.,* Chambre, *Débats,* 28 Dec. 1935, p. 2865; and his exchange of letters with Mussolini, Dec. 1935-Feb. 1936, Lagardelle, *Mission à Rome. Mussolini,* pp. 275-287.

[49] In addition to the sources cited above, consult the conflicting evidence in: Flandin, *Politique Française,* pp. 104-105, 177-178; Herriot, *Jadis,* II, 493-494; De Chambrun, *Traditions et Souvenirs,* pp. 192-209; testimony of M. Albert Lebrun to the Parliamentary Investigation, *Les Événements Survenus en France de 1933 à 1945,* IV, 959; testimony of M. Paul Baudoin, *ibid.,* VII, 2057-2059; Vansittart, *The Mist Procession,* pp. 515-516; Viscount Templewood, *Nine Troubled Years* (London, 1954), pp. 155-156; Aloisi, *Journal,* pp. 245-248 *et seq.* In a letter to Laval, 25 December 1935, Mussolini insisted that their understanding on the "free hand" had been verbal. "L'entretien que nous avons eu à Rome a été déterminé aussi par la nécessité d'une entente verbale, étant donné qu'en ce qui concerne la question du "désistement", il n'aurait pas été possible de dire tout dans des actes écrits." Lagardelle, *Mission à Rome. Mussolini,* p. 279.

[50] Protocol signed by Laval and Mussolini, Rome, 7 Jan. 1935, original and

Mussolini and Laval were determined to put some bite into their backing of Austria. They agreed to start negotiations for a military convention governing the case of a German attack on Austria. General Maurice Gamelin, who had just replaced General Weygand as chief of the French Army, initiated staff studies and made contact with his Italian counterpart, Marshal Badoglio. Gamelin worked out a plan to place a French Army corps on the Italian right flank next to Yugoslavia and an Italian Army corps on the French right flank between Belfort and Switzerland.[51]

The Rome Accords must be studied carefully for their evidence of Laval's attitude towards Germany. The pledge of common action to resist the *Anschluss* demonstrates that Laval did not seek a bargain at any price; he intended to negotiate from a strong position. On the other hand, he did not make this informal alliance with Mussolini in the spirit of preparing for an inevitable war with Germany, as Barthou had thought of it. With English assistance, Laval hoped to use the Franco-Italian entente as a means of channeling Hitler into an understanding.[52] If Hitler proved to be intransigent, then the entente would stand as protection against him.

On the surface, there was no reason why the Soviets should disapprove of the Rome Accords; they had long pursued friendly relations with Mussolini. However, M. Alphand, French Ambassador in Moscow, said that "the Soviet Government was disgruntled over the course of French policy and had regarded the results of the negotiations at Rome as in derogation of the Geneva protocol."[53] At Geneva, 16-19 January, Litvinov put severe pressure on Laval, perhaps even threatening a move towards Germany.[54] What the Soviets feared was that the Rome Accords would diminish French interest in a Russian alliance; they also suspected a return to the Four Power Pact.

---

translation printed by Watt, "The Secret Laval-Mussolini Agreement of 1935 on Ethiopia," pp. 75-76. The reference to "the treaty" is to the Versailles Peace Treaty with Germany.

[51] Gamelin, *Servir*, II, 163-165; Lagardelle, *Mission à Rome. Mussolini*, pp. 117-118.

[52] Notice Laval's remarks to the German Ambassador in Rome, 6 Jan. 1935, *G.F.P.*, III, 784-786.

[53] The reference is to the Franco-Soviet Protocol signed at Geneva, 5 Dec. 1934. Conversation between M. Alphand and the U. S. Chargé d'Affaires, Mr. Wiley, dispatch from the latter, 19 Jan. 1935, *F.R.U.S., 1935*, I, 176.

[54] *F.R.U.S., 1935*, I, 191-192; Szembek, *Journal 1933-1939*, pp. 22-23.

iv

One day in Berlin, the French Ambassador explained "that Laval could only proceed very slowly. He must go cautiously, step by step. It was not so easy . . . to pursue a policy of understanding. Laval still had to take into account a very powerful and violent opposition. . . ."[55] When Pierre Laval returned from Rome with Mussolini's friendship to display, he was strong enough to take another step.

On 13 January 1935, the Saar plebiscite recorded a vote of 90.35 per cent in favor of reunion with Germany. The Council of the League of Nations thereupon decided that the Saar territory should return to German sovereignty on 1 March. Hitler expressed his pride that "the call of the blood prevailed so overwhelmingly," but he promised that "the German Reich will raise no further territorial claims against France."[56] Two days later, at Geneva, M. Laval welcomed Hitler's gesture and called upon Germany to join the security pacts under negotiation. "The rapprochement of our two countries is, in effect, one of the essential conditions for the effective guarantee of peace in Europe. France is pacific; she pursues no egoistic goal."[57]

Laval turned back to Eastern Locarno at this time and sent off a reply to the German note of 10 September 1934. Although very conciliatory in tone, the French note did not contain any major concessions, which were hardly possible since the Germans objected to the basic idea of the pact.[58] Simultaneously, Laval tackled Colonel Beck during the League Council meeting in Geneva. Beck again insisted that Eastern Locarno would upset Polish relations with Germany and Russia. Poland would continue to subordinate her acceptance to the participation of Germany.[59]

Beck's refusal to bend in the slightest towards Eastern Locarno, followed by his warm reception of General Goering in Warsaw,

[55] Conversation between M. François-Poncet and Herr Gerhard Köpke, Director of Department II (West, South, and Southeast Europe) in the Foreign Ministry, 20 Dec. 1934, *G.F.P.*, III, 755.
[56] Broadcast of 15 Jan. 1935, *D.I.A., 1934*, pp. 65-66.
[57] Speech of 17 Jan. 1935, *ibid.*, pp. 67-69.
[58] French note of 15 Jan. 1935, presented the following day to State Secretary von Bülow, *G.F.P.*, III, 824-830. Baron von Neurath's minute on the note was "a lot of words with little persuasive power."
[59] Beck, *Dernier Rapport*, Appendix, pp. 283-285; Szembek, *Journal*, pp. 22-23; Laroche, *La Pologne de Pilsudski*, pp. 190-191; Herriot, *Jadis*, II, 495-496.

filled the cup to overflowing. The dispatches of the French Ambassador in Warsaw and the diary entries of the Polish Under-Secretary of State for Foreign Affairs, Count Jan Szembek, are filled with conversations that bear no relation to an alliance. Witness the devastating reproaches made by Ambassador Laroche, 2 February 1935.

> You always repeat that our alliance is at the base of your policy; however, the facts prove the contrary! ... For some time back, you have been constantly on the side of the adversaries of France. You never support her and that is having a profound influence on the psychological attitude of the French people with regard to Poland.[60]

Laroche complained that Warsaw's attitude on Eastern Locarno gave the impression of being carefully co-ordinated with Berlin.

Laval also conferred with Litvinov in Geneva. The latter vehemently renewed his demand that the Eastern Locarno negotiations not be allowed to drag on forever, and that France and Russia proceed to their own alliance. Laval assured the French cabinet on return that he had reached full accord with Litvinov, but British, Italian, and United States diplomats reported differently, emphasizing Litvinov's exasperation.[61] In any case, Laval was not to be tied; pressed from one direction he slipped off on another tack—to London.

Collaboration with the British admirably suited Pierre Laval. Their leaders shared his distrust of Russia, his determination to co-operate with Italy, and his desire for an understanding with Germany. Ironically, Laval was aided by the pro-British inclinations of his Premier, M. Pierre-Étienne Flandin, who was very suspicious of Germany. M. Flandin had set himself three objectives: "to tighten up the links of the Franco-British entente," to make an "intimate accord" with Italy, and "to bring to conclusion the negotiations with Russia."[62]

The Flandin-Laval visit to London was a remarkable conjuncture, for the British were equally busy with plans. Sir John Simon and Mr. Stanley Baldwin, insofar as he showed interest in foreign affairs, were convinced that a new effort was needed. Worried about Germany's air rearmament, hoping to avoid the cost and

[60] Conversation between M. Laroche and Count Szembek, 2 Feb. 1935, quoted by the latter, *Journal*, pp. 36-37.
[61] Notes of the French cabinet meeting of 22 Jan., Herriot, *Jadis*, II, 495; *F.R.U.S., 1935*, I, 176-178, 191-192; Aloisi, *Journal*, p. 252.
[62] *Politique Française*, pp. 169-170.

unpopularity of all-out British rearmament, they keenly desired an arms convention with Germany. Barthou had been an obstacle; now Laval offered an unexpected opportunity. As Sir John Simon told the German Ambassador, Leopold von Hoesch, "The time to try to influence Laval towards concessions was now, while he was still basking in the glory of his Rome successes. . . . The spirit of Barthou no longer reigned in the Flandin-Laval Cabinet and use must be made of this opportunity. The British Government would strive to make 1935 the year in which all problems were resolved."[63]

The British yearning for an understanding was stimulated by some private diplomacy, an interview between Hitler and Lord Lothian, a prominent Liberal peer.[64] Hitler played adroitly on two themes: his fear of Russia and his belief that England and Germany were natural partners. He also made some practical suggestions for an arms deal.

(1). The fleet is a vital necessity for England. Germany does not feel threatened by British superiority on sea. So long as Russia does not become a sea-power, we are prepared to accept the ratio, so far as the fleet is concerned, 35:100.

(2). Army. Just as we Germans recognize England's vital necessity of being supreme on sea, so England should realize that Germany must have a strong army. . . . It has to face a coalition of frightful strength, France and Russia. It must be capable of meeting this threat.

. . . .

(3). Air. This is a new arm, and we ask here for parity with England.[65]

When Lothian advanced the idea that Sir John Simon himself might come to Berlin, Hitler was very receptive.[66]

[63] Conversation of 10 Jan. 1935, *G.F.P.*, III, 797-798. Consult *F.R.U.S.*, *1935*, I, 182-183, 186, 188-192; Herriot, *Jadis*, II, 496; Thomas Jones, *A Diary with Letters, 1931-1950* (London, 1954), p. 139; Vansittart, *The Mist Procession*, pp. 482-485, 505-511. Vansittart and Churchill were very suspicious of Hitler's intentions and were convinced of the necessity for all-out British rearmament, but they were isolated. The Prime Minister, Mr. James Ramsay MacDonald, was declining in health and had lost most of his influence on foreign policy.

[64] Lord Lothian (Philip Kerr) was eager to explore all possibilities of an understanding with Hitler and had already talked to Ribbentrop, Hitler's unofficial envoy. J.R.M. Butler, *Lord Lothian* (New York, 1960), pp. 202-204; *G.F.P.*, III, 837-838, 885-887.

[65] Hitler also said that "he was prepared to give to England a binding guarantee that Germany would never attack Holland or Belgium." Lothian's notes of his talk with Hitler, 29 Jan. 1935, Berlin, Butler, *Lord Lothian*, Appendix III, pp. 330-337. Hitler made the same arms proposals to Lord Allen of Hurtwood, publisher and member of the Labor party, 25 Jan. 1935, *G.F.P.*, III, 798-799, 873-876.

[66] Lothian reported Hitler's proposals to Sir John Simon on 30 Jan. 1935, just in time to influence the talks with Laval and Flandin. *G.F.P.*, III, 887-889.

Given this combination of interests, it is not surprising that the visit of the French ministers to London was a success. MM. Flandin and Laval had three days of cordial talks with MacDonald, Baldwin, and Simon, including a luncheon of "salmon trout, mixed grill, very mixed, Kentucky ham which tasted like crystallized nectar, plum pudding and brandy sauce." But for its effect on Laval, said Baldwin, "we should never have got the important Declaration of February 3."[67]

At the end of their talks, 3 February 1935, the British and French ministers issued a wide-ranging Declaration.[68] They proposed "a general settlement freely negotiated between Germany and the other Powers."

This general settlement would make provision for the organization of security in Europe, particularly by means of the conclusion of pacts, freely negotiated between all the interested parties, and ensuring mutual assistance in Eastern Europe and the system foreshadowed in the Rome *procès-verbal* for Central Europe. Simultaneously, and in conformity with the terms of the Declaration of December 11, 1932, regarding equality of rights in a system of security, this settlement would establish agreements regarding armaments generally which, in the case of Germany, would replace the provisions of Part V of the Treaty of Versailles at present limiting the arms and armed forces of Germany. It would also be part of the general settlement that Germany should resume her place in the League of Nations with a view to active membership.[69]

The British and French ministers also advanced a novel concept— security in the air. They suggested that a group of states in Western Europe "undertake immediately to give the assistance of their air forces" to any one of them attacked by "unprovoked aerial aggression." Germany, Italy, and Belgium were invited to consider with England and France whether such an Air Pact "might not be promptly negotiated."

The Anglo-French Declaration was a substantial success for British policy. It placed the arms accord on an equal plane with security. Louis Barthou had been unwilling to admit this parallel relationship. He had agreed only that the conclusion of Eastern Locarno "would afford the best ground for the resumption of negotiations" for a disarmament convention with Germany.[70] Instead,

[67] Quoted by Jones, *A Diary with Letters, 1931-1950*, pp. 152-153.
[68] On the London talks consult *F.R.U.S., 1935*, I, 182-183, 188-192; *G.F.P.*, III, 910 ff.; Herriot, *Jadis*, II, 496-498; Marquess of Londonderry, *Wings of Destiny* (London, 1943), pp. 120-124.
[69] *D.I.A., 1935*, I, 25-27.   [70] See chap. ix above, p. 179.

Laval conceded that an arms accord could be negotiated "simultaneously" with the organization of security. The priority of Eastern Locarno was thus erased. The second score for British diplomacy was the distinction between Western and Eastern Europe. The exciting new Air Pact was limited to Western Europe.

On their side, the French were pleased by British willingness to give immediate assistance in case of an air attack. If the Air Pact were negotiated, it would be a major advance in the way of a direct, physical British guarantee of French security. With this exception, the Declaration seemed to represent a victory for Sir John Simon, a reversal of his loss to M. Barthou. In fact it was not, for there had been no contest. M. Laval was delighted to drop Barthou's shell and to find a new house in Sir John Simon's general settlement with Germany.

Great interest was aroused by the idea of an Air Pact. The proposal was quickly welcomed by the German, Italian, and Belgian governments.[71] Diplomats noticed that only in connection with the negotiation of the Air Pact was the adverb "promptly" used. It was, in fact, the intention of Sir John Simon and momentarily that of Laval to negotiate the Air Pact first.[72]

Laval's attitude emerged in the unusually frank explanations made by the First Secretary of the French Embassy in London, M. Roland de Margerie, to the Counsellor of the German Embassy, Prince Bismarck, 5 February 1935.[73] M. de Margerie made a subtle distinction between the four items first mentioned in the Declaration—Eastern Locarno, the Danubian Pact, an arms convention, Germany's return to the League of Nations—and, on the other hand, the Air Pact. The group of four were indivisible and must be negotiated simultaneously. However, "the air convention must be considered as a special arrangement which should be speedily concluded without regard to the negotiations on the other subjects."

Concerning the Eastern Pact, Margerie also let it be seen that the whole legacy left by Barthou was anything but welcome to Laval but that he could not abandon it for reasons of domestic policy. Neverthe-

[71] *S.I.A., 1935,* I, 126-127; *D.I.A., 1935,* I, 35-36; Aloisi, *Journal,* p. 254.

[72] See Simon's remarks to the United States Chargé d'Affaires in London, Mr. Atherton, *F.R.U.S., 1935,* I, 191.

[73] Conversation of 5 Feb. 1935, *G.F.P.,* III, 910-912. M. de Margerie was a career diplomat. He requested the talk with Prince Bismarck, in order "to explain more fully some details of last Sunday's Anglo-French communiqué." These facts and the tone of his explanations make it almost certain that he was acting on Laval's instructions.

less, the air convention which was expressly intended for "Western Europe" might make a breach in this policy because, as I well knew, the Russians had taken it in very bad part.

. . . .

Concerning the significance of the air convention in general, Margerie said it was intended to provide the French Ministers with a bridge for retreating from the position adopted by Barthou in his Note of April 17, on the grounds that the air convention created a new factor, and on the assumption that, once a convention on air security was obtained, this, as soon as it was feasible, must without further ado bring in its train military and naval assistance too.[74]

This was the furthest point of Laval's advances to the Germans. He had to retreat almost immediately.

When Laval received the German Ambassador in Paris, 12 February, he shifted to the position that all the proposals must be negotiated simultaneously. "Germany could not be allowed to accede to the air convention while dismissing one or other of the security projects as being of no interest to her."[75] Laval was forced to retreat by the French reaction against German tactics. The Berlin press had fixed upon the Air Pact as the only thing of value in the Declaration. On 14 February the German government commented on the Declaration in a note addressed to the British government alone. The security proposals were dismissed with a perfunctory promise to study them. The Air Pact, however, was warmly greeted; Germany would be quite willing to use "its aerial forces" in such a pact. The Germans requested "a direct exchange of views" with the British government.[76] A few days later, following up on Lord Lothian's hints, Baron von Neurath tendered an invitation to Sir John Simon to come to Berlin.

The German note was published and it sowed much jealously. At the cabinet of 19 February M. Herriot, who had so far accepted Laval's assurances, resumed his bulldog role. "I insisted . . . that our government affirm its thesis of the absolute solidarity of all the elements enunciated in the communiqué of 3 February. I obtained satisfaction."[77] M. Laval asked the British to insist that the Germans discuss all the issues, Eastern Locarno as well as the Air

[74] *Ibid.*, pp. 911-912.

[75] *Ibid.*, pp. 924-926. Laval made the invitation to Germany as attractive as possible. He pointed out the "great advantages" of the Air Pact; "above all it legitimized German air armaments."

[76] British Blue Book, *Cmd. 5143*, pp. 17-18; *G.F.P.*, III, 927-928.

[77] *Jadis*, II, 498-499; consult the semi-official leader, "Bulletin du Jour," *Le Temps*, 22 Feb. 1935.

Pact.[78] When Laval received Ambassador Köster 22 February, he complained that the German tactics "had created the impression amongst the French public and also in certain British circles that we wished to separate France from Britain." The London declaration was indivisible; "an air agreement could not be concluded in isolation from the other problems." Even so, Laval did not renounce his basic attitude of conciliation. "He was prepared to remove all misunderstandings; he hoped that the German Government would not ignore his desire for cooperation on a basis of mutual trust between the two countries."[79]

The Anglo-French Declaration was received with undisguised anxiety in Moscow. The Russians feared not only the re-establishment of British influence over French diplomacy but the distinction between Western and Eastern Europe. A diplomat in Moscow reported that Soviet leaders were worried "that Germany will escape from the encirclement that was the original Litvinov-Barthou conception of the Eastern Pact."[80] In a communiqué of 20 February the Soviet government argued that all parts of the London Declaration must be given equal value. Neglect of any one of the pacts mentioned in the Declaration was "likely to be regarded as open encouragement to break the peace in the area in question."[81] Litvinov matched Baron von Neurath by sending an invitation to Sir John Simon to come to Moscow after visiting Berlin.

Sir John acceded to the Franco-Russian pressure and requested an assurance that the German government was willing to discuss all of the points mentioned in the Declaration. Neurath agreed immediately and it was announced that the British Foreign Secretary intended to go to Berlin for talks on 8 and 9 March.[82]

Where was the Franco-Soviet pact in all this activity? It was still encased in Eastern Locarno, and that project was halfway down the fifth paragraph of the Anglo-French Declaration. Laval and Simon conferred about Eastern Locarno when the latter came to Paris to deliver a lecture, 28 February. They agreed upon a further dilution of the scheme in order to make it palatable to

[78] Herriot, *Jadis*, II, 501; *G.F.P.*, III, 953-958.
[79] *G.F.P.*, III, 956-957.
[80] Dispatch from the United States Chargé d'Affaires in Moscow, Mr. Wiley, 28 Feb. 1935, *F.R.U.S.*, *1935*, I, 194.
[81] Soviet Communiqué of 20 Feb. 1935, Degras, ed., *Soviet Documents on Foreign Policy*, III, 119; see also *D.I.A.*, *1935*, I, 36-38.
[82] British Blue Book, *Cmd. 5143*, pp. 18-19; *G.F.P.*, III, 958-959, 980, n. 3; *S.I.A.*, *1935*, I, 130-132.

Germany. Mutual assistance would be optional; Germany would be asked to pledge only non-aggression, non-assistance to the aggressor, and consultation.[83] Simon told a diplomat that Laval had stressed the need to arrange some sort of an Eastern Locarno. "The French had pointed out one of the particular reasons they were desirous of the conclusion of this [Eastern Locarno] was that they did not want to be forced into a Franco-Soviet pact. In fact, the conclusion of any such agreement would be against their present policy."[84]

Pierre Laval, then, did not try to kill the Franco-Soviet negotiations; he tried to lose them. He displayed a remarkably subtle touch in doing so and in substituting his own goals. Already, he had imparted to Franco-German relations a new tone of good will, he had extracted as fair a bargain as anyone was likely to get from Mussolini, he had kept Franco-Soviet negotiations within the framework of Eastern Locarno, and he had lost Eastern Locarno in the middle of a general settlement which would take months to unravel.

Then Hitler spoiled it all.

[83] *Rapport Torrès*, p. 165; *G.F.P.*, III, 999, 1005; *F.R.U.S., 1935*, I, 194-196.
[84] Conversation with the United States Chargé d'Affaires in London, Mr. Atherton, 5 March 1935, *F.R.U.S., 1935*, I, 195.

Eleven

THE PACT OF MUTUAL ASSISTANCE

The conciliatory policy of M. Pierre Laval rested on the fallacious assumption that Hitler still needed international approval for rearmament. In fact, the Chancellor had reached the conclusion that Germany was strong enough to admit rearmament and not be punished. On 26 February 1935 the German cabinet passed a secret decree which read in part: "On March 1, 1935, the Reichsluftwaffe will become the third branch of the Wehrmacht, at the side of the Reich Army and Reich Navy."[1] It has long been thought that the decision to announce German air rearmament was taken in reaction to a British White Paper on rearmament, issued on 4 March. The German decree, passed at a time when no crisis existed, reveals that Hitler made the decision simply because he was ready.

On 1 March 1935 at Saarbrücken, Baron Aloisi, acting on behalf of the Council of the League of Nations, formally transferred the Saar Territory to the German Minister of the Interior, Dr. Frick. Now that the Saar had been gathered in, the risk could be taken. An ideal pretext was provided when the British government published a memorandum on defense policy in preparation for a debate in the House of Commons. The White Paper, 4 March 1935, was a cautious justification of much-needed British rearmament. What gave it archival immortality was some plain talk about German rearmament inserted by the apprehensive chief of the Foreign Office, Sir Robert Vansittart.[2]

This re-armament, if continued at its present rate, unabated and uncontrolled, will aggravate the existing anxieties of the neighbours of Germany, and may consequently produce a situation where peace will be in peril. His Majesty's Government have noted and welcomed the declarations of the leaders of Germany that they desire peace. They can-

[1] G.F.P., III, 963-965.
[2] "We tried tactfully to make British flesh creep, but it wouldn't." Vansittart, *The Mist Procession,* p. 508. See G. M. Young, *Stanley Baldwin* (London, 1952), pp. 191-194.

not, however, fail to recognize that not only the forces but the spirit in which the population, and especially the youth of the country, are being organized lend colour to, and substantiate, the general feeling of insecurity which has already been incontestably generated.[3]

This cool statement of fact infuriated Hitler.

The reaction in Berlin was immediate. Baron von Neurath announced that Hitler was suffering from a cold and that Sir John Simon's visit to Berlin would have to be postponed. Universally, this was interpreted as a "diplomatic cold" which masked Hitler's fury.[4] (Later the German invitation was reissued for a visit at the end of the month.) On 9 March the British Air Attaché in Berlin, Colonel F. P. Don, was informed of the militarization of German aviation.[5] Next day the Air Minister, Hermann Goering, made the decision public. Blandly, he used the justification that the invitation to join a Western Air Pact implied the existence of a German air force.[6]

The reactions to this flagrant violation of the Versailles Treaty were surprisingly tranquil.[7] In any case, they were quickly overtaken by other events. On 12 March it was announced that the French cabinet had reached agreement on an increase in military service from one to two years. This decision had not been taken on sudden impulse; it was the result of an inexorable problem of manpower. The next four years would be the hollow years, *les années creuses*, symbols of the price of victory. Schoolrooms would have empty corners, hands would be missing at harvest, and the lines of recruits would be only half their normal length; all the result of the low birth rate of the years 1914-1918. From a normal figure of about 230,000, the average annual figure of the military classes inducted from 1936 to 1940 would fall to 118,000.[8] The hollow years coincided with a century-long decline in the birth rate. This combination put France in a peril unheard of in modern

[3] British White Paper entitled "Statement relating to Defence issued in connexion with the House of Commons Debate," reprinted in *D.I.A., 1935,* I, 38-47.
[4] François-Poncet, *Souvenirs d'une Ambassade à Berlin,* pp. 225-227; William E. Dodd, Jr. and Martha Dodd, eds., *Ambassador Dodd's Diary 1933-1938* (London, 1941), p. 227; *G.F.P.,* III, 979-980, 983-985.
[5] *Nazi Conspiracy and Aggression,* VIII, 386-387; *F.R.U.S., 1935,* II, 294-296.
[6] Goering chose an unusual channel to publicize the news, an interview given to Mr. G. Ward Price, correspondent for the London *Daily Mail.* S.I.A., *1935,* I, 140; François-Poncet, *Souvenirs d'une Ambassade à Berlin,* p. 226.
[7] Article 198 of the Versailles Treaty stated: "The armed forces of Germany must not include any military or naval air forces."
[8] General Maurin's report to the cabinet, dated 4 March 1935, cited by Herriot, *Jadis,* II, 509.

times—depopulation. Each year from 1935 through 1938, there were actually more deaths than births.[9]

Marshal Pétain had not thought it expedient to act in 1934, but now, though retired, he lent his unrivaled prestige. In an article in the *Revue des Deux Mondes,* 1 March 1935, the Marshal explained the exigencies which dictated a two-year term of military service. "Germany intends to let a permanent menace hang over Europe.... She respects only 'force.'"[10] In the cabinet discussions, Herriot gave Premier Flandin unstinted support and he was able to swing over some of the Radical-Socialists to favor this unpopular move. Herriot's backing made Flandin indebted to him and put Herriot in a strong position to protect his Franco-Soviet Pact.[11]

M. Pierre-Étienne Flandin announced to the Chamber of Deputies, 15 March 1935, that the government intended to use its powers under the 1928 defense law to prolong to two years the service of the classes inducted from October 1935 to 1939.[12] He requested a vote of confidence and won by 350 to 196. Most of the opposition in what was a very revealing debate came from Socialists and Communists. Léon Blum denied the necessity for longer service; it was a maneuver to impose on France "the militaristic direction." Instead, he pledged that the workers would rise as one man if Hitler attacked France.[13] Maurice Thorez, the Communist chieftain, also decried "the two years," but he vehemently repudiated Blum's right to speak for French workers. "We shall not permit the working class to be dragged into a so-called war to defend democracy against fascism."[14] What should French workers do in case of a war? Thorez said that they should try to overthrow the capitalist regime. The fact that this threat completely negated the concept of Franco-Soviet mutual assistance did not seem to bother him in the least.

[9] Tables in Ministère des Finances, Service National des Statistiques, *Mouvement Économique en France de 1929 à 1939,* p. 211.

[10] "La Securité de la France au cours des Années Creuses," in *Revue des Deux Mondes,* 1 March 1935, p. xx.

[11] Herriot, *Jadis,* II, 502-516; Gamelin, *Servir,* II, 156-159.

[12] The annual class of recruits was inducted in halves, in April and October. The service of the contingent to be inducted in April 1935 was increased to eighteen months. Speech by M. Flandin, *J.O.,* Chambre, *Débats,* 15 March 1935, pp. 1021-1022.

[13] *J.O.,* Chambre, *Débats,* 15 March 1935, pp. 1024, 1025. M. Édouard Daladier, leader of the left-wing opposition to Herriot in the Radical-Socialist party, also spoke and voted against the increase in service.

[14] *Ibid.,* p. 1038.

The debate also put the spotlight on a military weakness hither-to largely ignored—the defensive character of the French Army. The Maginot Line was nearing completion, but its implications for French strategy had not been publicly discussed. General Louis Maurin, Minister of War, was candid and prophetic when he rose to reply to the Army's critics.

We have been told that in 1913 we had the Napoleonic doctrine of the offensive. Perhaps. But it cost us dearly enough that we will not take it up again.

How can anyone believe that we are still dreaming of the offensive, when we have spent billions to establish a fortified barrier? Would we be foolish enough to go out beyond that barrier into I know not what sort of an adventure?[15]

Such a directive for the French Army would negate the value of Franco-Soviet mutual assistance as much as M. Thorez' call to the barricades.

One man demolished the fragile assumptions of this position. M. Paul Reynaud, a dapper conservative with a taste for unpopular causes, insisted that France must have the army of her foreign policy.

This afternoon speakers have presented . . . the role of our army as solely defensive, within our own territory. But that is not our policy. And one must have the army of one's policy. Is it just possible that we have abandoned the policy of assistance and pacts? Do we conceive of assistance as a one-way current, which we can demand from London but which we do not owe to Vienna, Prague, or Brussels?[16]

Reynaud proposed a specialized, mobile striking force, able to take the offensive quickly and thus to assist French allies.[17] This idea had been suggested by a tall young Colonel, Charles de Gaulle, who had failed to gain a hearing in the Army. Paul Reynaud was no more able to awaken the Chamber of Deputies; his proposal was met by deep and impartial skepticism.

Rephrased, the question posed by Reynaud went to the heart of the Franco-Soviet alliance. Was mutual assistance no longer mutual, was it something to be requested from Moscow but not

[15] *Ibid.*, p. 1045. Consult Challener, *The French Theory of the Nation in Arms, 1866-1939*, pp. 220-229.

[16] *J.O.*, Chambre, *Débats*, 15 March 1935, p. 1042.

[17] Reynaud submitted a project to the Army Commission of the Chamber of Deputies; it called for creation of a specialized corps of six armored divisions and supporting units. Later in the year the project was rejected. Paul Reynaud, *Mémoires*, I, *Venu de ma montagne* (Paris, 1960), pp. 420-440.

reciprocated? Suppose Germany should attack Russia: the minimum French obligation would be an immediate offensive into Germany to draw German troops to the west. But was the French Army now capable of an offensive?[18] The Soviet military men were aware of this weakness, although they did not seem to realize how fundamental were its causes. In an article published in *Pravda*, 31 March 1935, Marshal Tukachevsky included the following critical judgment: "The French Army, with its twenty divisions, its hastily assembled units, and slow rate of expansion by stages under mobilization, is already incapable of active opposition to Germany. On the contrary, before engaging in such an encounter it will lose a great deal of time in bringing its forces up to strength."[19]

Nothing could have better suited Hitler's purposes than the French decision to lengthen military service. On 13 March, the day after the French cabinet had announced its policy, Hitler sent his adjutant, Colonel Hossbach, a sudden order to meet him in Munich. There he confided his intention to restore conscription and expand the Reichswehr as soon as the French Chamber of Deputies made known its vote. Returning to Berlin, the Chancellor overruled the surprising opposition of the professional soldiers, who believed that the move was too sudden and feared foreign reaction.[20] The French Chamber of Deputies voted for the two years' service on the evening of 15 March, and Hitler's decision was approved by the German cabinet at noon the next day.

Late in the afternoon of Saturday, 16 March 1935, Hitler called in the French, British, Italian, and Polish Ambassadors and informed them of the historic action.[21] M. François-Poncet found

---

[18] This question came up in connection with the Franco-Italian entente, at a meeting of the Haute Comité Militaire, 6 April 1935. "M. Laval demanda si, au cas où l'Allemagne agissant en Autriche, l'Italie faisait appel à nous, l'Armée française serait en état de passer, sur notre front, à l'offensive pour lui porter secours. Le 'maréchal' Pétain prit alors la parole pour déclarer que nous avions une armée défensive. Il émit des doutes formels sur la possibilité d'une intervention efficace." Gamelin, *Servir*, II, 165.

[19] Degras, ed., *Soviet Documents on Foreign Policy*, III, 124-126.

[20] Friedrich Hossbach, *Zwischen Wehrmacht und Hitler 1934-1938* (Wolfenbüttel, 1949), pp. 94-96. See General Van Overstraeten, *Albert I-Leopold III: Vingt Ans de Politique Militaire Belge, 1920-1940*, p. 159.

[21] G.F.P., III, 1005-1006, 1015. In his instructions to the ambassadors in Rome, London, Paris, and Warsaw, Neurath pointed out: "No reference to the navy and the air force is made in the law because ... we are considering making certain proposals concerning the limitations of these two arms."

him "sure of himself, intense, solemn, conscious of the gravity of the moment."[22] The evening newspapers and radio spread the news by means of a "Proclamation to the German People." In it Hitler raked over the compulsory disarmament of Germany by the Versailles Treaty and the failure of the Disarmament Conference. He cited the recent rearmament measures in other states, particularly the Red Army's increase to 940,000 men and the increase to two years' service in the French Army. Then came the terse, powerful announcement.

1. Service in the defence force is performed on the basis of universal liability to defence duty.
2. The German Army on a peace footing, inclusive of the militarily organized police taken over into the Army, is composed of twelve corps and thirty-six divisions.[23]

On the following day the Chancellor and his generals reviewed a smart parade of several Army regiments and units of the new Luftwaffe.

The dramatic admission of German rearmament startled the whole world. One result was to wash away Pierre Laval's efforts to construct a bridge to Berlin. Had Hitler shown interest in the general settlement suggested by the Anglo-French Declaration, the negotiations could have been spun out for months. And who can tell what might have happened to the Franco-Soviet negotiations in the meantime? But the Nazi leader did not want a general settlement; the piece that he wanted he no longer had need to ask for, he simply took it. By flaunting his will, Hitler again applied the spur, and this time he kicked the French and the Russians into alliance.

ii

The Versailles Treaty forbade universal military training in Germany and limited her army to 7 divisions and a total of 100,000 men. Hitler's announcement meant that he would soon have an army of 36 divisions and about 600,000 men. The new Reichswehr would be as large as the entire French Army and much superior to the forces stationed in metropolitan France.[24] It would be nearly

[22] François-Poncet, *Souvenirs d'une Ambassade à Berlin*, pp. 228-229.
[23] Quoted in *S.I.A., 1935*, I, 141-142.
[24] Even with the two-year service in operation, the forces stationed in metropolitan France would only be 405,000 men. Marshal Pétain, "La Sécurité de la

the equal of the Italian Army, and far outdistance the tiny British Army. Only the Red Army, recently increased to nearly a million men, would outnumber the Reichswehr.

Hitler's defiance stirred anger and alarm in Moscow, Rome, and Paris, but not in London. The Russians had good reason to fear German rearmament. They had abetted it by giving the Reichswehr secret training stations in Russia from 1926-1933; they knew very well that the Germans were pioneering in aviation and tanks.[25] *Izvestya* asserted that only a preponderant coalition could stop Hitler.

Everything depends on whether or not the powers against whom this policy is directed will be able to work out quickly a system of mutual assistance against the event of German aggression.... Time demands a speedy consultation of the powers interested in the preservation of peace. Time demands rapid decision.[26]

M. Litvinov followed up on this plea by inviting M. Laval to make a visit to Moscow.[27]

In Rome the reaction was very hostile. Mussolini feared that Hitler's move would upset his own timetable for the conquest of Ethiopia. The Italians joined the French in pressing the British to cancel Sir John Simon's visit to Berlin and to join them in an immediate high level conference. The Italian Ambassador in Berlin delivered a formal note of protest, 21 March; it was very cool in tone, pointing out with injured pride that in the past Italy had championed German equality of rights. "The Italian Government ... feel it to be their duty to make the most comprehensive reservations with regard to the German Government's decision and its probable consequences."[28] The tough Italian reaction was re-

France au cours des Années Creuses," *Revue des Deux Mondes,* 1 March 1935, pp. xviii-xix. The strength of the British Army was 154,000 men and estimates of the Italian Army ran from 600,000 to 800,000 men.

[25] Consult chap. v above, pp. 95-97.

[26] Editorial in *Izvestya,* 18 March 1935, quoted in dispatch of the same date from the U.S. Chargé in Moscow, Mr. Wiley, *F.R.U.S., 1935,* II, 298; see also pp. 306, 312-314.

[27] *Rapport Torrès,* p. 165; Friedrich Berber, ed., *Europäische Politik, 1933-1938, Im Spiegel der Prager Akten,* pp. 45-46.

[28] *G.F.P.,* III, 1038-1039; see also pp. 1018-1019. Additional evidence on the Italian reaction may be found in: *F.R.U.S., 1935,* I, 200-202, 212-215, and II, 297, 305; Szembek, *Journal,* p. 49; Aloisi, *Journal,* 260-262; Vansittart, *The Mist Procession,* pp. 517-518.

ceived with joy in Paris and the Franco-Italian entente grew even more intimate in the next few months.

The British broke the ring. Their official reaction boiled down to expressing the hope that Hitler would still receive Sir John Simon in Berlin. There was a tussle over the decision; some said it was humiliating, but Baldwin and Simon took the view that there was still much to be gained by a personal exchange of views.[29] Franco-Italian pressure for cancellation of the visit was rejected, as was their request for a conference.[30] Instead, Sir John Simon sent a conciliatory note to Berlin which did not even mention the Versailles Treaty violation. His complaint was entirely directed against Germany's upsetting the negotiations which had grown out of the 3 February Declaration.

His Majesty's Government are most unwilling to abandon any opportunity which the arranged visit might afford of promoting general understanding, but in the new circumstances, before undertaking it ... they wish to be assured that the German Government still desire the visit to take place with the scope and for the purposes previously agreed.[31]

The Germans were delighted to receive such a soft answer, and Baron von Neurath replied on the spot that Hitler remained quite willing to talk about all aspects of the 3 February Declaration.[32] Accordingly, it was announced in London on 19 March that Sir John Simon and Mr. Anthony Eden would visit Berlin as planned, and that Mr. Eden would go on alone to Moscow. The only concession made to the French and Italians was that Mr. Eden would stop over in Paris on his way to Berlin for a short talk with Laval and Signor Suvich.

The British insistence upon going to Berlin as if nothing had happened was galling to the French. It made Flandin and Laval look like dupes. Laval, to be sure, would not have minded going to Berlin himself; but he could do so only in a season of good will, never after Hitler had pounded the table. Laval had been injured by Hitler, now he was insulted by Sir John Simon.

[29] Vansittart, *The Mist Procession*, p. 512; Viscount Simon, *Retrospect* (London, 1952), p. 202; Feiling, *The Life of Neville Chamberlain*, p. 256; J. E. Wrench, *Geoffrey Dawson and Our Times* (London, 1955), p. 321; London Times, *The History of the Times* (London, 1952), IV, Part II, 890-893; Geyr von Schweppenburg, *The Critical Years* (London, 1952), pp. 28 ff.; *G.F.P.*, III, 997-1000, 1018-1021, 1040-1041.

[30] *F.R.U.S.*, *1935*, I, 200-202, and II, 305; Aloisi, *Journal*, pp. 260-261.

[31] British note of 18 March 1935, reprinted in *D.I.A.*, *1935*, I, 66.

[32] *G.F.P.*, III, 1015-1016.

The reaction of public opinion in France was very agitated. The Paris press, particularly on the Center and Right, denounced Hitler's action in indignant fashion and called for urgent diplomatic countermeasures. In the *Journal des Débats,* M. Pierre Bernus insisted that the consultations of the Western Powers "must extend to all the countries resolved to protect peace from the blows of those who prepare war systematically."[33] M. Henry de Jouvenel, the former Ambassador to Italy, wrote that France must "take the elementary precaution of organizing mutual assistance in Europe."[34] The president of the Senate Foreign Affairs Commission, M. Henry Bérenger, proposed the immediate creation of an anti-German league: France, England, Italy, Russia, the Little Entente, and the Balkan Entente.[35] M. Emile Buré, the outspoken editor of *L'Ordre,* begged the leaders of the cabinet to redouble their preparations. "They have pushed through the two years law; now they must turn their attention to our allies, organize them and arm them."[36] M. René Pinon, political commentator for the *Revue des Deux Mondes,* slapped at the "radical error of method and psychology" committed by Sir John Simon. "The time has come to place England, in a friendly way, face to face with her responsibilities; if she declines them, it will be up to the continental powers to organize security and peace by a system of balance based on alliances."[37]

The reaction was fully as sharp in official circles. The United States Ambassador in Paris reported, 20 March, that "the French attitude ... was characterized yesterday by despair and smouldering resentment against England for its decision to go ahead on negotiations with Germany alone without consulting France or Italy."[38] The diplomats and journalists at the League of Nations believed that "the French resentment against England ... is much deeper than the press or public statements reveal. ... It is primarily based on the French belief that the British Government in arrang-

[33] *Journal des Débats,* 18 March 1935.

[34] Article in *L'Excelsior,* quoted in the "Revue de la presse," *Le Temps,* 18 March 1935.

[35] Article in *L'Agence Économique et Financière,* quoted in "Revue de la presse," *Le Temps,* 19 March 1935.

[36] Article in *L'Ordre* quoted ibid.

[37] "Chronique de la Quinzaine," *Revue des Deux Mondes,* 1 April 1935, pp. 718, 720.

[38] *F.R.U.S., 1935,* II, 305. Consult also the semi-official "Bulletin du Jour," *Le Temps,* 20 March 1935; Aloisi, *Journal,* pp. 260-262; *Ambassador Dodd's Diary, 1933-1938,* pp. 231-233; François-Poncet, *Souvenirs d'une Ambassade à Berlin,* pp. 230-232.

ing Simon's visit to Berlin after Hitler's declaration had violated the consultation agreement with France."[39]

At a decisive three-hour cabinet on 20 March, the initiative was taken away from Laval. According to Herriot's notes, Laval came to the cabinet looking depressed; "he seems to be very embarrassed and that is hardly surprising." Laval tried to minimize the deflection of his policy; he proposed only "a protest and a consultation." The Premier, M. Flandin, demanded a more energetic move—to bring the event before the League of Nations as a threat to the peace.[40] M. Édouard Herriot then demolished Laval's proposals. A protest? Hitler would laugh. A consultation? The British tactics made it impossible. Principle, duty, and interest impose the appeal to the League of Nations. "It is there that we have the most friends and there that we meet Soviet Russia, our surest and most courageous backer." Vigorously supported by M. Louis Marin, a conservative nationalist, Flandin and Herriot swung the debate. The cabinet decided to request a special session of the Council of the League.[41]

Pierre Laval, characteristically supple, bent to the wind and accepted the cabinet's will. That was not all; apparently he himself proposed that he should accept Litvinov's invitation and go to Moscow.[42] The cabinet agreed and the communiqué released to the press included the statement: "The Council [of Ministers] authorized M. Pierre Laval to accept the invitation which has been addressed to him to come to Moscow in the near future."[43] It was a way of saying: "We shall now conclude the pact with Russia."

The French Foreign Minister personally announced the decision to the Chamber of Deputies, 22 March 1935. The debate was enlivened by the fiery Rightist Deputy, M. Franklin-Bouillon, whose duels with M. Briand had made him famous as a symbol of nationalism. M. Franklin-Bouillon demanded a coalition of all peoples faced by the German danger.

[39] Dispatch from Mr. Hugh Wilson, United States Minister to Switzerland, 21 March 1935, Geneva, *F.R.U.S.*, *1935*, I, 204.

[40] Note Flandin's growing suspicion of Laval, confided to Herriot 6 March 1935. On the morning of the cabinet meeting, 20 March, Herriot went to see Flandin privately and apparently they agreed on a common line of policy. Herriot, *Jadis*, II, 509, 517.

[41] Herriot's notes of the cabinet meeting of 20 March 1935, *ibid.*, II, 517-518.

[42] "Laval . . . fait accepter son voyage à Moscou." *Ibid.*, II, 518.

[43] *Le Temps*, 21 March 1935.

How many times did I hear it repeated during the military debate [of 15 March]: "They have 66 million, we have only 40 million. We are doomed to perish."

What stupefying reasoning on the part of men who lived through the war! Have they already forgotten that it was a coalition of allies which conquered barbarism . . . ? In the east, to begin with, there are 160 million Russians. . . .[44]

M. Laval spoke in bald and relative terms. "In 1931, I made the journey to Berlin. In 1935, I will make the journey to Moscow." He let it be seen that it was with reluctance that he had to turn aside from the policy of reconciliation with Germany.

By her gesture, Germany, I hope, has only slowed down the work to which we remain passionately attached. . . . They know in Germany that no one is more determined than I to realize the necessary rapprochement between our two peoples.[45]

Four days later he spoke in the same diffident tone to the Senate.[46] It was thus in a spirit of resignation that M. Laval resolved to go to Moscow.

The French riposte began with the delivery of a stiff note of protest in Berlin, 21 March 1935.[47] Simultaneously, M. Laval requested the Secretary-General of the League of Nations to call an extraordinary session of the Council on the grounds that the German action "threatens to disturb international peace."[48] Two days later Mr. Anthony Eden came to Paris for a brief talk with M. Laval and M. Alexis Léger and the Italian Under-Secretary, Signor Suvich. Eden was made fully aware of the resentment aroused by British tactics; he and Sir John Simon were not to consider themselves spokesmen for France and Italy in their talks at Berlin. In order to repair the damaged coalition, it was agreed that the heads of the three governments should meet at Stresa in northern Italy on 11 April.[49]

[44] *J.O.*, Chambre, *Débats*, 22 March 1935, p. 1200. M. Paul Bastid, Radical-Socialist Chairman of the Foreign Affairs Commission, backed Laval's plans. "La seule politique qui s'impose est celle d'une solidarité permanente. . . . Le voyage annoncé de Pierre Laval à Moscou cadre avec cette politique; plus exactement il la complète et la couronne." *Ibid.*, p. 1207.

[45] *Ibid.*, p. 1209.

[46] *J.O.*, Sénat, *Débats*, 26 March 1935, p. 395. Consult also Laroche, *La Pologne de Pilsudski*, p. 208, and "Bulletin du Jour," *Le Temps*, 23 March 1935.

[47] *G.F.P.*, III, 1031-1032; *D.I.A.*, *1935*, I, 67-68; François-Poncet, *Souvenirs d'une Ambassade à Berlin*, p. 232.

[48] *D.I.A.*, *1935*, I, 66-67.

[49] Aloisi, *Journal*, pp. 261-262; François-Poncet, *Souvenirs d'une Ambassade à*

Sir John Simon and Mr. Eden met the German Chancellor for long, frank talks in Berlin, 25-26 March 1935. Hitler did most of the talking. With no apology, he repeated his arms formula: 35 per cent of the British fleet; in the air, parity with England and France; on land, a strong army. He would accept nothing less than the thirty-six divisions just announced. When asked point-blank about actual German air strength, he replied that the Luftwaffe had already achieved parity with the Royal Air Force, a claim that made a deep impression in London.[50]

The British ministers found Hitler adamantly opposed to most of the projects for security. He was still willing to join the Air Pact, but was very hostile to the Danubian Pact and Eastern Locarno. He harped on the Russian menace, pointing to the vast potential of Russian manpower and industry. "Russia was the country which could start a war with the least risk to herself. . . ."[51] At the end of the talks, however, Baron von Neurath gave Simon a brief outline of the sort of Eastern pact that Germany would accept. He suggested a ten-year pact of non-aggression, consultation, and non-support of the aggressor; there would be no mutual assistance.[52]

Sir John Simon returned to London sobered by Hitler's belief in his mission to lead Germany's revival.

It is very dangerous to peace in Europe, and it is all the more dangerous for being very sincere. . . . The practical result of our Berlin visit is to establish that Germany greatly desires a good understanding with Britain, but that she is determined to go her own course in rearmament; that she expects in time to get all Germans within her borders, including Austria; that she does not fear isolation and has no intention of joining in collective security. . . .[53]

Berlin, p. 232; Szembek, *Journal*, p. 49; *G.F.P.*, III, 1085-1086, 1090-1091.

[50] This account of the Simon-Eden-Hitler talks is based upon: *G.F.P.*, III, 1043-1080, 1091-1103; *F.R.U.S.*, *1935*, I, 249-254, and II, 322 ff.; Simon, *Retrospect*, pp. 200-203; Lord Strang, *Home and Abroad* (London, 1956), pp. 66-67; Paul Schmidt, *Hitler's Interpreter*, pp. 16-26; François-Poncet, *Souvenirs d'une Ambassade à Berlin*, pp. 233-234; General Van Overstraeten, *Albert I-Léopold III: Vingt Ans de Politique Militaire Belge, 1920-1940*, pp. 160-161; Szembek, *Journal*, pp. 52-56; Londonderry, *Wings of Destiny*, pp. 126-129.

[51] Notes of the German interpreter, Dr. Paul Schmidt, *G.F.P.*, III, 1050. Later, Hitler said: "Russia and France would probably soon be united in military respects." *Ibid.*, III, 1071.

[52] Text *ibid.*, III, 1103, and in British Blue Book, *Cmd. 5143*, pp. 19-20.

[53] From a note made by Sir John Simon immediately after his return from Berlin, *Retrospect*, pp. 202-203.

The British Foreign Secretary revealed his anxiety by sending a message to M. Laval reaffirming the "tight solidarity of France and England in the search for peace and security."[54]

Mr. Anthony Eden journeyed on from Berlin to Moscow for talks with Stalin, Molotov, and Litvinov, and then returned home via Warsaw and Prague. He found the Russians afraid of Hitler's intentions and convinced that only an armed coalition could stop him.[55] At Prague, Eden was assured by Dr. Edward Beneš, Czech Foreign Minister, that Czechoslovakia still desired to join the Eastern Pact.[56] In contrast, Eden's conversations with Marshal Pilsudski and Colonel Beck revealed no slackening of Polish hostility to the project.[57]

The journeys of Sir John Simon and Mr. Eden, contrary to prediction, thus turned out to favor French and Russian policies. Sir John Simon now was apprehensive of Hitler's ambitions and in no mood to criticize the French for their fears; Anthony Eden shared that reaction and was impressed by Stalin's realism. The British still did not like the Franco-Soviet alliance, but they no longer tried to block it.

The last French effort to conciliate Poland also failed to produce any new factor. Colonel Beck again said that Poland could not join Eastern Locarno as long as Germany refused. When Ambassador Laroche informed him that the French cabinet had decided to conclude a pact with Russia alone, Beck replied that Poland remained "profoundly attached" to her alliance with France. "If the French government desired an alliance with Russia, it was up to them to see that it was concluded in a manner compatible with the Franco-Polish alliance."[58] The only accomplishment was an agreement that Laval should stop in Warsaw on his way to Moscow.

M. Laval and the Soviet Ambassador in Paris, M. Potemkin, began the final negotiations at the end of March. The visit of M.

[54] Quoted by Herriot from Laval's report to the cabinet, 26 March 1935, *Jadis*, II, 519.
[55] Szembek, *Journal*, pp. 53-58; *F.R.U.S.*, *1935*, I, 224, and II, 326, and III, 103; Strang, *Home and Abroad*, p. 68; John Connell, *The 'Office', A Study of British Foreign Policy and Its Makers, 1919-1951* (London, 1958), pp. 158-159.
[56] *F.R.U.S.*, *1935*, I, 225-229.
[57] *Ibid.*, pp. 222-225; Szembek, *Journal*, pp. 52-59; Beck, *Dernier Rapport*, pp. 89-91.
[58] Conversation of 27 March 1935, Laroche, *La Pologne de Pilsudski*, pp. 208-209.

Laval to Moscow was set for about 20 April, after the conferences at Stresa and Geneva; this would make it possible for Laval to sign the pact in Moscow. The drafting of the pact immediately ran into difficulties which stemmed from divergent conceptions of the alliance. Litvinov wanted to write an "automatic" pact. He proposed that the obligation to render mutual assistance should be briefly and precisely worded, so as to leave no time for delay and no loophole to escape from the obligation. On the other hand, Laval and the Quai d'Orsay officials did not wish to be tightly committed. They were concerned to have the pact loosely worded, so that it would not contradict the League Covenant, the Franco-Polish alliance, and the Locarno Rhine Pact.[59] The latter was their most serious preoccupation. Technically, if France assisted Russia by invading Germany, the British might go to the aid of Germany. This was unlikely, but there was good reason to fear that the British might withdraw from Locarno.[60]

Within the French cabinet, Herriot was determined to crown the rapprochement. His influence was growing over the Premier, whose position had been hurt by the German rearmament and another financial slump; Flandin was grateful for Herriot's public statements of support. Herriot was haunted by the inferiority of France vis-à-vis Germany in population and industry.

> I consult the map. I see only one country which can bring us the necessary counterweight and create a second front in case of war. That is the Soviet Union. I have been saying it and writing it since 1922. People call me a communist or an imbecile. In the old days, the Tsar, despot that he was, agreed to ally with a Republic.[61]

Coming to these conclusions, he went frequently to see the Soviet Ambassador, Vladimir Potemkin, and served as a mediator between him and Laval.

At the cabinet meeting of 6 April, M. Laval reported on the Franco-Soviet negotiations. A draft of the pact had been constructed, based on the Covenant of the League. He was resisting the Soviet pressure for an automatic alliance. "[Laval] wants to treat with the Soviets, if only to reinforce the Little Entente and to prevent a German-Russian accord. But at heart—and he admits it—

[59] Herriot, *Jadis*, II, 523 ff.; Laroche, *La Pologne de Pilsudski*, p. 212; *F.R.U.S.*, *1935*, I, 260-261, 270.

[60] The relation of the Franco-Soviet Pact to the Locarno Rhine Pact is discussed below, pp. 246-250.

[61] Herriot, *Jadis*, II, 523.

he dreads the eventual effect of a bolshevik army on the French army."[62]

On 9 April the cabinet discussed the international situation in preparation for the Stresa conference. Laval communicated a Soviet *aide-mémoire* couched in a "severe" tone; Moscow demanded "precise engagements." Premier Flandin declared that the pact must be placed in the framework of the League. At the end of the discussion, Laval gave the following assurance: " 'Whatever happens at Stresa, . . . we shall sign a pact of mutual assistance with the Soviet Union.' "[63] The cabinet approved the decision and authorized Laval so to inform Ambassador Potemkin.

If any new stimulus were needed, it was provided by the signature of a new commercial accord between Germany and Russia, 9 April 1935.[64] This agreement extended a credit of 200,000,000 marks to the Soviet Union for purchases in Germany. Actually, there were no political implications, but no one could be certain and the specter of Rapallo was conjured up immediately.

At Stresa, on beautiful Lake Maggiore, Mussolini extended a luxurious hospitality to his guests: Prime Minister Ramsay Mac-Donald, Sir John Simon, and Sir Robert Vansittart from London, Premier Flandin, M. Pierre Laval, and M. Alexis Léger from Paris.[65] Mussolini, his "chameleon ego at its most colorful," was thoroughly anti-German but contemptuous of British pacifism; to Vansittart it looked as if "Mussolini wanted to see just how far we would go in resisting German expansion."[66]

After four days of negotiations, 11-14 April 1935, the conference produced several resolutions. The three governments announced that they would pursue a "common line of conduct" at the special session of the League Council, restated the necessity of "maintaining the independence and integrity of Austria," and proposed further negotiations for a Western Air Pact and an Eastern Pact. They declared "complete agreement in opposing, by all prac-

[62] From Herriot's notes of the cabinet meeting, 6 April 1935, *ibid.*

[63] Quoted by Herriot in his notes of the cabinet meeting, 9 April 1935, *ibid.*, II, 525.

[64] *G.F.P.*, III, 935, 960, 1000, 1028, 1088; W. Höffding, "German Trade with the Soviet Union," *Slavonic and East European Review*, XIV (Jan. 1936), 477 ff.

[65] This account of the Stresa conference is based on: Flandin, *Politique Française*, pp. 171-173, 177-178; Herriot, *Jadis*, II, 527; Simon, *Retrospect*, pp. 203-204; Vansittart, *The Mist Procession*, pp. 516-521; Aloisi, *Journal*, pp. 264-266; *F.R.U.S.*, *1935*, I, 249-254; *S.I.A.*, *1935*, I, 156-161; Lagardelle, *Mission à Rome. Mussolini*, pp. 122-127.

[66] Vansittart, *The Mist Procession*, p. 518.

ticable means, any unilateral repudiation of treaties which may endanger the peace of Europe." The British and Italian governments added a special warning to Hitler, by reaffirming their obligations as guarantors of the Treaty of Locarno.[67]

The ramifications of the Stresa agreements need not detain us here. The significance of the words "of Europe" is well known. Mussolini was massing in Eritrea an army of 250,000 men to invade Ethiopia; it was he who inserted the words "of Europe" and he rightly interpreted British and French silence as tacit consent to his adventure outside Europe. British acquiescence was either accidental or the product of a vague desire to accommodate Mussolini; French acquiescence was deliberate and part of a concrete bargain.

MM. Laval and Flandin both conferred with Mussolini, approved the progress already made in military negotiations, and decided that they should be pushed to conclusion. Franco-Italian accords for military and air collaboration against German aggression in Austria or on the Rhine were signed in May and June.[68] These conventions were the logical military extension of the Rome Accords of January 1935. At Stresa the Franco-Italian entente glittered more brightly than Paul-Boncour and Barthou ever could have anticipated. The approaches to Rome and to Moscow continued to follow parallel roads to success.

For the Franco-Soviet negotiations, the most important result of the Stresa conference was, unexpectedly, a concession from Berlin. Sir John Simon, in reporting on his talks with Hitler, brought up the German proposal for a multilateral non-aggression pact in Eastern Europe. M. Laval asked whether Germany would maintain that offer even though other governments signed separate pacts of mutual assistance. Sir John Simon wired to Berlin and received a conciliatory reply. Baron von Neurath reiterated his dislike of mutual assistance pacts, but he said that they would "not deter the German Government on its side from concluding pacts of non-aggression."[69] This rather surprising German concession may have stemmed from nervousness or from desire to smooth relations with the British; Hitler still hoped to

[67] The Stresa resolutions are printed in *D.I.A., 1935,* I, 80-82.

[68] Flandin, *Politique Française,* pp. 172-173; Gamelin, *Servir,* II, 166-171; Herriot, *Jadis,* II, 535; Aloisi, *Journal,* p. 270; Van Overstraeten, *Albert I—Léopold III,* p. 163; Lagardelle, *Mission à Rome. Mussolini,* pp. 118, 141, 149.

[69] Statement by Baron von Neurath, 12 April 1935, British Blue Book, *Cmd. 5143,* p. 23.

242 Alliance Against Hitler

bargain with them on naval power. At any rate, the German reply eased Laval's task. "M. Laval said that this cleared up the position. France now had latitude to make with Russia a bilateral arrangement of mutual assistance without hindering the negotiation and conclusion of a multilateral pact of non-aggression."[70]

Now the scene shifted from Stresa to Geneva, where the Council of the League of Nations convened on 15 April to discuss German rearmament.[71] After two days of debate, the Council unanimously approved a resolution presented by the three Stresa powers. The resolution condemned the German action as a "threat to European security." The Council appointed a Committee to propose "the economic and financial measures which might be applied should, in the future, a state, whether a member of the League of Nations or not, endanger peace by the unilateral repudiation of its international obligations."[72] Maxim Litvinov was the most vehement prosecutor of Germany, suggesting that the rearmament just revealed was not designed for German security but "for the infringement of frontiers, the fulfillment by violent methods of the idea of *revanche....*"[73]

And so the ring was closed, and it seemed to the French Ambassador in Berlin, M. André François-Poncet, that the Germans could feel it.

April 1935, Stresa and Geneva, mark the high point of European solidarity against the ambitions of the Reich. Germany saw herself denounced, guarded, isolated. Her public opinion was acutely impressed. Her press burst out in protests and imprecations which betrayed vexation and rage. Never did her leaders, her diplomats, her "official" journalists seem to me more unsure of themselves, more discouraged.[74]

Alas, there was nothing to show that Hitler himself was discouraged. He had predicted protests and he ignored them.

[70] Extract from the notes of the Anglo-French-Italian conversations at Stresa, 12 April 1935, *ibid.*, pp. 24-25. See also *F.R.U.S., 1935*, I, 244-246.

[71] Consult *S.I.A. 1935*, I, 161-166; *F.R.U.S., 1935*, I, 249-258, 265-269; Aloisi, *Journal*, pp. 266-268; François-Poncet, *Souvenirs d'une Ambassade à Berlin*, pp. 234-235; Walters, *A History of the League of Nations*, II, 606-613.

[72] Resolution adopted by the League Council, 17 April 1935, *League of Nations Official Journal*, May 1935, Eighty-Fifth (Extraordinary) Session of the Council, pp. 551-552. The vote was 13 to 0, Denmark abstaining and Germany not being represented; legally, Germany was still a member of the League until Oct. 1935, the end of the two-year period of notice of her withdrawal.

[73] Speech of 17 April 1935, *ibid.*, p. 556.

[74] *Souvenirs d'une Ambassade à Berlin*, p. 235. Consult also *F.R.U.S., 1935*, II, 330, 332; *Ambassador Dodd's Diary*, pp. 247-248; Gamelin, *Servir*, II, 171; *G.F.P.*, III, 1109.

M. Laval had a very busy time at Geneva, for in addition to the Council meetings he was conferring with MM. Litvinov, Beneš, and Titulescu. The Romanian Foreign Minister, who had visited Paris earlier in the month, was urging Laval to make the Franco-Soviet pact as rapidly as possible. He told United States diplomats that "if France did not do so Romania and all the small states of the Danubian region would have to submit to dictation from Germany and follow the German line rather than the French in order to save themselves from German aggression."[75] Titulescu thus had moved in a full circle since the days of October 1932 when he had prevented the signature of a Romanian-Russian Non-aggression Pact.[76] Titulescu and Beneš arranged a joint meeting of the permanent councils of the Little Entente and the Balkan Entente at Geneva, 15 April 1935. The five states thus represented—Czechoslovakia, Romania, Yugoslavia, Greece, and Turkey—announced that they "attach a particular importance to the early conclusion of treaties of mutual assistance in the north-east of Europe. . . ."[77]

Czechoslovakia was prepared not only to support the Franco-Soviet Pact but to imitate it. Recently, Dr. Edward Beneš had accelerated his country's rapprochement with Russia. Czechoslovakia had adhered to the Franco-Soviet Protocol of 5 December 1934, and a Soviet-Czech Treaty of Commerce and Navigation was signed on 25 March 1935. At Geneva, Beneš confirmed the rumors of alliance by announcing that negotiations were under way for a Czech-Soviet Pact of Mutual Assistance.[78]

Pierre Laval's most productive talks in Geneva were those with Maxim Litvinov. The Soviet Foreign Minister renewed his demand for precise engagements, for an "automatic" pact. Laval insisted that France could not agree to assist Russia 'automatically'; her action must not expose her to sanctions from the Locarno guarantor powers, England and Italy. Despite the divergence, substantial progress was made, and when Laval returned to Paris he carried an almost complete draft of the Pact.[79]

[75] Statement of M. Titulescu to the U.S. Ambassador to France, Mr. Straus, and the United States Ambassador to Russia, Mr. Bullitt, in Paris, 6 April 1935. Dispatch of 9 April 1935, from Ambassador Straus, 751.61/191 Archives of the Department of State, Washington, D. C. See also Herriot, *Jadis*, II, 489, 558.
[76] See chap. iv above, pp. 64-66.   [77] *D.I.A.*, *1935*, I, 86.
[78] *Le Temps*, 19 April 1935. Consult Hubert Ripka, *East and West*, pp. 28-30; Friedrich Berber, ed., *Europäische Politik 1933-1938 im Spiegel der Prager Akten*, p. 46.
[79] Herriot, *Jadis*, II, 529-530.

At the cabinet meeting of 19 April 1935, M. Pierre Laval read out the draft and seemed pleased with his work. Herriot was delighted "to see Laval so happily transformed." The President of the Republic, M. Albert Lebrun, made some adverse comments, noting the fact that Russia did not have a common frontier with Germany. General Louis Maurin, Minister of War, was skeptical, contrary to the Army's general line of support, but he did not oppose the pact.[80] Balancing these reserves was the unqualified approval of M. Louis Marin, head of the largest conservative and nationalist party, the *Fédération Républicaine*. Marin even suggested that the pact be reinforced by military accords. At the end of its discussion, the cabinet authorized Laval to sign the pact.[81]

The cabinet had scarcely adjourned when Herriot heard from the Soviet Ambassador that everything was off. At the last moment, the Quai d'Orsay had inserted a new formula "about the necessity to wait for the recommendations of the League of Nations; they [the Russians] are willing to accept the idea but do not want it to be expressed in such a brutal form." Herriot spent the afternoon vainly trying to mediate. That evening Litvinov, who was still in Geneva and was planning to come to Paris, suddenly left for Moscow in a huff. "Vrai coup de théâtre."[82]

The incident had the immediate effect of postponing Laval's visit to Russia, which had been scheduled for 25 April. There were rumors of a complete break, but the two governments were much too far along the road to court such a loss of prestige. When Litvinov returned to Moscow, he received Stalin's permission to accept the French conditions if necessary.[83] The final calculations in the Kremlin are a matter of speculation, but diplomats who talked to Soviet leaders in the spring of 1935 agree in reporting a genuine fear of German aggression in two or three years. The Russians were especially afraid of a simultaneous attack by Germany and Japan.[84]

[80] *Ibid.*, II, 530. "Le général Maurin ne croit pas beaucoup à la valeur de l'armée russe; en revanche, il redoute l'action du bolchévisme sur les troupes françaises." *Ibid.*, II, 530. Maurin's skepticism was not shared by the new chief of the French Army, General Maurice Gamelin, who had succeeded General Weygand on 21 Jan. 1935. Gamelin was convinced of the necessity of the Franco-Soviet alliance. Gamelin, *Servir*, II, 130-133, 172, 177-181; see also chap. ix above, pp. 195-197, for discussion of the Army's support for the alliance in 1934.

[81] From Herriot's notes, *Jadis*, II, 530.

[82] *Ibid.*

[83] *Ibid.*, II, 531; *F.R.U.S.*, 1935, I, 270.

[84] *F.R.U.S.*, 1935, I, 224, 271-272, 283-285, and II, 312-314, 326, and III, 106-

In Paris, Herriot and Flandin pressed Laval to compromise.[85] The Premier was determined to match the entente with Italy by one with Russia. He was not thinking of direct Soviet assistance to France, but of indirect benefits. The pact would weaken Germany by making impossible the revival of Rapallo. He also hoped that it would bolster Poland and Czechoslovakia, make them better able to fulfil their role as sentinels on Germany's borders. For Flandin the Franco-Soviet Pact was primarily "a guarantee of Russian non-intervention against the neighbors of Germany."[86] Without it their defenses against German aggression would be crippled by their fear of Russian attack.[87]

Paradoxically, at the end Pierre Laval dropped his hostility to the Franco-Soviet Pact. The principal cause of the 19 April break was not Laval but the permanent officials of the Quai d'Orsay. Laval was influenced by the desire for a success, another voyage which would garnish his international reputation. He was ambitious to become Premier again and, for that, good relations with Herriot were essential.[88]

In the last days the center of delay was the Secretary-General of the Quai d'Orsay, M. Alexis Saint-Léger Léger. Léger was meticulous in working out a formula loose enough to satisfy the British. He had been attached to Eastern Locarno, surprisingly attached to it in view of its incongruities. His ideal was a multilateral pact including Russia, Poland, and Czechoslovakia, welding the new to the old, and he was not happy about being left alone

---

111, 122; Szembek, *Journal*, p. 53, 85. Note that on 23 March 1935 the Soviet government agreed to the sale of its interest in the Chinese Eastern Railway to the Japanese puppet state, Manchukuo.

[85] "Je rencontrai, sur ce terrain, la plus mauvaise volonté de M. Laval, mais, soutenu par M. Herriot, . . . je réussis à imposer à M. Laval la signature du Pacte franco-soviétique (2 mai 1935)." Flandin, *Politique Française*, p. 170. Probably Flandin had in mind the period in March and early April. After meeting Litvinov in Geneva, 15-17 April, Laval did not hold back the negotiations.

[86] Author's interview with M. Pierre-Étienne Flandin, in Paris, 8 Dec. 1950. M. Flandin added: "We never wanted to give Russia a guiding hand in our destinies. We never wanted to bring the Russian Army into the center of Europe."

[87] It is possible that Flandin hoped that France could transfer to Russia the major burden of aiding Poland and Czechoslovakia in case they were attacked by Germany. Compare his remarks in *Politique Française*, p. 170, with those of M. Paul-Boncour, quoted in Beck, *Dernier Rapport*, p. 73, n. 1.

[88] Cameron, "Alexis Saint-Léger Léger," in Craig and Gilbert, eds., *The Diplomats, 1919-1939*, p. 386. There is a story that Laval signed the pact in order to assure his re-election, 5 May, as Mayor of Aubervilliers, a Paris suburb where the Communists were strong. This explanation is difficult to credit; see, however, Flandin, *Politique Française*, p. 194, n. 1, and *G.F.P.*, III, 926.

with Russia. Léger recognized the necessity of the alliance but he wanted to shape it very carefully so as to eliminate any dangers for France.[89]

Sir John Simon used the interlude to renew his efforts to safeguard Locarno. He instructed the British Ambassador "to let M. Laval know frankly at this stage the exact nature of our preoccupation, i.e., that France should not be induced to subscribe to any agreement which might oblige her to go to war with Germany in circumstances not permitted by article 2 of the Treaty of Locarno." M. Léger assured Sir George Clerk that there was no cause for anxiety. "French Government had made it an absolute condition that Franco-Soviet Agreement must be subordinated not only to the working of Covenant but also to that of Locarno Treaty."[90]

The negotiations were resumed in Paris, 27 April, by MM. Laval and Léger and Ambassador Potemkin. Nonetheless, when Herriot returned from Lyons three days later, disagreements still existed on the safeguarding of Locarno; and he again interceded between Laval and Potemkin. Finally, the Russians gave up their resistance on that point and agreement was reached the next day.[91] At 6:30 P.M., 2 May 1935, in the Foreign Minister's room at the Quai d'Orsay, M. Pierre Laval and M. Vladimir Potemkin placed their signatures on the Franco-Soviet Treaty of Mutual Assistance.

iii

The Franco-Soviet Pact consisted of a Treaty of Mutual Assistance and a Protocol of Signature, which was the agreed interpretation of the treaty.[92] The pact was to come into force after ratification and to have a duration of five years; if not denounced then, it would remain in force indefinitely until denunciation.

The contract was written in the language of the Covenant of the League of Nations. Article I of the treaty concerned a threat

[89] Cameron, "Alexis Saint-Léger Léger," in Craig and Gilbert, eds., *The Diplomats,* pp. 383, 386.
[90] Telegram from Sir John Simon, 26 April, and reply from Sir George Clerk, 27 April 1935, British Blue Book, *Cmd. 5143,* pp. 25-26.
[91] Herriot, *Jadis,* II, 531; *F.R.U.S., 1935,* I, 270.
[92] The protocol was handled in the same manner as the treaty; it was signed by Laval and Potemkin and was to be ratified. The Franco-Soviet Pact was ratified by the Chamber of Deputies, 27 Feb. 1936, and by the Senate, 12 March 1936; it was ratified by the Soviet government, 8 March 1936. Ratifications were exchanged in Paris, 27 March 1936.

or danger of attack; France and Russia would consult immediately and bring the crisis to the attention of the League Council.[93] Article II dealt with an actual attack; the two governments pledged mutual assistance in case the League Council failed to reach a decision (Article 15, paragraph 7 of the Covenant.) In Article III, the two governments repeated their pledge of mutual assistance, this time in case the League Council reached a decision to recommend sanctions against the aggressor (Articles 16 and 17 of the Covenant.) Specific references to attack by "a European State" made it clear that France would not aid Russia in the Far East. In the Protocol of Signature it was further defined that "European State" really meant Germany. The Franco-Soviet Pact thus was directed against Germany alone.[94]

The heart of the Treaty of Mutual Assistance was placed in Article II:

In the event of France or the U.S.S.R., in the circumstances specified in article 15, paragraph 7, of the League of Nations Covenant, being the object, in spite of the genuinely peaceful intentions of both countries, of an unprovoked attack on the part of a European State, the U.S.S.R., and, reciprocally, France, shall immediately give each other aid and assistance.[95]

This was a straightforward statement, but in the protocol M. Léger and his experts had diluted it. Article 15, paragraph 7 of the Covenant stated that, if the League Council failed to reach a unanimous decision about a dispute, "the Members of the League reserved to themselves the right to take such action as they shall consider necessary for the maintenance of right and justice"—i.e., self-defense and mutual assistance. The Russians demanded that the protocol define exactly (by a time limit) how long the two countries had to wait before it was clear that the League Council

[93] The treaty and protocol were immediately published, at Moscow in *Pravda,* 4 May 1935, and at Paris in *Le Temps,* 5 May 1935. The French and Russian texts, equally valid, were registered with the Secretariat of the League of Nations and were published in *L.N.T.S.,* CLXVII, 395-403. The French text of the treaty and protocol, from the source just cited, may be consulted in Appendix II.

[94] Paragraph 4 of the Protocol of Signature. The parliamentary report of M. Henry Torrès stated: "L'engagement contracté le 2 mai par la France et l'U.R.S.S. ne concerne donc que l'hypothèse d'une agression non-provoquée de la part de l'Allemagne." *Rapport Torrès,* p. 166.

[95] The English translation used is that given by the Quai d'Orsay to the British Ambassador in Paris, British Blue Book, *Cmd. 5143,* p. 27.

had failed to reach a decision. The French refused to agree to a time limit and the protocol referred to the problem in an ambiguous manner.

It is further agreed that the two contracting parties will take joint action to ensure that the Council issue their recommendations with all the speed required by the circumstances of the case, and that, should the Council nevertheless, for some reason, make no recommendation or fail to reach a unanimous decision, effect shall nevertheless be given to the obligation to render assistance.[96]

This formula left France free to decide for herself what she required of the Council in the way of speed.

The most important French safeguard[97] concerned the Locarno Treaty, signed by France, Germany, England, Italy, and Belgium, 16 October 1925. Litvinov demanded that Locarno not be mentioned by name. The French made this face-saving concession and still secured their protection by an interpretation in the protocol couched in general terms.

The joint purpose of both Governments being in no way to invalidate by the present treaty the obligations previously undertaken by France and the U.S.S.R. towards third countries, in published treaties, it is agreed that effect shall not be given to the provisions of the aforesaid treaty in a way which, being inconsistent with the treaty obligations assumed by one of the contracting parties, would expose the latter to sanctions of an international character.[98]

This was an obvious reference to Locarno and to the possibility that the Franco-Soviet Pact might expose France to British and Italian sanctions.

The Locarno Treaty provided that if either France or Germany attacked the other, England, Italy, and Belgium would go to the assistance of the party attacked if they decided that the attack was "an unprovoked act of aggression."[99] This provision raised the question: if Germany attacked Russia, and France then attacked

[96] Paragraph 1 of the Protocol of Signature, *ibid.*, p. 28.

[97] The Franco-Polish alliance apparently was protected by Paragraph 4 of the protocol. This question cannot be definitely decided until publication of the secret Franco-Polish Military Convention of 1921. Consult, *Rapport Torrès*, pp. 166-167; Gamelin, *Servir*, II, 466-467; Szembek, *Journal*, pp. 68-73.

[98] Paragraph 2 of the Protocol of Signature, British Blue Book, *Cmd. 5143*, pp. 28-29.

[99] Article 4, paragraph 3, of the Locarno Treaty.

Germany, in application of the Franco-Soviet Pact, would England, Italy, and Belgium be forced to go to the aid of Germany? The answer was no, so long as it was Germany that attacked Russia first. For, in that case, the French attack on Germany would not be "an unprovoked act of aggression."[100] France, then, could give assistance to Russia without fear of sanctions if England, Italy, and Belgium agreed that Germany had attacked first. The French would not be held back by the Belgian opinion and at the moment they were sure of Italian sympathies; it was the British reaction that they feared. In effect, then, the protocol made French assistance to Russia conditional upon French consultation with the British government.[101]

In view of British inclinations to sympathize with Germany, the Quai d'Orsay's anxiety on this score was legitimate. The German press played up to the British by harping on the charge that the Franco-Soviet Pact contradicted the Locarno Treaty. Hitler hit this very point in his speech of 21 May 1935. "As a result of the military alliance between France and Russia, an element of legal insecurity has been brought into the Locarno Pact. . . ."[102]

Sir John Simon was questioned about the Franco-Soviet Pact on the day of its signature and he assured the House of Commons that the pact would not force England to go to the assistance of Germany.

If Germany attacks Russia and in view of a Franco-Russian treaty of mutual assistance France goes to the assistance of Russia by attacking Germany, the Locarno Treaty does *not* put this country in those circumstances under any obligation to go to the assistance of Germany.[103]

[100] Article 2 of the Locarno Treaty stated that the Franco-German promise not to go to war was not binding in three cases: (1) self-defense; (2) action in pursuance of Article 16 of the League Covenant, and (3) "Action as the result of a decision taken by the Assembly or by the Council of the League of Nations or in pursuance of article 15, paragraph 7, of the Covenant of the League of Nations, provided that in this last event the action is directed against a State which was the first to attack."

[101] France had the right to judge for herself whether Germany was the first to attack. "Mais avant de l'exercer, il n'en est pas moins qu'elle se trouverait appelée à vérifier sur-le-champ si son appréciation des circonstances de l'agression allemande concorde bien avec celle de ses co-contractants du Pacte Rhénan [Locarno], c'est-à-dire non seulement les garants [England and Italy] mais encore la Belgique." *Rapport Torrès*, p. 166.

[102] *D.I.A., 1935*, I, 169.

[103] *Parliamentary Debates, Official Report*, House of Commons, Fifth Series, 301, 2 May 1935, columns 681-682. (Italics inserted.)

Later, in a note to the German government, the British government stated that they were satisfied "that there is nothing in the Franco-Soviet Treaty which either conflicts with the Locarno Treaty or modifies its operation in any way."[104] The Italian and Belgian governments also informed Berlin that they considered the Franco-Soviet Pact compatible with Locarno.[105]

Sir John Simon's statement was received with delight in Paris and Moscow. Maxim Litvinov told the United States Ambassador that he and the French had been trying for a month to get a British declaration. "At last we got it." Litvinov added that "the obligations undertaken by France to come to the support of the Soviet Union had been without binding character until the declaration of Sir John Simon, but that Sir John's statement made French support of the Soviet Union in case of an attack by Germany absolutely certain."[106]

Czechoslovakia now boldly made a third in the league against Germany. On 16 May 1935 Foreign Minister Beneš and the Soviet Minister, M. Alexandrovsky, signed in Prague a Pact of Mutual Assistance. The treaty was a reproduction of the articles of the Franco-Soviet Treaty as was most of the Protocol of Signature. The protocol, however, contained one significant difference. It stipulated that the treaty would come into force only if France rendered assistance to the country attacked.[107] The Czech-Soviet Pact was thus subordinated to the operation of the Franco-Czech Pact of 1925 or of the Franco-Soviet Pact. Ratifications of the Czech-Soviet Pact were exchanged during a visit to Moscow by Dr. Edward Beneš, 8-10 June 1935.[108] Thus, in the month of May 1935, there emerged an axis Paris-Prague-Moscow.

[104] Note from Sir Samuel Hoare (who succeeded Sir John Simon as Foreign Secretary) to Ambassador von Hoesch, 5 July 1935, British Blue Book, *Cmd. 5143*, p. 45.
[105] Italian memorandum of 15 July and Belgian memorandum of 19 July 1935, both addressed to the German government, *ibid.*, pp. 46-47.
[106] Conversation between M. Litvinov and Ambassador William C. Bullitt, in Moscow, 4 May 1935, *F.R.U.S., 1935*, I, 270.
[107] "Les deux gouvernements reconnaissent que les engagements d'assistance mutuelle joueront entre eux seulement en tant que ... serait prêté de la part de la France assistance mutuelle à la partie victime de l'agression." Paragraph 2 of the Protocol of Signature, *L.N.T.S.*, CLIX, 360.
[108] Consult *F.R.U.S., 1935*, I, 271-272, 284; Degras, ed., *Soviet Documents on Foreign Policy, 1917-1941*, III, 134-136; Paul E. Zinner, "Czechoslovakia: the Diplomacy of Eduard Benes," in Craig and Gilbert, eds., *The Diplomats 1919-1939*, pp. 110, 120-121; F. J. Vondracek, *The Foreign Policy of Czechoslovakia, 1918-1935* (New York, 1937), pp. 404-406.

iv

The Franco-Soviet Pact was greeted with approval by most sections of French public opinion, as revealed in the Paris press. The party reactions were much the same as they had been in the summer of 1934.[109] The only significant change was an increase in support from the Right.

On the Left, most of the Radical-Socialists maintained their enthusiasm for the policy advanced by their leader, M. Édouard Herriot.[110] M. Léon Blum, head of the Socialists, displayed the same cool, skeptical attitude he had worn since the beginning of the rapprochement. He insisted that the pact would be valuable only if France and Russia should revive the Disarmament Conference and work for general disarmament.[111] The Communists were pleased, though bewildered at the implications.[112] They were just finishing a bitterly fought campaign for the municipal elections of 5 and 12 May 1935. The party had spent the time well since the dramatic Unity of Action Pact with the Socialist party in July 1934. Ardently exploiting the broad appeal of the new Popular Front, the Communists revealed a dynamism which made a deep impression on the left-wing Socialists and even the left-wing Radical-Socialists. In the municipal elections the Communists made by far the largest gain of all parties. In towns over 5,000 inhabitants, Communists won control of the Municipal Council in 90 towns, a net gain of 43.[113]

On the Extreme Right, intransigent hostility was still the response. Despite German rearmament, *L'Action Française* and *Le Jour* denied that the alliance with Russia could bring France any benefit.[114] But as Jacques Bainville, the royalist historian, admitted ruefully, the warnings went unheeded. "The public was not moved. It did not even pay attention."[115]

[109] See chap. ix above, pp. 193-195.

[110] M. Yvon Delbos, a prominent moderate in the party, wrote detailed justifications of the alliance in *La Dépêche de Toulouse*, 29 April and 23 May 1935. See also the articles in praise of the pact by Mme Geneviève Tabouis, in *L'Oeuvre*, 18 and 20 April 1935.

[111] *Le Populaire*, 5 May 1935.   [112] *L'Humanité*, 3 May 1935.

[113] Figures given to the cabinet meeting of 17 May 1935, by the Minister of Interior, M. Regnier, Herriot, *Jadis*, II, 536-537; Georges Dupeux, *Le Front Populaire et les Élections de 1936* (Paris, 1959), p. 85.

[114] Notice the examples in Micaud, *The French Right and Nazi Germany, 1933-1939*, p. 46.

[115] Article by Jacques Bainville in *Candide*, 9 May 1935, quoted *ibid.*

The conservatives (as distinct from the reactionaries of the Extreme Right) generally accepted the pact as an unpleasant necessity. On the Center and Right, *L'Echo de Paris* and *Revue des Deux Mondes* were now joined by *L'Ordre* and *Le Journal des Débats*.[116] In the latter M. Pierre Bernus, who had rejected Barthou's Russian policy, finally rallied to the alliance after Hitler's proclamation of German rearmament.[117] M. Émile Buré responded to the same stimulus and swung *L'Ordre* into the Franco-Soviet camp. "As the German peril grows, the French people will attach proportionally more importance to the Franco-Russian Pact."[118] From the *Revue des Deux Mondes*, M. René Pinon issued the classical analysis of a traditional nationalist: all ideological disadvantages must be rigorously subordinated to the calculations of foreign policy. The Franco-Soviet pact would serve first as a forceful warning to Germany. But suppose that Hitler gambled on war. "On that day, the Russian mass, even if her army does not go into the line, would make the decisive weight in the balance.... The Europe of Stresa is strong enough to defend itself against German aggression..., but the mass of the U.S.S.R. must not go over to the opposite [German] side."[119] One of the most striking aspects of the Franco-Soviet Pact was its favorable reception by most French conservatives. Once bitterly hostile to an alliance with Moscow, they had been driven to accept it by the resurgence of Germany.

v

A week after signature of the pact, M. Pierre Laval set off for the East. Accompanied by M. Alexis Léger, he spent two days in Warsaw talking to Colonel Beck and Count Szembek. Laval assured his hosts that the Franco-Soviet Pact did not contradict the Franco-Polish alliance. He had no pro-Russian sympathies; he had signed the pact only because it was "the best guarantee" against German-Russian collaboration.[120] Marshal Pilsudski was too sick to

[116] *Le Temps* approved the pact as it had approved the rapprochement. However, the "Bulletin du Jour" editorials in *Le Temps* were so frequently inspired by the Quai d'Orsay that they cannot be cited as representative examples of public opinion.

[117] See his article of 3 May 1935, *Journal des Débats*.

[118] Article by Émile Buré in *L'Ordre*, quoted in "Revue de la Presse," *ibid.*, 5 May 1935.

[119] M. René Pinon, "Chronique de la Quinzaine," *Revue des Deux Mondes*, 15 May 1935, p. 479.

[120] Conversation in Warsaw, 10 May 1935, Szembek, *Journal*, pp. 71-72. See

talk, and on 12 May the great old eccentric—socialist, soldier, dictator—died. On returning from Moscow, Laval stopped at Warsaw and Cracow to join the mourning for the hero of reborn Poland.[121]

As Pierre Laval reached Moscow, 13 May 1935, he may have thought back to the days before 1914 when he, Stalin, Pilsudski, and Mussolini had all been members of the Socialist Second International. At any rate, the visit was a bright success. M. Laval was lavishly entertained for three days in the Russian capital and carried on conversations with Stalin, Molotov, and Litvinov. The Russian dictator made a sharp impression; "Stalin is wise, cold, detached and ruthless," Laval told a Polish friend.[122]

Laval's success came from bearding Stalin on a touchy subject. Laval said that Frenchmen were not impressed by the pretense that Stalin had no control over foreign Communists. "French public opinion certainly would not understand if Stalin did not now give orders to the Communists in France to cease opposition to the army budget and to the 2-year service law." Laval told the U. S. Ambassador that Stalin simply said, "I agree"; and the communiqué issued on 15 May revealed his concession.[123]

Comrade Stalin expressed complete understanding and approval of the national defence policy pursued by France with the object of maintaining its armed forces at a level consistent with its security requirements.[124]

In view of the savage Communist attacks on the two years' service, Stalin's statement was a humiliating disavowal of his French minions.

When the Laval-Stalin communiqué was published, *L'Humanité*

also Laroche, *La Pologne de Pilsudski*, pp. 214-218; Beck, *Dernier Rapport*, pp. 91-93, 288.

[121] At Cracow Laval had a two-hour conversation with General Hermann Goering, Hitler's personal representative at the funeral; Laval reaffirmed his undiminished interest in Franco-German reconciliation. Consult Szembek, *Journal*, pp. 81-87; Aloisi, *Journal*, pp. 272-273; Schmidt, *Hitler's Interpreter*, pp. 29-32.

[122] Laval to his host at Cracow, Count Alfred Potocki, *Master of Lancut* (London, 1959), p. 207. On Stalin, Laval told Count Szembek: "Oh, oh! très fort; c'est un très grand bonhomme; mais c'est le type du conquérant asiatique—une espèce de Tamerlan." Szembek, *Journal*, p. 85.

[123] Conversation between M. Laval and Ambassador William C. Bullitt, in Moscow 15 May 1935, *F.R.U.S., 1935*, I, 278. Laval told Count Potocki: "He [Stalin] gave me the impression that he was not only master of Russia but that his writ ran also in France." *Master of Lancut*, p. 207.

[124] Communiqué issued jointly by Stalin and Laval, 15 May 1935, Degras, ed., *Soviet Documents on Foreign Policy, 1917-1941*, III, 131-132; *Le Temps*, 17 May 1935.

lurched from one explanation to another. Lenin's decision to adopt the "New Economic Policy" in 1921 was a favorite analogy. In a long apologetic article, Vaillant-Couturier explained that it was necessary for the Soviet Union "to gain time, to postpone war...."[125] Finally, the party appealed to that best of all formulas, "Stalin is right," and settled down to live with the duty of being patriotic.[126]

It was, however, the Socialists who came off the worst, for they were scandalized by Stalin's move and equally by the blind obedience of the Communists. M. Léon Blum reacted to the Stalin-Laval communiqué with dismay and unbelief. "The more I think it over, the less I understand.... Thus, Stalin disapproves those who refused their vote to the two-year [law].... He approves, against us, the government which we have fought and whose representative will now return from Moscow displaying his good-conduct medal."[127] The more consternation on the Left, the happier were French conservatives. They took the Laval-Stalin communiqué as proof that their support of the Franco-Soviet Pact was realistic.

One man was even more shocked than Léon Blum: the exile Leon Trotsky, miserable in his semi-custody in the mountains near Grenoble. "Even though I am sufficiently familiar with the political cynicism of Stalin, his contempt for principles, and his near-sighted practicality, I still could not believe my eyes when I read these lines. The cunning Laval has found a way to approach that vain and limited bureaucrat."[128]

The second important result of Laval's voyage was kept strictly confidential. It concerned the vital question of a military accord. Stalin said that, while he agreed with Laval's peaceful interpretation of the pact, it would be best to prepare for the worst. Military arrangements to give the alliance its full power should be discussed. Although undoubtedly reluctant, Laval agreed to conversations between the two general staffs.

[125] *L'Humanité*, 18 May 1935.

[126] "Within three days of Stalin's pronouncement they had adopted this new line without audible murmurs, and the streets were placarded with posters proclaiming, 'Staline a raison.'" James Joll, "The Making of the Popular Front," in James Joll, ed., *St. Antony's Papers* No. 5, *The Decline of the Third French Republic*, p. 54.

[127] *Le Populaire*, 17 May 1935. "If one may talk about traumatic experiences in politics, surely the effect of Stalin's statement upon the left should be considered a model case." Marcus, *French Socialism in the Crisis Years, 1933-1936*, p. 119.

[128] Diary entry of 17 May 1935, *Trotsky's Diary in Exile, 1935* (Cambridge, Mass., 1958), p. 120.

I agreed to them, at the same time pointing out that staff conversations would only realize their full value after conclusion of the accord between the U.S.S.R. and Czechoslovakia. Litvinov then informed me of the agreement which he and M. Beneš had made, and I declared that I was ready to propose to the Government the opening of these staff conversations under conditions of the customary discretion.[129]

It was quite appropriate that Laval followed this commitment by a trip to the military aerodrome at Molino, where he watched demonstrations of the Red Army's planes and parachute troops.[130]

When M. Pierre Laval left Moscow, the Franco-Soviet rapprochement had reached its climax. In May 1935, forty-one years after the alliance with Tsarist Russia, the Third French Republic was the ally of Soviet Russia.

[129] Telegram of 16 May 1935 from M. Laval in Moscow to M. Pierre-Étienne Flandin, the Premier, in Paris, quoted by the latter at the Parliamentary Investigation Commission, *Les Événments Survenus en France de 1933 à 1945*, I, 142-143. Note Laval's remarks to the United States Ambassador in Moscow, *F.R.U.S., 1935*, I, 279.

[130] M. Alexis Léger, Secretary-General of the Quai d'Orsay, told the United States Ambassador in Moscow, Mr. William C. Bullitt, that the French government thought the Russian planes of inferior quality. However, "arrangements would now be made for the sending of French airplane engineers and foremen to Soviet factories who could use Russian material and manpower for an immense output of first-rate planes." Telegram from Ambassador Bullitt, Moscow, 14 May 1935, 751.6111/75 Archives of the Department of State, Washington, D. C.

[131] The ratification of the Franco-Soviet Pact became the first chapter in the story of its fate; see chap. xii.

Twelve

FAIR WEATHER FRIENDS

The origins of the Franco-Soviet Pact of Mutual Assistance present an almost classic display of balance-of-power diplomacy. As long as Germany was weak, France and Russia had traded insults and indifference. France had nothing to fear from the struggling Weimar Republic, disarmed, occupied, and forced to pay reparations. The Russians, indeed, fell into rewarding collaboration with Germany—the notorious Rapallo policy of diplomatic, economic, and secret military ties.

In 1930 the situation started to change. French troops evacuated their last post on the Rhine in June 1930; the Nazis won six million votes in the election of September 1930; and in March 1931 Germany and Austria tried to stage an economic *Anschluss* by announcing a Customs Union. The Quai d'Orsay began to attribute a bit more importance to Russia; hesitantly, almost furtively, negotiations for a trade accord and a non-aggression pact were opened in June 1931. The commercial talks came to nothing, but the Franco-Soviet Non-Aggression Pact was signed in Paris, 29 November 1932.

It was the appointment of Adolf Hitler as Chancellor of Germany that gave the Franco-Soviet rapprochement real drive. His program of expansion was directed at the destruction of France as a great power and at the colonization of Russia. For the first time the Russians became afraid of Germany. Threatened by the Japanese thrust into Manchuria, beset by famine, and preoccupied by the immense troubles of industrialization and collectivization, they sorely needed an ally in Europe. Abruptly, in the summer of 1933, Maxim Litvinov, the Soviet Foreign Minister, pressed Paris for a tight military alliance. The French reaction to Hitler was slower, not excited until his dramatic withdrawal from the World Disarmament Conference and the League of Nations, 14 October 1933. This was the event which spurred the Foreign Minister, M. Joseph Paul-Boncour, to seek alliance. The Soviets jumped to grasp the offer, and formal negotiations for a mutual assistance pact began early in December 1933.

The crucial step was taken by M. Louis Barthou, who came to the Quai d'Orsay as a result of the riots of 6 February 1934. Animated by his correct and horrified judgment of Hitler, the doughty veteran, who had been a cabinet minister in the days of the first Franco-Russian alliance, set himself to build a ring around Germany. He was backed by a cabinet committed to the anti-German course, dominated by conservatives such as the Premier, Gaston Doumergue, Louis Marin, André Tardieu, and Marshal Pétain.

Barthou was urged to go even faster by M. Édouard Herriot, who had entered the cabinet as a symbol of the moderate Left. The man who had "recognized" Soviet Russia in 1924, Herriot had been alienated by the intransigence of the French Communists. Late in 1932 he dismissed his doubts and opened a sustained, effective campaign for an alliance with Russia. Herriot was obsessed by the German danger and by the weakness of France. Leader of the largest French party, the Radical-Socialists, he was essential to the existence of the Doumergue cabinet and the Flandin cabinet which held power from February 1934 to June 1935. He never released his powerful pressure, and the Franco-Soviet Pact owed more to Édouard Herriot than to any other man.

Louis Barthou would not have hesitated in his drive for the Russian alliance, but his precise plans remain a secret. As he welcomed King Alexander of Yugoslavia to France, 9 October 1934, he and his guest were assassinated. By chance, the Foreign Ministry fell to an opponent of the alliance, M. Pierre Laval. His reluctance was matched by Herriot's vigilance and by the fidelity to Barthou's program displayed by the new Premier, M. Pierre-Étienne Flandin. Nonetheless, Laval's subtlety was a marvel to watch. He spun out the negotiations and made known his desire for a reconciliation with Germany.

Pierre Laval did not neglect the balance of power, but he wanted to play it only in Western Europe. His solution was Italy. In the Rome Accords of January 1935 and subsequent military agreements, he won something close to an alliance. Laval's aim was to use Italy, and England as well, to "channel" Germany into a more conciliatory mood and possibly a four-power understanding. If that did not work, France could fall back on Italy and England. He did not want an alliance with Russia because he feared that it would provoke Hitler and facilitate the spread of communism in France.

Pierre Laval's policy rested on the comfortable assumption that Germany needed French benevolence. Having watched over secret rearmament for two years, Adolf Hitler decided that Germany was strong enough to admit it. On 9 March the existence of the Luftwaffe was announced and on 16 March 1935 he proclaimed the reinstitution of conscription and set the new level of the Reichswehr at 36 divisions, nearly 600,000 men.

Hitler's decision to withdraw from Geneva had led to the opening of the alliance negotiations; his decision to announce German rearmament forced their conclusion. There was a tempest of resentment in Paris, and the cabinet imposed a firm anti-German policy on Laval. He bent to the wind, and the Franco-Soviet Pact of Mutual Assistance was signed in Paris, 2 May 1935.

Could the French have found other, less risky allies than Italy and Russia? Not if they wished to remain a great power, not if they hoped to tilt the balance against Hitler. The only alternative was abdication of all French influence in Central and Eastern Europe, which would inevitably lead to retreat from the Near East as well.

The French had no choice because there were no other allies available. Time after time, British cabinets made it bleakly clear that they would not give France any further security beyond the equivocal promise of Locarno. Even if the British had been generous, they would have been promising only moral support. Aside from their Navy, the British had virtually no military forces to offer. In any case, London had no intention of being drawn into an anti-German coalition. Vacillation obscured this at times but ended by doubling its impact on the disappointed French. When they worked with the British on a project, there would be a German explosion and the French would look up to find the British gone, hastily trying to patch up things with the Germans.

Needless to say, the French could expect no aid from Washington. The United States had even less military strength than the United Kingdom. Moreover, Franklin Roosevelt did not intend to offer anything to the French; during his first term American foreign policy was thoroughly isolationist. In the years of Hitler's rise, United States influence was less active in Europe than at any other period since 1919.

Why not rely on the original French alliance system? Belgium, Poland, and the Little Entente had been adequate in the decade of German weakness, but they could not pretend to hold Hitler. The Belgians were weary of standing as a sentinel against Germany. Their government, by its repeated requests for the right to have a veto on the operation of the Franco-Belgian Military Convention, had sapped its moral value.

The Poles, too, wanted to be "independent"; in contrast to the Belgians they cast themselves in an active, militant role. A long-term tendency to resent French tutelage and a short-term opportunity for a deal with Hitler combined to lead to the German-Polish Non-Aggression Declaration, 26 January 1934. Marshal Pilsudski and Colonel Beck applied the new policy with bluntness and, in the case of the latter, obvious satisfaction in embarrassing the French. They did not break off the alliance with France (in fact their independent policy was impossible without it as a guarantee). But though the paper was not torn, almost no trust survived. The Quai d'Orsay felt that Poland wanted all the security of the alliance with none of its dangers. It has been said that the Franco-Polish alliance hindered Franco-Soviet rapprochement. On the contrary, its moral collapse speeded the latter.

As for the Little Entente, that was only a coalition against Hungary. Each had a nightmare of a different color: for Romania it was Red Russia; for Yugoslavia it was Mussolini and his black shirts; for Czechoslovakia the brown-shirted Nazis of Germany. All three had been battered by the depression, and Yugoslavia and Romania were highly vulnerable to German trade pressure. Only Czechoslovakia was a willing ally against Germany. And the final indignity was the Polish-Czech quarrel, an exchange of contempt and self-righteousness. In short, there was no French alliance system.

In her search for security against resurgent Germany, France could count on little more than advice from London and Washington, and her existing allies were weak and disunited. On cold calculation of military, industrial, demographic power only Italy and Russia offered hope. French statesmen decided to seek both alliances and they did so successfully. April and May 1935 formed the high point of the French attempt to balance Hitler's power. Only one month separated the Stresa conference, where the Franco-Italian alignment was shown to brilliant advantage, from the

Franco-Soviet Pact of Mutual Assistance. Momentarily, Hitler was encircled.

Once French leaders realized that they needed Russia, all the old obstacles dropped away. For years Soviet repudiation of Tsarist Russia's debts and the fear of communism had been paraded as "insuperable" obstacles to a Franco-Soviet entente. French investors held some ten billion francs of Tsarist Russian securities, and in the previous decade the issue had wrecked several negotiations. It is fascinating to watch it disappear completely, as a political factor, after the French became afraid of Germany and appreciative of Russia's weight. (The debts did continue to function as an economic factor, making it impossible to grant Russia credits and thus hampering trade.) Never once did the debts trouble the negotiation of the mutual assistance pact. When national security was threatened, money—and it was a great deal of money—faded to secondary stature.

It was much more difficult to subordinate the communist factor, but it was done. Part of the success was due to the traditional nationalist attitude adopted by most French leaders, part was due to favorable circumstances. To understand the result, it is necessary to turn in detail to the relationship between foreign and domestic policy.

ii

In the twentieth century, or more accurately since the advent of democracy and the mass circulation press, no foreign policy can be considered in a vacuum. Of all allies, Soviet Russia was the most likely to agitate public opinion. Yet it would be wrong to suppose that here lay the contrast between the Franco-Soviet Pact and the Franco-Russian alliance of 1894. An ideological conflict troubled the prewar alliance—the incompatibility between Tsarist autocracy and the bourgeois, increasingly democratic Third Republic. In France many men of the Left balked at embracing the Tsar of Bloody Sunday. Jean Jaurès, Georges Clemenceau, Anatole France held up to shame the pernicious effects of the Franco-Russian alliance. They deplored the fact that in shoring up autocracy it shackled Russian democracy; they claimed that it also would lead to autocracy in France.

Stalin had something the Tsar could not pretend to, control

over a French party. The French Communists were notorious for their attacks on the French Army and their contempt for patriotism. Was it wise to ally with a country to which some Frenchmen in effect had transferred their allegiance? For years, the danger had seemed too great; Hitler turned it into a lesser evil.

It might have been expected that the Franco-Soviet Pact would be the work of the left-wing. Instead, the Left played a subordinate part in its origins and conclusion. This was logical, for the Left repudiated the balance of power, power politics, secret diplomacy, and other emanations of the devil. The French Socialists looked on the pact with deep suspicion. It would provoke Germany to retaliation and thus lead to an arms race and war. Searching for the most damning epithet, M. Léon Blum often called the pact a re-apparition of the prewar Franco-Russian alliance. The Socialists also disliked co-operation with Stalin because of their acid rivalry with Stalin's party in France. After their reconciliation with the Communists in July 1934, they became less suspicious but they were never enthusiastic.

The Left did contribute two architects of the pact: Édouard Herriot, a Radical-Socialist, and Joseph Paul-Boncour, an independent Socialist. Both men, however, were moderates, pragmatists, more republican than radical, and intensely patriotic. Herriot occasionally waxed sentimental about Russia, but this stemmed from wishful thinking, not from any sympathy with communism. Herriot and Paul-Boncour sought the power of Russia; the fact that it was now Soviet Russia was irrelevant to them.

The Franco-Soviet Pact was largely the work of conservatives. The responsibility for authorizing the negotiations and their conclusion was taken by the Doumergue and Flandin cabinets. Both were oriented to the Right. Several of the champions of the pact were conservatives: Louis Barthou, Pierre-Étienne Flandin, and Louis Marin in the cabinet; Henri de Kerillis, Pertinax, and René Pinon of the press.

The paradox of conservative support for the Franco-Soviet Pact is resolved by two considerations. After all, the Center and Right were dominated by traditional nationalists. These men reacted sensitively to the German challenge, and they took the customary position that domestic politics and ideological factors must be subordinated to exigencies of foreign policy. They accepted without question the role of a great power for France; to play the role they knew that France required powerful new allies. The conservatives respected power, and it was obvious that only Russia and Italy had enough power to stop Hitler. Many of them welcomed alliance with Fascist Italy. With reluctance, they accepted the necessity of alliance with Communist Russia. They had not forgotten the Russian contribution to the victory of the Marne in 1914; for them the analogy to the prewar Franco-Russian alliance was a compliment.

The second factor which affected the conservatives was an accident. It happened that the Franco-Soviet rapprochement closely coincided with the nadir of the French Communist party. Plagued by dissidence, poor leadership, and the Comintern line of complete intransigence towards other parties, the party hit bottom during the period 1928-1933. In the elections of 1924, the Communists had won 26 seats in the Chamber of Deputies; in 1928 they fell to 12 and in 1932 down to 10. From June 1932 to May 1936, there were only 10 Communist deputies (9 after the defection of Doriot) in contrast to 131 Socialists. Not until 1935 did the first Communist, Marcel Cachin, enter the Senate. The men who made the pact were almost all parliamentarians, and it is likely that their image of the Communist threat in France was shaped by what they encountered in parliament. There the Communists were a nuisance but no more.

The trouble with the Communist problem was that by its very nature it was not likely to remain quiescent. Implicit in the conservatives' attitude was a qualification. They would accept the Franco-Soviet Pact so long as the French "soviets" were only a nuisance.

iii

The more one probes, the more "qualifications" emerge on the French side. Of course, the Russians had their reservations too. Stalin was not known for keeping his word. He had dropped the Rapallo policy of collaboration with Germany only with reluctance, and some of his advisers were never satisfied with France as the equivalent. However, as long as Hitler remained hostile, the Russians had no choice. Once they decided to go after the French alliance, they pressed for a tight, automatic accord; after the pact was signed, they immediately demanded a military convention to complement it. Whatever their ultimate intentions, the Russians acted as if they took the pact seriously.

In Paris, only Herriot and Barthou accepted the alliance without conditions, without inserting a veto. Four vetoes emerge on the French side, two of them potentially destructive. They were the British veto, the Italian veto, the Communist veto, and the military veto.

The British veto was most prominent in the case of M. Alexis Léger, Secretary-General of the Quai d'Orsay; M. Pierre-Étienne Flandin also placed a very high value on harmony between London and Paris. There was the practical consideration of the Locarno Treaty; execution of the Franco-Soviet Pact might violate Locarno and, at the least, lead the British to withdraw from it. To Léger it was a more profound proposition; he was determined to protect the deep ties of interest and culture with England. "No new ally was worth the price of estrangement from Britain."[1] One has the feeling that Léger, faced with a crisis involving Russia, would have immediately consulted the British and given much weight to their advice. The British veto, however, depended entirely upon individual attitudes. Louis Barthou would have acted first and informed the British later.

The Italian veto was a curious business. The French rapprochements with Italy and Russia had run to success on parallel lines; in parliament and the press they had been linked together consistently. It is quite possible that this constant juxtaposition prevented a sharp confrontation (to the favor of the Russians). The Ethiopian crisis, which became acute in October 1935, shattered the Franco-Italian entente, despite Laval's desperate search for a compromise. It also placed Russia and Italy in conflict at the League of Nations. Now the question had to be squarely faced, and for many conservatives it seemed as if it were the first time they had considered the Russian alliance solely on its own. The confrontation was revealing; their latent prejudices seemed to be released and many rejected alliance with Russia alone.

The third qualification was potentially destructive. The conservative assumption that the French Communists would remain weak proved entirely wrong. Swelled by unemployment and by their new Popular Front appeal to all anti-fascists, the French

[1] Cameron, "Alexis Saint-Léger Léger," in Craig and Gilbert, eds., *The Diplomats, 1919-1939*, p. 383.

Communists started a surging recovery. Ironically, it was not visible until the Franco-Soviet Pact had been made. Three days after its signature some evidence emerged clearly for the first time. In the municipal elections of 5 and 12 May 1935, the Communists ran powerfully, more than doubling the number of town councils under their control. The left-wing Radical-Socialists began to push their party into the Popular Front, and in a great manifestation in Paris, 14 July, Maurice Thorez, Léon Blum, and Édouard Daladier marched side by side. Their parties, Communist, Socialist, and Radical-Socialist, signed an electoral alliance in January 1936. In the general elections, 26 April and 3 May 1936, the Popular Front won control of the Chamber of Deputies. The Communists jumped from 10 to 72 seats, and took votes away from their allies. They increased their popular vote from 783,000 in 1932 to 1,469,000, while the Socialists fell off slightly, 2,034,000 to 1,997,000, and the Radicals lost heavily, 2,315,000 to 1,955,000.

The conservatives did not need to see the election statistics—they had become alarmed by the end of 1935. Many were convinced that the Communists were running the Popular Front and were on their way to take over France. Within nine months their image of the Communist party changed from a handful of noise-makers to that of a powerful menace. With that changing image came a d fferent response to the Russian alliance.

The Chamber of Deputies debate on ratification of the Franco-Soviet Pact, 11-27 February 1936, was turbulent. In the debate and the press commentary on it, most of the Center and the Right rejected the pact. When the vote was taken, the pact was ratified by 353 to 164, with 45 abstentions, many deputies in the Center and on the Right either voting no or abstaining.[2] Men such as Louis Marin and Henri de Kerillis who had vigorously supported conclusion of the pact, now spurned their own creation. The disenchanted conservatives argued that the alliance was too risky. It would give Stalin the means for dragging France into war, into a crusade against fascism; it would give the Communists respectability and thus speed their resurgence. Most of them simply ignored their previous argument that such risks had to be assumed in order to gain Russian aid against Nazi Germany. But one of them, M. de Kerillis, admitted the dilemma frankly: "At the same

[2] Prominent conservatives who voted to ratify the Pact were MM. Pierre Étienne Flandin, Georges Mandel, François Piétri, and Paul Reynaud.

time that she [Russia] offers us a guarantee against the German danger, she threatens us with the Soviet danger. And between the danger of Hitler and the danger of Stalin we do not wish to make a choice."[3]

As Charles Micaud has shown, "the opposition of the nationalist leaders to the Franco-Soviet Pact in February, 1936, was a dangerous and momentous step toward the abandonment of their traditional foreign policy."[4] Until 1936, the conservatives had followed the traditional practice of subordinating ideology to national interest. Now they seemed to place a higher value on defeating their domestic enemy than on defeating their national enemy. A consequence of this shift was renunciation of the free use of the balance of power.

The core of the majority voting to ratify the Franco-Soviet Pact came from the Radical-Socialists and the Socialists. The pact became what it had never been in its origins, a pact of the Left.[5] When it was signed, it had been an instrument of balance-of-power diplomacy; by the time it entered legally into force, 27 March 1936, it had become a domestic football. "Domestic and foreign policy thus had become intertwined, each sacrificing its integrity and coherence to the other."[6]

The fourth veto was a private affair: the French refusal to add a military convention. One of the most interesting aspects of the Franco-Soviet rapprochement was the French Army's support. Trained to think in terms of power, the military men discounted the value of Belgium, Poland, and the Little Entente and realized that England could offer France almost no immediate military assistance. They vigorously pushed the Italian alliance, and they sought a strong ally to threaten Germany from the east. They had been alarmed by the secret Reichswehr–Red Army collaboration and they wished to render a revival of it impossible.

When Hitler and the Russians broke off co-operation in 1933, the French Army leaders recognized a rare opportunity. They sup-

[3] *L'Echo de Paris*, 10 Feb. 1936.

[4] Micaud, *The French Right and Nazi Germany, 1933-1939*, p. 84.

[5] The Senate ratified the pact, 12 March 1936, by a vote of 226 to 48, with 34 abstaining. As a result of the German remilitarization of the Rhineland, 7 March, several conservatives, led by M. Alexander Millerand, changed their position and voted to ratify the pact. The Soviet government ratified the pact by decree of 8 March 1936; ratifications were exchanged in Paris, 27 March 1936.

[6] Luther Allen, "The French Left and Soviet Russia," *World Affairs Quarterly*, XXIX (July 1959), 121.

ported M. Paul-Boncour when he opened the negotiations for an alliance. They backed Barthou's policy, and at the signature of the Franco-Soviet Pact one of its most important advocates was the new chief of the French Army, General Maurice Gamelin.

Paradoxically, the Army never displayed any desire for a military convention. Communist propaganda and infiltration posed a threat; a military convention would involve constant exchanges of staff officers and technicians, channels that could be exploited for espionage. But there was a more profound reason: many military men did not think they needed a military convention, because they did not think they needed a Russian offensive. With a rigidly defensive army, the basic French plan was to hold the Maginot Line, move up into Belgium to man a defensive position there and then wear down the German attacks. Convinced of the superiority of the defensive, because of its superiority in the World War, they strove only to weaken Germany. The Russians could contribute much to this goal by forcing the German Army to deploy for a two-front war. Moreover, Germany would not be able to draw raw materials and food supplies from Russia. To accomplish these aims, no military convention was necessary, merely a Franco-Soviet entente.

The attitude of the political leaders on this question was divided. Ironically, they did not yet realize how rigidly defensive was their own army. Flandin, Herriot, and Barthou seem to have considered a military convention desirable; Paul-Boncour was cautious about it, and it was the last thing that Laval wanted.

Whatever their preferences, none of the French negotiators ever plainly warned the Russians that they would refuse to sign a military convention. When Pierre Laval went to Moscow in May 1935, Stalin pressed him to make the pact efficient by working out military arrangements for the case of a war. Laval agreed; specifically he agreed "to propose to the government the opening of these staff conversations under conditions of the customary discretion."[7] Shortly after he returned, Laval became Premier as well as Foreign Minister, and thus could have implemented his promise with ease. Yet he gave instructions to the War Minister and to General Gamelin to postpone the staff conversations. After ratification of the pact, the decision rested with the Popular Front cabinets. It was precisely the military aspect of the pact that the Left

[7] Telegram of 16 May 1935 from M. Laval in Moscow, quoted by Flandin, *Les Événements Survenus en France de 1933 à 1945*, I, 142-143.

disliked. Preliminary staff conversations were begun in January 1937 but after three meetings they were not continued. The Franco-Soviet Pact never received its logical complement—a military convention to co-ordinate the movement of the two armies in case of attack by Hitler's legions. This void made a stark contrast to the Franco-Russian Military Convention of 1892, constantly revised by staff conversations.

Not all the French leaders made qualifications. Louis Barthou and Édouard Herriot were so acutely apprehensive of Hitler's threat, so anxious to secure a strong ally, that they had no time to be apprehensive about the nature of the ally. They would walk with the bear if he would protect them from the beast. Their colleagues, however, set the tone of the French attitude towards the pact. The vetoes had a composite effect; one might say that they left the following impression: "We will apply the Franco-Soviet Pact if the British approve, if Mussolini is also our ally, if the Communists do not frighten us, and without any military planning."

iv

Despite the qualifications, the Franco-Soviet Pact of Mutual Assistance was made. Out of humble origins—the liquidation of a minor tariff war—had emerged a slow rapprochement. Hitler's accession transformed this movement, gave it vitality and created the desire for alliance. His flaunting of rearmament brushed aside the last doubts. The Franco-Soviet Pact was the second alliance against Hitler. The Rome Accords had united France and Italy in an informal alliance against the *Anschluss* of Austria to Germany. The day after Laval left Moscow, Russia and Czechoslovakia signed their pledge of mutual assistance against the enemy of the Slavs. The balance of power was moving in precise and logical grooves. The aggressor had appeared, he had frightened his victims, and they had dropped their own quarrels to cling together.

The Franco-Soviet Pact was a tribute to the potential power of Germany and to the Nazi program of conquest. Hitler goaded into alliance two states who previously had little in common. Time alone would tell whether the common fear would be enough.

APPENDIX I. THE FRANCO-SOVIET PACT OF NON-AGGRESSION

Le Président de la République Française et le Comité Central Exécutif de l'Union des Républiques Soviétiques Socialistes,

Animés de la volonté de consolider la paix,

Convaincus qu'il est dans l'intérêt des deux Hautes Parties Contractantes d'améliorer et de développer les relations entre les deux pays,

Respectueux des engagements internationaux qu'ils ont précédemment assumés et dont ils déclarent qu'aucun ne fait obstacle au développement pacifique de leurs relations mutuelles et ne se trouve en contradiction avec le présent Traité,

Désireux de confirmer et de préciser, en ce qui concerne leurs rapports respectifs, le Pacte général de renonciation à la guerre du 27 août 1928,

Ont résolu de conclure un Traité à ces fins et ont désigné pour leurs plénipotentiaires, savoir:

Le Président de la République Française:

M. Edouard Herriot, député, président du Conseil, ministre des affaires étrangères;

Le Comité Central Exécutif de l'Union des Républiques Soviétiques Socialistes:

M. Valerien Dovgalevsky, ambassadeur extraordinaire et plénipotentiaire de l'Union des Républiques Soviétiques Socialistes près le Président de la République Française;

Lesquels, après avoir échangé leurs pouvoirs, reconnus en bonne et due forme, sont convenus des dispositions suivantes:

Article premier.

Chacune des Hautes Parties Contractantes s'engage vis-à-vis de l'autre à ne recourir en aucun cas contre elle, soit isolément, soit conjointement avec une ou plusieurs tierces Puissances, ni à la guerre, ni à aucune agression par terre, sur mer ou dans les airs et à respecter l'inviolabilité des territoires placés sous sa souveraineté ou dont elle assume la représentation extérieure et contrôle l'administration.

Art. 2.

Si l'une des Hautes Parties Contractantes est l'objet d'une agression de la part d'une ou de plusieurs tierces Puissances, l'autre Haute Partie

Contractante s'engage à ne prêter ni directement, ni indirectement aide ou assistance à l'agresseur ou aux agresseurs, pendant la durée du conflit.

Si l'une des Hautes Parties Contractantes se livre à une agression contre une tierce Puissance, l'autre Haute Partie Contractante pourra sans préavis dénoncer le présent Traité.

Art. 3.

Les engagements énoncés aux articles I et II ci-dessus ne peuvent en aucune façon limiter ou modifier les droits et obligations découlant pour chacune des Hautes Parties Contractantes des accords conclus par elle avant l'entrée en vigueur du présent Traité, chaque Partie déclarant d'ailleurs par les présentes n'être liée par aucun accord comportant l'obligation pour elle de participer à une agression entreprise par un Etat tiers.

Art. 4.

Chacune des Hautes Parties Contractantes s'engage, pour la durée du présent Traité, à ne participer à aucune entente internationale ayant pratiquement pour effet d'interdire l'achat ou la vente de marchandises ou l'octroi de crédits à l'autre Partie et à ne prendre aucune mesure ayant pour effet d'exclure celle-ci de toute participation à son commerce extérieur.

Art. 5.

Chacune des Hautes Parties Contractantes s'engage à respecter à tous égards la souveraineté ou l'autorité de l'autre Partie sur l'intégralité de ses territoires tels qu'ils sont définis à l'article premier du présent Traité, à ne s'immiscer en aucune façon dans ses affaires intérieures, à s'abstenir notamment d'une action quelconque tendant à susciter ou à favoriser toute agitation, propagande ou tentative d'intervention ayant pour but de porter atteinte à son intégrité territoriale ou de transformer par la force le régime politique ou social de tout ou partie de ses territoires.

Chacune des Hautes Parties Contractantes s'engage en particulier à ne créer, protéger, équiper, subventionner ou admettre sur son territoire ni des organisations militaires ayant pour objet la lutte armée contre l'autre Partie, ni des organisations s'arrogeant le rôle de gouvernement ou représentant le tout ou partie de ses territoires.

Art. 6.

Les Hautes Parties Contractantes, ayant déjà reconnu, dans le Pacte général de renonciation à la guerre du 27 août 1928, que le règlement ou la solution de tous les différends ou conflits, quelle que soit leur nature ou leur origine, qui pourront surgir entre elles, ne devra jamais être recherché que par des moyens pacifiques, confirment cette disposition et, pour lui donner effet, annexent au présent Traité une Convention relative à la procédure de conciliation.

Art. 7.

Le présent Traité, dont les textes français et russe feront également foi, sera ratifié et les ratifications en seront échangées à Moscou. Il prendra effet à dater dudit échange et restera en vigueur jusqu'à l'expiration d'un délai d'une année à partir du jour où l'une des Hautes Parties Contractantes aura notifié à l'autre son intention de le dénoncer. Cette notification ne pourra toutefois avoir lieu avant l'expiration d'un délai de deux années à compter du jour de l'entrée en vigueur du présent Traité.

En foi de quoi, les plénipotentiaires ont signé le présent Traité et y ont apposé leurs sceaux.

Fait à Paris, en double expédition le 29 novembre 1932.

(L.S.) (Signé) E. Herriot
(L.S.) (Signé) V. Dovgalevsky

APPENDIX II. FRANCO-SOVIET TREATY OF MUTUAL ASSISTANCE

Le Président de la République Française et le Comité Central Exécutif de l'Union des Républiques Soviétiques Socialistes,

Animés du désir d'affermir la paix en Europe et d'en garantir les bienfaits à leurs pays respectifs en assurant plus complètement l'exacte application des dispositions du Pacte de la Société des Nations visant à maintenir la sécurité nationale, l'intégrité territoriale et l'indépendance politique des Etats,

Décidés à consacrer leurs efforts à la préparation et à la conclusion d'un accord européen ayant cet objet et, en attendant, à contribuer, autant qu'il dépend d'eux, à l'application efficace des dispositions du Pacte de la Société des Nations,

Ont résolu de conclure un Traité à cet effet et ont désigné pour leurs Plénipotentiaires, savoir:

Le Président de la République Française:
M. Pierre Laval, Sénateur, Ministre des Affaires Étrangères.
Le Comité Central Exécutif de l'Union des Républiques Soviétiques Socialistes:
M. Vladimir Potemkine, Membre du Comité Central Exécutif, Ambassadeur extraordinaire et plénipotentiaire de l'Union des Républiques Soviétiques Socialistes près le Président de la République Française.

Lesquels, après avoir échangé leurs pleins pouvoirs reconnus en bonne et due forme, sont convenus des dispositions suivantes:

Article premier.

Au cas où la France ou l'U. R. S. S. serait l'objet d'une menace ou d'un danger d'agression de la part d'un Etat européen, l'U. R. S. S. et réciproquement la France s'engagent à procéder mutuellement à une consultation immédiate en vue des mesures à prendre pour l'observation des dispositions de l'article 10 du Pacte de la Société des Nations.

Art. 2.

Au cas où, dans les conditions prévues à l'article 15, paragraphe 7, du Pacte de la Société des Nations, la France ou l'U. R. S. S. serait, malgré les intentions sincèrement pacifiques des deux pays, l'objet d'une agression non provoquée de la part d'un Etat européen, l'U. R. S. S. et réciproquement la France se prêteront immédiatement aide et assistance.

Art. 3.

Prenant en considération que, d'après l'article 16 du Pacte de la Société des Nations, tout Membre de la Société qui recourt à la guerre contrairement aux engagements pris aux articles 12, 13 ou 15 du Pacte est *ipso facto* considéré comme ayant commis un acte de guerre contre tous les autres membres de la Société, la France et réciproquement l'U. R. S. S. s'engagent, au cas où l'une d'elles serait, dans ces conditions et malgré les intentions sincèrement pacifiques des deux pays, l'objet d'une agression non provoquée de la part d'un Etat européen, à se prêter immédiatement aide et assistance en agissant par application de l'article 16 du Pacte.

La même obligation est assumée pour le cas où la France ou l'U. R. S. S. serait l'objet d'une agression de la part d'un Etat européen dans les conditions prévues à l'article 17, paragraphes 1 et 3, du Pacte de la Société des Nations.

Art. 4.

Les engagements ci-dessus stipulés étant conformes aux obligations des Hautes Parties Contractantes en tant que Membres de la Société des Nations, rien dans le présent traité ne sera interprété comme restreignant la mission de celle-ci de prendre les mesures propres à sauvegarder efficacement la paix du monde ou comme restreignant les obligations découlant pour les Hautes Parties Contractantes du Pacte de la Société des Nations.

Art. 5.

Le présent Traité, dont les textes français et russe feront également foi, sera ratifié et les instruments de ratification seront échangés à Moscou aussitôt que faire se pourra. Il sera enregistré au Secrétariat de la Société des Nations.

Il prendra effet dès l'échange des ratifications et restera en vigueur pendant cinq ans. S'il n'est pas dénoncé par une des Hautes Parties Contractantes avec un préavis d'un an au moins avant l'expiration de cette période, il restera en vigueur sans limitation de durée, chacune des Hautes Parties Contractantes pouvant alors y mettre fin par une déclaration à cet effet avec préavis d'un an.

En foi de quoi, les Plénipotentiaires ont signé le présent Traité et y ont apposé leurs sceaux.

Fait à Paris, en double expédition le 2 mai 1935.

(L.S.) (Signé) Pierre LAVAL
(L.S.) (Signé) V. POTEMKINE

APPENDIX III. PROTOCOLE DE SIGNATURE

Au moment de procéder à la signature du Traité d'assistance mutuelle franco-soviétique en date de ce jour, les Plénipotentiaires ont signé le Protocole suivant qui sera compris dans l'échange des ratifications du Traité.

I

Il est entendu que l'effet de l'article 3 est d'obliger chaque Partie Contractante à prêter immédiatement assistance à l'autre en se conformant immédiatement aux recommandations du Conseil de la Société des Nations, aussitôt qu'elles auront été énoncées en vertu de l'article 16 du Pacte. Il est également entendu que les deux Parties Contractantes agiront de concert pour obtenir que le Conseil énonce ses recommandations avec toute la rapidité qu'exigeront les circonstances et que, si néanmoins le Conseil, pour une raison quelconque, n'énonce aucune recommandation ou s'il n'arrive pas à un vote unanime, l'obligation d'assistance n'en recevra pas moins application. Il est également entendu que les engagements d'assistance prévus dans le présent Traité ne visent que le cas d'une agression effectuée contre le territoire propre de l'une ou de l'autre Partie Contractante.

II

L'intention commune des deux Gouvernements étant de ne contredire en rien, par le présent Traité, les engagements précédemment assumés envers des Etats tiers par la France et par l'U. R. S. S. en vertu de traités publiés, il est entendu que les dispositions dudit Traité ne pourront pas recevoir une application qui, étant incompatible avec des obligations conventionnelles assumées par une Partie Contractante, exposerait celle-ci à des sanctions de caractère international.

III

Les deux Gouvernements, estimant désirable la conclusion d'un accord régional qui tendrait à organiser le sécurité entre Etats contractants et qui pourrait comporter ou que pourraient accompagner d'autre part des engagements d'assistance mutuelle, se reconnaissent la faculté de participer, de leur consentement mutuel, le cas échéant, à de semblables accords dans telle forme, directe ou indirecte, qui paraîtrait appropriée, les engagements de ces divers accords devant se substituer à ceux résultant du présent Traité.

IV

Les deux Gouvernements constatent que les négociations qui viennent d'avoir pour résultat la signature du présent Traité ont été engagées, à l'origine, en vue de compléter un accord de sécurité englobant les pays du nord-est de l'Europe, à savoir l'Union des républiques soviétiques socialistes, l'Allemagne, la Tchécoslovaquie, la Pologne et les Etats baltes voisins de l'Union des républiques soviétiques socialistes; à côté de cet accord devait être conclu un Traité d'assistance entre l'Union des républiques soviétiques socialistes, la France et l'Allemagne, chacun de ces trois Etats devant s'engager à prêter assistance à celui d'entre eux qui serait l'objet d'une agression de la part de l'un de ces trois Etats. Bien que les circonstances n'aient pas jusqu'ici permis la conclusion de ces accords, que les deux parties continuent à considérer comme désirable, il n'en reste pas moins que les engagements énoncés dans le Traité d'assistance franco-soviétique doivent être entendus comme ne devant jouer que dans les limites envisagées dans l'accord tripartite antérieurement projeté. Indépendamment des obligations découlant du présent Traité, il est rappelé en même temps que, conformément au Pacte franco-soviétique de non-agression signé le 29 novembre 1932 et sans porter par ailleurs atteinte à l'universalité des engagements de ce Pacte, au cas où l'une des deux Parties deviendrait l'objet d'une agression de la part d'une ou de plusieurs tierces puissances européennes non visées dans l'accord tripartite ci-dessus mentionné, l'autre Partie contractante devra s'abstenir, pendant la durée du conflit, de toute aide ou assistance directe ou indirecte à l'agresseur ou aux agresseurs, chaque Partie déclarant d'ailleurs n'être liée par aucun accord d'assistance qui se trouverait en contradiction avec cet engagement.

Fait à Paris, le 2 mai 1935.

(Signé) Pierre LAVAL
(Signé) V. POTEMKINE

BIBLIOGRAPHY

I. *Official Documents*

France

Ministère des Affaires Etrangères

Pacte d'Entente et de Collaboration paraphé à Rome le 7 juin 1933. Paris: Imprimerie des Journaux Officiels, 1933. (Livre Bleu Français.)

Les Négociations relatives à la Réduction et la Limitation des Armements. Vingt-quatre pièces (14 octobre 1933–17 avril 1934). Paris: Imprimerie nationale, 1934.

Ministère des Finances

Service National des Statistiques. *Mouvement Economique en France de 1929 à 1939.* Paris.

Assemblée Nationale

Session de 1947. No. 2344. *Rapport fait au Nom de la Commission chargée d'Enquêter sur les événements survenus en France de 1933 à 1945,* par M. Charles Serre, Rapporteur général. 2 vols. Paris: Presses Universitaires de France, 1947.

Rapport fait au Nom de la Commission chargée d'Enquêter sur les événements survenus en France de 1933 à 1945. Annexes (Dépositions.) Témoignages et documents recueillis par la Commission d'enquête parlementaire. 9 vols. Paris: Presses Universitaires de France, 1947.

Chambre des Députés

Journal Officiel de la République Française, Chambre des Députés, Débats Parlementaires, Paris: Imprimerie des Journaux Officiels.

Journal Officiel de la République Française, Chambre des Députés, Documents Parlementaires, Paris: Imprimerie des Journaux Officiels.

Sénat

Journal Officiel de la République Française, Sénat, Débats Parlementaires, Paris: Imprimerie des Journaux Officiels.

Journal Officiel de la République Française, Sénat, Documents Parlementaires, Paris: Imprimerie des Journaux Officiels.

Germany

Documents on German Foreign Policy 1918-1945. Series C, 1933-1937. The Third Reich: First Phase. Published jointly by the British Foreign Office and the U. S. Department of State (London and Washington), 1957 *et seq.* 3 volumes to date.

Great Britain

Foreign Office

Documents on British Foreign Policy 1919-1939. Edited by E. L. Woodward and Rohan Butler. Second Series (1930-1938), 9 volumes to date. London: His Majesty's Stationery Office, 1946 *et seq.*

Parliament

Parliamentary Debates, House of Commons, Official Report.
Parliamentary Debates, House of Lords, Official Report.
Parliamentary (Command) Papers:
  Cmd. 5143, *Correspondence showing the course of certain Diplomatic Discussions directed towards securing an European Settlement,* Miscellaneous No. 3 (1936). (British Blue Book.)

Poland

Ministry for Foreign Affairs

Official Documents concerning Polish-German and Polish-Soviet Relations 1933-1939. (Polish White Book.) London: Hutchinson and Co., Ltd., no date [1940]. Published by Authority of the Polish Government.

United States

Department of State

Foreign Relations of the United States. Diplomatic Papers, 1931, 1932, 1933, 1934, 1935. Washington, D. C.: Government Printing Office, 1946-1953.
Foreign Relations of the United States. Japan: 1931-1941. 2 vols. Washington, D. C.: Government Printing Office, 1943.
Foreign Relations of the United States. The Soviet Union 1933-1939. Washington, D. C.: Government Printing Office, 1952.
Unpublished Archives of the Department of State. (By permission.)

League of Nations

Official Journal (Records of the Council).
Official Journal. Special Supplements (Records of the Assembly).
Conference for the Reduction and Limitation of Armaments. Records.
  Series A. Verbatim Records of Plenary Meetings.
  Series B. Minutes of the General Commission.
  Series C. Minutes of the Bureau.
  Series D. Minutes of the Political Commission.
Treaty Series.
World Economic Survey 1932-1933.
International Trade Statistics (annual).

II. *Political Trials*

International Military Tribunal. *Trial of the Major War Criminals before the International Military Tribunal, Nuremberg, 1945-1946. Proceedings and Documents in Evidence.* 42 volumes. Nuremberg: International Military Tribunal, 1947-1949.

Nazi Conspiracy and Aggression. A collection of documentary evidence and guide materials prepared by the American and British prosecuting staffs for ... the International Military Tribunal at Nürnberg. 8 volumes. With "Opinion and Judgment" and Supplements A and B. Washington: U. S. Government Printing Office, 1946-1948.

République Française. Haute Cour de Justice. *Procès du Maréchal Pétain. Compte rendu in extenso des Audiences.* Paris: Imprimerie des Journaux Officiels, 1945.

Extracts from the stenographic records:

Mazé, Pierre, and Genebrier, Roger. *Les Grandes Journées du Procès de Riom.* Préface de Édouard Daladier. Paris: La Jeune Parque, 1945.

Ribet, Maurice. *Le Procès de Riom.* Paris: Flammarion, 1945.

Les Procès de Collaboration. Fernand de Brinon, Joseph Darnand, Jean Luchaire. Compte rendu sténographique. Collection des Grands Procès Contemporains publiée sous la direction de Maurice Garçon. Paris: Albin Michel, 1948.

Le Procès Laval. Compte rendu sténographique. Collection des Grands Procès Contemporains publiée sous la direction de Maurice Garçon. Paris: Albin Michel, 1946.

Le Procès Flandin devant la Haute Cour de Justice (23-26 Juillet 1946). Paris: Librairie de Medicis, 1947.

III. *Documentary Collections*

Baynes, Norman H. *The Speeches of Adolph Hitler. April 1922– August 1939.* 2 volumes. London, New York: Oxford University Press, 1942.

Berber, Friedrich, ed. *Europäische Politik 1933-1938, im Spiegel der Prager Akten.* Essen: Essener Verlagsanstalt, 1942.

Degras, Jane, ed. *Soviet Documents on Foreign Policy, 1917-1941.* 3 volumes. Issued under the auspices of the Royal Institute of International Affairs. London, New York: Oxford University Press, 1951-1953.

Dokumente der Deutschen Politik. (Annual) Berlin: Junker und Dünnhaupt, 1937-1943.

Geheimer Briefwechsel Mussolini-Dollfuss. Mit einem Vorwort von Vizekanzler Dr. Adolf Schärf; Erläuternder Text von Karl Hans Sailer. Anhang: Aus den Memoiren Starhembergs. Wien: Verlag der Wiener Volksbuchhandlung, 1949.

Royal Institute of International Affairs. *Documents on International Affairs.* (Annual) London: Oxford University Press, 1929-

IV. *Memoirs and Works by Statesmen and Political Figures*

Aloisi, Baron Pompeo. *Journal (25 Juillet 1932–14 Juin 1936)* traduit de l'italien par Maurice Vaussard. Introduction et notes par Mario Toscano. Paris: Plon, 1957.

Armengaud, General. *Batailles Politiques et Militaires sur l'Europe. Témoignages (1932-1940.)* Paris: Du Myrte, 1948.

Barmine, Alexander. *One Who Survived: The Life Story of a Russian under the Soviets.* New York: G. P. Putnam's Sons, 1945.

Barthou, Louis. *Lettres à un Jeune Français.* Paris: Éditions Pierre Lafitte, 1916.

Barthou, Louis. *Le Politique.* Paris: Hachette, 1923.

Barthou, Louis. *Promenades autour de ma Vie. Lettres de la Montagne.* Paris: Les Laboratoires Martinet, 1933.

Beck, Joseph. *Dernier Rapport: Politique polonaise 1926-1939.* Neuchatel: Éditions de la Baconnière, 1951.

Belin, Jean. *My Work at the Sûreté.* Translated by Eric Whelpton. London: George G. Harrap and Co., Ltd., 1950.

Blum, Léon. *L'Histoire Jugera.* Paris: Diderot; Montreal: de l'Arbre, 1945.

Blum, Léon. *L'Oeuvre de Léon Blum.* I. *Mémoires; La Prison et Le Procès; À L'Échelle Humaine. 1940-1945.* Paris: Editions Albin Michel, 1955.

Bonnet, Georges. *Défense de la Paix.* 2 vols. Geneva: Les Éditions du Cheval Ailé, 1946, 1948.

Brinon, Fernand de. *France-Allemagne, 1918-1934.* Paris: B. Grasset, 1934.

Brinon, Fernand de. *Mémoires.* Paris: L. L. C., 1949.

Brüning, Heinrich. "Ein Brief," *Deutsche Rundschau,* LXX, Heft 7, Juli 1947.

Caillaux, Joseph. *Mes Mémoires.* 3 vols. Vol. III, *Clairvoyance et Force d'Ame dans les Épreuves, 1912-1930.* Paris: Plon, 1947.

Cecil, Robert, Viscount. *A Great Experiment: An Autobiography.* London: Jonathan Cape, 1941.

Chambrun, Charles de. *Traditions et Souvenirs.* Paris: Flammarion, 1952.

Charles-Roux, F. *Huit Ans au Vatican 1932-1940.* Paris: Flammarion, 1947.

Churchill, Winston S. *The Second World War.* 6 vols. Vol. I, *The Gathering Storm.* Boston: Houghton Mifflin, 1948-1953.

Cot, Pierre. *Le Procès de la République.* 2 vols. New York: Éditions de la Maison Française, Inc., 1944.

Coulondre, Robert. *De Staline à Hitler: Souvenirs de deux Ambassades 1936-1939.* Paris: Librairie Hachette, 1950.

Curtius, Julius. *Bemühung um Österreich: Das Scheitern des Zollunionplans von 1931.* Heidelberg: Carl Winter, Universitätsverlag, 1947.

Curtius, Julius. *Sechs Jahre Minister der Deutschen Republik.* Heidelberg: Carl Winter, Universitätsverlag, 1948.

Delbos, Yvon. *L'Expérience Rouge.* Paris, 1933.

Dirksen, Herbert von. *Moscow, Tokyo, London: Twenty Years of German Foreign Policy.* London, New York: Hutchinson and Co. Ltd., 1951.

Dodd, William E., Jr., and Dodd, Martha, eds. *Ambassador Dodd's Diary 1933-1938.* London: Victor Gollancz, 1941.

Edge, Walter. *A Jerseyman's Journal.* Princeton: Princeton University Press, 1948.

Fabry, Jean. *De la Place de la Concorde au Cours de l'Intendance.* Paris: Les Editions de la France, 1942.

Flandin, Pierre-Étienne. *Politique Française, 1919-1940.* Paris: Les Éditions Nouvelles, 1947.

François-Poncet, André. *Souvenirs d'une Ambassade à Berlin: Septembre 1931–Octobre 1938.* Paris: Flammarion, 1946.

François-Poncet, André. *De Versailles à Potsdam: La France et le problème allemand contemporain 1919-1945.* Paris: Flammarion, 1948.

Gamelin, General Maurice. *Servir.* 3 vols. Vol. II, *Le Prologue du Drame (1930-Août 1939).* Paris: Plon, 1946.

Gaulle, Charles de. *Vers l'Armée de Métier.* Paris: Berger-Levrault, 1934.

Henderson, Sir Nevile. *Water under the Bridges.* London: Hodder and Stoughton, 1945.

Herriot, Édouard. *La Russie Nouvelle.* Paris: J. Ferenczi et Fils, 1922.

Herriot Édouard. *La France dans le Monde.* Paris: Hachette, 1933.

Herriot, Édouard. *Eastward from Paris.* Translated by Phyllis Megros. London: Victor Gollancz Ltd., 1934. (French edition: *Orient.* Paris, 1934).

Herriot, Édouard. *Jadis.* 2 vols. Vol. II, *D'Une Guerre à l'autre, 1914-1936. Paris:* Flammarion, 1952.

Hilger, Gustav, and Meyer, Alfred G. *The Incompatible Allies: A Memoir-History of German-Soviet Relations 1918-1941.* New York: The Macmillan Co., 1953.

Hitler, Adolf. *Mein Kampf.* Unabridged and annotated edition. New York: Reynal and Hitchcock, 1941.

Hossbach, Friedrich. *Zwischen Wehrmacht und Hitler 1934-1938.* Wolfenbüttel und Hannover: Wolfenbütteler Verlagsanstalt, 1949.

Hymans, Paul. *Mémoires.* 2 vols. Brussels: Éditions de l'Institut de Sociologie Solvay, 1958.

Jones, Thomas. *A Diary with Letters, 1931-1950.* London: Oxford University Press, 1954.

Kerillis, Henri de. *Français, Voici la Verité....* New York: Éditions de la Maison Française, Inc., 1942.

Kordt, Erich. *Wahn und Wirklichkeit.* Stuttgart: Union Deutsche Verlagsgesellschaft, 1948.

Kordt, Erich. *Nicht aus den Akten....* Stuttgart: Union Deutsche Verlagsgesellschaft, 1950.

Lagardelle, Hubert. *Mission à Rome. Mussolini.* Paris: Plon, 1955.

Laroche, Jules. *La Pologne de Pilsudski: Souvenirs d'une Ambassade, 1926-1935.* Paris: Flammarion, 1953.

Laroche, Jules. *Au Quai d'Orsay avec Briand et Poincaré.* Paris: Hachette, 1957.

Laval, Pierre. *Laval Parle... Notes et Mémoires rédigés à Fresnes d'août à octobre 1945.* Paris: La Diffusion du Livre et Librairie Ch. Béranger, 1948.

Lebrun, Albert. *Témoignage.* Paris: Plon, 1945.

Léger, Alexis. *Briand.* Aurora, New York: V. and J. Hammer, Wells College Press, 1943.

Litvinov, Maxim. *Against Aggression: Speeches of Maxim Litvinov.* New York: International Publishing Co., 1939.

Loizeau, General. "Une Mission Militaire en U.R.S.S.," *Revue des Deux Mondes,* 15 September 1955, pp. 252-276.

Londonderry, Marquess of. *Wings of Destiny.* London: MacMillan, 1943.

Luciani, Georges. (Pierre Berland, pseud.) *Six Ans à Moscou.* Paris: Picart, 1937.

Manstein, Erich von. *Aus einem Soldatenleben.* Bonn: Athenäum-Verlag, 1958.

Milićević, Vladeta. *A King Dies in Marseilles: The Crime and Its Background.* Bad Godesberg: Hohwacht, 1959.

Nadolny, Rudolf. *Mein Beitrag.* Wiesbaden: Limes Verlag, 1955.

Noël, Léon. *L'Agression Allemande contre la Pologne: Une Ambassade à Varsovie 1935-39.* Paris: Flammarion, 1946.

Ormesson, Wladimir d'. *France.* Translated by J. Lewis May. London, New York: Longmans, Green and Co., 1939.

Overstraeten, General van. *Albert I—Léopold III: Vingt Ans de Politique Militaire Belge. 1920-1940.* Brussels: Desclée De Brouwer, no date.

Papen, Franz von. *Memoirs.* Translated by Brian Connell. London: Andre Deutsch, 1952.

Paul-Boncour, J. *Entre Deux Guerres: Souvenirs sur la Troisième République.* 3 vols. Paris: Plon, 1945, 1946.

Pertinax (André Géraud). "France, Russia and the Pact of Mutual Assistance," *Foreign Affairs,* XIII, No. 2 (January 1935).

Pertinax (André Géraud). *Les Fossoyeurs. Défaite Militaire de la France; Armistice, Contre-Revolution.* 2 vols. New York: Éditions de la Maison Française, 1943.

Pétain, Marshal Henri-Philippe. "La Sécurité de la France au cours des Années Creuses," *Revue des Deux Mondes,* 1 March 1935.

Potocki, Count Alfred. *Master of Lancut.* London: W. H. Allen, 1959.

Raeder, Erich. *Mein Leben.* 2 vols. Vol. I. *Bis zum Flottenabkommen mit England 1935.* Tubingen: Verlag Fritz Schlichtenmayer, 1956.

Rauschning, Hermann. *Germany's Revolution of Destruction.* Translated by E. W. Dickes. London: William Heinemann Ltd., 1939.

Rauschning, Hermann. *The Voice of Destruction.* New York: G. P. Putnam's, 1940.

Réquin, General E. *D'une Guerre à l'Autre (1919-1939): Souvenirs.* Paris: Charles-Lavauzelle, 1949.

Reynaud, Paul. *Au Coeur de la Mêlée.* Paris: Flammarion, 1951.

Reynaud, Paul. *Mémoires, I, Venu de ma Montagne.* Paris: Flammarion, 1960.

The Ribbentrop Memoirs. Introduction by Alan Bullock. London: Weidenfeld and Nicholson, 1954.

Ripka, Hubert. *East and West.* London: Lincolns-Prager, 1944.

Rosenberg, Alfred. *Der Zukunftsweg einer deutschen Aussenpolitik.* Munich: F. Eher, 1927.

Roton, General G. *Années Cruciales: La Course aux Armements (1933-1939), La Campagne (1939-1940).* Paris: Charles-Lavauzelle, 1947.

Schmidt, Paul. *Statist auf Diplomatischer Bühne 1923-45: Erlebnisse des Chefdolmetschers im Auswärtigen Amt mit den Staatsmännern Europas.* Bonn: Athenäum-Verlag, 1949. (English Edition: *Hitler's Interpreter.* London: Heinemann, 1951.)

Schuschnigg, Kurt von. *Austrian Requiem.* Translated by Franz von Hildebrand. London: Victor Gollancz Ltd., 1947.

Schweppenburg, Geyr von. *The Critical Years.* London: Allan Wingate, 1952.

Seeckt, Generaloberst von. *Deutschland zwischen West und Ost.* Hamburg: Hanseatische verlagenstalt, 1933.

Selby, Sir Walford. *Diplomatic Twilight 1930-1940.* London: John Murray, 1953.

Simon, Viscount. *Retrospect: The Memoirs of the Rt. Hon. Viscount Simon.* London: Hutchinson, 1952.

Speidel, Helm. "Reichswehr und Rote Armee," *Vierteljahrshefte für Zeitgeschichte,* I, No. 1, January 1953.

Starhemberg, Ernst Rüdiger Prince von. *Between Hitler and Mussolini: Memoirs of Ernst Rüdiger Prince Starhemberg.* New York: Harper and Brothers, 1942.

Strang, Lord. *Home and Abroad.* London: André Deutsch, 1956.

Szembek, Count Jean. *Journal 1933-1939.* Translated from the Polish by J. Rzewuska and T. Zaleski. Paris: Plon, 1952.

Tabouis, Geneviève. *Ils l'ont appelée Cassandre.* New York: Éditions de la Maison Française, 1942.

Tabouis, Geneviève. *Vingt Ans de "Suspense" Diplomatique.* Paris: Éditions Albin Michel, 1958.

Temperley, Major-General A. C. *The Whispering Gallery of Europe.* London: Collins, 1938.

Templewood, Viscount. *Nine Troubled Years.* London: Collins, 1954.
Thorez, Maurice. *Oeuvres de Maurice Thorez.* Paris: Editions Sociales, 1950—.
Tissier, Pierre. *I Worked with Laval.* London: George G. Harrap and Co., 1942.
Torrès, Henry. *Pierre Laval, La France Trahie.* New York: Brentano's, 1941.
Trotsky, Leon. *Trotsky's Diary in Exile, 1935.* (Translated from the Russian by Elena Zarudnaya.) Cambridge, Mass.: Harvard University Press, 1958.
Vansittart, Lord Robert. *The Mist Procession.* London: Hutchinson, 1958.
Weizsäcker, Ernst von. *Erinnerungen.* Munich: Paul-List Verlag, 1950.
Weygand, General Maxime. *Mémoires.* 3 vols. Vol. II. *Mirages et Realité.* Paris: Flammarion, 1957.
Zuylen, Baron Pierre van. *Les Mains Libres: Politique Extérieure de la Belgique, 1914-1940.* Paris: Desclée de Brouwer, 1950.

V. *Biographies, Histories, and other studies*

Albrecht-Carrié, René. *France, Europe and the Two World Wars.* Paris: Librairie Minard, 1960.
Allen, Luther. "The French Left and Soviet Russia," *World Affairs Quarterly,* XXIX (July 1959).
Anonymous. *La Vérité sur Fernand de Brinon.* Paris, 1947.
Askew, William C. "Secret Agreement between France and Italy on Ethiopia," *Journal of Modern History,* XXV (March 1953).
Baron, Charles. *Au Pays de l'Or Noir.* Paris: Librairie polytechnique Ch. Béranger, 1934.
Baumont, Maurice. *La Faillite de la Paix (1918-1939).* 2 vols. Paris: Presses Universitaires de France, 1945. 3rd edition, 1950.
Baykov, A. *Soviet Foreign Trade.* Princeton: Princeton University Press, 1946.
Beloff, Max. *The Foreign Policy of Soviet Russia, 1929-1941.* 2 vols. Issued under the auspices of the Royal Institute of International Affairs. New York, London: Oxford University Press, 1947-1949.
Bettelheim, Charles. *Bilan de l'Économie Française, 1919-1946.* Paris: Presses Universitaires de France, 1947.
Binion, Rudolph. *Defeated Leaders: The Political Fate of Caillaux, Jouvenel and Tardieu.* New York: Columbia University Press, 1960.
Borkenau, Franz. *European Communism.* London: Faber and Faber Ltd., 1953.
Braunthal, Julius. *The Tragedy of Austria.* Appendix: "Mussolini and Dollfuss, An Episode in Fascist Diplomacy," by Professor Paul R. Sweet. London: Victor Gollancz Ltd., 1948.
Bréal, August. *Philippe Berthelot.* Paris: Gallimard, 1937.
Brogan, D. W. *The Development of Modern France, 1870-1939.* London: Hamish Hamilton, 1940.

Bullock, Alan. *Hitler: A Study in Tyranny.* New York: Harper and Brothers; London: Odhams Press Ltd., 1952.

Butler, J. R. M. *Lord Lothian (Philip Kerr) 1882-1940.* New York and London: St. Martin's Press, 1960.

Cameron, Elizabeth R. *Prologue to Appeasement: A Study in French Foreign Policy.* Washington, D. C.: American Council on Public Affairs, 1942.

Carr, Edward Hallett. *German-Soviet Relations between the Two World Wars, 1919-1939.* Baltimore: The Johns Hopkins Press, 1951.

Castellan, Georges. "Von Schleicher, von Papen et l'Avènement d'Hitler," *Cahiers d'Histoire de la Guerre.* No. 1, 1949.

Castellan, Georges. *Le Réarmement Clandestin du Reich, 1930-1935.* Paris: Plon, 1954.

Celovsky, Boris. "Pilsudskis Präventigkrieg gegen das nationalsozialistische Deutschland (Entstehung, Verbreitung und Widerlegung einer Legende)", *Die Welt als Geschichte,* XIV (1954).

Challener, Richard D. *The French Theory of the Nation in Arms, 1866-1939.* New York: Columbia University Press, 1955.

Chambrun, M. et Mme René de, compilers. *La vie de la France sous l'Occupation.* 3 vols. Paris: Plon, 1957.

Chastenet, Jacques. *Raymond Poincaré.* Paris: Julliard, 1948.

Coates, W. P., and Coates, Zelda. *A History of Anglo-Soviet Relations.* London: Lawrence and Wishart, 1943.

Connell, John (pseudonym for J. H. Robertson). *The 'Office': A Study of British Foreign Policy and its Makers, 1919-1951.* London: Allen Wingate, 1958.

Craig, Gordon A. *The Politics of the Prussian Army, 1640-1945.* London: Oxford University Press, 1955.

Craig, Gordon A. *From Bismarck to Adenauer: Aspects of German Statecraft.* Baltimore: The Johns Hopkins Press, 1958.

Craig, Gordon A., and Gilbert, Felix, eds. *The Diplomats 1919-1939.* Princeton: Princeton University Press, 1953.

Davis, Kathryn W. *The Soviets at Geneva: The U.S.S.R. at the League of Nations, 1919-1933.* Geneva: Librairie Kundig, 1934.

Deist, Wilhelm. "Schleicher und die deutsche Abrüstungspolitik im Juni/Juli 1932," *Vierteljahrshefte für Zeitgeschichte,* VII, April 1959.

Dupeux, Georges. *Le Front Populaire et les Élections de 1936.* Paris: Armand Colin, 1959.

Duroselle, Jean-Baptiste. *Les Relations Germano-Soviétiques de 1933 à 1939.* Recueil d'études sous la direction de J.-B. Duroselle. Paris: Armand Colin, 1954.

Duroselle, Jean-Baptiste. *Histoire Diplomatique de 1919 à nos jours.* Paris: Dalloz, 1957.

Duroselle, Jean-Baptiste. *Les Frontières Européennes de l'U.R.S.S. 1917-1941.* Paris: Armand Colin, 1957.

Feiling, Keith. *The Life of Neville Chamberlain.* London: Macmillan, 1946.

Fischer, Louis. *Men and Politics: An Autobiography.* New York: Duell, Sloan and Pearce, 1941.

Galtière-Boissière, J., ed. *Dictionnaire des Contemporains.* Paris, 1950.

Gasiorowski, Zygmunt J. "Did Pilsudski Attempt to Initiate a Preventive War in 1933?" *Journal of Modern History,* XXVII, June 1955.

Gasiorowski, Zygmunt J. "The German-Polish Non-Aggression Pact of 1934," *Journal of Central European Affairs,* XV, April 1955.

Gauché, General. *Le Deuxième Bureau au Travail, 1935-1940.* Paris: Dumont, 1953.

Goedorp, Victor. *Figures du Temps.* Paris: A. Michel, 1943.

Goguel, François. *La Politique des Partis sous la Troisième République.* 2 vols. Paris: Éditions du Seuil, 1946.

Grimm, Frédéric. *Hitler et la France.* Preface de J. von Ribbentrop. Paris: Plon, 1938.

Hamilton, Mary Agnes. *Arthur Henderson.* London: Heinemann Ltd., 1938.

Hartlieb, W. W. *Das Politische Vetragssystem der Sowjet-Union, 1922-1935.* Leipzig: R. Noske, 1936.

Hayes, Carlton J. H. *France, A Nation of Patriots.* New York: Columbia University Press, 1930.

Heiden, Konrad. *Der Fuehrer.* Translated by Ralph Manheim. New York: Lexington Press, 1944.

Herzog, Wilhelm. *Barthou.* Zurich: Verlag die Liga, 1938.

Höffding, W. "German Trade with the Soviet Union," *Slavonic and East European Review,* XIV.

Holborn, Hajo. *The Political Collapse of Europe.* New York: Alfred A. Knopf, 1951.

Joll, James, ed. *The Decline of the Third Republic.* London: Chatto and Windus, 1959.

Jouvenel, Bertrand de. *D'une Guerre à l'autre.* 2 vols. Vol. II, *La Décomposition de l'Europe Libérale.* Paris: Plon, 1941.

Kochan, Lionel. *Russia and the Weimar Republic.* Cambridge, England: Bowes and Bowes, 1954.

Langer, William Leonard. *The Franco-Russian Alliance, 1890-1894.* Cambridge, Mass.: Harvard University Press, 1929.

Lapaquellerie, Yvon. *Édouard Daladier.* Paris: Flammarion, 1939.

Laure, Géneral, in collaboration with General Audet, Lieut. Colonel Montjean, and Lieut. Colonel Buot de l'Epine. *Pétain.* Paris: Berger-Levrault, 1941.

Lewis, W. Arthur. *Economic Survey, 1919-1939.* London: George Allen and Unwin, 1949.

[Litvinov, Maxim ?] *Notes for a Journal.* Introduction by E. H. Carr. London: André Deutsch, 1955.

Mackenzie, Compton. *Dr. Beneš.* London: George G. Harrap, 1946.

Mahaney, Wilbur L., Jr. *The Soviet Union, the League of Nations and Disarmament 1917-1935.* Philadelphia: University of Pennsylvania Press, 1940.

Mallet, Alfred. *Pierre Laval.* 2 vols. Paris: Amiot-Dumont, 1955.

Marcus, John T. *French Socialism in the Crisis Years, 1933-1936: Fascism and the French Left.* New York: Praeger, 1958.

Micaud, Charles A. *The French Right and Nazi Germany, 1933-1939.* Durham, N. C.: Duke University Press, 1943.

Michon, Georges. *The Franco-Russian Alliance 1891-1917.* Translated by Norman Thomas. London: George Allen and Unwin Ltd., 1929.

Miliukov, Paul. *La Politique Extérieure des Soviets.* 2nd edition. Bibliothèque d'Études sur la Russie contemporaine, Tome 1. Paris: Librairie générale de droit et de jurisprudence, 1936.

Millikan, G. W. "The Science of Soviet Politics," *Foreign Affairs,* XXXI, April 1953.

Ministère des Finances, Service National des Statistiques, *Mouvement Économique en France de 1929 à 1939.* Paris: Imprimerie Nationale, 1941.

Namier, L. B. *Europe in Decay: A Study in Disintegration, 1936-1940.* London: Macmillan, 1950.

Osgood, Samuel M. *French Royalism under the Third and Fourth Republics.* The Hague: Martinus Nijhoff, 1960.

Planté, Louis. *Un Grand Seigneur de la Politique: Anatole de Monzie, 1876-1947.* Paris: Raymond Chavreuil, 1955.

Poole, Dewitt C. "Light on Nazi Foreign Policy," *Foreign Affairs,* XXV, No. 1.

Pope, Arthur Upham. *Maxim Litvinov.* New York: L. B. Fischer, 1943.

Potiemkine, Vladimir (published under the direction of): *Histoire de la Diplomatie.* Translated from the Russian into French by I. Levin, J. Tarr, and B. Metzel. 3 vols. Paris: Librairie de Médicis. 1947.

Privat, Maurice. *Pierre Laval.* Paris: Neuilly, 1931.

Privat, Maurice. *Pierre Laval, Cet Inconnu.* Paris: Fournier-Valdès, 1948.

Renouvin, Pierre. *Histoire des Relations Internationals.* Tome Huitième, *Les Crises du XXᵉ Siècle.* II. *De 1929 à 1945.* Hachette, 1958.

Roberts, Henry L. *Roumania.* New York, 1951.

Roos, Hans. "Die 'Präventivkriegspläne' Pilsudskis von 1933," *Vierteljahrshefte für Zeitgeschichte,* III, October 1955.

Rossi, A. *Physiologie du Parti Communiste Français.* Paris: Self, 1948.

Royal Institute of International Affairs. *Survey of International Affairs* (Annual). London: Oxford University Press, 1925—.

St. Antony's Papers, Number 5. *The Decline of the Third Republic.* Edited by James Joll. London: Chatto and Windus, 1959.

Salisbury-Jones, Guy. *So Full a Glory: A Biography of Marshal de Lattre de Tassigny.* London: Weidenfeld and Nicholson, 1954.

Salvemini, Gaetano. *Prelude to World War II.* London: Victor Gollancz Ltd., 1953.

Schmitt, Bernadotte E., ed. *Poland.* Berkeley: University of California Press, 1945.

Sharp, Walter Rice. *The Government of the French Republic.* New York: D. Van Nostrand Co., 1938.

Siegfried, André. *Tableau des Partis en France*. Paris: Bernard Grasset, 1930.

Slovès, H. *La France et l'Union Soviétique*. Préface de Henry Torrès. Paris: Les Éditions Rieder, 1935.

Spengler, Oswald. *The Hour of Decision*. Translated from the German by C. F. Atkinson. London: George Allen and Unwin Ltd., 1934.

Suarez, Georges. *Les Hommes Malades de la Paix*. Paris: Bernard Grasset, 1933.

Suarez, Georges. *Briand, Sa Vie—Son Oeuvre, avec son Journal et de nombreux documents inédits*. 6 vols. Vol. VI, *L'Artisan de la Paix, 1923-1932*. Paris: Plon, 1952.

Tarr, Francis de. *The French Radical Party, from Herriot to Mendès-France*. London: Oxford University Press, 1961.

The Times (London). *The History of the Times. The 150th Anniversary and Beyond, 1912-1948*. Part II, *1921-1948*. London: The office of *The Times*, 1952.

Thomson, David. *Two Frenchmen: Pierre Laval and Charles de Gaulle*. London: The Cresset Press, 1951.

Vogelsang Thilo, ed. "Neue Dokumente zur Geschichte der Reichswehr, 1930-1933", *Vierteljahrshefte für Zeitgeschichte*, II, 1954.

Vogelsang, Thilo, ed. "Hitlers Brief an Reichenau vom 4. Dezember 1932," *Vierteljahrshefte für Zeitgeschichte*, VII, October 1959, 429-437.

Vondracek, Felix J. *The Foreign Policy of Czechoslovakia, 1918-1935*. New York: Columbia University Press, 1937.

Walter, Gerard. *Histoire du Parti Communiste Français*. Paris: Almery Somogy, 1948.

Walters, Francis P. *A History of the League of Nations*. 2 vols. London, New York: Oxford University Press, 1952.

Warth, Robert D. *The Allies and the Russian Revolution*. Durham, N. C.: Duke University Press, 1954.

Watt, D. C. "The Anglo-German Naval Agreement of 1935: An Interim Judgment," *Journal of Modern History*, XXVIII, June 1956.

Watt, D. C. "The Secret Laval-Mussolini Agreement of 1935 on Ethiopia," *The Middle East Journal*, XV, Winter 1961.

Werth, Alexander. *France in Ferment*. London: Jarrolds, 1934.

Werth, Alexander. *Which Way France?* New York and London: Harper and Bros., 1937.

Wheeler-Bennett, John W. *The Pipe Dream of Peace*. New York: William Morrow and Co., 1935.

Wheeler-Bennett, John W. *Hindenburg: The Wooden Titan*. London: Macmillan, 1936.

Wheeler-Bennett, John W. *Munich: Prologue to Tragedy*. New York: Duell, Sloan, and Pearce, 1948.

Wheeler-Bennett, John W. *The Nemesis of Power: The German Army in Politics, 1918-1945*. London: Macmillan, 1954.

Wiskemann, Elizabeth. *The Rome-Berlin Axis: A History of the Relations between Hitler and Mussolini*. London, New York: Oxford University Press, 1949.

Wolfe, Martin. *The French Franc between the Two Wars, 1919-1939.* New York: Columbia University Press, 1951.
Wolfers, Arnold. *Britain and France between Two Wars: Conflicting Strategies of Peace since Versailles.* New York: Harcourt, Brace, 1940.
Wrench, John Evelyn. *Geoffrey Dawson and Our Times.* London: Hutchinson, 1955.
Young, G. M. *Stanley Baldwin.* London: Rupert Hart-Davis, 1952.

VI. *Periodicals*

The Bulletin of International News (London: Royal Institute of International Affairs).
Bulletin périodique de la presse russe (Paris: prepared by the French Foreign Ministry).
Cahiers du Bolchévisme (Paris, publiée par la C. C. du parti communiste français).
Les Documents Politiques, Diplomatiques et Financiers (Paris).
L'Europe Nouvelle (Paris).
Foreign Affairs (New York: Council on Foreign Relations).
L'Illustration (Paris).
Journal of Central European Affairs (Boulder, Colorado).
Journal of Modern History.
Osteuropa (Berlin).
Revue des Deux Mondes (Paris).
Revue d'Histoire de la Deuxième Guerre Mondiale (Paris: Presses universitaires de France).
Revue Politique et Parlementaire (Paris).
The Slavonic and East European Review (London).
Soviet Studies (Oxford).
Soviet Union Review (Washington, D. C.: Soviet Union Information Bureau, 1923-1934).
Vierteljahrshefte für Zeitgeschichte (Stuttgart).

VII. *Newspapers*

Le Temps.
Le Journal des Débats.
L'Echo de Paris.
L'Humanité.
Le Populaire.
L'Oeuvre.

VIII. *Bibliographical Collections*

Degras, Jane. *Calendar of Soviet Documents on Foreign Policy 1917-1941.* London, New York: Royal Institute of International Affairs, 1948.
Grierson, Philip. *Books on Soviet Russia 1917-1942: A Bibliography and a Guide to Reading.* London: Methuen and Co., 1943.
Slusser, Robert M., and Triska, Jan F. *A Calendar of Soviet Treaties, 1917-1957.* Stanford, California: Stanford University Press, 1959.

INDEX